THE TIE THAT BOUND US

THE TIE THAT BOUND US

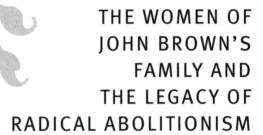

THE WOMEN OF
JOHN BROWN'S
FAMILY AND
THE LEGACY OF
RADICAL ABOLITIONISM

BONNIE LAUGHLIN-SCHULTZ

CORNELL UNIVERSITY PRESS
Ithaca and London

First published 2013 by Cornell University Press

Printed in the United States of America

Library of Congress Cataloging-in-Publication Data

Laughlin-Schultz, Bonnie, 1975– author.
    The tie that bound us : the women of John Brown's family and the legacy of radical abolitionism / Bonnie Laughlin-Schultz.
        pages cm
    Includes bibliographical references and index.
    ISBN 978-0-8014-5161-4 (cloth : alk. paper)
    1. Women abolitionists—United States—Biography.
    2. Brown, John, 1800–1859—Family. 3. Brown, John, 1800–1859—Relations with women. 4. Brown family.
    5. Antislavery movements—United States—History—19th century. 6. Women—United States—Political activity—History—19th century. I. Title.
    E451.L38 2013
    973.7'1160922—dc23   2013001918

Cornell University Press strives to use environmentally responsible suppliers and materials to the fullest extent possible in the publishing of its books. Such materials include vegetable-based, low-VOC inks and acid-free papers that are recycled, totally chlorine-free, or partly composed of nonwood fibers. For further information, visit our website at www.cornellpress.cornell.edu.

Cloth printing   10 9 8 7 6 5 4 3 2 1

For Bill and Henry

❧ CONTENTS

❧ ILLUSTRATIONS

THE TIE THAT BOUND US

Introduction
Searching for the Brown Women

> I feel proud when I think that his blood runs in my veins. Oh! may I always act in a way to be worthy of such a Father. He was no doubt *hung* last Friday, his only crime was that of being a human and not a devil.
>
> —Annie Brown to Thomas Wentworth Higginson, December 1859

Traditional accounts of American abolitionist John Brown's raid at Harpers Ferry highlight one particular scene: Brown holed up in the engine house while two of his sons, Oliver and Watson, lay dying, a testament to Brown's sacrifice on behalf of the antislavery cause. But it was another scene that mesmerized many Americans in 1859: that of Brown's wife, four daughters, and two daughters-in-law awaiting and receiving word of the outcome of Brown's raid, an audacious gamble for which they had labored for more than a decade. Brown's wife, Mary, daughters Ruth, Annie, Sarah, and Ellen, and daughters-in-law Bell and Martha passed the night of October 16, 1859, at their home in North Elba, New York. Though a believer in the antislavery cause, Mary Brown worried not just about her husband and sons but about the fate of their whole family, a fate she knew to be contingent on the events soon to unfold. Eldest daughter Ruth, a mother of three who had recently confessed her desire to "do something for the cause," may nonetheless have been glad that her husband, Henry—wounded in his work alongside Brown in Kansas—was safe at home.[1]

Her sister Annie and sisters-in-law Martha and Bell—Isabella—did not have this luxury. Bell had recently received a letter from her husband, Watson. He confided that, but for "a desire to do something for others, and not live wholly for my own happiness," he would have remained at

1

home with her and their newborn son, Freddy.[2] Sympathetic Americans, aware of his agonizing death outside the engine house at Harpers Ferry, would soon read reprints of Watson's poignant letter. Upon meeting Bell the next year, Louisa May Alcott would proclaim that her "patient, heart-broken face" was "a whole Harper's Ferry tragedy in a look."[3] Oliver's wife, Martha, almost seventeen and expecting her first child, had only recently returned to the family home from his side. She and Annie, almost sixteen, waited anxiously to hear about the fates of the Brown sons and the other men they had come to know during their months as house-keepers at a farmhouse outside Harpers Ferry. Abolitionist Thomas Wentworth Higginson would soon highlight Martha's poignant stoicism. While being shown Oliver's daguerreotype, he reported, "I glanced up sidelong at the young, fair-haired girl, who sat near me by the little table—a wife at fifteen, a widow at sixteen; and this was her husband, and he was KILLED." Higginson continued, "As the words were spoken in her hearing, not a muscle quivered, and her finger did not tremble as she drew the thread."[4]

Thirteen-year-old Sarah and five-year-old Ellen, Brown's youngest children, likely understood the gravity of the family's situation. In the weeks to come, Ellen, assisted by her older sisters, would write to her imprisoned father. "I hope we may so live as to profit by the kind and good advice you have so often given us, and at last meet in heaven," she wrote, closing with a "Farewell!" from "your affectionate daughter, Ellen."[5] Her letter would be widely circulated as proof of the family's devotion to the antislavery cause, and mention of Brown's widow and fatherless children would appear in countless abolitionist tributes. At a relief meeting for Brown's family, Ralph Waldo Emerson astutely summarized what drew so many. "It is impossible," he noted, "to see courage, and disinterestedness, and the love that casts out fear, without sympathy."[6]

In the days that followed Brown's raid, many Americans professed interest in the Brown women. Yet the women are missing from the prevailing popular narrative about John Brown. That he had sons who died in his work is commonly known, as is the fact that he had a large family. When antislavery statesman and writer Richard Henry Dana visited John Brown's family in the summer of 1849, he noted that "there were a great many sons and daughters," so many so that despite his overnight stay with the family, "I never knew how many."[7] Biographers, abolitionists, and Brown aficiona-dos, past and present, have looked to Brown's family as his private antislavery army. Given this military metaphor, it is unsurprising that much of the interest has been with the Brown sons, with those who fought alongside their father as well as those who refused to follow him to Harpers Ferry.[8] Whether Brown is characterized as a patriot, terrorist, or both, he is almost always portrayed as occupying an entirely male sphere. John Steuart Curry's famous Kansas statehouse mural of a bearded patriarch—arms outstretched, with Bible in one hand and gun in the other, feet upon the bodies of Union and Confederate dead—continues to represent the Brown that most Americans know. The recent explosion of scholarly interest in Brown tied to the sesquicentennials of Harpers Ferry and the Civil War has largely ignored the women in his family.

It was in reading several new works about Brown a number of years ago that I started to wonder about these neglected women.[9] I began with questions about antebellum women's participation in antislavery violence, reasoning that Mary, Ruth, and Annie's experiences would shed light on the motivations and understandings with which antebellum women approached militant antislavery in the 1850s. As is so often the case, I soon realized that these were not the right, or only, questions, because the women's story revealed much more. Their personal and public experiences, their choices as well as their lack of choices, offer insight into nineteenth-century American women's lives and into how memory of radical antislavery and the Civil War was incorporated into popular understandings about Brown and his kin.

Mary Brown was in many ways the most ordinary of women. Never one to claim a public spotlight, she was fated to a life outside of history before her role as Brown's wife thrust her into antislavery, the great reform movement of the nineteenth century. Like many women, Mary and her daughters spent their daily lives in household toil, and her antebellum life was defined by a seemingly endless cycle of childbearing. Plain in speaking (and even in appearance, as many biographers have delighted in observing), Mary Brown did not stand out from the crowd.[10] Neither did her daughters. In part, this was a function of class. Ruth, Annie, Sarah, and Ellen endured lifelong battles with poverty and led day-to-day lives that were, on the surface, typical. In an age where some women moved from antislavery activism to women's rights, neither Mary nor her daughters took this bold leap. Aside from their unconventional immediate antislavery sentiment and the courage that such beliefs required, they were surprisingly conventional. As such, they spent the years after the Civil War advocating a common cause among women: temperance. They did not tackle it in the John Brown-esque manner of someone such as Carrie Nation; instead, they joined local temperance societies and abstained from drinking.

Mary Brown and her daughters would likely be obscured from the historical record but for their connection to John Brown. In the 1840s and 1850s, they were among a small percentage of Americans who adopted antislavery sentiment, an even smaller percentage who worked on its behalf, and a still-smaller group that embraced a belief in militant abolitionism. Alongside Brown, they embraced an unorthodox creed, one that viewed African Americans as their equals and that ultimately advocated violent means to end slavery. Their link to the notorious John Brown meant that even after his execution in 1859, they could not retreat into obscurity. Harpers Ferry propelled them into a remarkable circle, where they crossed paths with famous abolitionists and became celebrities of a sort. At times, the Brown women welcomed the unusual dimensions of their lives; at other moments they chafed against them. Regardless of what they preferred at any given moment, the tension between their ordinary class-bound roles and the extraordinary dimensions of their existence shaped their lives. This juxtaposition is at the heart of this book.

What we can know about their antislavery beliefs and, especially, their response to Brown's violence is an integral part of their story. A close examination of the choices that Mary, Ruth, and Annie made in the 1850s reveals their internal struggle over what commitment to antislavery violence would entail. In 1857 abolitionist and Brown backer Franklin Sanborn noted that Mary, Ruth, and Annie were "hardworking, self-denying, devoted women, fully sensible of the greatness of the struggle in which Capt. Brown is engaged, *and willing to bear their part in it.*"[11] In the 1840s and 1850s, Mary and Ruth labored at home so that Brown and his sons could be away fighting slavery, and daughter Annie worked alongside Brown's raiders in 1859. But they experienced the decades in which the family was drawn into antislavery militancy from a perspective different from that of their men. While the Brown men were away, the Brown women toiled at home, their efforts allowing Brown's commitment to antislavery endeavors near and far. Their indirect "supply side" support meant that his work could proceed, and the abolitionists who praised Mary Brown as his fervent supporter were technically correct.[12] She and her stepdaughter Ruth gradually came into radical abolitionism, ultimately accepting, if not fully embracing, Brown's violent means.

Reading the *Liberator* and *Uncle Tom's Cabin* helped further Ruth's devotion to antislavery, but the Brown women did not participate in antislavery in the manner adopted by famous antislavery women from Angelina Grimké to Sojourner Truth or even so-called "ordinary" women.[13] Mary and Ruth may have made items for an antislavery fair, and Mary once heard American Anti-Slavery Society (AASS) lecturer Lucy Stone.[14] But beyond this, they had no involvement in any kind of female antislavery circle. There is no record of a Brown woman attending a convention, signing a petition, or taking the radical step of speaking out against slavery in public, despite the fact that other female abolitionists in Ohio and elsewhere did all this and more. Instead, far removed from any urban antislavery society, they provided logistical support for one of the most radical agitators in American history. While lecturers, petitioners, and fairgoers alike argued that the cause of the slave was "peculiarly woman's cause," the Brown women did not evoke antislavery as any kind of special gendered mission.[15] Ruth once asserted that the Brown women would fight slave catchers even if their only weapon was hot water, and, in an 1858 letter, she begged to be included in Brown's antislavery militancy, acknowledging her gender as an obstacle rather than a special enabler.[16]

In that same year, Brown assessed how his antislavery work had affected Mary, then in her early forties and his wife of twenty-five years. "I have," he wrote, "kept her tumbling here and there over a stormy and tempestuous sea."[17] Brown chose an apt metaphor. In the years before Harpers Ferry, Mary and Brown's daughters made many sacrifices in the "stormy and tempestuous sea" of the family's commitment to militant abolitionism. Aware that their hardships would multiply in the wake of the failed raid, John Brown conducted a jailhouse letter-writing campaign to generate sympathy—and money.[18] His prison letters succeeded in creating an outpouring of aid for his family despite some abolitionists' hesitation about his means. Such aid became a fact of life for the Brown women, as they ever after faced what eldest Brown son John Jr. termed "the cloud of debt."[19]

Though he worked to "manufacture" his martyrdom, John Brown does not appear to have anticipated the long-lasting celebrity that attached itself to his family.[20] Just as Americans had wanted to "see" and read about John Brown in the days after his raid, in the decades after 1859 many in America were curious to see his family.[21] When Mary arrived in Charles Town, Virginia (now West Virginia), to see Brown in jail, artists sketched her for an eager public, and writers published lengthy stories about her.[22] Brown's execution did not diminish interest in his family. Countless periodicals published articles about their whereabouts and remembrances, and communities gathered money and built homes for the Brown women because of their connection to a man whom one newspaper would call the "frightener of the great state of Virginia."[23] Their lifelong celebrity was molded by Americans' fierce fascination with and feelings about the war, and the Brown kin became special sites of memory.[24]

In Brown's time as now, he was a compelling yet troubling figure. His willingness to die on behalf of African American slaves—and, moreover, to kill for their freedom—set him apart from almost everyone else in antebellum America. In the days surrounding Brown's execution, many vilified him as a mad fanatic; others idealized him as a man of righteous action, a Moses or Samson. In the aftermath of Brown's raid and the Civil War that followed, the Brown women, the abolitionist coterie, and Americans overall grappled with whether Brown's violence was justified and what the postwar commitment to African American equality should be. These questions became intertwined: opinion on the former was often linked to the latter, and expressions of sympathy for Brown or his family often symbolized broader egalitarian aims. In looking to Brown, Americans created and constructed the past while also acting to shape the present, whether it was 1859, 1879, or 1899.[25]

As symbols of John Brown, his wife and daughters were entangled in the widespread memory making.[26] Those who supported Brown or who worked on behalf of African American equality celebrated the Brown children. African American groups, along with other sympathetic Americans, sent the Brown daughters money to assist them in times of hardship; in doing so, they were being charitable and, just as important, were making a claim to how Brown ought to be remembered. But public response was not always positive. A few years after their migration to Red Bluff, California, Mary and her daughters were harassed to the point that they chose to move again, and attacks on Brown only grew in the 1880s and 1890s. As the dominant majority increasingly sanctioned Jim Crow laws and beliefs, some Americans placed John Brown alongside other reminders of the racial and slave origins of the Civil War, pushing them further away from public memory of what the war had been about.[27]

The Brown women were not only pawns in the battle over Brown's legacy. They, too, had a vested interest in how he was remembered. Though she guarded her privacy, when approached Mary Brown defended Brown's actions and insisted that her family had fully supported him. Ruth, too, looked for occasions to justify his actions, and she allowed temperance advocates in her home of Pasadena, California, to advertise her participation in the local WCTU as part and parcel of Brown's legacy. Annie was even more active in her efforts to shield her father, writing letters for public consideration and urging Brown biographers to set the record straight. Youngest daughters Sarah and Ellen dodged some of the memory-making work, though when pressed, both vehemently backed their father.

This book is a collective biography of sorts, opening with Mary Brown's marriage to John Brown in 1833 and concluding with the death of the last Brown woman, Annie, in 1926. Many in the academy criticize biography for its all-inclusive nature, with the implication being that what is incorporated is at times unimportant, unsuitable, and not useful for analysis.[28] But a close examination of the Brown women's lives offers not only a compelling and poignant story but a window "into the larger cultural and social and even political process of a moment in time."[29] Their lives were implicated in the cultural, social, and political processes of the broad Civil War era: the rise and experience of antislavery activism and the process of remaking the nation in the decades that followed.

The chapters that follow are snapshots from the Brown women's lives, chosen because they reveal important elements of their story as well as this broader sweep of Civil War–era history. Chapter 1 examines the Brown family's antislavery culture, the world in which Mary operated and into which Brown's daughters were born. Alongside an outline of the Browns' lives in the 1830s and 1840s, I highlight Mary's role in the family's early antislavery activism, challenging portrayals of her as merely compliant—or simply defiant. Chapter 2 incorporates the experience of Mary and of Brown's eldest daughter, Ruth, in the 1850s, the decade in which Brown morphed into a violent abolitionist. Chapter 3 looks at the Harpers Ferry raid through the perspective of daughter Annie, the only Brown woman to directly participate in antislavery violence. Chapters 4 and 5 are more collective, looking at the experiences of the women of Brown's family in late 1859 and the two decades that followed, as they interacted with abolitionists, reacted to Brown's execution and notoriety, and then tried to create new lives for themselves in the face of their connection to him. The final chapters highlight two Brown women, Mary and Annie. Chapter 6 examines Brown's legacy and late nineteenth-century uses of his memory by depicting a cross-country trip taken by his widow in 1882, while chapter 7 looks at Annie's adult life alongside her interactions with Brown biographers and the public memory of her father. Though this book is arranged chronologically, it is not an exhaustive account of the Brown women's lives. I only briefly outline the adult lives of Sarah and Ellen, who are also largely absent from early chapters because they were too young to meaningfully participate in the family's antislavery activism. And I only gesture to the last decades of eldest daughter Ruth's life, as I chose to focus on Annie to highlight themes related to Brown memory and his family's continued celebrity at the turn of the twentieth century.

Because of their famous patriarch, many of the Brown women's letters have been preserved, and notice was frequently given them during the women's lifetime.[30] However, as the letters of "semiprivate" individuals rather than public figures in their own right, they are not the focal point for any collection or preservation of records.[31] Much of the evidence about the Brown women's lives comes from sources and individuals connected to John Brown, and with few small exceptions these letters are housed in collections named for John Brown or his researchers.[32] I have been fortunate to be able to access many letters that resulted from the Brown women's connections to abolitionists and Brown aficionados. Nevertheless, it is a painful certainty that many more private letters, among the women themselves and others, have been lost. To circumvent these gaps in knowledge, I have tried, through language, to cue the reader to what I think of as informed speculation; for example, I use the phrase "must have" as opposed to "did." I have also tried to re-create some aspects of their lives by looking at local histories and other tangential source materials.

The polemical nature of some of my sources also calls for strict scrutiny. Early Brown biographies offer a wealth of information to the researcher, but though each of the writers claimed to be after the "truth," their pro-Brown and anti-Brown motivations surely skewed their presentations of "fact." Additionally, the Brown children's own recollections are not pure, objective sources. Their need to defend their father's life and legend, as well as guilt about their participation in Brown's work, no doubt colored their narration of the past.[33] But as Jeremy Popkin writes, "Autobiographies and memoirs may be classified as dubious sources for historical research, but they are sources nonetheless, and often irreplaceable ones."[34] In their post–Harpers Ferry letters and recollections, I search for a double meaning: first, I use them to comment about Brown and the women's work for his cause, and second, I employ them to analyze the women's experiences and their links to Brown's memory at any given moment in time.[35]

Even at the close of this project, Mary Brown in particular remains frustratingly enigmatic. In the sixty-five letters in her hand that I have been able to find, she uses a no-frills style that offers frustratingly little insight into her interior sensibility. As such, her letters stand in particular contrast to those written by middle-class and elite abolitionists. The letters and speeches that prominent abolitionists penned in the days and years surrounding Brown's death are full of rhetorical flourish and elaborately detailed sentiment. With Mary Brown, this is almost never the case; it is part of why elite abolitionists such as Thomas Wentworth Higginson and Lydia Maria Child proved so condescending in their assessment of her. What we can and cannot know about Mary and the other Brown women is an important element in the work that follows.[36]

In most places, I have aimed to de-center John Brown in order to retain my focus on Mary, Ruth, Annie, Sarah, and Ellen Brown and what their histories, rather than Brown's per se, reveal. Nevertheless, I would be remiss if I were unmindful of the ways in which the history of the Brown women is essential to understanding John Brown. In various sections throughout this work I address how their experience sheds light on the character, motivations, and legacy of Brown himself, contending that the domestic life of John Brown is important to understanding his public persona, that the "personal is political," so to speak. I also believe that an examination of the Brown women reveals the meaning of his raid and the conflicted legacy of his violent means on behalf of a "good" cause in the decades that followed his death.

One final note. Because of their rich, revealing nature, I make frequent use of quotations by all of the Browns. Though Brown's daughters were astonishingly well educated given their class status (the three youngest as a result of abolitionist charity), none of them had access to the kind of schooling typical of the elite abolitionists with whom they interacted. Their letters—and especially those by Mary, who had little formal training—reveal this gap. In quoting from their letters, I have chosen to make no changes to their spelling, grammar, and style. In some ways, I fear this does the women a disservice; it seems part of why abolitionists and even contemporary biographers have felt comfortable in dismissing Mary Brown in particular as "slow" or dull. But I believe that there is no other way to be accurate as I offer their story.

When seventeen-year-old Mary Ann Day met and married the widower John Brown in 1833, she had no idea of all that her life as matriarch of the blended Brown clan would entail. She likely expected it to continue as it was, confined largely to a private domestic sphere where she could expect to tend house, bearing children and enduring the brunt of the family's poverty. But in her marriage to Brown and in her quiet affirmation of the family's culture of antislavery, her life would move in directions she never could have imagined. She would live not only in Ohio's Western Reserve but in two remote American regions: far upstate New York and northern California. She would travel all over the country, and reporters would fight to gain access to her. She would never claim a public platform to advocate for African American equality, but Americans all over the country would link her family to Brown's movement, however they defined it.

Chapter 1

The Brown Family's Antislavery Culture, 1831–49

Decades after its occurrence, John Brown Jr. recounted an important incident from his family's past. His father had asked him, his stepmother Mary, and the eldest Brown siblings to "make common cause with him in doing all in our power to 'break the jaws of the wicked and pluck the spoil out of his teeth.'" Reared to hate slavery and extol self-sacrifice, the Browns quickly agreed. "After prayer," John Jr. continued, "he asked us to raise our right hands, and he then administered to us an oath, . . . in substance it bound us to secrecy and devotion to the purpose of fighting slavery by force and arms to the extent of our ability."[1] The drama inherent in this moment is almost irresistible: John Brown stands to declare war on slavery, and then kneels and vows with a noticeably pregnant Mary and children John Jr., Jason, Owen, Frederick, and Ruth.[2] Unceasing debate over whether an oath was actually sworn (and, if so, when) obscures the important truth summarily contained within his children's problematic claims about it.[3] From early on, John Brown's beliefs and his family's evolving antislavery culture shaped the lives of his wife and children.

In the oath story Mary Brown usually appears as a prop, silently supporting Brown's work, or kneeling, pregnant, as his eldest sons pledge to give their lives in antislavery battle.[4] Scenes of Brown's sons riding alongside him in Kansas or dying with him at Harpers Ferry frequently appear in works on Brown: the father in the forefront, the sons in the background, and the women largely absent.[5] De-centering the Brown men demonstrates how Brown's wife and daughters came into radical antislavery after decades of commitment to the religious faith, equity, and self-sacrifice that undergirded the Brown family culture. These would ultimately lead Brown to a violent radical abolitionist creed, one that he expected his wife, daughters, and sons to support. Though all would defend him in the aftermath of Harpers Ferry, in the decades leading up to the raid, their response to Brown's persistent requests that they wage war against slavery in ways big and small was not that simple.

The Brown family culture was formed against the backdrop of poverty and life in rural antebellum America. Mary Ann Day, Brown's second wife, was born in Granville, New York, after which her family soon moved to Meadville in western Pennsylvania. Her daughter Sarah described her as having grown up "in narrow means & hard work, with almost no schooling."[6] An older daughter in the large family of a blacksmith, Mary married Brown when she was seventeen, after years of caring for her younger siblings.[7] Brown's household, like hers, was poor and crowded. When they married in the summer of 1833, Mary became stepmother to Brown's five children: twelve-year-old John Jr., nine-year-old Jason, seven-year-old Owen, four-year-old Ruth, and two-year-old Frederick.

Very little is known about their mother, Dianthe Lusk Brown.[8] After John Brown was born in Torrington, Connecticut, his family had moved to Hudson, a community in Ohio's Western Reserve, when he was just four. Growing up in the reform-minded community of Hudson, Brown attended school with some of the Lusk family. A widow cooked and cleaned for the young bachelor Brown, and her daughter Dianthe occasionally accompanied her.[9] Brown claimed to have come to admire Dianthe for her industriousness, "excellent character; earnest piety; & good practical common sence" in an autobiographical letter written to twelve-year-old Henry Stearns in 1857.[10] They were wed in the Congregational church in Hudson in 1820; he was twenty and she nineteen. They married against the wishes of Dianthe's brother, Milton, who apparently had qualms about turning over care of his sister to a young man with a "commanding disposition" and an "austere" sense of right and wrong.[11]

Ten months later Dianthe gave birth to their first son, John Jr., beginning a pattern that would dominate the lives of most of the Brown women. Five more children soon followed: Jason, Owen, Frederick, Ruth, and Frederick (named for the first Frederick, who had died as a toddler). In the midst of this, Dianthe adapted as the family moved from Hudson to a new settlement that Brown helped survey in New Richmond, Pennsylvania. There he worked as a tanner, postmaster, land surveyor, and sometime teacher. Along with another local man, George Delamater, Brown opened a school, the first in western Pennsylvania's Richmond Township, and he helped establish an Independent Congregational Society in 1832, hosting the services at his tannery.[12] It was here in New Richmond that Brown's first daughter, Ruth, was born in 1829.

Brown's first marriage ended like so many others in the nineteenth century, with his wife's death in childbirth. Ruth was only three when, in August of 1832, she was called to her mother's bedside to witness as Dianthe "bade 'farewell to earth.'"[13] Dianthe was buried in her wedding dress along with the unnamed infant.[14] John Brown, who grieved her loss deeply, was left with three-year-old Ruth, toddler Frederick, and young sons John Jr., Jason, and Owen. As the historian Catherine Clinton has noted, though the "pattern of disruption and displacement was common for children of the era," it was "nevertheless painful."[15] This was certainly the case for Dianthe's children, who ever after would remember their mother with special tenderness.

Brown soon began relying on a housekeeper for assistance, and in a providential move, she brought her younger sister Mary to assist her. The pair married within a year of Dianthe's death. Though the Browns would later tell a story of how a shy Mary had taken a day to read Brown's letter proposing marriage, it appears to have been a remarriage based on "urgent practical needs," much like that of Abraham Lincoln's widower father and countless others, rich and poor, in antebellum America.[16] For Mary it might have offered a welcome opportunity to escape her family's crowded household, even if it also entailed being stepmother to five children, the eldest of whom was just five years her junior.

Ruth and her brothers' reactions to Mary's arrival formed an early and enduring part of the Brown family dynamics.[17] The phenomenon of stepfamilies was widespread in the nineteenth century. Anecdotal evidence from biographies of famous Americans such as Abraham and Mary Todd Lincoln indicates that the relationships between stepmothers and stepchildren varied widely. Mary was not as "singularly unsuccessful" a stepmother as Eliza Humphreys Todd, but no surviving letter or reminiscence credits her with bringing the kind of "healing" and order that Sarah Bush Johnston restored to Lincoln's life.[18] In the years after their mother's death, Dianthe's children became closely knit. Though they were kind to and helped care for the siblings born out of John and Mary's marriage, they also acted as a unit among themselves. It is unclear whether that was born out of any ill feeling toward Mary, fond recollection of their mother, or something else.[19] Whatever the immediate reaction Mary faced, it had to be a challenge to the seventeen-year-old to manage Brown's five children. It would prove the first of many tests.

"Equity," Antislavery, and Gender Politics

In the decades that followed Brown's second marriage, his five children with Dianthe were joined by half sisters Annie (1843), Sarah (1846), and Ellen (1854), along with ten other children. In dealing with their children, Mary Brown found that she had an attentive partner. The popular notion of John Brown as a patriarch is a caricature relying on testimony taken down many years after the fact. Pro-Brown writers use scraps of evidence to idealize him as tender if unsmiling. Anti-Brown writers have furthered their portrayal of a villain by highlighting all the ways in which Brown was rigid, authoritarian, and even cruel.[20] Neither they nor the popular notion of the stern, bearded Brown fully reveals his role in the family.

Mary witnessed many moments of tenderness from her vantage point as Brown's wife. In an age that placed increasing emphasis on affective ideals in parenting, John Brown loved and took great pleasure in his children.[21] When away from home, he wrote letters to his children and seemed delighted by their responses. Pet names such as "Little Chick" and "Kitty" and queries about the children peppered his letters to Mary.[22] John and Mary's son Salmon, born in 1836, recalled that his father often sang to the children at bedtime, drawing them onto his lap and taking care to pay attention to them.[23] Family letters indicate that this was his practice well into the 1850s, when his time at home was brief and the number of young children shrinking. Annie, born in 1843, described how her father would even use his hands to make shadow puppets on the wall to amuse his children in the evenings.[24] All of Brown's children agreed that he exemplified tender devotion whenever illness befell them.[25]

Upon assuming her place in the household, Mary learned that Brown's affection was accompanied by a gruffer component, one that chronicled wrongdoing and doled out punishment (often corporal) in response. He wrote to Mary in November 1838, "Nothing will give me half as much pleasure as to hear that God is still granting you health and peace, & a disposition to do your duty to him and to each other." Continuing affectionately—but instructing rather dourly nonetheless—he concluded, "Say to all my little folks that I want much to see them, and tell Ruth and Fred not to forget the verse their father taught them last."[26] When Brown saw his children steering

John Brown's family

	Date of birth	Place of birth	Death
Dianthe Lusk	1801	Hudson, OH	Died after childbirth, Aug. 10, 1832
John Jr.★	July 25, 1821	Hudson, OH	Died in Put-in-Bay, 1895
Jason★	Jan. 19, 1823	Hudson, OH	Died in Akron, OH, 1912
Owen★	Nov. 4, 1824	Hudson, OH	Died in Pasadena, CA, 1889
Frederick (I)	Jan. 9, 1827	New Richmond, PA	Died March 31, 1831, age 4
Ruth★	Feb. 18, 1829	New Richmond, PA	Died in Pasadena, CA, 1904
Frederick★ (II)	Dec. 21, 1830	New Richmond, PA	Died in Kansas Aug. 30, 1856
Infant son	Aug. 7, 1832	New Richmond, PA	Stillborn, Aug. 7, 1832
Mary Ann Day	1816	Granville, NY	Died in San Francisco, 1884
Sarah (I)	May 11, 1834	New Richmond, PA	Died of dysentery, Sept. 1843, age 11
Watson★	Oct. 7, 1835	Franklin Mills, OH	Died at Harpers Ferry, 1859
Salmon★	Oct. 2, 1836	Hudson, OH	Died in Portland, OR, 1919
Charles	Nov. 3, 1837	Hudson, OH	Died of dysentery, Sept. 1843, age 5
Oliver★	March 9, 1839	Franklin Mills, OH	Died at Harpers Ferry, 1859
Peter	Dec. 7, 1840	Hudson, OH	Died of dysentery, Sept. 1843, age 2
Austin	Sept. 14, 1842	Richfield, OH	Died of dysentery, Sept. 1843, age 1
Annie★	Dec. 23, 1843	Richfield, OH	Died in Eureka, CA, 1926
Amelia	June 22, 1845	Akron, OH	Died, scalding, Oct. 1846, age 1
Sarah★ (II)	Sept. 11, 1846	Akron, OH	Died in Saratoga, CA, 1916
Ellen (I)	May 20, 1848	Springfield, MA	Died, April 30, 1849, age 11 mos.
Infant son	April 26, 1852	Akron, OH	Died few weeks after birth, May 17, 1852
Ellen★ (II)	Sept. 25, 1854	Akron, OH	Died in Saratoga, CA, 1916

Sources: Evan Carton, *Patriotic Treason: John Brown and the Soul of America* (New York: Simon & Schuster, 2006); Damon Nalty, *The Browns of Madronia* (Saratoga, CA: Saratoga Historical Foundation, 1995); Stephen Oates, *To Purge the Land with Blood: A Biography of John Brown* (New York: Harper & Row, 1971); Annie Brown Adams Binder, Mattole Valley Historical Society, Petrolia, CA; Clarence Gee notes on Brown children genealogy, Brown-Gee Collection, Hudson Library and Historical Society, Hudson, OH; and assorted newspaper obituaries from *America's Historical Newspapers* online database.

★ Lived to adulthood.

off course, he stepped in to correct them, either in epistle or corporeal form, depending on his (or their) whereabouts. Lying was a special offense in the Brown household. Many Brown biographers recount an incident in which three-year-old Jason was whipped, soundly, for recounting a dream as if it were real.[27] The Brown daughters also had their own memories of the importance of truth telling. Ruth recalled that Brown "used to whip me quite often for telling lies."[28] Annie recounted that one time she accidentally misread while reading aloud from the Bible; her father, who, despite his daughter's claim, thought it was no accident and that she was deliberately lying, boxed her ears.[29] Without exception, Mary Brown is never remembered as disciplining the children (or, for that matter, stepping in to protect them from Brown's wrath). But Brown looked to her to enforce his rules when he was away from home, and his letters frequently requested reports and confided hopes about the children's behavior.

The Brown family culture centered on discipline. Historian Stephen Frank notes that if "nineteenth-century parents wanted anything, they wanted their children to be obedient and to grow up to lead socially useful lives."[30] Additionally, John Brown thought of each child as he thought of himself: as someone constantly exposed to and needing to fight temptation. In Brown's famous 1857 autobiographical letter, he presents his early life in this light, recalling at length the various failings of his youth.[31] That his children were resisting temptation and "improveing" remained his lifelong preoccupation.[32] After offering some directions to his sons about "the business at home" in 1850, he offered this typical reminder: "I hope all of you will bear in mind the shortness, & the great uncertainty of life."[33]

Brown's apprehension about temptation and moral improvement was deeply rooted in his and Mary's religious beliefs, which Tony Horwitz has recently characterized as "a faith ever vigilant against sin and undue attachment to the things of this world."[34] His frequent urgings and reproofs of his children stemmed from their shared Congregational upbringing. Images of Brown happily embracing corporal punishment are often linked to his Puritan outlook and belief in an Old Testament God.[35] Both John and Mary Brown stood out from the core abolitionist beliefs that had emerged from the Second Great Awakening and associated reforms. Though he was not untouched by the Second Great Awakening revival, John Brown was no evangelical and did not participate in the "antebellum spiritual hothouse" from which faiths as diverse as Methodism and spiritualism emerged.[36] Instead, his faith was rooted in a modified Calvinism that had taken root in various Congregational and

Presbyterian congregations in the years after the American Revolution. Though it continued to stress the innate sinfulness of humankind, a newfound sense that humans could overcome their wicked nature was added.[37] This is reflected in Brown's continual urgings that his children "improve." To improve and, more important, to be useful would also become a motif in Mary Brown's post–Harpers Ferry life.

Mary's letters confirm that she, like Brown, placed importance on her family's religious education and believed in a kind of Calvinistic Golden Rule. She and Brown carefully taught their children the New Testament admonition to "remember those that are in bonds as though bound with them."[38] When Ruth brought home a piece of calico material that she had found at school, her father encouraged her to think not of her joy but of the sorrow of the girl who had lost it. (Needless to say, the material was returned to its owner.) Mary, too, encouraged such practice. In the late 1840s, Watson and Annie Brown attended a local grammar school in Springfield, Massachusetts, where their father was engaged in a wool business. At school they met a poor girl named Maggie Cole. "One night when we were going home from school," Annie later recalled, "Watson told me he thought if I was willing to put my spending money with his, that we might buy a warm dress for Maggie."[39] After consulting with Mary and getting her permission, Annie and Watson bought a dress for her the next morning on their way to school. Even in their own financial hardship, the lesson in the Brown household was service to others. Years later, Mary and Ruth would defer furnishing their own parlor in order to lay aside money to aid African Americans in North Elba.[40]

In John Brown's household, such decisions evolved from a family culture based on what son Salmon described as "equity," behaving as if all people were equal in God's eyes.[41] Some of the family's farm chores were segregated by sex, but other indoor household chores were not. Though the Browns occasionally had a hired woman to assist Mary with chores, their class status meant that none of them had the luxury of considering themselves above any particular task, and this coincided nicely with the ideal of equity. Frederick Douglass, visiting the Brown household in 1847, noticed this immediately. In his *Life and Times*, he idealized the roles that their poverty likely necessitated: "The mother, daughters, and sons did the serving, and did it well. They were evidently used to it, and had no thought of any impropriety or degradation in being their own servants."[42] After supper had ended, it was the boys who cleared the table and washed dishes. Remarking on their distinctiveness years later, Douglass added, "This style of housekeeping struck me as a little odd."[43] But to Brown it was a matter of principle as well as poverty, demonstrating his beliefs about humankind. At the Kennedy farmhouse outside Harpers Ferry, he would insist that one of his raiders assist his daughter in serving the nightly meal.

The lessons that John and Mary Brown taught their children about equity in the 1830s and 1840s led naturally into lessons about antislavery. They married in 1833, the year in which the American Anti-Slavery Society (AASS) was founded by William Lloyd Garrison and others who were calling for an immediate end to slavery.[44] Two years prior, in the opening issue of his abolitionist periodical the *Liberator*, Garrison had proclaimed a new urgency for the abolitionist mission. Garrison famously proclaimed that although some might "object" to his strong language, "I do not wish to think, or speak, or write, with moderation. . . . I am in earnest—I will not equivocate—I will not excuse—I will not retreat a single inch—AND I WILL BE HEARD."[45] Garrison's proclamation gestures to his method of moral suasion to convince Americans of the sinfulness of slavery; he vowed not to "*think, or speak, or write*, with moderation." While antislavery sentiment and calls for immediate emancipation remained associated with a small minority, most adherents to the cause adopted Garrison's pacifist ideals and tactics.[46] John Brown would ultimately dismiss these means and push his household toward direct interference with American slavery: words and moral suasion were not enough.

Brown later claimed that his beliefs stemmed from a childhood experience where, while driving cattle and spending the night at a man's house, he had seen a slave boy his own age treated badly and beaten.[47] His father Owen, who had had a similar brush with the brutality of slavery, nurtured Brown's leaning. Mary does not appear to have had the same kind of early encounter, but by the mid-1830s she had become familiar with both Garrison and Brown's antislavery doctrine. Brown subscribed to Garrison's *Liberator*, likely reading many of its stories and editorials aloud to his gathered family throughout the 1830s.[48] The 1837 killing of Elijah Lovejoy by an anti-abolitionist Illinois mob affected Brown profoundly.[49] But even before that, as early as 1834, he had spoken to his family of his hopes to "devise some means whereby I might do something in a practical way for my poor fellow-men who are in bondage."[50]

In the late 1830s, he and Mary provided an object lesson in "equity" that shaped his children's early antislavery ideals. In their home of Franklin Mills, Ohio, they attended a Congregational church. At that time, an African American couple was working on the Brown farm, and one Sunday the woman attended the Browns' church. Because the pews were segregated by race, she was seated toward the back of the church. This, Ruth later recalled, "aroused Father's indignation at once," and he took action. He invited the couple to attend church with his family the next week, and he pointedly walked them to the Brown pew. "The whole congregation were shocked," Ruth, who was nine at the time, recalled, "and the minister looked very angry, but I remember Father's firm determined look."[51] After the Browns' move to Hudson the following year, they were informed that their membership in the Franklin Mills church had been revoked, presumably in retaliation for their bold stance.[52] Ruth and the rest of the Browns saw this as the cost of antislavery adherence.

By 1840, Brown's wife and daughters were aware that they would be expected to perform self-sacrifice on account of American slaves; the specific shape of this duty would emerge over the next two decades. In April of that year, Brown was in Virginia surveying land. "I think," he wrote to his family, "we can find a place in it that will answer all the purposes for which we kneed."[53] He was already talking with his family about their need to combat slavery, even on southern soil, and about the need to live and work among African Americans. In the coming decades, his resolution would increase, giving shape to the remainder of the Brown women's lives. As he moved toward more radical belief in the 1840s, Mary and the children struggled with the demands of his extraordinary cause. No one would prove as unwavering as the family patriarch, but all the Browns would ultimately respond to his call.

Because of the Browns' emphasis on equity, it is tempting to portray Mary Brown as embracing a nascent feminism or to position John Brown as an ardent supporter of women's rights, demanding equality for his daughters in the public sphere at large after having his sons perform chores typically relegated to women in the private realm.[54] In the past decade, Brown's extraordinary antislavery beliefs have received much attention. He has been the subject of multiple full-length studies that single him out for his ability to transcend the racism that was predominant in nineteenth-century America—and rightly so.[55] There is much to admire in the antislavery creed that John Brown practiced and taught his family.[56] With his studied attention to "equity," Brown was not unlike other radical abolitionists who looked to their families as a springboard from which to perfect society.[57] But in a time when some radical abolitionists also looked to subvert traditional gender roles, or used their wedding ceremonies to renounce patriarchy, Brown did not, in large part because he was more than comfortable with both.[58] Though he expected Mary to endure hardship, he also sought to position her in the background, supporting his work: he thought of her as his equal before God, but not in earthly affairs, perhaps.[59] He never appeared publicly on behalf of women's rights in the way that Frederick Douglass did, nor did he enact anything we might recognize as feminism in his private life.[60] Comfortable with and even empowered by the enactment of patriarchy, Brown does not stand out as extraordinary in his beliefs about gender; instead he seems almost common. Mary does as well.

His dealings with his eldest son and daughter reveal Brown's gender politics clearly. Ruth left home in the mid-1840s to attend the Grand River Institute in Austinburg, Ohio, perhaps to train to work as a teacher.[61] In 1847, John Brown wrote his eighteen-year-old daughter a letter that revealed his vision of a daughter's place in the world. "I will just tell you what questions exercise my mind in regard to an absent Daughter," he wrote. He then listed eight queries for Ruth to consider, arranging them, he said, according to importance: "What feelings and motives govern her? In what manner does she spend her time? Who are her associates? How does she conduct in word and action? Is she improving generally? Is she provided for with such things as she needs, or is she in want? Does she enjoy herself, or is she lonely and sad? Is she amongst real friends, or is she disliked, and dispised?" These questions reveal an expected side of John Brown: was Ruth being motivated by the right ideals? Was she "improving?" But a softer side shows, too, as he reflected his concern that she was enjoying herself. Referring to himself as "a certain anxious father," John Brown warmly urged her to write. He ended with an unexpected vote of confidence: "If you have a satisfactory answer to them in your own mind, he can rest satisfied."[62] Though gender bending to be a "true and anxious mother" to Ruth, Brown confined his expectations of her and his other daughters to the private realm. He expected Ruth to work on "improving" herself, but he did not ask much of her in the way of public work. He would command that from his sons—work in his business and, later, personal bodily risk for antislavery.[63]

As a result, Brown's relationship with his sons had much more tension. They were routinely dispatched to one place or another to deal with Brown's business matters, and occasionally this interfered with their desire to make their own economic path. Brown also routinely chastised his older sons over their religious failings.[64] Brown biographer Oswald Garrison Villard reported that at Harpers Ferry, Watson informed his father, "The trouble is, you want your boys to be brave as tigers, and still afraid of you."[65] Tellingly, when his eldest son first left home, there is no record of a tender-toned letter such as Ruth received. Instead, Brown displayed quite a different tenor. In 1841 John Jr. took a position teaching in Ohio, where, just twenty years old, he struggled with asserting control in his classroom. As with Ruth, Brown portrayed himself as full of "intence anxiety" for his son's welfare. But by welfare he did not mean John Jr.'s happiness. He looked to the situation as a divinely ordained "test of the sway you may be expected to exert over mind in afterlife" and a trial to determine his manliness. "If," he continued,

> you cannot now go into a disordered country school and gain its confidence, & esteem, & reduce it to good order, & waken up the energies & the verry soul of every rational being in it yes of every mean ill behaved, ill governed, snotty boy & girl that compose it, & secure the good will of the parents, then how how how are you to stimulate Asses to attempt a passage of the Alps. If you run with footmen & they should wery you how should you contend with horses. If in the land of peace they have wearied you, then how how how will you do in the swelling of Jordan.[66]

Brown imagined here a public life for his sons different from that of his daughters, one that made him demand from John Jr. many responses that he did not ask of Ruth. It is thus not surprising that his sons professed a little more weariness in regard to their father than Ruth did. In his account of a visit to their home in 1859, Thomas Wentworth Higginson recounted that one of Brown's sons admitted that "we boys felt a little pleased some-times . . . when father left the farm for a few days." Higginson added that after this admission, Ruth spoke up, "reproachfully," and interjected, "we girls *never* did."[67]

When it came to his marriage, Brown was somewhat affected by the nineteenth-century development of "companionate marriage."[68] Many scholars point to one letter from him to Mary, likely written in 1846, as evidence of this affection and even partnership.[69] This letter is different from a typical Brown letter full of directives and inquiries. Instead, he offers very tender language. He opened, "It is once more Sabbath evening, and nothing so much accords with my feelings as to spend a portion of it in conversing with the partner of my choice, and the sharer of my poverty, trials, discredit, and sore afflictions." Brown's use of "the partner of my choice" is striking. He offered more praise a few lines later: "I do not forget the firm attachment of her who has remained my fast and faithful affectionate friend, when others said of me, 'Now that he lieth, he shall rise up no more.'"[70] As he had credited his first wife, Dianthe, with having a good influence on him, Brown now characterized Mary as an ever-faithful partner enabling his life's work.[71] But in haste to see Brown as a feminist-minded romantic, we cannot overlook the pragmatic fact that much rode on Mary's ability to manage his household.[72] The context for this particular letter was a time in which her "firm attachment" was being tested as it never had before, as Brown's antislavery commitment demanded more than ever before and as she endured illness and heart-breaking loss.

Rising Antislavery and "Sore Afflictions"

By 1840 five children—Sarah, Watson, Salmon, Charles, and Oliver—had joined the already bustling Brown household. Mary went on to have a total of thirteen children.[73] She spent the first years of her marriage in New Richmond, Pennsylvania, where she had met Brown, but in 1835 they moved to Franklin Mills, Ohio. Over the next eight years, Mary and her children moved back and forth between Franklin Mills, Hudson, and Richfield, all towns in northeastern Ohio, following Brown in his attempts to find work as a tanner, shepherd, and land surveyor. In addition to being characterized by dislocation, these were also years marked by profound loss. Between 1843 and 1849 Mary Brown lost six children, one at birth, four to an outbreak of illness, and one to a household accident, all the while balancing multiple pregnancies and shifting her household between several Ohio locations. In the face of these sorrows—or because of them—John Brown became more entrenched in antislavery sentiment and ever-bolder work on behalf of the antislavery cause.[74] Though abolitionists such as Wendell Phillips would claim after Brown's raid that Mary had been ever supportive of his cause, during the 1840s she seems to have had doubts, not about the wisdom of Brown's antislavery position but—quite understandably, given her circumstances—about its impact on her family's life.

In three weeks in September 1843, Mary Brown went through what she would later describe as the most trial-filled period of her life.[75] Six months pregnant, she saw eight members of her family fall ill. The cramped quarters of their home, as well as the needs of her family and potential illness of her own, made any momentary respite impossible, and Mary, surely filled with anxiety, tended to five-year-old Charles, critically sick with dysentery. He died a week later. Mary then watched helplessly as three more of her children became gravely ill: eleven-year-old Sarah, two-year-old Peter, and one-year-old Austin. Less than two weeks after the loss of Charles, Austin died, followed the next day by Peter and, a day later, Sarah. All three, Brown noted, were buried in the same grave. "They were all children towards whom perhaps we might have felt a little partial," he wrote to his eldest son, "but they all now lie in a little row together."[76]

Brown made sense of his loss through religion, like many in antebellum America. Though he acknowledged to John Jr. that this was "to us all a bitter cup indeed, and we have drunk deeply," he noted that one thing provided him comfort. "Sarah (like your own Mother) during her sickness," he wrote, "discovered great composure of mind, and patience, together with strong assurance at times of meeting God in Paradise." He added, "We fondly hope that she is not disappointed."[77] How Mary felt when she heard him reflect on this aloud can only be imagined, though one suspects that she instinctively recoiled. Even in an era when most mothers lived under what Judith Leavitt calls the "shadow" of maternity, and many children did not live to adulthood, to lose four children in two weeks was uncommon, extraordinarily tragic.[78] Mary would later recall, "That was the time in my life when all my religion, all my philosophy, all my faith in God's goodness, were put to the test." Years later, Mary would still recall the grievous loss of "my little ones . . . but three months before the birth of another child."[79]

That child was Annie, Mary's eighth child.[80] Despite her profound grief, Mary kept busy with a newborn as well as eight-year-old Watson, seven-year-old Salmon, and five-year-old Oliver. Eldest daughter Ruth had departed for school, so Mary was without her source of help in years prior. Another familiar chore soon added to her workload: preparing to move, this time to Akron, Ohio, where she would stay behind while Brown worked to establish a wool-trading business with wealthy businessman Simon Perkins in Springfield, Massachusetts.[81] Eldest son John Jr. was dispatched to Springfield to oversee the Perkins and Brown warehouse, and Mary and the children moved into a small home rented from Perkins.[82] At some point in 1845, Ruth returned to Akron, perhaps when Mary again became pregnant and needed an extra set of hands. Two Brown daughters were born in the next two years. Amelia was born in June 1845, followed by Sarah in September 1846. Mary may still have been in bed recovering from Sarah's birth when, one room over, daughter Amelia was taken from her. Sarah, like her older sister Annie, was born into a house full of melancholy.

Mary had put seventeen-year-old stepdaughter Ruth in charge of many household chores, including laundry. Even nineteenth-century domestic guru Catharine Beecher referred to laundering as the "American housekeeper's hardest problem," one that consumed "staggering amounts of time and labor."[83] It was the chore that middle-class women outsourced as soon as they were able. The Browns could not afford such a luxury, and Ruth was likely preparing water for laundry when a dreadful accident occurred. A pot of boiling water fell from the stove, scalding sixteen-month-old Amelia as she played on the floor. The baby, fondly nicknamed "Kitty," died within minutes; her pained cries were audible to a horrified Ruth, two-year-old Annie, six-week-old Sarah, and her mother. Though some Brown biographers have faulted Ruth for "carelessness," this was no more than an unfortunate accident as an overworked young woman tackled a physically demanding chore.[84]

Mary was not up to writing the news to Brown, nor was Ruth. (If the record that survives is representative, Ruth maintained a lifelong silence about the incident.) Owen, the eldest son at home, was assigned the task. After receiving the news, Brown wrote from Springfield to address his "dear afflicted wife & children." Brown wrote that he was "struck almost dumb" by the news that "one more dear little feeble child I am to meet no more till the dead small & great shall stand before God." He instructed, "This is a bitter cup indeed, but blessed be God: a brighter day shall dawn; & let us not sorrow as those that have no hope." With compassion, Brown acknowledged "Divine Providence seems to lay a heavy burden; & responsibility on you my *dear Mary*; but," he continued, ever moralizing, "I trust you will be enabled to bear it in some measure as you ought." Concerned about his eldest daughter, he added that he hoped no one would blame Ruth.[85] Nearly two months later, Ruth wrote to her father and requested "as much good advice as I will give."[86] It seemed her way of trying to make up with him, to seek out what he wanted to give his children: instruction. Whatever Mary had written to him, Brown said that it provided him "mournful satisfaction." Apparently she at least mirrored his language of Providence and acceptance of the loss— in his words, "as she ought."[87] On the basis of Mary's later statement about this being a time that tested her faith, one might wonder if she exaggerated her peace to her husband.

Mary remained preoccupied by grief for months. She confided in her husband, who conceded "the sudden and dreadful manner" of Amelia's death but chided that she, like he, needed to "bow my head in submission and hold my peace." He concluded, "Mary, let us try to maintain a cheerful self-command while we are tossing up and down; and let our motto still be Action, Action,—as we have but one life to live."[88] Later, faced with the sorrow of Harpers Ferry, Mary would look to doing to see her through; in the years after 1859, her motto was undeniably "Action, Action." But in 1849 she would take a different action from what Brown envisioned.

After the devastating losses and financial downturns of the 1840s, John Brown, too, transferred his grief into "Action, Action."[89] He hatched a plan to move his family again, this time over five hundred miles to North Elba, in Essex County in upstate New York, where Gerrit Smith had established a land-grant colony for African Americans. By 1848, only twenty or thirty farms had been established there; start-up costs were high, and the land and climate harsh.[90] But Brown saw something in the far-off Adirondack region: a place to live equitably alongside African Americans, to redeem his family financially and claim a place in antislavery insurgency.

While Brown planned this next move, Mary cared for the children. She had been struck with a "bilious fever" that lingered after Amelia's death and had remained sick in the years that followed.[91] Now pregnant for a tenth time, she heard of another child's brush with death. Oliver had accidentally eaten hemlock. John Brown described the boy's recovery as "like one raised from the dead, almost."[92] After this scare, Mary must have been particularly relieved to deliver a healthy girl, whom they named Ellen.[93]

By fall John Brown had grown eager to examine North Elba in person. Mary and six-month-old Ellen traveled with him as far as Whitehall, New York, where they remained behind with Mary's brother Orson while her husband traveled into what Ruth described as "the Adirondac wilderness." Ruth recollected his enthusiasm for the "grand mountain scenery" and his sense "that he was needed there to encourage and help by his experience the few colored families who had already settled in the wilderness, and those who might move there the following spring." But on the trip home, Ellen fell ill with consumption, and it proved fatal. She was the sixth of Mary's children to die. When she was buried, Ruth later noted, "father broke down completely, and sobbed like a child. It was very affecting to see him so over-come, when all the time before his great tender heart had tried to comfort our weary, sorrowing mother, and all of us."[94]

In the months after Ellen's death, Mary continued to be unwell from some combination of weariness, sorrow, and disease. In the summer of 1849, the Massachusetts writer and attorney Richard Henry Dana visited the Browns at North Elba. (His visit was not intentional; lost in the woods, he stumbled upon the Brown home.) He described Mary as an "invalid" and noted that twenty-year-old Ruth, a "bonny" redhead, was in charge of an "unlimited family of children."[95] John Brown's departure to Europe in August 1849 to sell more wool—on top of the death of Ellen and the move to North Elba—did nothing to help Mary's uncertain health. Within days of his departure from their new Adirondack homeland, she, too, left it behind.

Flight

Mary Brown's flight to David Ruggles's water cure establishment in Northampton, Massachusetts, stemmed from near-desperation to obtain relief. Between 1840 and 1900, nearly 213 "water cure establishments" appeared in the United States, concentrated in New York, New Jersey, Pennsylvania, and Massachusetts.[96] They were popular with many reformers interested in not just antislavery but diet and other "bodily reforms," and they promised users they could "wash and be healed."[97] Abolitionists backed the building of African American David Ruggles's establishment; Garrison himself had been a patient there the previous year.[98] Ruggles, a onetime bookstore owner, grocer, and longtime antislavery writer and activist, had opened his water cure in 1845. There, cold water wraps, sprays, soaks, and plunges into pools of water (the "ladies plunge" was $6 \times 10 \times 3\frac{1}{2}$ feet deep), as well as attention to diet, exercise, and clothing, were employed to cure patients of neuralgia and numerous other bodily ills.[99]

How Mary knew about the water cure is not clear. Advertisements for Ruggles's establishment appeared in the *North Star* and other reforming papers, and Northampton was only a short distance from Springfield, Massachusetts, where she had been living prior to the Browns' move to North Elba. Ruggles had assisted the fugitive Frederick Douglass, who could have mentioned him to Mary during his visit to the Browns' home. Or she may have heard townspeople discussing Ruggles, whom the *Water-Cure Journal* described as a "man of color, faithful, honest, intelligent, and persevering; one of the earliest practitioners of water, and always had so far as we can learn, remarkably good success."[100] Mary's stepsons Jason and John Jr. were also intrigued by the newfangled practice of hydropathy, so she may have discussed it with them.[101] If she talked it over with Brown, he likely dismissed the water cure as an unnecessary fad. Because of the planning and cost involved, Mary's departure could not have occurred without some forethought. Ruggles only accepted patients who wrote to him of their symptoms in advance. She also had to pull together the necessary payment—at $5.50 a week, a hefty payment for a poor woman. (The fees were significant enough that Sarah Grimké had complained about their prohibitive cost.[102]) How Mary paid the fee—or if Ruggles offered any kind of discount—is unknown, though once there, she wrote to John Jr. to request additional funds on at least one occasion.[103]

Significantly, she left for the water cure without her husband's knowledge. She left it up to John Jr. to inform his father that she had traveled alone from Essex with the "principal design" of going to Ruggles's water cure. This, he wrote, "she seems *bent* upon as her only salvation. Said that she must do something at once, or she would not live but a little while." John Jr. and his wife, Wealthy, attempted to talk Mary out of her decision, to no avail. "She persisted in her resolution so strongly," he added, "that we had to fix her off with all things necessary as well as we could and she went and has been there ever since."[104] In a few weeks, she began to feel better.[105] Her growing sense of well-being emboldened her. Mary wrote to John Jr., "I am glad you have let him know where I am," adding forthrightly, "he has never believed their was any disease about me but I think if he was here now he would to change his mind."[106] Brown came to see her once before returning to North Elba alone. If he expected her to depart with him, he was disappointed; she remained with Ruggles until November.

Ruth tended to the family in Mary's absence and kept her apprised of all that went on in North Elba, sending newsy letters full of information about neighbors in "Timbuckto" and her own family. She was especially careful to include news of five-year-old Annie and three-year-old Sarah. Both of them were "remarkably good," she wrote Mary, assuring her that they were eating fruit and had stopped crying before bedtime. "I think we get along first rate here, much better than I expected," Ruth concluded, but reassured Mary that she was missed.[107] Over a month later, she added, "if you want to come back as much as we all want too see you, you would not stay long after you get well. . . . I know Said and Anna do for they often speak of you."[108] She also let Mary know that the Brown rules were being followed in both parents' absence. "I have been too meeting every Sunday, and the boys have when they could," she wrote, noting, "I have told several, that we did not receive '*sunday calls*' nor shall we with *my* consent, while you, are gone." Ruth was supportive of Mary's decision to go to the water cure, despite all the extra work it created for her. And she encouraged her not to rush home, whether from enjoyment of life without Mary's presence or a sympathetic assessment of her stepmother's needs. "We *all*," she added, "want to see you very much, but, *do not come until you get well* if the doctor can cure you for it is an opportunity you may not get again."[109]

Mary's twelve-week stint in Northampton provided her with a number of benefits. One element was respite. Though both men and women flocked to water cures, the historian Susan Cayleff describes them as "a physiological and psychological sanctuary" for nineteenth-century women in particular.[110] They addressed women's life experiences: they offered treatments for complicated pregnancies, frank discussions of childbirth and female problems, and even treatment of conditions such as a prolapsed uterus. If Mary went to Ruggles's establishment in part as a response to concerns about her many pregnancies, the focus on "self-help" may have assisted her.[111]

There she was also exposed for the first time to a genuine reformist circle beyond that of her immediate household. Though Brown and his family were fervent in their antislavery beliefs, Mary Brown had had little exposure to the reform radicals like those she would see in Northampton. One such radical was Lucy Stone, who spoke in Northampton in early November 1849.[112] Stone had been speaking throughout Massachusetts in the fall of 1849, lecturing on antislavery and women's rights.[113] A week or so prior to her talk at Northampton, Stone had even been vocal in her criticism of religion, which, she had argued, made "'man-stealers missionaries, woman-whippers ministers, and cradle-plunderers church members.'"[114] If Stone lodged such a complaint at Northampton, it probably first took Mary Brown aback. But she likely also felt affirmed, thinking upon the Browns' expulsion from their church in Franklin Mills. The *Liberator* reported that Stone had "good meetings" the week in which she spoke at Northampton, but Mary may have also heard opposition from the audience.[115] Mary declared it the "first time that I ever heard a Woman speak." She did not detail Stone's message, but she noted, "I liked her very well."[116] After her return to North Elba, Mary would not be part of such a reformist group again for another decade, but her time at the water cure may have given her a sense that women could be more active participants in reform. This is not to say that it propelled her toward radical beliefs about women. Though Lucy Stone made an impression, Mary Brown never worked on behalf of woman suffrage. But perhaps she became more outspoken as a result. A few months after her return, Ruth wrote to her sister-in-law Wealthy, "You have no idea how large she is in her feelings since she came home from the Cure."[117]

In his 1910 biography of Brown, Oswald Garrison Villard idealized Mary Brown as possessing "rugged physical health and even greater ruggedness of nature," adding that she "was as truly of the stuff of which martyrs are made as was her husband."[118] But her 1849 departure to the water cure reveals a different Mary, one acting in opposition to the family culture of self-sacrifice and duty. Pressured by financial constraints, grieving the loss of a half dozen children, and ever on the move, Mary had experienced her share of tribulations prior to 1849; yet in some ways her life was ordinary for a woman of her times. Still, her connections to her husband's mission heightened the demands placed on her. Though he mythologized her strength, Villard may not have been all wrong in his assessment that the demands on Mary required her to be "rugged." And the water cure respite stands out because it was her one indulgence during decades of work to rear dutiful children and to perform the home-front tasks that enabled her husband to become an antislavery warrior.

Such demands would only increase in the next decade. Like many other women in nineteenth-century America, Mary Brown would lose another infant child; unlike many others, she would also mourn the death of two grown sons and a stepson, all sacrificed on the antislavery battlefield. Her husband's mission would create new constraints, as Mary and young daughters Annie and Sarah faced multiple moves, long periods of Brown's absence, and an even less certain financial outlook. By the time the last Brown, Ellen, was born in 1854, the family culture centered on John Brown's growing activism. Mary and Ruth acquiesced as he risked his life and the lives of Brown sons and husbands on multiple antislavery missions. In 1849, as she returned from the water cure, Mary had no way of knowing the lengths to which John Brown would go to combat slavery, and all the sacrifices he was yet to require of her and the children.

❦ CHAPTER 2

North Elba, Kansas, and Violent Antislavery

Mary Brown returned from the water cure and rejoined a family that was putting its long-nurtured antislavery sentiment into action, first by moving to the African American settlement at North Elba and then by becoming increasingly militant in antislavery practice. As ever, ordinary life continued alongside this extraordinary trajectory. Mary and soon Ruth were preoccupied by childbearing, illness, and the day-to-day routine. Brown's absences—for work and his antislavery mission—became more frequent, and Mary and Ruth were left to maintain the antislavery family base at North Elba and endure the continuing repercussions of the family's poverty. In doing so they remained in the background, acquiescing if not implicitly endorsing Brown's radical decisions. But their domestic work proved necessary to his mission, allowing him to roam far from home throughout the 1850s.

The decade proved pivotal for the Brown women as well. Ruth, along with John Jr.'s wife, Wealthy, and Jason's wife, Ellen, became the first Brown women to embrace militant antislavery. Throughout the decade, Ruth's fervency deepened. Mary and Annie ultimately followed her lead. Back from the water cure in 1849, Mary, one suspects, still viewed the Brown family's North Elba outpost with some skepticism. But by 1858, according to early Brown biographer Richard Hinton, she would fold bandages as Brown prepared to go to Harpers Ferry, implicitly endorsing his violent plans.[1] Daughter Annie grew to a teenager against the backdrop of the Kansas years. By 1859, she would play a critical role in Brown's raid and be the only one of the Brown women to take a direct role in his battle against slavery. The childhoods of the youngest Brown daughters, Sarah and Ellen, born in 1846 and 1854, respectively, took place amid this increasing family devotion to violent antislavery.

Taking a Stand at North Elba

Though they took pride in the fact that they were living out the family ideal of equity, the fierce winters of their new home were hard on the Browns. When they arrived in 1849, Richard Hinton, a British-born journalist (later to be Brown's comrade in Kansas), noted that Essex County had "but few roads, schools, and churches, and only a few good farms." "The life of the settler at North Elba," he added, "was pioneer work. . . . The forest had to be cut down and the land burnt over; the family supplies must be produced, mainly, within the household itself. Sugar was made from the maple trees; from the wool they raised, the women spun and wove garments; sheep and cows especially were the farmer's wealth."[2] During the six months of the year not comprising winter, the younger Brown sons planted grass, oats, potatoes, and some vegetables. The Brown daughters gathered fruit from the meadows and forests. Mary's illnesses continued, but with John Brown away, much was required of her regardless. As he had not had the time or resources to build them lodging, the family of nine first lived in a rented home. The small log house, Ruth recalled, featured "one good-sized room below, which answered pretty well for kitchen, dining-room, and parlor; also a pantry and two bedrooms; and the chamber furnished space for four beds,—so that whenever 'a stranger or wayfaring man' entered our gates, he was not turned away."[3]

Ruth remembered that the house at first seemed "dark and cheerless to us," but they soon settled in.[4] A few years after their arrival, Ruth campaigned for John Jr. and Wealthy to join them in their Adirondack home. Even in her attempts to persuade them, she was forced to admit that living there had its difficulties. Though it was a "cold and frosty country," Ruth contended that a good living could be made and added that there were "preaching every sabbath and schools."[5] To Wealthy's queries about whether it was perhaps too cold, Ruth's then-husband Henry Thompson admitted that, though it was May, their ground was "frozen as hard as a brick bat." He further confessed that their rooster had frozen to death, "thus paying the penalty of living in this inhospitable clime." Looking at the bright side,

Ruth appended, "What Henry wrote was true, and I shall not attempt to dispute it, but he had the blues pretty hard just then because it was so cold."[6] Ruth did not look to attract her brother and sister-in-law solely out of her desire for their companionship; she saw the Brown family mission there as important. John Brown frequently reminded his family that their work at North Elba did not just focus on economic renewal. Instead, they aimed to establish a model African American community, of which he hoped to serve as leader.[7] "As soon as we had got fairly settled," Ruth later recalled, "father began to think what he could do to help the new colored settlers to begin work on their lands."[8]

Though they had lived in the antislavery stronghold of Hudson and had interacted with African Americans before, North Elba was different. Here, the Browns met daily with those whose lives were marked by the existence of slavery and racism. Though Gerrit Smith had hoped to give land to many families, only a few dozen at most were present in the early 1850s, and by 1870 only a few remained. It is hard to re-create life there, especially from the African American settlers' perspective.[9] It is clear that the Browns developed close relationships with some in the community, including the family of Lyman Epps. The 1855 census lists Epps as a forty-one-year old mulatto who had resided at North Elba for six years with his wife, Ann, and four children.[10] Though it was the younger Browns who had been playmates of the Epps children, John Jr. and Ruth would maintain a lifelong correspondence with Lyman Epps Jr., who referred to their father as "one of the truest friends our race has ever known."[11] Numerous residents worked with the Brown sons or inside the Brown home, including Mrs. Reed, a widow who assisted Ruth in managing the household when Mary was ill, and a Mrs. Wait.[12] The Browns also socialized with the North Elba community. Salmon Brown recalled attending meetings at the local schoolhouse where everyone ate picnic style.[13] The Browns were also close to at least one fugitive slave who had made his way to the Adirondacks, though most of the settlers were free. The first morning that they awoke there, Ruth and Annie Brown had met Cyrus. Hearing that Cyrus was a runaway slave from Florida, John Brown hired him to work on the farm.[14] With his addition, Ruth recalled, "there were ten of us in the little house," but "Cyrus did not take more than his share of the room, and was always good-natured."[15]

In their relationship with North Elba's African American community, the Brown family put into practice a lifetime of Brown's unorthodox belief that all people deserved equal treatment. In their North Elba home, all—male and female, black and white—sat around the same dinner table.

A visitor who passed a few days with them in the summer of 1849 reported this practice with an admiration tinged with surprise. Richard Henry Dana was struck by the Browns' careful attention to surnames: the African American guests and Dana were all addressed as "Mr." Dana also glimpsed the beginnings of the Brown family commitment to a more militant antislavery. While eating, Dana overheard Ruth inquiring from a passerby if he had seen her father. The man told them that Brown, accompanied by "two negroes . . . a man and woman," would arrive soon. Dana noted, "Ruth smiled, as if she understood him," implying that these were fugitives the family was assisting. Dana also witnessed Brown's arrival. "Late in the afternoon," he recalled, "a long buckboard wagon came in sight, and on it were seated a negro man and woman, with bundles; while a tall, gaunt, dark-complexioned man walked before . . . while a youth followed by the side of the wagon."[16] It was these two, along with Cyrus, who joined the Browns for dinner.

One year later the activity Dana witnessed took on a new urgency. The passage of the Fugitive Slave Act in 1850 made Ruth and the other Browns more aware of the dangers that African Americans such as Cyrus faced. The law marked a concession to the South, part of the Compromise of 1850 to resolve sectional tensions over slavery exacerbated by land gains after the Mexican War. It "put federal muscle on the side of slave owners" and forced northerners to cooperate in the return of escaped slaves. Historian Bruce Laurie adds, "The controversial law rattled Yankees like nothing else had."[17] Many abolitionists reacted to the law by adopting more militant language. Wendell Phillips, for instance, argued that an African American under threat from a federal marshal was justified to shoot the marshal.[18] John Brown applauded the law for its effect on the antislavery movement. He noted in a letter to Mary that the law had roused many to the cause: "It now seems that the Fugitive Slave Law was to be the means of making more Abolitionists than all the lectures."[19] But he also considered its effects on African Americans, reminding his family "to imagine themselves in the same condition," threatened with enslavement.[20]

Ruth and the other Browns talked over Brown's plan to fight back against the Fugitive Slave Law. In Springfield, Brown organized a group of forty-four African American men into the League of Gileadites, and he encouraged them to train to use arms. Brown biographer David Reynolds adds that Brown converted his wool warehouse in Springfield into an Underground Railroad stop.[21] When he returned to North Elba, Ruth recalled, "he went round among his colored friends there who had been fugitives, urging them to resist the law, no matter by what authority it should be enforced. He told them to arm themselves with revolvers, men and women, and not to be taken alive."[22]

Brown's growing commitment to armed resistance was not limited to himself: *all* Browns were expected to defend their North Elban neighbors against slave catchers. Ruth noted that Brown "bade us resist any attempt that might be made to take any fugitive from our town, regardless of fine or imprisonment."[23] Notably, she needed no such persuasion. Taught from infancy to "remember those in bonds as if bound with them," Ruth was especially struck by the dangers that now faced Cyrus.[24] She stated: "Our feelings were so roused that we would all have defended him, though the women folks had resorted to hot water."[25] Though Brown had assigned her to home-front defense, Ruth envisioned herself as active on behalf of the antislavery cause. Though she denigrated "hot water" as a woman's weapon, she still claimed it as hers.

As she found her antislavery feelings roused to extraordinary lengths, twenty-one-year-old Ruth also experienced the most ordinary of life events: courtship. Her courtship with Henry Thompson stands in marked contrast to that of John and Mary Brown. Ruth confided her interest in Henry, part of a longtime North Elba farming family with antislavery inclinations, to John Jr. and Wealthy. The Thompsons were also comparatively well established at North Elba, as Henry's father had arrived in nearby Lewis in 1824. Roswell Thompson was relatively successful, ultimately owning a thousand acres and many cattle. Henry had at least nine siblings, and one of his sisters would later marry Watson Brown.[26] Writing to her brother and sister-in-law in March of 1850, Ruth confided, "I will be candid . . . and tell you that we are *engaged to each other for life*." Valuing emotion in a way that Mary may not have been able to in her 1833 "courtship" with the widower Brown, she added, "I used to think that I should never see the person that I loved well enough to have, but I believe, I have, at least. He is a gentleman in every respect. he is kind, *affectionate*, and *whole-sould*, and what you call a 'progressive-being.'"[27]

Though Henry had a "verry excellent farm" about four miles from land Brown had acquired, Ruth and Henry planned to build on the Brown claim instead, perhaps as a way to maintain the family's work with the North Elba community.[28] Despite the constraints of her family's poverty, Ruth prepared to "go to house keeping" and created a trousseau. Seven-year-old Annie and four-year-old Sarah watched and perhaps even assisted as Ruth and Mary made new pillowcases, sheets, linen tablecloths, and other items for her home. She also had some furniture and household

FIGURE 1.   Ruth Brown Thompson, ca. 1850. Ella Thompson Towne Scrapbook, John Brown Family Collection, The Huntington Library, San Marino, California. Reproduced by permission of The Huntington Library.

items. To Wealthy, she wrote, "I have also a very nice table, a wash stand a large looking glass, . . . chairs and other things that will not be worth while to mention. So you see Wealthy I need not complain." Her father's daughter, Ruth then declared herself above such material considerations: "Yet for all this we shall not be happy if furniture, and land, and houses,

Figure 2. Henry Thompson, ca. 1850. Ella Thompson Towne Scrapbook, John Brown Family Collection, The Huntington Library, San Marino, California. Reproduced by permission of The Huntington Library.

are our highest aim. . . . That is not the case with *us*. Pure genuine *love* is upper most."[29]

In her close friendship with Wealthy and in a courtship based on "love," Ruth, unlike her stepmother Mary, exemplified mid-nineteenth-century middle-class ideals.[30] Ruth's acquaintance with Wealthy had likely begun when Ruth was living in Ohio with her brother John, attending school at the Grand River Institute around 1846.[31] Their letters are reminiscent of the closeness described in Carroll Smith-Rosenberg's seminal article on nineteenth-century female friendship.[32] At one point they had a falling out, and in a letter of apology, Ruth asked Wealthy, "Who is there that I can call sister, if it be not you?"[33] When John and Wealthy decided to move to Ohio in the late 1840s, Ruth declared their impending move as "a sad thought," lamenting, "You have blasted, all of my fond hopes, and all I can do is submit to it."[34] She would ever after try to persuade them to adopt North Elba as home.[35] Unable to prevail on them, she and Henry ultimately traveled to Ohio to visit, and the two growing families exchanged frequent letters.[36]

She found more in their relationship to inspire her than that which she saw between her father and Mary. Writing to Wealthy, Ruth confided, "It was with you and John that I first became convinced that true genuine happiness could exist between husband & wife but I now believe it after witnessing it in you and from your own account." What she had with Henry lived up to their model. "I think that I have found one true confiding heart one that I love fondly," she continued, adding, "He is I think well adapted . . . to me, allowing me to be my own judge."[37] Ruth's words reveal that "genuine happiness" had not always prevailed in the Brown household. And though John Brown would occasionally acquiesce to Mary—most notably when she disagreed about what to do with his body after his death—he did not aspire to let her "be my own judge." After her wedding in September 1850, Ruth continued to define her marriage according to the companionate ideal in vogue in the mid-nineteenth century.[38] Almost a year after her marriage, she wrote to Wealthy, "The more Henry's character unfolds itself to me the better I *love* him."[39] The losses Ruth experienced may have somewhat softened her relationship with her stepmother. In 1851 she gave birth to a son who lived only a few months. Writing a few weeks after her loss, John Brown confessed that he was "afflicted" alongside the Thompsons. He added, "As in this trouble you are only tasting of a cup I have had to drink deeply, and very often, I need not tell you how fully I can sympathize with you in your anxiety."[40]

Since the time of Amelia's death Ruth had looked to her father for both guidance and approval. More than any of her brothers, she mirrored Brown's religious beliefs. When her brothers fell away from Brown's creed and began to challenge his orthodoxy, Ruth took actions of which her father would have approved: she wrote them pleading letters in which she expounded on the errors of their religious ideas. In one lengthy letter in 1853, she reminded her brother of the "principles" that had been taught them, even "around the death-bed of our departed Mother."[41] John Brown looked to her when he was frustrated about his sons' loss of faith, apparently feeling that Ruth could understand what he was enduring. "Why will not my family endeavor to secure *his* favor, and to effect in the *one only* way a perfect reconciliation?" he once wrote to her.[42] After Henry was saved at a North Elba revival in 1853, Ruth's position as religious heir was further confirmed.[43]

Ruth and Henry also followed her father in their growing antislavery fervency. In 1853, they wrote to John and Wealthy of their pleasure in reading Harriet Beecher Stowe's antislavery novel *Uncle Tom's Cabin*. Ruth's sense of what means antislavery advocates should employ came across clearly as she reported their recent foray into neighborhood discussion of Stowe's novel. Perhaps some of Henry's siblings were among the discussants, or the Brewsters, another white family. It does not appear to have been an inter-racial gathering. Some of her neighbors, she wrote, had said that though they felt for the plight of the slave, "they think the Abolitionists have done a great deal of harm in coming out so strong and in taking such high ground they have only riveted the chains tighter." Ruth found this to be nonsensical. Dismissing her neighbors' views as ineffectual, she described "moral suasion" as a "verry mild means a plan which I think will do about as much good as it wold to try to pacify a raging tiger with the promise of a good meal by and by."[44] Years later, another Brown daughter, Annie, would compare Brown to this tiger and assert that she, like Ruth, would prefer him to be on her side if she were faced with trouble. If Mary read *Uncle Tom's Cabin* (which, given the hardships she faced in the early 1850s, seems unlikely), any thoughts that she had about it have disappeared from the historical record.

In the early 1850s, Ruth's antislavery sentiments had grown without much direct contact with her increasingly fiery father. Brown felt pressed to leave North Elba in order to resolve his financial obligations and settle lawsuits stemming from his partnership with Simon Perkins. Most of the Browns moved back to Akron in March of 1851, with the Brown sons driving cattle overland and Mary and "the little girls," as John Brown called Annie and Sarah, traveling by train.[45] Mary may have welcomed the move back to a larger society, particularly after seeing Ruth's pregnancy and loss.[46] If he was reluctant to depart, Brown may have derived some comfort from the fact that Ruth and Henry were stationed there, symbols of the family's antislavery beliefs.

Even as her husband moved toward radical action, Mary's life remained dominated by the ebb and flow of pregnancy, childbirth, and recovery. In

May of 1852, John Brown wrote to John Jr. and Wealthy to let them know that they had another brother. But although the baby was "the largest and strongest boy she ever had," he had contracted the measles and whooping cough. Brown noted, "Our little one has dark hair and eyes like Watson's," adding, quite movingly, that "notwithstanding our large number, we are very anxious to retain him."[47] A few days later, the yet-unnamed infant succumbed. Sarah, too, became sick with the measles and whooping cough, and though "we were quite anxious on her account," John Brown wrote to John Jr. that they were "much more alarmed" for Mary, who started having bleeding in her lungs within a few days of the baby's death.[48] It took her the summer to recover. Writing to Ruth that August, John Brown reported, "Your mother is still more or less troubled with her difficulties, but is able to keep up about and accomplish a good deal."[49] Annie and Sarah, he added, were attending school while the Brown boys prepared the animals for the Ohio State Fair. Though Mary's health did rebound, in early 1854 she became ill again, likely an effect of her thirteenth pregnancy.[50] Ellen was born in September 1854, the twentieth and last of Brown's children.[51]

Paddling Their Own Canoe

Soon after Ellen's birth, John Brown prepared his family for a final move back to North Elba to rejoin Henry, Ruth, and their son Johnny. He seemed determined that Mary play a part in his antislavery activism by housekeeping at North Elba and standing, like Ruth and Henry, as a symbol of his commitment to African Americans.[52] If Mary was reluctant, she apparently did nothing to prevent the move; she may have bargained with Brown to delay the move until after Ellen's birth, or she may have been glad to be moving close to Ruth and her growing family.[53] During her second tenure at North Elba, Mary would witness Ruth's growing antislavery commitment, one marked by abstract ideological belief as well as specific support of a militant antislavery mission that would take her father and brothers, and some of the Brown women, to Kansas. Together, Mary and Ruth would read letters detailing their husbands' armed antislavery efforts, and they would sustain the loss of the first Brown son on the antislavery battlefield. Though Brown had long talked of his war on slavery, it only now became their reality.

Ruth and Henry eagerly welcomed Mary Brown and her children— teenagers Watson, Salmon, and Oliver, as well as ten-year-old Annie, eight-year-old Sarah, and new baby Ellen—back to the area. Prior to their return, Ruth wrote to assure Mary that she would have more comfortable quarters in North Elba than during her first sojourn there. Henry was building his in-laws a house. "I am really glad that you are coming here," Ruth wrote, "for we need you here." She concluded with a few words for her three young sisters. "Well An and Saidy," she wrote, "I expect to see you before long, and also the little girl. I expect she is something nice from father's description."[54]

As the Browns prepared to move, Kansas emerged as an antislavery battleground. After the Kansas-Nebraska Act (1854) mandated that the people of each territory would be free to determine whether slavery was permitted, pro-slavery Missourians poured into Kansas. When a pro-slavery constitution was fraudulently enacted, many northerners saw it as the further encroachment of "the slave power" that had been growing since the Fugitive Slave Act of 1850.[55] Antislavery advocates in the Northeast formed the New England Emigrant Aid Company to send New Englanders to Kansas to provide enough voters to ensure that Kansas's entry as a slave state would be blocked. Notably, it sent them armed. As Nicole Etcheson has demonstrated, northerners and southerners came with different notions of liberty, but both were determined to ensure it for their side, slave or free.[56] Brown's idea

FIGURE 3.   Annie, Mary, and Sarah Brown, ca. 1851. Library of Congress.

that "war" must be declared on slavery had a growing number of backers.[57] Ultimately, it was in Kansas that Brown would embrace violent means—and broadswords.

Long before the infamous events along Pottawatomie Creek, Brown's sons John Jr., Jason, Salmon, Frederick, and Owen had made plans to travel to Kansas. In October 1854, Owen, Frederick, and Salmon departed from Ohio. Though motivated by the chance to help ensure that a free Kansas came into the Union, they were also clearly prompted by economic opportunity. After their arrival, John Jr. reported, "Salmon, Fredk, and Owen say that they never was in a country that begun to please them as well."[58] Interweaving antislavery zeal with pragmatism, he continued, "And I will say, that the present prospect for health, wealth, and usefulness much exceeds even my most sanguine anticipations. I know of no country where a poor man endowed with a share of common sense & with health, can get a start so easy."[59] John Jr. and Jason had followed their brothers by boat, as they brought their wives Wealthy and Ellen and their children.

As they traveled, Jason and Ellen lost their oldest child, Austin, to cholera. They had disembarked to bury Austin in Missouri and, in so doing, encountered a group who had been told to extend no kindness to "northern men."[60] Upon reaching Kansas territory, John Jr. assessed it favorably but added that he had seen many pro-slavery men "armed to the teeth with Revolvers, Bowie Knives, Rifles and Cannon." His chosen remedy was to coordinate an antislavery army to rival them. "Here are 5 men of us," he added, "who are not only fully anxious to prepare, but are thoroughly determined to fight."[61] By that August, Oliver would write to Mary and Ruth to report approvingly on Underground Railroad activity in Kansas.[62]

Even before his sons sent such reports, Brown had been torn: he longed to live at North Elba, and yet he felt inclined to go to Kansas and actively battle the "slave power." In August 1854, he had urged John Jr. and his other sons toward Kansas, but he noted, "*I feel committed to operate in another part of the field.*"[63] Now he wavered. He wrote to Ruth and Henry, mulling over the matter and hinting at the obligation that he felt to the people of North Elba. (Whatever duty he felt to Mary and his young children, he did not say.) He asked for the opinion of Ruth and Henry as to which place he was "more likely to benefit the colored people *on the whole*." Indicating a continued closeness with the Adirondack settlers, he requested that Ruth and Henry "learn from Mr. Epps & all the colored people (so far as you can) how they would wish, & advise me to act in the case, all things considered," adding, "As I volunteered in their service . . . they have a right to vote, as to course I take."[64] That November he still felt "pretty much determined to go back to North Elba," but by the following summer he had changed his mind.[65] This was a fateful move. His actions in Kansas would connect Brown with the abolitionists who would fund the Harpers Ferry raid and provide aid to his family in the years that followed.[66]

Though some antislavery men would bring their families to Kansas to engage in the fight, it would be five years before Brown asked any woman of his family to directly engage in, rather than indirectly support, his antislavery work.[67] Instead, Mary and Ruth maintained homesteads in the absence of their husbands. In late summer of 1855, they assisted as John Brown, his son Oliver, and son-in-law Henry departed North Elba for Kansas. Twenty-year-old Watson was left behind to assist Mary and daughters Annie, Sarah, and Ellen, as well as Ruth and Johnny. For once it was Ruth, rather than Mary, who was expecting a child as John Brown departed home. He left the Brown women with a final admonishment. "If it is so painful for us to part with the hope of meeting again," Ruth later recalled him saying to his gathered family, "how dreadful must be the feelings of hundreds of poor slaves who are separated for life!"[68] This occasion marked the first of three times in Mary's life when she would watch as men of her family departed North Elba to fight slavery. By the time Brown and his sons returned from this first mission, he had begun to acquire the fame and celebrity that would, in the wake of Harpers Ferry, extend to her and the Brown daughters.

The Brown women faced a number of challenges as they tried to manage their households and farms with only the assistance of Watson. Mary took charge of the family homestead, exchanging letters with John Brown and her sons, going over day-to-day arrangements, and pleading for any money that could be spared to help support them. Ruth and Mary enlisted the help of twelve-year-old Annie and nine-year-old Sarah for household chores and caring for Ellen and Johnny, both toddlers. Mary likely assisted her step-daughter in the delivery of Ella, born in the spring of 1856. (Grace followed in 1858.) Ella would grow up alongside her aunt Ellen, and Mary and Ruth benefited from having an extra set of hands to care for their youngest daughters.[69]

While their husbands fought their battles in Kansas, the women's daily lives were preoccupied with domestic management and scraping by. Mary's letter to Brown in May 1856 is typical. After reporting that all were "midling well," she added that the two youngest Browns were ill, Ellen suffering from worms and Ella being "dreadfull cross." Mary then detailed how the Brown farm fared. They had made sixty-four gallons of sugar as well as some molasses and vinegar, and Old Spott, one of the cows, had begun giving "a nice mess of milk." And, Mary assured Brown, "Watson is not idle I can tell you." He had sown four acres with rye, and was preparing to plant carrots, turnips, and potatoes in their garden. In addition, he had been working for one of the Thompsons, perhaps in exchange for other work on the Brown farm.

Mary's lifelong poverty had prepared her to make do with little, but she now found herself stretched to the limit. She defended the North Elba Browns for their financial endeavors, but admitted that they were hard pressed in Brown's absence. Reduced to five dollars, Mary admitted that Watson had written to Brown's father to ask for money. "We have tried to use what means we had as economical as we knew how to & tried to keep out of debt," she argued, but added, "What we have now received will pay up all of our debts & some over to get leather for shoes. The girls & I have not had any since we came here & have made all Ellen has had this winter out of cloth."[70] As Frederick Brown noted in a letter home to them, with all but one Brown man off fighting, Mary and Ruth were left "alone to paddle your canoe."[71] Brown valued the domestic work that the women (and Watson) at North Elba did, acknowledging Mary's "widowed" state and the inherent hardships and loneliness as the price of the family's antislavery work.[72] But he also urged Mary to get by on as little as possible.

Though their front against slavery was a world away, the urgency of the antislavery battle in Kansas was soon brought to life in letters from men and Brown daughters-in-law Wealthy and Ellen. In August 1855, Oliver wrote to North Elba about the Kansas Browns' own gloomy financial straits, and the following month, Mary heard from John Jr. about an encounter with an area slaveholder.[73] Once John Brown arrived in Kansas that fall, his letters quickly became filled with news of the antislavery battle being waged in Kansas Territory. Writing to North Elba in October 1855, Brown made no attempt to conceal the Brown sons' militant endeavors. He reported that the previous Tuesday had been an election day, and, "hearing that there was a prospect of difficulty we all turned out most thoroughly armed (except Jason, who was too feeble)." As they read the men's letters aloud to Watson and his sisters, Mary and Ruth could not have overlooked the Brown men's willingness to undertake violent defense of Kansas. Brown closed with these words of consolation: "You are all very dear to me, and I humbly trust we may be kept and spared to meet again on earth; but if not, let us all endeavor earnestly to secure admission to that eternal home."[74] Though this was in some ways typical rhetoric, the prospects of his death must have seemed suddenly real.

The Kansas letters brought home the Brown men's commitment to violent means on behalf of the antislavery cause. In one especially long letter from December 1855, Brown detailed how about three weeks prior, in response to a murder of a pro-slavery man and the jailbreak of his killer, Kansas governor Shannon had ordered out about two thousand men. Going into detail, Brown stated that a battle had been "hourly expected." John Jr. (who had traveled ahead of them on horseback to Lawrence) got word that "our help was immediately wanted." The letter related:

> On getting this last news it was at once agreed to break up at Johns Camp, & take Wealthy, & Jonny to Jasons Camp, (some Two Miles off); & that all the men but Henry, Jason, & Oliver, should at once set off for Lawrence under Arms, those Three being wholly unfit for duty. We then set about providing a little Corn Bread; & Meat, Blankets, Cooking Utensils, running Bullets, loading all our Guns Pistols etc. The Five set off in the Afternoon, & after a short rest in the Night (which was quite dark) continued our march untill after daylight next Morning when we got our Breakfast, started again; & reached Lawrence in the Forenoon all of us more or less lamed by our tramp.

Lest the North Elba Browns be in doubt that the men were prepared for violent action, John Brown added that he, John Jr., Jason, Salmon, and Frederick "had each a gun, with two large revolvers in a belt exposed to view, with a third in his pocket, and as we moved directly on to the bridge." Praising his sons and the Free State forces, he continued, "I never expect again to see an equal number of such well behaved, cool, determined men; fully as I believe sustaining the high character of the Revolutionary Fathers."[75] He promised to mail a newspaper account of their exploits back to North Elba.

Mary, Ruth, and Annie were also aware that the Brown daughters-in-law were applying the family ideal of self-sacrifice for principled belief in a free Kansas Territory.[76] Assessing the danger they faced and commenting wryly on the North Elba weather, Wealthy wrote to Watson that "we might as well die here in a good cause as freeze to death there."[77] Though Ellen admitted that their house had only a dirt floor, it was an improvement on their original quarters, as, she wrote, it had "quite a good chimney in it so that I can cook a meal without smoking my eyes almost out of my head."[78] Mary and Ruth, each sensitive to a mother's loss of a child, may have considered Austin's death as Ellen's antislavery sacrificial offering. In time Wealthy especially began to write of her support of the cause. This surely made a special impression on Ruth, her close friend. Writing to another friend in March 1856, Wealthy thundered,

> Those *miserable Missourians, barbarous scamps* many and wicked are their threats but whether they *dare* attempt to intrude on the people of Kansas again I know not. reports say that they are busily engaged preparing—getting together arms men, and means, to make another desperate effort to drive out the Free State men here. but let them come, the people here are quite well supplied with arms, and have for the last six months had millitary [sic] Companies formed and are ready and determined to go forward and defend their rights even if it must be by bloodshed.[79]

Wealthy did not go as far as some Kansas women and take up arms herself, but her words nonetheless relayed the severity of their situation.[80]

In June 1856 Mary received a letter recounting all that had passed in the fighting in Lawrence and telling her of the imprisonments of John Jr. and Jason. After they had gone to the relief of Lawrence, John Brown wrote, the two men had been taken prisoner after both of their homes were burned "to ashes."[81] Pro-slavery forces, he continued, were after "our scalps," and since the capture of his two eldest sons and the wounding of Ruth's husband, Henry, "we have, like David of old, had our dwelling with the serpents of the rocks and wild beasts of the wilderness; being obliged to hide away from our enemies." He continued, "We are not disheartened, though nearly destitute of food, clothing, and money." Almost as an aside, he casually mentioned that they were suspected of murdering five at Pottawatomie. This is all that he would acknowledge in writing about Pottawatomie, other than a cryptic mention in this same letter that God would not charge them with "innocent blood."[82] When they returned to North Elba, Henry Thompson would tell stories about their times and travels in Kansas, but he did not include details drawn from his participation in the murders of James Doyle, two of Doyle's sons, and Allen Wilkinson and William Sherman on Pottawatomie Creek.

Mary and Ruth drew a renewed sense of the urgency of the antislavery fight from the letters that they received in the summer of 1856. A letter from the gentle Jason to Ruth detailed how he had been taken prisoner. Jason confided that John Jr., harshly beaten soon after his capture, had fallen into fits of madness. Even this had not saved him, and Jason reported that he had seen "my Brother knocked and kicked shamefully for feigning insanity (as they said); and making noise." Thinking of Wealthy must have affected Ruth profoundly. Jason despaired, "How much longer will the worthless doughfaces of the North cry 'we have nothing to do with Slavery.'" He detailed the worsening conditions in Kansas. "Murders and robbery are very frequent now. We are obliged to keep under arms night and day," he wrote, adding, "Ellen and Wealthy have done exceedingly well about taking care of the children and what stock and other things we have left. . . . They would gladly go home; but feel safer here than on the *way* home. No women have been injured yet; so far as I know." Jason concluded, "We expect to fight till the last. All active FS men are marked for destruction. I shall not leave Kansas till it is free or I fall in the field."[83] As Jason was known for his gentle disposition and abhorrence of violence, his sentiments were striking.

After a summer in which Ruth and Mary had read reports of the Kansas wars, in September 1856 John Brown wrote home to report that Frederick had been killed in an attack by the "Ruffians" at Osawatomie, the biggest Brown sacrifice to date.[84] He did not linger detailing the death but instead divulged details of his counterattack. Collecting a group of men who were serving under him, Brown attacked the "Ruffians" within an hour of Frederick's death. Boasting that they had killed or wounded between seventy and eighty men, he added, "Jason fought bravely by my side during the fight, and escaped with me, he being unhurt. I was struck by a partly-spent grape, canister, or rifle shot, which bruised me some, but did not injure me seriously." "Things seem rather quiet just now," he concluded, "but what another hour will bring I cannot say."[85] From jail John Jr. would comfort his father that "Poor Frederick has perished in a good cause, the success of which cause I trust will yet bring joy to millions."[86] Was this a transformational moment for the Brown women? It is hard to imagine it in any other way. Ruth had first seen pro-slavery forces threatening Cyrus and others at North Elba; now, they had taken one of her brothers. Owen wrote to Mary that Brown was gaining a reputation as "the most daring courageous man in Kansas," and the men also sent home news clippings telling of their exploits.[87] Celebrity had begun to attach itself to the Brown family.

Though most of the letters that the women wrote to the Kansas Browns have been lost, we may surmise that they advised the men to bear up and assured them they were carrying on well at home; the tone of their letters, John Brown wrote, "I like exceedingly."[88] As ever, Brown appreciated contact with his family. Writing to Mary in February 1856, he claimed himself "particularly grateful when I am noticed by a Letter from you," adding that thoughts of visiting North Elba could almost "unman" him. But he very quickly turned back to talking of the "new; & shocking outrages at Leavenworth: & that the Free State people there have fled to Lawrence, which place is again threatened with an attack. Should that take place we may soon again be called uppon to 'buckle on our Armour;' which by the help of God we will do."[89] He let Mary Brown know that he was sacrificing their togetherness for the cause, and she was urged to "buckle on" her own "Armour" and deal with all the hardship.

The passage above is Brown at his most tender, though one of Henry's letters to Ruth surpasses it. Henry opened, "I hardly no how to express my feelings while reading your last letter. Words or language is too barren with me to express the half I feel." He added, "After reading your letter I could hardly go to sleep and when I did my mind wandered back to my mountain home. I saw my dear Ruth and pressed (her) to my heart and imprinted kiss after kiss on her noble brow." From this dream, though, he awoke "to find myself in Kansas far far from the dearest object of my affection." Like Brown, Henry admitted that he missed his wife, along with his "dear boy" Johnny. "Oh: how I miss your society and advice," he confided to Ruth, "for I feel you have great influence over me. . . . Should I be spared to fulfill my mission (for I feel I have a sacrifice to do to *Baal*) I should go home and be content to spend the remainder of my days in providing for my *loved ones*." If these sentences alone failed to remind Ruth of the dangers Henry faced, he instructed her that he would be on the move soon and urged her to "give yourself no uneasiness about me."[90]

Ruth's response was equal parts tender and affirming of Henry's devotion to his "duty." She confided that, in reading accounts of the Kansas troubles in the papers, she felt quite "anxious" for Henry. "I do very much want to see you, Dear Husband," she confessed, "and I often feel as though I could not be separated any longer from *one that is so dear to me*." Their son, she noted, "talks a great deal about you, and says, 'I wish Father could see my little Sister.'" Ruth acknowledged how hard it was having Henry away, but encouraged him to remain. "I know," she wrote, "that your motive was a good one, in going and I shall always love and respect you for doing what you felt to be your duty." Belief that he was sacrificing for a noble cause helped but did not make it easy to endure his absence. She concluded, "Oh! I long to have you come home, and if you think best come for all will welcome you gladly, but if you think you cannot I will try to think all is for the best, and may the Lord ever be with, and guide you."[91] It is unclear from Ruth's letter how she defined Henry's "duty," though it seems likely that it was one to the antislavery cause and, perhaps as important, to her father.

Henry Thompson returned shortly thereafter. Back home with a rifle ball from the battle of Black Jack still in his shoulder, he served as a living testament to the antislavery struggle in which the family was engaged. An additional monument was soon added when a stone was erected in Frederick's honor, reading "Born Dec. 31, 1830, and Murdered at Osawatomie, Kansas, Aug. 30, 1856, For his adherence to the cause of freedom."[92] After Henry's return, Ruth listened with other family members as he told some of his best stories about his travels to and adventures in Kansas to visitor Franklin Sanborn.[93] Henry might have included a tale of his near-arrest early in their Kansas travails. He had challenged "old man Doyle" (who died at Pottawatomie, perhaps at Henry's hands) when Doyle asserted that African Americans were naturally inferior. His brother-in-law Salmon and Henry heard of the arrest warrant, "and concluded it would be a good thing for me to go over and give myself up." Salmon traveled with him so he could report on what happened, and "in case they arrested me, the whole company was to come over in the morning, march into the court, and hand me a couple of revolvers; we would then adjourn the court summarily." Resolving his listeners' suspense, Henry continued, "But the court had weakened, Judge Cato had gone—and I heard no more about the warrant."[94] Such stories cemented Ruth's determination to serve what she would soon term "the cause."

Reflecting back on all that had passed in 1858, Ruth wrote to her father, "I do feel that God has been with you thus far, and will still, be with you in your great and benevolent work."[95] By this point she could have no doubt that this "great and benevolent work" involved violence and danger. But she declared devotion to Brown and "the cause." During Sanborn's visit, she, like Henry, "entertain[ed]" him "with anecdotes of her father."[96]

Mary Brown, Enigma

When John Brown returned to North Elba from Kansas in 1856, he felt no wavering about whether he should stay there or go elsewhere to fulfill his antislavery duty. Instead, over the next few years he crisscrossed the country from Kansas to New England and back again. He spent time in Iowa and Missouri, from which he led close to a dozen slaves to freedom in Canada. He also continued consulting with New England abolitionists such as George Stearns and Thomas Wentworth Higginson, hinting at his plans to lead a raid to help slaves escape in the mountains of Virginia. Though Mary had never been accustomed to luxury, the financial straits that she faced in these years were especially difficult, particularly as Brown's father Owen, a source of aid, had died in May 1856. From Osawatomie, Brown wrote to her in September 1858, talking over some matters involving the farm and their debt, and closed by encouraging her, "Do the best you can: & *neither be hasty or get discouraged*."[97] He also began his own fund-raising efforts on her behalf.[98] Writing to Franklin Sanborn in May 1857, he mentioned that he had written to another backer, George Stearns, to request that a $1,000 donation Stearns had promised "for the permanent assistance of my Wife & children" be "promptly raised."[99]

By the time of his request, John Brown's fame had begun to grow, particularly among a small but influential circle of New England abolitionists. Few of them had met his family, though they had been introduced through Brown's letters and speeches to their sacrifices to make Brown's work possible.[100] Franklin Sanborn vouched for them as worthy recipients for charity. In a circular to raise funds for the Brown women, he declared their devotion: "Both Mrs. Brown and Mrs. Thompson (whose husband was wounded in the battle of Black Jack, and who has two children)," he wrote, "are hard working, self-denying, devoted women, fully sensible of the greatness of the struggle in which Capt Brown is engaged, and willing to bear their part in it."[101] Such characterization of the Brown women would become commonplace among Brown's supporters, then and in the months that followed Harpers Ferry.

For such sacrifices Mary emerges from the historical record as "willing to bear [her] part" in Brown's work. She did so in the most practical way, maintaining the family home and living on a small and uncertain income during Brown's frequent absences. By the mid-1850s she was unquestionably sensible, concerned most of all with pragmatic details of day-to-day life at North Elba: what to plant and when, how she would feed her family, and what she would do to assist Ruth as each of her children was born. Perhaps this practicality came naturally to Mary, or perhaps it was molded during her marriage to John Brown. The same can be said about her reticence. John Brown described her in the late 1850s as someone who, "though not above getting her head over the *wash tub*; will never till [tell] her *trials or her wants* to the world." This, he added, "I know by the experience of the past two Years."[102] By this time, Mary was beginning to realize that her survival would hinge on not keeping such "trials" and "wants" to herself.

But to Brown's funders it was also important that Mary be "worthy" of Brown. This meant that she not only logistically supported but believed in all of his work. John Brown offered Sanborn an anecdote to assure him that Mary did both. He recounted that Mary had "made up her mind" that he should go to Virginia long before 1859, and "when I did go, she got ready bandages and medicines for her wounded."[103] Did Mary actually do this?

And if she did so, did it express *ideals* as well as *pragmatism*? In the records that survive—and in all likelihood, in those that have been lost—Mary Brown's feelings are hard to decipher. That she was reticent, perhaps even shy, comes across clearly. But what she actually thought about Brown, his work, and the antislavery cause prior to 1858 is not clear. She stood alongside him when he seated African Americans at their church in Franklin Mills in 1838, and she maintained the family home throughout the 1850s while he was away. These are not small things, and they certainly enabled Brown's antislavery mission, at home and beyond. How she *felt* about all of this in some ways seems like a luxury in which Mary Brown did not indulge.

In the weeks (and years) after Brown's raid, it would become important to abolitionists, and even to the Brown women themselves, to assert that their support of John Brown had been unwavering and constant. By 1885, Sanborn would eloquently compare Mary to the Old Testament figure of Ruth as well as Homer's Penelope.[104] Such heavy-handed comparisons diminish her lived experience, ignoring the real sacrifice in her choice to sustain Brown or even her lack of choice in the matter. For Mary as well as Brown's sons, a willingness to do all that Brown asked would not come easily. In the years after Harpers Ferry, Mary Brown herself would claim her support had been absolute. But the veracity of this claim is questionable—and impossible to prove. Simply put, Mary Brown remains an enigma.

There was one Brown woman who would do all her father asked. In the mid-to-late 1850s, Annie Brown started writing letters to her brothers who were far from home in Kansas and elsewhere. For the most part, her letters echo an ordinary girlhood, describing outings and her daily life to brothers who, like so many northeastern sons, had moved away from the family farm to pursue their own livelihoods. But Annie's letters also refer to interracial overnight camping trips and were addressed to brothers enlisted in a radical, violent cause. By 1858, she would write, knowingly, "Where are Father and Owen and what are they doing? We have not heard from them for some time. Father has got an idea that letters are taken out at the P.O. and that we do not get them."[105] The following year, Annie Brown would adopt her father and brothers' violent creed as her own—and to her siblings' chagrin, she would ever after claim that she had a special role in her father's extraordinary work.

❧ CHAPTER 3

Annie Brown, Soldier

One day in the summer of 1859 Annie Brown was hard at work sewing at the hideout for Brown's raiders. Out of the blue, two small wrens flew all over and "appeared to be in great distress." "We went out," Annie recollected, and "found that a snake had crawled up the post and was just ready to devour the little ones in the nest." John Brown quickly killed the snake. Then he turned to his daughter and said that he thought it "very strange the way the birds asked him to help them, and asked if I thought it an omen of his success."[1]

Franklin Sanborn included this anecdote in his 1885 *Life and Letters of John Brown*. He described it as a "touching incident," one that highlighted Brown's bravery and his certainty of belief in the antislavery cause. Few have gone beyond recounting it to look closely at the female actor or to consider the Brown women's experience of the Harpers Ferry raid.[2] Annie had traveled along with her sister-in-law Martha from North Elba to serve directly alongside her father in his war on slavery. Five miles outside Harpers Ferry, she worked as lookout and cook, antislavery idealist and laundress. In her labor in the months before his raid, Annie experienced a trial-by-fire inauguration into abolitionist activism and, perhaps more notably, an antislavery creed that not only tolerated but embraced violent means. While her older sister Ruth had come of age in a more traditional way—marrying and "going to housekeeping"[3]—Annie's coming of age came through her embrace of a much less conventional form of housekeeping, one designed to conceal a radical agenda. She was like many antebellum women who worked in reform, in that her assertion of "housekeeping" involved a clever use of domestic rhetoric to claim a place in radical, public activity. But she differed in that hers was not just a rhetorical device: her very position as housekeeper clothed her involvement in violent antislavery.[4] Her life blended the mundane tasks of cooking and laundry with work as a lookout, and this extraordinary juxtaposition shaped both her present and her future. In the months around the raid, she and brothers Owen, Oliver, and Watson applied family lessons about self-sacrifice and embraced the violence inherent in Brown's definition of their family's special duty. In the course of this, Annie grew close to many of Brown's antislavery soldiers; she would ever after take pride in her months as an "outlaw girl."[5]

News of Brown's raid would soon grip the nation, but planning for it had controlled the Brown women's lives for years, if not decades. While Mary, Ruth, and the other Browns endured what biographer David Reynolds has termed a "hardscrabble" existence, John Brown had traveled not just to Canada and Iowa but to antislavery centers such as Boston, where he courted abolitionists who helped fund his antislavery enterprise.[6] In the summer of 1859, Brown used the alias of "Isaac Smith" to rent a farm about five miles from Harpers Ferry. Brown planned to seize the federal arsenal there and arm local slaves in order to incite widespread rebellion. He had the financial backing of Thomas Wentworth Higginson, Franklin Sanborn, George Stearns, Gerrit Smith, Theodore Parker, and Samuel Howe, a group known to history as the "Secret Six."[7] In addition to consultations with Harriet Tubman and Frederick Douglass, he had also persuaded well over a dozen men from as far away as Iowa, Kansas, and even Canada to join his makeshift antislavery army.[8] He expected further reinforcements from his family, long trained in sacrifice on behalf of principle.

When Brown announced his intentions he found his sons divided. Owen, thirty-four, and newly married sons Oliver, twenty, and Watson, twenty-three, quickly agreed to participate.[9] Brown was not surprised that Jason, whose aversion to violence was well known, deferred.[10] However, he was likely taken aback by the defection of Salmon, who pleaded familial obligations. Henry Thompson also declined his invitation. In early 1858, John Brown had asked Ruth to "let Henry go 'to school'" again, using the coded language that Ruth had invented while Henry was waging war against slavery alongside Brown in Kansas.[11] Ruth's response highlighted her conflicting desires: to earn her father's approval, to protect her growing family, and to claim an active role for herself and not just Henry. She explained, "Were it not for my little children, I would go almost anywhere with Henry, if by going I could do . . . any good." She then questioned, "could I not do something for the cause?"[12] After years of home-front work for Brown's cause, Ruth suddenly asked for a role at a different front. But she then yielded to practical considerations.

It is hard to know how to interpret her request. Surely Ruth did not think that her father would arm her, yet her request seems to have been earnestly made. After hearing about the Brown sons' trials in Kansas, did she yearn to sacrifice directly rather than indirectly? Did she suddenly wish to be treated as a Brown *son*? Although some scholars have taken Ruth's refusal to immediately agree to Henry's absence in the face of her father's "hard question" as indication that the Brown women overall did not support Brown's newest mission, the whole of Ruth's response offers indication to the contrary.[13] In the end, even John Brown seems to have concurred that it was better that Ruth and Henry stay behind, overseeing the farm and lending assistance to Mary. Brown may have been appeased by the substitution of two of Henry's brothers, Dauphin and William. In retrospect Ruth's calculation of the risk to Henry would prove correct: both of his brothers lost their lives fighting alongside her father.

In mid-June John Brown and his son Oliver departed, stopping to pick up Owen in Ohio before emerging in Chambersburg, Pennsylvania, reborn as "Isaac Smith and sons." They had not been gone long before Oliver reappeared at North Elba with a surprising request. Suddenly, Brown asked of Mary what he had recently denied to Ruth: an active role in the mission. "I find," Brown wrote, "it will be indispensable to have some women of our own family with us for a short time." After instructing Mary on what to pack and chiding her to maintain his guise, he added, "I want you to come right off. It will be *likely* to *prove* the most valuable service you can ever render the world."[14]

Mary remained at North Elba, and the ambiguity of her response has long frustrated Brown biographers.[15] Despite Brown's entreaty, perhaps she feared leaving five-year-old Ellen and twelve-year-old Sarah, or Watson's wife Bell and her newborn Freddy. Mary seems to have believed that she was needed more at home and that the stakes for her family were as high as those for the slaves. Like her flight to the water cure, this episode demonstrates that her submission to Brown was not complete; she did not see his "I want you to come right off" as an order that commanded obedience.[16] She continued to have faith in Brown's broad antislavery cause. The month previously, she had confided her hope that Brown "be blessed with health & success in the good & great cause your [*sic*] are engaged in."[17] She signed that with the pseudonym "Mary D. Smith," implicitly endorsing Brown's plan as well as acknowledging the danger that he faced.

Regardless of Mary's reason for refusing Brown's entreaty, it appears as if he anticipated it. In the middle of his letter he offhandedly inserted, "if you cannot come, I would be glad to have Martha and Anne come on."[18] And it was so: in the third week of July 1859, Oliver, Martha, and Annie set out for the Kennedy farmhouse. If Brown was at all angry with Mary or surprised at the girls' appearance, this did not prevent him from writing to assure her that they had arrived safely.[19] Their arrival in Maryland opened up the most momentous chapter of Annie's life.

Annie and Her "Invisibles"

The farmhouse that Brown rented was located about half a mile from the foot of the Blue Ridge Mountains, far enough away from the neighbors to be secluded—or so he thought. He believed Annie and Martha could help maintain the ruse that "Isaac Smith" and his sons were scouting for mining opportunities and land, and he carefully introduced them as the Smith daughter and daughter-in-law. To neighbors he claimed that the boxes of rifles and weapons in the living room were furniture awaiting his wife's inspection.[20] Though some of the raiders were housed in a building across the road, most of them were to live at the farmhouse. Brown and the girls quickly outfitted an upstairs loft for them.[21] Annie, Martha, and Oliver shared a downstairs bedroom. Interviewed in 1908, Annie recalled, "Oliver and Martha slept in one side of the room and I in the other side, of the same room, My bed was under the last window." Taking pride in her sacrifice there, she added, "I had a calico curtain around my bed, my only luxury."[22]

Luxury aside, she and Martha put in long days of work. The girls first made beds of coarse cotton filled with hay for themselves and for the men. For their beds downstairs, Martha and Annie also sewed sheets. Neither the men nor the girls had pillows, so they relied on carpet sacks or coats to cushion their heads on the primitive beds.[23] As Annie and Martha worked, more men arrived. Some came on foot, while others were picked up in nearby Chambersburg. Most arrivals were brought in secretly, particularly the African American raiders. Annie and Martha made a cover for Brown's wagon so that he could bring in his men without attracting attention.[24] Though Annie cried herself to sleep the first night, homesick and flea-bitten, she soon settled into life at the farm.

FIGURE 4.   Annie Brown, age 15, 1859. Library of Congress.

FIGURE 5. Martha and Oliver Brown, 1859. Library of Congress.

As she had grown up poor in a small house packed with family, the cramped quarters of the Kennedy farmhouse were not a novelty. She and Martha quickly turned to the tasks that would dominate their days. After an initial culinary debacle, Martha took over much of the cooking. Annie handled serving and cleaning. As would have been familiar to Annie from her childhood, one of the men was assigned to help them with chores and the ever-expanding laundry duty.[25] At least one of the men always assisted, washing while Annie and Martha spread clothes out to dry in the sun, ready at a moment's notice to bring them in so that so many clothes would not generate suspicion among the neighbors.[26]

Annie took pride in her role as woman of the house. Perhaps she remembered the bustle at the Brown family home as her older sister Ruth prepared to set up housekeeping with Henry, and thought of herself as undertaking the same. Or she saw herself as bringing domesticity (limited as it was) to the rough-and-tumble farmhouse. Her first week had been memorable, as she and Martha had endeavored to demonstrate their culinary skills to the three Browns and Jeremiah Anderson, a raider recruited from Brown's days in Kansas. Annie recalled that while the men went to Harpers Ferry to buy a stove and other essentials, "Martha and I went to the house and tried to surprise them with a dinner which we tried to cook in an old fire place. . . . We succeeded after making several attempts in getting a poor fire to burn, and boiled some potatoes and onions, which tipped nearly over several times, spilling out a few each time. I was trying to make some kind of bread when the boys arrived bringing bread . . . relieving us of that source of worriment to older housekeepers than we. We ate our dinner camp fashion," she concluded, "and began housekeeping in real earnest."[27] The mid-nineteenth century saw the publication of numerous cookbooks and housekeeping guides for a growing middle class, but none envisioned the kind of family that Annie now governed.

Annie saw her role as a woman offering—and demanding—civilization, regardless of the radical nature of their true mission. She normally swept the floor around dinnertime, but one day she balked at the chore, seeing that tobacco had been spat all over the floor after an afternoon of card playing. That night before serving supper, she held up the light to reveal her unswept floor and declared, "Gentlemen, I am willing to wait upon you,—that is what I am here for; I will do anything that is reasonable, but I am not willing to be a mop-rag for you; I do not want this thing to occur again."[28] New arrival Alfred Hazlett apologized the next morning. Despite the crimp the young women put on rougher behavior, Hazlett and the other raiders took comfort from their presence. Perhaps playing the role of middling-class bachelors made the real dangers that they faced as well as the monotony of hiding in the loft bearable. In his 1861 memoir, Osborne Anderson noted his gratitude for the grapes, chestnuts, and flowers that Annie and Martha gathered.[29] In return, Annie would defend Brown's raiders—their couth as well as their motives—for the rest of her life.

Describing her evenings "spent on the porch or sitting on the stairs, watching and listening," Annie proudly recalled, "I was there to keep the outside world from discovering that John Brown and his men were in their neighborhood . . . he *depended* on me to watch."[30] In engaging Brown women to move beyond the private sphere on behalf of antislavery, John Brown had gauged wisely. Martha and Annie's work was critical in keeping the raiders' secret, for despite their remote location, neighbors did appear. A Mrs. Nichols proved a frequent source of trouble. One morning she appeared unannounced, and although Annie signaled to the raiders to scurry upstairs, John Cook did not flee to the loft in time.[31] "I had to think of a good many things *instantly* in those days," she later recounted. As Mrs. Nichols stood between Cook and the ladder to the loft, Annie shooed him into her bedroom "in the corner near the window at the back of the house and only a short distance to the ground on that side." Pulling her calico curtains (her one luxury) around the bed, she bid Cook to keep silent. Then Annie entertained Mrs. Nichols while Martha made a "rumpus" in the kitchen, allowing Cook to escape out the window amid the noise.[32]

A Mrs. Huffmaster also frequently appeared without warning, sometimes while a suspicious amount of laundry was out to dry. "So minute of a record of this curious, little woman's doings may seem trifling to you after so many years have come and gone," Annie conceded self-consciously, "but I assure you she was not a trifle in our daily life then although she filled a small space in the world physically." She seemed to have the uncanny ability to time her visits at breakfast or dinner, when the men were downstairs eating and perhaps off guard. Annie recalled, "I would then shut the door and the men would disappear noiselessly up the stairs, taking the dishes, victuals, tablecloth, and all with them, while Martha and I entertained her on the porch or in the kitchen." She often appeared with her children, causing Martha to dub her "the little hen and chickens."[33] Once, one of the "chickens" made it halfway up the stairs to the loft before Annie deftly cut him off. On another memorable occasion, Annie and her brothers performed songs for the Huffmaster family, who had apparently heard raiders Aaron Stevens and Charles Tidd singing and had come to the house to request an encore. Though Stevens and Tidd laughed upstairs while listening to the Browns' off-key reprise of their singing, Annie took the threat posed by the Huffmasters seriously.[34]

Annie set herself the additional task of keeping the raiders within the confines of the house, especially as some had a penchant for wandering off from the farm during daylight. Alfred Hazlett and William Leeman in particular "were the hardest ones to keep caged," she recalled in 1895, adding that she and Martha "were so self-conscious that we feared danger when no man pursued or even thought of it."[35] Her older brother Owen also stepped in and assisted her once, walking all the way to Antietam to buy corn so that some of the more adventurous—or foolhardy—raiders would not be tempted to leave their upstairs hideaway to steal it from the neighbors.[36] On another occasion, restless Kansas recruit Charles Tidd stood out on the porch and read a newspaper, too weary of confinement to show proper fear of exposure. Annie tried to warn him about Mrs. Huffmaster's propensity to appear, but to no avail. "Just then I looked up and saw her coming along the path by the fence," she recollected. "Tidd said, 'Blast that woman, what a torment she is,' and slipped back into the kitchen and up a ladder into the loft."[37]

While Annie took pride and even joy in her secret antislavery mission—she proudly titled Brown's raiders her "invisibles"—she was not at all light-hearted.[38] As children in the Brown household, Oliver and Annie had been taught that any lie, even one of omission, was sinful. Living a lie rankled her conscience. "It was sometimes a hard matter for me," she recalled, "to reconcile myself to the fact that the father who had always before this taught me to speak the truth should place me in a position where I was obliged to constantly tell lies, go by a false name, and live a false life." She confessed, "I used to wonder if God would bless a work that had to be done that way."[39] But at the time and in years to come, Annie found comfort from her sense of duty to her father's work and from the idea that Brown had "depended" on her.[40] For the first time, she felt as though her father trusted her. She cherished a particular recollection of his bowing to her judgment of how to deal with Mrs. Huffmaster after the woman had glimpsed one of the African American raiders. Acting on his request that she "account for it some way" or to "bribe her not to tell, if possible," Annie went to Mrs. Huffmaster's house. Though she felt sure she had smoothed over the matter, she added, "We lived in constant fear and dread after that."[41]

As at North Elba, Brown brought the men together to read from the Bible and pray every morning. The raiders gathered downstairs to eat both breakfast and dinner.[42] John Henry Kagi, John Brown's "lieutenant," occasionally sent newspapers from nearby cities, and John Brown subscribed to the *Baltimore Daily*. Other raiders subscribed to religious publications. Aaron Stevens also brought Thomas Paine's *Age of Reason*, which the men read and debated. Despite the serious nature of the plans and drills, Annie and Martha witnessed the men indulging in merriment: "They played checkers and cards, sang songs, and told stories for amusement and on stormy nights when the 'old man' was gone, held something that sounded like a circus, upstairs, for exercise and amusement."[43] It might have reminded Annie of scenes at North Elba, when her brothers carried on when her father was away. Or perhaps it seemed like a whole new life to the teenager, the youngest of Brown's soldiers.

But for most of the day, the men stayed hidden, concentrating on logistics as well as ideology. "The greater part of the men," Cook recalled from prison, "kept out of sight during the day, for fear of attracting attention."[44] They stayed upstairs in the loft, listening attentively as Stevens (a former soldier who had met Brown in Kansas) led them through "a quiet, though rigid drill" based on a military manual.[45] At other times, Osborne Anderson recalled, "we applied a preparation for bronzing our gun barrels—discussed subjects of reform—related our personal history; but when our resources became pretty well exhausted, the ennui from confinement, imposed silence, etc., would make the men almost desperate." He noted that their discussions of slavery grew particularly heated. "At such times, neither slavery nor slaveholders were discussed mincingly," he recalled.[46] Annie was privy to such conversations, and they confirmed her sense that she had embarked on an important mission, part and parcel of longtime Brown family plans.

The men's faith in Brown's cause cemented her own, as did increasing contact with the institution of slavery. Annie and Martha became acquainted with Dangerfield Newby, a free African American raider whose wife and children were enslaved in Virginia. A letter from his wife telling him of her impending sale inspired him to join Brown. Newby told his story to Annie on at least one occasion, and she recalled, "Poor man, he used to get very low spirited and impatient at what appeared to him the long delay and preparation. We tried to cheer him up, for we really liked him."[47] (Newby was the first of Brown's raiders to die, his wife's letter in his pocket.[48]) In a letter that arrived for Bell, Watson related Newby's story to the women at North Elba and also noted that a slave had been found dead in a nearby orchard, the day after his wife had been sold into the Deep South. Watson recounted that his death made five murders and one suicide among slaves in the area since their arrival; this, he said, solidified their faith in their mission.[49] Oliver, too, wrote to North Elba, assuring them that "our work is going on very slowly, but we think satisfactorily." He added, "I hope you will all keep a stiff lip, a sound pluck, and believe that all will come out right in the end."[50]

Brown's men and their housekeepers were well aware that they also needed a "stiff lip" and "sound pluck." Jeremiah Anderson, for one, wrote several letters from Maryland in which he referred to the possibility of death. "If my life is sacrificed it cant be lost in a better cause," he wrote to his brother with surprising frankness. He continued, "Our motto is, We go into win at all hazards; so if you *should* hear of a failure it will be after a *desperate* struggle and loss of capital on both sides."[51] One afternoon Annie felt overwhelmed by the seriousness of what they were about. She fled her farmhouse post for the nearby woods. There, she sat under a butternut tree thinking about the raiders' mission and her own role in it, fighting a near-suicidal despair. Watching the "great fleecy clouds drifting overhead," she slowly calmed herself, aware that giving in to her feelings would endanger the mission her family had been working toward for decades. "I had come so far to help him," she reminded herself, vowing, "I could and would be brave enough to endure the rest, whatever it might be."[52] Considering herself a soldier for Brown's cause, Annie held herself to high standards of valor, then and in the months to follow, though she would occasionally be overtaken by the memories of what she had seen and experienced just outside Harpers Ferry.

Such earnest devotion to a shared cause and its leader created a strong bond between the raiders and their housekeepers. Annie grew especially close to Aaron Stevens, and Iowa Quaker brothers Edwin and Barclay Coppoc referred to both of the young women as their sisters.[53] Tidd took particular delight in calling Oliver and sixteen-year-old Martha "Mother and Father" to tease them, and the nicknames stuck. After the birth of her first child, Martha would ask Annie to write to Tidd with news of his "little sister."[54] This affection underlined the real unity felt by Brown's raiders. Anderson exulted that "when all had collected, a more earnest, fearless, determined company of men it would be difficult to get together." To this he added, "I thank God that I have been permitted to realize to its furthest, fullest, extent, the moral, mental, physical, social harmony of an Anti-Slavery family, carrying out to the letter the principles of . . . the Anti-Slavery cause."[55]

Anderson's glorification notwithstanding, harmony did not always prevail. In her new "Anti-Slavery family," Annie was exposed to a broad new world of ideas. The father to whom Annie was accustomed—the one her brother Salmon described with the motto "Father is right"—was undoubtedly present.[56] Once after the raiders had teased her about exaggerating the size of the fleas she had been catching, Annie stuck a pin through one to demonstrate the accuracy of her assessment. Brown rebuked her cruelty in "revenging [herself] on even a flea."[57] But at the farmhouse, Annie also observed overt challenges to Brown's patriarchal authority. Though John Brown had been disappointed by some of the family's decisions regarding participation at Harpers Ferry, the last time a family member had overtly defied his will was when Mary stole off to David Ruggles's water cure in 1849. It is unclear what Annie, just five at the time, might have seen pass between her parents upon Mary's return. She likely came to the Kennedy farm with a sense of Brown, who had been gone for so much of her childhood, as unchallenged by his family when he was present at home.

As Brown had always advised, cajoled, and thundered at his older children about their religious straying, it was the raiders' free-wheeling religious discussions that were most striking to Annie. Brown's men were a varied lot but united by one thing: not a one held Brown's religious views.[58] Jeremiah Anderson was a freethinker, the Coppocs were Quakers, and several of the men dabbled in spiritualism. Aaron Stevens exposed Annie, Martha, and Oliver to the spiritualist publication *Banner of Light*.[59] Annie grew increasingly confident in expressing her own religious outlook. Writing to Higginson right before her father's execution, Annie unapologetically confessed that she was no longer "what is commonly termed a *Christian*."[60] She described an "old Calvanistic" camp meeting to her spiritualist compatriot Stevens and then exclaimed,

> When Oh: when will people throw off such a mantle of darkness, and *rise* above such *absurdities*? I do not see how any one can allow their souls to be so cramped and contracted and then say that it is all "for the glory of God." I have a better opinion of God than that. I do not believe that there is any God that requires us to choke out all our reason and even good common sense for his *glory*. Why it could do him no good and must do us a great harm. Give *me* the *true Infidels* God. *Nature* in its most perfect form.

She wryly added, "You must remember that I have got 'revived' on the subject of religion."[61] The impact of her Kennedy farm encounters was evident for the rest of Annie's life, as she remained a proud freethinker on religion.

Though her "revival" would later trouble her father, he was then preoccupied with a larger rebellion. Only some raiders had known the full extent of his plans prior to their arrival in Maryland, and even those who had been forewarned evidently began having second thoughts about the logistics of Brown's plans.[62] At one point Tidd, convinced they would be "caught in a pen," stormed off. With a headiness that stemmed from her newfound freedom, Annie voiced her agreement with him. Owen, ever loyal despite his own doubts, scolded her and stated that *he* intended to stand by their father.[63]

John Brown ultimately called a farmhouse meeting, resigning his post in an elaborate drama that ended with him being recalled as leader. Owen recalled, "though we were not satisfied with the reasons he gave for making our first attack there, all controversy and opposition to the plan from that time was ended."[64] Though Annie would continue to be a freethinker on matters of religion, after Owen's rebuff she unfailingly defend her father against any detractors.

The Raid as Seen from North Elba

From their home in North Elba, the other Browns had kept up with the raiders as best as they could, always happy to receive letters but unsure of how Brown's plans were coming together.[65] But they knew when the raid was imminent: Martha and Annie reappeared at North Elba in the first week of October, sent home from Maryland in anticipation of the attack.[66] All the raiders gathered the night before the girls departed, and Stevens and Tidd serenaded the two girls.[67] With all the Brown women back at North Elba, the waiting began. They resolved to maintain "sound pluck," knowing that news might travel slowly to their remote home. (Indeed, it would take a week for word of the raid's failure to reach them.) They passed the time, surely, by pressing Martha and Annie for details of life at the Kennedy farm. Martha stayed with Ruth and Henry Thompson, while Mary's crowded quarters hosted not only Annie but also Bell, and her and Watson's young son Freddy. William Thompson's wife, Mary, may also have been a frequent visitor.

After all their years of preparation and sacrifice, it is hard to imagine the Brown women's emotions as they awaited word, especially upon receipt of some final letters from their raider kin. In a letter dated October 1, Brown reassured Mary that he would "do all in my power for you" and noted that he had sent four blankets for Martha, Annie, Bell, and Salmon's wife, Abbie. Martha, he added, was "to have the first choice," because she, now noticeably pregnant, was "fairly entitled to *particular* notice." Already regretting his lenient farmhouse stance, he instructed Annie "to become a sincere, humble, earnest, and consistent Christian."[68] He added ominously that she should save the letter to remember him by. One week before the raid, Oliver wrote to Martha that he carried her picture everywhere, and he besought her to get plenty of rest "in your present situation." "Finally, Martha," he closed poignantly, "do try to enjoy yourself. Make the most of everything."[69] In the months after Brown's raid, such letters would be publicized, turning Martha and the other formerly unknown Brown women into celebrities.

Brown's attempt to seize the federal arsenal began on October 16, 1859. By mid-morning the next day it was clear that his "breathtakingly ambitious plan" was indeed, as Frederick Douglass had warned, destined to fail.[70] Within two days the raid was over: Brown had been trapped after holing up in the engine house, and he was imprisoned and badly wounded. Over the two-day standoff, numerous casualties had mounted: seven locals (including free African American Hayward Shepherd) had been killed during the course of the raid, as were Brown's sons Oliver and Watson, the Thompson boys, and six other raiders.[71] Captured along with Brown were a severely wounded Aaron Stevens, Edwin Coppoc, and African Americans John Copeland and Shields Green. Seven of Brown's men escaped, though two (John Cook and Albert Hazlett) were recaptured and ultimately hanged along with the captured men.[72] Owen, the eldest Brown son participant, was one of the escapees.

From Boston to Charleston, much of the nation's urban population found out about the raid in bits and pieces from newspapers.[73] Some northern Republicans and Unionists distanced themselves from Brown in the wake of southern condemnation, but all seemed mesmerized by the figure of Brown. As Paul Finkelman has argued, John Brown helped to "manufacture martyrdom" from his prison cell, writing countless letters that, while nominally addressed to family members, abolitionists, and others, were clearly intended for a wider audience.[74] In jail Brown was forced to become exactly what he had once condescended to: a man of *words* in lieu of *action*. Writing to Mary Stearns, he seized the chance to create a legend. "I have asked," he wrote, "to be spared from having any mock; or hypocritical prayers made over me, when I am publicly murdered: & that my only religious attendants be poor little, dirty, ragged, bareheaded, & barefooted Slave Boys; & Girls led by some old greyheaded Slave Mother."[75] These words enshrined him as a heroic martyr to many, and they helped to create a sense of obligation to his family, especially its women.

Abolitionist women especially became fascinated by Brown. Sarah Grimké's admiration was such that she later claimed to communicate with Brown in the spirit world.[76] Grimké was not the only one so captivated. Abolitionist stalwarts Lydia Maria Child and Rebecca Spring stand out for their elaborate professions. "We cannot help reverencing the *man* while we disapprove of his *measures*," antislavery author Child reasoned.[77] But despite this small hesitation, she found herself taken by Brown: "I long to be at the *Telegraph* office every ten minutes," she wrote.[78] And she was far from unique: she soon found herself "overwhelmed with letters, mostly expressive of admiration of the old hero, and sympathy for his family."[79] Writing to Spring, Child confided, "Though habitually a good sleeper, I now lie for hours, watching the stars." To honor the "noble, disinterested, kind hearted, brave old man," she planned a display of "photographs, busts, medallions, & c of the noble old martyr in every corner of my dwelling, as a testimonial to all who enter."[80] Spring was equally effusive, writing countless letters and sending packages to the jailed raiders, Brown, and his family.[81] Their sometimes maudlin profusions quickly extended beyond Brown to his and his raiders' families. Though Mary and her daughters would occasionally resent the intrusiveness of widespread curiosity about them, such sentimental profusions also translated into much-needed financial donations.

As Garrisonian abolitionists found themselves admiring Brown, and angry southerners castigated him, the Brown women continued to wait for word that the raid had even occurred. They found out after the mail arrived, almost a full week after the raid had begun. On the Tuesday after Brown's attack, Ruth recalled, Martha went to the post office and heard a rumor of an attack and Brown's arrest. As rumors had surfaced before, Martha did not immediately believe it. Later in the week, Martha returned to the post office. According to Ruth, she opened a New York newspaper and "the first thing upon which her eyes rested was the head-lines announcing the death of her husband and Watson Brown, the capture of John Brown, and the failure of the raid. She returned to Mrs. Thompson's house almost beside herself with grief, and the news was sent to Mrs. John Brown."[82] Annie, the family's fastest reader, read aloud. "I read that long account from beginning to end, aloud, without faltering," she later remembered. "We were most of us struck dumb, horror-stricken with a grief too deep & hard to find expression in words or even tears."[83] Ruth, too, was in shock. Some forty years after the fact, Ruth recalled, "My father had often spoken of the possibility of failure and the certainty of his being hanged in such an event, and had endeavored to prepare our minds for it, but I did not think failure possible. I felt that God had proven unfaithful; that it was bitterly unjust that father should be brought low after all his sufferings and unselfish struggles, and that the wicked slave-power should triumph."

After a sleepless night, Ruth and her family went over to the Brown home, where they found Mary "pallid as death." But the family's sorrow was mingled with pride. Ruth stated, "Our grief was heavy, but we did not feel humiliated nor disgraced; and even though my father died a felon's death, none of us ever felt but that he was a noble martyr."[84] A week later, they received more newspapers from Higginson, including a transcript of Brown's post-capture interview in which he declared himself an instrument in the hands of Providence, enacting the Golden Rule.[85] "That sounds just like father," one of them chimed, thinking back to their childhood lessons of equity.[86]

By the time these reports reached North Elba, Brown had been indicted for conspiring to incite insurrection. He and his captured raiders were jailed in Charles Town, Virginia. With the exception of Higginson, the "Secret Six" scattered, fearing exposure or arrest. John Jr. waited anxiously for the arrival of federal marshals despite the fact he had never gone to Harpers Ferry, and Frederick Douglass soon sailed for England. Owen hid out in the Pennsylvania backcountry with a few of the other escaped raiders. Brown's trial concluded on November 2. Sentenced to death in one month's time, he made an address to the court, proclaiming to a national audience the righteousness of his mission.[87] In a letter that concluded with word of his sentence, he assured his family that he felt "quite cheerful in the assurance that God reigns."[88]

The Brown women put on a brave face for their growing public. The Brown daughters worked together to help five-year-old Ellen compose a letter. It opened, "Father, I deeply sympathize with you." Ellen (or, more likely, some combination of her sisters) continued, "I hope we may so live as to profit by the kind and good advice you have so often given us, and at last meet in heaven."[89] Conscious of their newfound fame, they crafted Ellen's letter with the knowledge that it would be reproduced. Annie also avowed her faith in Brown's cause: "All you were guilty of," she wrote to her father, "was, doing your duty to your fellow-men. Would that we were all guilty of the same." She reported that her sisters-in-law, especially Martha, bore "their grief like heroines." She closed by asking her father to give her "love to Stevens and the other prisoners."[90]

Annie's stoical letter masked a great deal of grief. The fifteen-year-old who had fled to the woods before Brown's raid could not escape its outcome. Thoughts of her father and her friend Aaron Stevens in prison, of her brother Owen and Osborne Anderson on the run, and of her two dead brothers overwhelmed her. Without Watson—the one Brown she had felt truly understood her—Annie exchanged a series of letters with "friend" Higginson, deriving comfort from her sense of herself as part of the broad antislavery family that had waged war against the slave power.[91] Just two days after Brown's execution, she wrote, "For my part I feel proud when I think that his blood runs in my veins"; writing again a month later, she closed, "Yours for bleeding humanity."[92] But it was not easy for her, as focusing on the cause made her think about her time at the "head quarters war department" and the worthy men she had known there—most of whom were now dead.[93] To Higginson she declared that people were surprised at Brown's "daring to invade Virginia with only twenty-three men; but I think if they knew what sort of men they were, there would be less surprise. *I* never saw such men."[94] Annie also exchanged letters with imprisoned raider Stevens. A few weeks after her father's burial she confided, "if it were not for the thought that it was doing a great good I could not endure it."[95] Stevens responded, addressing her as "my dear sister" and working to bolster her spirits. He wrote, "I hope you will cheer up and learn all you can and help advance this world in *truth* and *righteousness*." Knowing that he would soon hang, he added that he would see her in the spirit world.[96]

But correspondence with fellow antislavery soldiers did not alleviate her suffering. Decades later Ruth recalled, "Annie's grief was terrible to see. She had known every man who fell in the fight, had been present at all their conferences, and was like a sister to many of them. . . . She went about the house pale, silent, and tearless. She neither slept nor ate, and I feared for her reason."[97] Concerned, Ruth arranged for a local music teacher to play "The Dying Warrior" while Annie was around. She recalled how "the pathos of this sweet old song broke up the fountain of Annie's grief, and she cried with a passion I shall never forget. She often said afterward that had it not been for that song she would certainly have gone insane, but the fit of crying relieved the tension of her feelings."[98] Her feelings would continue to overwhelm her in the year to come, when, almost stuck in her past, she would find herself unable to escape her memories of Brown's men.[99]

Ever after, Annie saw her months at the Kennedy farm as the most important of her life. All that followed paled in comparison, and over time Annie grew committed to telling her story, to Brown biographers and to the broader public. Her desire to "bear witness" was likely linked to her sense that she had lived through traumatic events.[100] Famous for her connection to Brown, she frequently felt as though her direct participation as Kennedy farmhouse housekeeper and "watchdog" was wrongly overlooked. Though Owen had to hide out and John Jr. had to stand guard against any federal marshals out to arrest him, Annie was ignored in the roundup that followed the raid. In the trial, congressional hearings, and press that immediately followed Brown's raid, little if any mention was ever made of her role in assisting Brown's raiders, likely because the image of a female conspirator was unimaginable to most.[101] Annie resented the dismissal on both her and Martha's behalf.[102]

Though she did not march to Harpers Ferry in October 1859, Annie's work in the Maryland countryside may have allowed Brown's raiders to do so, and the work of Mary and Ruth at North Elba helped smooth over the Brown men's absences. In the "John Brown Year" that followed, Annie and the other Brown women had to adjust to their new position as celebrities within the abolitionist circle. Leaving solitary antislavery activism behind, Mary would battle to remain independent and financially afloat. A similar struggle would soon extend to each of her daughters as they looked to create new lives under the shadow of memory of their father.

❧ CHAPTER 4

Newfound Celebrity in the John Brown Year

A few weeks after Brown's capture the Brown women received an unexpected visitor. Thomas Wentworth Higginson appeared as emissary for a group of abolitionists who hoped that an appeal from his wife would persuade John Brown to agree to a rescue plot.[1] After his few days in their Adirondack home, Higginson declared the Brown women to possess the "same simple, upright character" as Brown himself.[2] Though he had lived in the "good society" of abolitionists throughout his life, Higginson proclaimed, "never did I see such perfect simplicity & absolute disinterestedness."[3] Mary Brown, eager to see her husband, made the long trek to Charles Town in Higginson's company. In the near-month that it took her to arrive at Brown's side, she began what must have seemed like a new life. Crowds angled to catch a glimpse of the Brown matriarch as she traveled, and newspapers eagerly reported on her jailhouse meeting with her husband.

After Brown's hanging, the now-widow's journey back to North Elba dispelled any illusion that the Brown women would soon return to obscurity.[4] Brown's body was sent to Philadelphia by train. Worried that its presence would incite trouble, the Philadelphia mayor insisted that the body be sent on to New York.[5] Mary and a party that included abolitionists Wendell Phillips and James McKim then took a train to Vergennes, Vermont, and began a slow trek by wagon, sleigh, and ferry toward North Elba.[6] "At the places where they stopped," the American Anti-Slavery Society annual report later noted, "the news of their arrival brought together large numbers of the people . . . eager to do honor to the memory of the departed hero, and show respect and sympathy for his bereaved wife."[7] Finally, on December 7, the party arrived at North Elba. The *New York Weekly Tribune* painted the scene of the Brown women's reunion: Mary descended from the carriage "with difficulty, being much agitated. . . . Instantly there was a sharp, low cry of 'Mother!' and in answer, another in the same tone of mingled agony and tenderness, 'O! Annie!' and the mother and daughter were locked in a long, convulsed embrace. Then followed the same scene with the next daughter."[8]

Such scenes were commonly reported during what abolitionists termed "the John Brown Year." The Brown women were thrust into a national spotlight, held up by many as symbols of Brown's noble cause and as worthy recipients of charity. This was never truer than with New England's anti-slavery literary elite, who embraced Brown's family along with his cause. Lydia Maria Child spoke for many when she wrote, "My pity flows like a fountain for those widows and children who have for years worked hard and lived in destitution, for the sake of sustaining husbands and fathers . . . in their noble efforts to help poor hunted slaves."[9] As depictions of "suffering slaves" had inspired antislavery fervor, images of the Brown women's distress now furthered abolitionist devotion.[10] Soon the Browns' tragic losses would not seem so singular, as the Civil War claimed countless husbands, sons, and fathers, but in 1859 his widow and daughters' grief remained a captivating part of the Brown story.[11] But this was not all that made them fascinating. As antislavery adherents in the 1850s, the Brown women had had little contact with other abolitionists. Now they were newly drawn into a literary, middle-class, and predominantly urban antislavery circle. While they were held up as noble because of their poverty and ties to rural life, as "rustic" beings they were not entrusted to commemorate Brown properly or to carve out their own post–Harpers Ferry life.

Mary Brown's Long Journey

When Mary first left North Elba, escorted by Higginson, to begin the long journey south to see her husband in jail, the two of them had made their way overland to Burlington, Vermont, and from there to Boston by train. Onboard, Mary had begun to experience the fame—and notoriety—that would follow her for the rest of her life. When the conductors learned of her identity, they insisted that she ride for free.[12] This was just the first of many instances in which her connection to Brown would offer a tangible lifeline. Later, as she made her way south from Boston with Higginson, Mary would learn of Brown's death sentence.[13] Onboard the train, Higginson provided a newspaper with word of the sentence. "She read it," he reported, "and then the tall, strong woman bent her head for a few minutes on the seat before us; then she raised it, and spoke calmly as before."[14] Higginson would describe Mary Brown's stoicism to many in the months that followed. He would also highlight her rusticity.

In Boston, Mary Brown had been welcomed into its abolitionist fold. In the city in which Garrisonian nonresistance had been born, many turned out, curious to meet the wife of Brown.[15] To Annie and thirteen-year-old Sarah, Higginson reported that their mother "had quite a *levee* at the American House. . . . Some twenty-five or thirty people found out she was there and came in to see her," including some of the Secret Six. Beginning a series of meetings that Mary would slowly grow accustomed to, "they kept giving her money, handkerchiefs, gloves, shoes, & *kisses*. One old Mr. Fiske gave her $20 & a pair of gloves (!!) & came back twice to give good advice. Mr. Amos Lawrence made her go & have a large photograph picture taken, to match that one of your father, and you are to have copies of it by & by. She had over $100 given to her in all."[16] Franklin Sanborn also wrote of the "kindness" Mary had been shown in Boston, telling her son Salmon that she "everywhere finds sympathy" because of John Brown's noble behavior. Sanborn added, "I envy you your descent from him."[17] Similar sentiments—as well as general curiosity—drew crowds who came to see her in Boston. Laden with gifts, she departed the city.[18]

As she set out southward with Higginson, Mary's thoughts surely turned to her reunion with Brown. Though she had often gone months without seeing him, this latest absence had been especially wearying. If she mentally rehearsed a speech, her plans to deliver it were soon put on hold. While en route, Higginson received a telegraph informing him that "Mr Brown says for gods sake don't let Mrs Brown come."[19] Brown confided, "If my Wife were to come here just now it would *only tend* to distract *her mind, ten fold*; & would *only add* to my affliction; & cannot *possibly* do me any *good*."[20] Brown also recognized the importance of Mary's image and even the celebrity that his family now held.[21] He wrote to his family, "If she comes on here, she must only be a gazing-stock throughout the whole journey, to be remarked upon in every look, word, and action, and by all sorts of creatures, and by all sorts of papers, throughout the whole country."[22] Brown was also unusually pragmatic. "The sympathy that is now aroused in your behalf may not always follow you," Brown instructed his children. They should capitalize on it while they could and not divert funds to cover the expense of her trip.[23]

Mary Brown was stranded. Having reached Philadelphia by the time she got word of Brown's "no," she remained there through much of November. She stayed with James McKim and then Lucretia Mott, who offered sympathy despite her Quaker nonresistance stance. Rebecca Spring also summoned Mary to Eagleswood, New Jersey, where the noted Quaker reformer lived on the grounds of the former Raritan Bay socialist commune.

Aside from their sex and age, Rebecca Spring and Mary Brown made a strikingly divergent pair. Mary arrived at Eagleswood with limited schooling and a shabby dress that revealed her lifetime of poverty. In contrast, Spring had an elite family pedigree and an extensive education. Her father, Arnold Buffum, had been the first president of the New England Anti-Slavery Society, while her sister was reform lecturer Elizabeth Buffum Chace. While Mary had spent the past decades in relative isolation, in the 1840s Spring had lived in New York City, serving as an "American salonière" and counting as her friends Lydia Maria Child, Julia Ward Howe, and Horace Greeley.[24] She had traveled throughout Europe in 1845 in the company of Margaret Fuller and had stood in William Wordsworth's home and listened to him recite poetry.[25] Back in the United States, Spring had participated in two communal experiments. The second, the Raritan Bay Colony, had failed a few years earlier, but its progressive school, Eagleswood, was still in operation. She and her husband, Marcus, lived on its grounds in a mansion.[26] Rebecca Spring—confident, elite, well-dressed, and highly conscious of her role as a "charming lady"[27]—was quick to dismiss the likes of a Mary Brown.

Spring regaled Mary with tales of her own visit to Brown as the unlikely duo worked to prepare a trunk full of clothing and supplies to send to Charles Town.[28] Spring had not requested permission or sent notice, so John Brown had no opportunity to deny her entry. Spring highlighted how she had charmed her way out of the many dangers she had faced. Though at first no one, not even a fellow Quaker, wanted to assist her in getting to Brown, in time she won admission and presented Brown with a collection of autumn leaves. Spring likely boasted to Mary that her charm had worked on Brown, noting that she had quickly rid him of "the shyness that I believe he felt in the presence of strangers."[29] Spring recalled in 1899 that she had expected Brown to be "rude and uncouth," but that she had instead been impressed by his simplicity and "unostentatious courage."[30] Spring expected Brown's wife to be equally "uncouth." In such a spirit of helpfulness, she offered advice that Brown should be buried in an expensive brown suit. Knowing the Browns' poverty, she and her husband Marcus offered to provide it. Mary informed Spring, "It would grieve him to receive so expensive a present, as he never wore fine clothes." Standing up for Brown's principles, Mary insisted upon a cheaper, coarser suit.[31] After a week of observing Mary, Spring described her as "a quiet motherly woman," adding that she had "lived a life of devotion to him, his will being hers."[32] In the future, after Mary emerged as less "quiet" than Spring might have preferred, she would take back this assessment and instead dismiss her as coarse, just like Brown's suit.[33]

Mary continued to take consolation from her steadfast faith as she awaited Brown's execution far from her family. "I have often thought that I should rather hear that you were dead than fallen into the hands of your enemies," she confided to Brown, "but I don't think so now. The good that is growing out of it is wonderful." She noted with evident pride that his last speech to the court "is talked about and preached about every where and in all places."[34] Like Moses, she continued, he would not live to see the slaves free, but God's hand was also in that: "Man deviseth his way, but the Lord directeth his steps." Though she had felt herself tested in the 1840s when so many of her young children died, she never recalled the hard months of 1859 in the same manner. Nevertheless, she did appear to find the fact that Brown had seen Spring rather than her galling. Writing to Brown from Spring's, she noted that she was with "the kind lady who came to see you, and minister to your wants, which I am deprived of doing." The deprivation seemed especially tough, she added, because "you have nursed and taken care of me a great deal; but I cannot even come and look at you. O, it is hard! But I am perfectly satisfied with it, believing it best." Although she continued to declare that the Lord's will be done, she added, "I would serve you gladly if I could."[35]

Not a week from Brown's execution, Mary remained in Philadelphia. She wrote to Brown of her desire to remain there until the "sad event."[36] But as Mary waited, Brown suddenly rescinded his "no." On November 21, 1859, he wrote that the heightened state of "public feeling" in Charles Town was another reason for her not to come, adding, "but I did not intend saying another word to you on that subject."[37] But a few days later his desire for her presence had grown. He stated, this time more emphatically, "I will close this by saying that if you *now feel* that you are *equal* to the undertaking do *exactly as you FEEL disposed to do* about coming to see me. . . . *I am entirely willing.*"[38] Mary, accompanied by a small party that included *National Anti-Slavery Standard* correspondent James McKim, traveled to Virginia.[39] Security was tight and suspicions high; Mary surely noted the presence of so many soldiers.[40] On December 1 she received a military escort to the jail. After she was searched for weapons, Brown's jailor Captain Avis served as the sole witness to the reunion of Mary and John Brown. His account of the event was soon in demand.[41]

Brown tried to cheer her regarding his "hard fate," and she related news from North Elba.[42] Though he may not have anticipated his family's celebrity status, Brown certainly was attentive to his own fame, then and for posterity. He gave to her all of his papers and letters, mindful that Mary's new role would involve preserving his memory.[43] He also charged her with assuming her role as Brown matriarch: "Mary," he stated, "I hope you will always live in Essex County. I hope you will be able to get all our children together, and impress the inculcation of the right principles to each succeeding generation."[44] The pair also discussed practical matters, clashing over Brown's request that Mary arrange that his body, along with those of the dead Browns and Thompsons, be burned for an easy return to and burial at North Elba. As she had with Spring, Mary asserted her will. To Brown's request she responded, "I really cannot consent to do this. I hope you will change your mind on this subject. I do not think permission would be granted to do any such thing." She reminded Brown of all she had to now contend with, continuing, "For my sake, think no more of such an idea."[45] Brown consented.

One of John Brown's concerns had been that Mary would be a "gazing-stock," an apt description of the celebrity that she and his family now inhabited. Newspapers covered her visit alongside other stories leading up to his execution, and public interest in seeing Brown's wife heightened as news of her visit spread.[46] Reporter Theodore Tilton soon published an interview with Mary to satiate the public appetite. In it, he questioned Mary about Brown's supposed insanity and reported that she did not believe it.[47] He also worked to satisfy curiosity about her appearance. While images of John Brown abounded, few knew what his wife looked like. "She is tall, large and muscular, giving the impression at first sight of a frame capable of great strength and long endurance," Tilton wrote. Then, allowing a seemingly intimate look at her sorrow, he added, "Her face is grave and thoughtful, wearing, even in this hour of her trial, an expression of soberness rather than of sadness, as if, like her husband, she had long since learned how to suffer and be calm."[48] (This said, he revealed that she had once left a room sobbing.) James McKim also published an account of his time with Mary Brown. "Apparently unconscious that she is an object of observation, her demeanor is marked by unaffected propriety and natural dignity," McKim noted, highlighting Mary's simplicity and lack of savvy as proof of her noble nature.[49]

Curiosity about Brown's wife was such that her arrival drew even more interest than the ongoing preparation of the gallows. The *Liberator* reported that arrangements for the hanging had been "watched with great public

FIGURE 6. "Arrival of Mrs. Brown in Charlestown," *New York Illustrated News*, December 17, 1859. Boyd Stutler Collection, West Virginia State Archives.

interest, but their attraction ended at once, when, at noon, the knowledge that John Brown's wife was expected became general."[50] By 3 p.m., a crowd had gathered, eager to glimpse a living link to Brown's radical abolitionism. What followed calls to mind the modern media frenzy. A group of soldiers told the wife of the owner of the hotel where Mary lodged "that if she would give Mrs. Brown her meals in the dining room & charge for sights of her, she could make a handsome sum by it."[51] The *Boston Evening Courier* and other newspapers carried full accounts of Mary's visit to the jail, sentimentalizing moments of when the Browns met and parted. The *Courier* reported that "they seemed considerably affected when they first met, and Mrs. Brown was, for a few moments, quite overcome, but Brown was as firm as a rock."[52]

Mary believed that Brown's martyrdom was part of a divine plan, but she worried about one earthly matter: what would happen to his body. She enlisted the aid of other abolitionists and wrote to Virginia governor Henry Wise to request that the bodies of her two sons, the two Thompsons, and Brown be turned over "for decent & tender interment among their kindred."[53] Wise agreed, writing an order to that effect.[54] However, Mary only proved successful in reclaiming Brown's body, a source of much unhappiness in an age where corpses were granted both secular and sacred meanings.[55] Oliver and a number of other raiders were thrown unceremoniously into a large pit in an undisclosed location.[56] Annie Brown confided that they found it hard to bear that the men were "buried in the land of the slave."[57] Even worse, Watson's body was missing, taken by students at the local medical college.

Although she had succeeded in wresting at least one Brown body from the state of Virginia, Mary's struggle had only begun. She clashed with those antislavery activists who wanted to have an elaborate funeral and lay Brown to rest in a prominent cemetery. "Barnum-like proposals" were brought forward, including plans to parade Brown's body throughout the North.[58] An abolitionist named Henry Wright had suggested that antislavery speakers raise money to pay for a burial with requisite pomp and grandeur, and he had further suggested that Wendell Phillips persuade Brown to cede his body to the AASS. Seemingly as an aside, he added that someone should notify Brown's wife and family.[59] Higginson, too, tried to persuade her to have Brown buried at Mount Auburn, a large cemetery in Cambridge.[60] But Mary insisted on a private burial at North Elba, leaving Thaddeus Hyatt to declare that "another John Brown it seems was needed to take charge of John Brown's mortal remains."[61] What Hyatt missed was that Mary may have seen herself as that "another John Brown," acting—as she had in her determination that Brown be buried in a plain suit—on behalf of his wishes.

Mary got her wish for a North Elba funeral, but elite abolitionists made the most of it. Brown's favorite hymns, including "Blow, Ye, the Trumpet Blow," were sung; Ruth reported that the "voices of those dear children" singing provided her with much comfort. This may have been all the more so because those singing were the children of their black neighbor Lyman Epps.[62] After the hymn both McKim and Phillips spoke. Phillips used the Browns to rally others to the antislavery cause in an address that was widely reprinted. He proclaimed that Brown must have "lived wholly for one great idea," with a family that "serenely" accepted their roles. "I feel honored," he added, "to stand under such a roof." After asking his audience to pray for a "new baptism" of commitment to the antislavery cause, he again referred to Brown's Adirondack surroundings and his family. "We dare not say bless you, children of his home! You stand nearer to one whose lips God touched, and we rather bend for your blessing."[63]

Though a few had been angered by Mary's refusal to abide by abolitionists' wishes, most abolitionists glossed over the conflict. In the *National Anti-Slavery Standard*, McKim acknowledged that the "friends of the slave" in New York "had expected that some opportunity would be afforded, here, for public manifestations of respect for the remains of the martyr." But, he continued, they had instead adhered to Brown's "own dying wish" and "the earnest desire of Mrs. BROWN that his children and grandchildren might be permitted to look upon his features before decomposition." So, his story went, they took the body "quietly, speedily, and unostentatiously, to the family residence for interment." Rewriting history a bit, he added that this was "deemed most in accordance with the simple, undemonstrative grandeur of the old man's character."[64]

Inside the Abolitionist Circle

After her return to North Elba, Mary's days were full. Though grieving, she would later recall that she was glad to have "others for me to love and do for."[65] Word of the capture of John Cook and Edwin Coppoc, two of Brown's raiders who had made a jailbreak, came soon after Brown's funeral. This heightened their concerns about the safety of Owen, still on the run. Ruth confided: "*One* is wandering somewhere, & our anxiety for him is very great."[66] With expectant mother Martha as well as widow Bell and her son Freddy now living under her roof, Mary simultaneously had more mouths to feed and fewer sons to depend on. The Browns' North Elba home now boasted three widows and three daughters, with only Salmon and Henry Thompson (each of whom had their own family) to assist them. Though accustomed to scraping by on the small funds Brown managed to send home, Mary realized it would now be a wholly new struggle to make ends meet, with no end to Brown's absence and with the weight of her family's future squarely on her shoulders.[67]

Though Mary struggled with abolitionists over Brown's body and burial, in the weeks after his execution her new place in the abolitionist circle offered her comfort. From North Elba the Brown women read accounts of the many public memorial gatherings held on the eve of Brown's execution and in its aftermath. Mary probably heard of the large meeting at Boston's Tremont Temple the night after Brown's execution. The *Evening Courier* reported that an "immense crowd" attended the meeting, so many that "the air was so close and suffocating that quite a number fainted."[68] The *Morning Journal* added that even after the temple became "crowded in every part, hundreds remained in the vestibules and about the door, unable to gain admittance." Garrison himself read Brown's address to the court.[69] The Brown women also took pride in the literary outpouring that James Redpath captured in *Echoes of Harper's Ferry*. Ruth especially appreciated such tributes as Lydia Maria Child's poem "The Hero's Heart." In it, Child repeated the story that as Brown stepped through the jail door on his way to the gallows, he had stooped to kiss an African American baby held by her mother. Reports of this (utterly mythical) event circulated widely.[70]

The Brown women were thus drawn into a large antislavery network. In the days after Brown's death, many abolitionists wrote to introduce themselves and to extend elaborate condolences. Brown's Kansas compatriot (and future biographer) Richard Hinton addressed them as "dear bereaved friends" and noted that though they were "not personally known to each other, yet a common sorrow makes us all near to one another." After referring to Brown as "our Hero," he added, "you have winging to you in your Mountain Home, the prayers and fraternal wishes of the friends of Truth every where."[71] Other visitors followed, including Secret Six member George Stearns and his wife, Mary.[72] Ruth noted that they had been so pleased to see "Father's cherished friend," adding, "It is a great comfort to know that we have so many dear friends."[73] Annie had already made a similar request of Wendell Phillips. "Give my love to all friends to the *cause*," she instructed him, "and tell Mrs. Child to *be sure* come up here."[74]

The Brown women drew special consolation from a gathering at Brown's grave on July 4, 1860. Abolitionist donations made a family reunion possible. John Jr. and Wealthy, Jason and Ellen, and Jennie Dunbar (an acquaintance of hanged raider Aaron Stevens) traveled from Ohio to join Mary and her daughters, Henry and Ruth, and Salmon and Abbie at North Elba.[75] Mary Brown's growing group of grandchildren also joined in the occasion, along with her stepson Owen, the only Brown to have escaped Harpers Ferry. Fugitive raiders Barclay Coppoc, Frances Merriam, and Osborne Anderson also made the pilgrimage. In addition, a whole host of abolitionist speakers and a crowd that the *Liberator* estimated to number one thousand strong gathered at Brown's grave. Numerous speeches were made and letters were read from abolitionists who could not attend. Then Brown's oldest son was called forth. Though the *Liberator* reprinted the abolitionists' letters word for word, it merely summarized John Jr.'s comments, informing its readers that he thanked those gathered. Owen, too, was called for, and his "quaint speech and illustrations," as well as his eccentricity, were reported.[76] Following the speeches and parade of living raider relics, the gathering adjourned. But though the crowd dispersed, the popularity of Brown's grave as a site of pilgrimage did not diminish over the following years. William Lloyd Garrison would even travel there in 1862.[77]

From those who could not come to them, the Brown women received countless letters. Ruth noted that Higginson's "soul-cheering letters" had "cheer[ed] our sad hearts."[78] To James McKim, Annie added, "We have a shower of sympathizing letters every week."[79] Horatio Nelson Rust, who had fought alongside Brown in Kansas, began what would be a lifelong correspondence with the Brown women. "We feel much sympathy for you in your continued affliction," he wrote to Mary. "May God give you strength for each day as it comes."[80] Such letters were so common that the Browns were pressed for enough time to reply. As Mary explained to James McKim, "we get some twenty six letters most every week, so you see we have some writing to do." She closed, "Give my love to all inquiring friends."[81] The existence of "inquiring friends" meant much to Mary and the other Brown women: it signified that Brown's sacrifice had not been in vain and he was not forgotten. Summarizing her feelings about this outpouring, Mary wrote in late 1860 that they "have had many friends & sympathizers & . . . in our affliction to help us bear up."[82]

While the sympathy for Brown offered psychological comfort to the Browns, it also formed a tangible lifeline. Abolitionists, African Americans, and others sent small sums of money to Mary; this had been ongoing since Brown's imprisonment. Abolitionists distributed circulars: one in Boston proclaimed that it was "scarcely necessary to inform you that JOHN BROWN'S FAMILY are destitute."[83] Meetings were also conducted to raise money from gathered crowds.[84] On November 18, one of the first was held in Boston's Tremont Temple. Speaker Ralph Waldo Emerson reminded the crowd of Brown's place in the broad antislavery family and appealed to the audience to provide relief to Brown's *literal* family.[85] And writing to the *New York Times*, Thaddeus Hyatt proclaimed, "The story is here in its simplest and saddest form. Widows and fatherless children! Slain for a principle! The heads of the entire family slain! All the male members cut off! And this in the Nineteenth Century, and this amid a free people!" He then queried, "Friends at the North, what will you do for John Brown's family?" and offered to exchange a likeness "of the old man, presented to me by his own hands," to all who sent him a dollar for a relief fund.[86] Hyatt raised $2,600 from such sales and contributed his earnings to a broader John Brown fund recently established, raising its total to over $6,000.[87] In the months after Brown's death, the fund continued to grow. Higginson noted, "Money seems to be flowing for them from all directions & that is something, because beside their severe bereavement they greatly need money." Alluding to the Brown women's odd celebrity, he added, "I have had some queer letters about them, one from a man in Winchester offering to adopt one of the daughters & teach her telegraphing."[88]

Though grateful for such support, Mary Brown found herself frustrated by the methods of disbursement. Unlike a similar fund that would be gathered for and then handed over to William Lloyd Garrison in the 1870s, a committee oversaw the distribution of sums, determining who got what and when.[89] In February 1861 Mary wrote to Samuel Sewall that she had written to Redpath to request two hundred dollars "from some source" to help her survive the winter "and to so fix things on the farm that we can . . . not always be entirely dependent on others."[90] The following June, she exhibited increasing frustration. After thanking George Stearns for paying a particular expense, she justified her use of "a great deal of money." "I *have* and I am," she explained, "getting things in shape so that we shall not be dependent on any fund for all our living." Part of her plan was "to buy some sheep and to get a horse and wagon with which we kneed [*sic*] very much." She showed a newfound confidence in her ability to navigate as family matriarch, adding, "I have gone on with the approval of all that are dependent on me for a living to fix the house and to improve our farm so that we shall not have to buy everything that we eat, drink or wear."[91] Two months later she still had not been able to buy the sheep. Mary wrote to Sanborn, exasperated: "If I had five hundred dollars to invest I should invest it on my farm instead of investing it in Boston or any other place at six per cent interest. . . . I should like some now to buy sheep with wool is low this year but I don't think that it always will be. I could have got from fifteen to twenty per cent interest last year on a dollar if I had had the money in our sheep."[92] Over the next few years, Mary Brown would become increasingly frustrated with her inability to eke out a living from the North Elba farm.

As Mary tried to make the North Elba farm self-sustaining, the Brown women occupied themselves with the additional project of copying Brown-related letters. Mary even sent a few letters by Brown and raiders such as Osborne Anderson to papers for publication.[93] But in her work to commemorate Brown, she soon landed in the middle of an abolitionist battle. Even before they had achieved their goal of ending slavery, abolitionists began to commemorate their own movement, and Brown's now-famous family—especially his widow and daughters—became pawns. Caught in the middle of competing factions, Mary was politely assertive, determined to carry out what she thought were Brown's wishes. By the end of the year, this would bring her into renewed (and less conciliatory) contact with Rebecca Spring.

A biography was in the works even before Brown's execution. His family was courted for an official endorsement as well as materials. Mary soon found herself caught between would-be biographers James Redpath and Lydia Maria Child and clamoring advocates of each. Both Redpath and Child felt eminently qualified to produce the work, and each promised that some profits would go to the raiders' families, though the cash-strapped Child likely hoped to also maximize on Brown's sudden fame for her own gain.[94] While George Stearns was visiting her family at North Elba, Mary received a letter from Child that Redpath supporter Stearns intercepted.[95] Mary apparently found Stearns persuasive and authorized Redpath rather than Child to go forward. In doing so Mary offended not only Child but also James McKim, a Child advocate.[96] Child's ire comes across clearly in some of her personal letters.[97] She wrote to her niece, "I have found it a very thankless business to write a Biography for the benefit of a family."[98] Her earlier praise of Mary Brown as a "brave-hearted Roman matron" was gone, replaced by her more ambiguous characterization of the Browns as a "family of high-toned Calvinists and warriors."[99]

Redpath ultimately published not just one but two officially sanctioned works about Brown, while Child produced none.[100] Redpath dispatched his wife to North Elba to gather materials. She was the first of many would-be writers and aficionados to appear at a Brown doorstep. Annie cheekily described her visit, writing, "Mrs. Redpath has been here to gather facts for his book, we like her very much. The only fault I could find was she used a great deal too much of that abominable stuff called flattery."[101] In spite of this transparency she left North Elba with a treasure trove. Mary tried to direct the tone of the work, choosing particular letters that she wanted included. But her sense of urgency was such that she sent Redpath some originals instead of copies, beginning a lifelong pattern in which the family parted with letters they were then unable to reclaim.[102] She also tried to patch up her quarrel with the pro-Child faction, writing to McKim, "I certainly did not mean to ingure any ones character or feelings & am very sorry for it."[103] The biography battle revealed tensions within the abolitionist movement. McKim and Child sought a sense of continued relevance, an affirmation that their decades-long work for the movement still mattered, that the Garrisonian moment had not passed. Though initially some Garrisonians had distanced themselves from Brown, now and in the future they eagerly claimed him, using their ties to him to validate the importance of the antislavery movement and its moment in history.

Mary Brown knew that education could prove particularly vital to her impoverished daughters. It offered the only chance they had to escape poverty. She did not mull over their future needs in solitude. Various abolitionist factions weighed in on what should happen to Annie and Sarah, and she soon found herself in a second abolitionist quagmire. Brown had shrewdly realized that his daughters would need more schooling, whether from an unusually practical sense or from whatever impulse led him to send Ruth to school. What he desired, Brown had written Mary from prison, was "a very plain, but perfectly practical, education . . . enough of the learning of the schools to enable them to transact the common business of life, together with that thorough training in good business habits which best prepares both men and women to be useful, though poor, and to meet the stern realities of life with a good grace."[104] Brown entrusted this task to Mary; he had written to Spring, "I feel disposed to leave the education of my dear children to their mother, and to those dear friends who bear the burden of it."[105]

But as Mary moved forward she butted heads with others in the abolitionist circle who thought that they, rather than she, knew what Brown had really wanted and what was best for his daughters. And as they were prepared to "bear the burden of it," they claimed a role in her decision making. This was also because Brown had included them in his planning from the Charles Town jail. He had written to Rebecca Spring of his "earnest hope" that his daughters would "become strong, intelligent, expert industrious Christian housekeepers," concluding, "I want them to become matter of fact women."[106] By "matter of fact women" Brown likely meant that he wanted his daughters to be not only intelligent but faithful and not frivolous, as he outlined to Mary. Over the next two years Mary Brown worked to shape her family's destiny. She would be blocked by members of the antislavery circle who thought they had a better sense of Brown's wishes—and even of what "housekeeping" constituted—than his poor, "rustic" widow.

Mary received advice and offers of schooling for Annie and Sarah from abolitionists Rebecca Spring, Parker Pillsbury, Theodore Weld, and Franklin Sanborn, though none seemed more preoccupied with Mary's choice than Spring.[107] Spring wrote to Mary the day before Brown's hanging, enclosing a copy of Brown's letter. Whether she was trying to console or command Mary is unclear. "I told him," she wrote, "you would bear this affliction just as he would wish. . . . I hope all I have said to him will be true."[108] Unsurprisingly, Spring lobbied for her school, Eagleswood. Coeducational and racially integrated, it had already attracted many abolitionist children, including Lucretia Mott's niece Ellie Wright.[109] Famed abolitionist and reformer Theodore Dwight Weld acted as head teacher, and both Angelina and Sarah Grimké taught there. Spring would soon have hanged raiders Aaron Stevens and Alfred Hazlett buried on its grounds; she would refer to it as a "sacred spot."[110] She insisted that Mary heed her advice that her Eagleswood was the place Brown would have wished his daughters to attend.

At first it appeared that Mary would go along with Spring's proposal, or at least Spring wishfully interpreted matters this way. "At last she has written that she believes it was Mr Brown's wish they should come here to Mr. Weld's school," Spring wrote to Higginson, continuing, "I have written to hasten them." She added, "They can be here a year with what has been given by us." She then noted, more than a little possessively, "They are not to board at the boarding house, but where they can do a part of their own washing, ironing, &c, as we believe Mr Brown would prefer." She stated emphatically, "I say would I mean does. *He* wrote to me 'I want them to become strong, industrious, expert Christian housekeepers.'"[111] Spring may have been referring to the "manual labor principle" employed at Eagleswood.[112] The manual labor movement—popular especially with reformers such as Weld in the 1830s—had been intended to combine classical education with physical labor, to train hearts alongside heads. Though the movement was losing momentum by the 1850s, Weld's school remained one where students did some labor to earn their keep and to improve their physical health.[113] Although in the midst of her biography battle, Lydia Maria Child also weighed in on this choice, approving of Weld's school. "I should judge that the influences there would be extremely good," the author of the popular *The Frugal Housewife* wrote.[114]

But two weeks later a frustrated Spring wrote to Higginson that she had not heard from Mary. In early February, she expressed even greater displeasure: the Brown daughters had been stolen out from under her.[115] She reported, "I was surprised to receive a letter from Mrs. Brown, North Elba, last evening, which she says Mr Stearns of Boston had visited them, and advised her to send her daughters to Mr Sanborn's school; and that they would go as soon as ready." She added disingenuously, "I never urged her, I wished her to decide for herself. I hope it is for the best though. . . . I cannot see how she can find a better teacher than Mr Weld, or a better school."[116] She and Child corresponded about Mary's choice, as did others within abolitionist circles.[117] As with the biography, Mary was pressured by different factions. Opposing Spring's lobby were some of Brown's "intimate friends"—likely George Stearns and Thomas Wentworth Higginson—who favored Concord, where Franklin Sanborn had a school.[118]

Mary made her choice carefully in the face of these pressures. After thanking a correspondent for yet a third offer, Mary wrote that "according to the best information I can get of places and locations and chances, I have come to the conclusion to send them to Concord."[119] As Sandra Harbert Petrulionis has demonstrated in her book on Concord's antislavery movement, the Massachusetts town might have seemed like a potential haven because of its antislavery connections and close ties to Brown.[120] Mary may have derived comfort and even pleasure from sending Annie and Sarah into an antislavery stronghold that boasted the likes of Sanborn, Ralph Waldo Emerson, and Henry David Thoreau, the last of whom had famously proclaimed her husband akin to Christ. Perhaps wiser (or more wary) because of the biography furor, Mary embarked on a public relations campaign. She carefully wrote to McKim, "I did not send them to Concord to school because I did not think Mr Welds school was not a good one I think it is."[121]

It appears that Annie and Sarah also had some voice in their fate. Sarah, a budding artist, may have thought Sanborn's school would afford her more opportunity to take the drawing lessons she coveted. One compelling clue comes from a letter written by Martha, Oliver's widow, to James McKim. "The girls think after hearing so much about Mrs —— that they would rather go to some other place besides Eagleswood."[122] Though Martha obscured the name, it could have only been Rebecca Spring. Perhaps Mary's account of her time with Spring had not been glowing, or had stressed their differences in class and demeanor. Spring certainly faulted Mary for the decision. Though she had initially pronounced Mary as a fitting wife for Brown, later in her life she would dismiss her as "a coarse sort of woman . . . without much sensibility."[123]

Life among the "Antislavery Set"

Annie and Sarah arrived in Concord in late February 1860, less than three months after their father's execution, and joined a school with about fifty pupils.[124] Once there they found themselves the center of attention. Much like Mary Brown, Annie was first comforted and then discomfited by this position. Brown's daughters took courses in English and music, and Sarah also enrolled in drawing, a passion she would pursue for years to come.[125] For the first two weeks they boarded at the Emersons, where they made the acquaintance of daughters Ellen and Edith and enjoyed "interesting" discussions at supper each night. Ralph Waldo Emerson, Sarah would recall in later years, was very sympathetic to them. Even after they moved into a boardinghouse he greeted her on the street, though, she recollected, he was typically so lost in thought as to be unaware of others.[126]

Although Concord boasted its own famous figures, the presence of John Brown's daughters did not go unremarked. Annie and Sarah piqued the curiosity of many Concord residents. Louisa May Alcott, who Annie first met at a party given for them by the Thoreaus, pressed her for details about Harpers Ferry.[127] Ellen Emerson was also intrigued. Writing to a cousin, she mentioned, "They are very willing to talk and it is very interesting to hear them. The eldest, who is sixteen, kept house for her father at Harper's Ferry all summer, and knows all about it." Perhaps influenced by all the talk about John Brown and his "rustic" family, Ellen looked to Annie as some type of exotic creature. "The other side of her is just what I've always wanted to see, a girl brought up in the primitive spinning, weaving, sheep-tending, butter-making times, which she certainly has been, in every particular, even to the Calvinism."[128] Describing Annie as some kind of "other," she noted, "Mother is exceedingly interested in such a child." But there was a problem: in their country clothes the Brown girls did not fit in, their dress betraying their class status as well as noble rusticity. Ellen Emerson continued, "Alice and Edith have been occupied for the last week in dressing them in Boston fashion, that they should look *like the rest of the world* when they go to school on Monday."[129]

When it came to descriptions of Mary Brown and her daughters, words such as "primitive," "rustic," and "simple" had an underbelly. In his 1848 *Dictionary of Americanisms*, John Russell Bartlett offers hints of how Higginson and Concord society understood it. "Rustic" first shows up as a comparative: "among the educated as well as among the uneducated and rustic classes." It also appears in definitions of two words: "clodhopper" and "countrified."[130] Even late in his life, though Higginson conceded that he "was never more impressed with the spectacle of womanly dignity than in Mrs Brown," he noted, "But she was rustic. That story is simply a statement of the simple, rustic truth."[131] Though some, such as Child, Garrison, and the Alcotts, would struggle financially, there was never any doubt that they were of a different tier than Mary Brown: literate, well educated, almost members of a Boston antislavery intelligentsia best described by Lawrence J. Friedman as a "clique" comfortable with the "genteel New England urban middle class."[132] In their discussions of domesticity and rusticity, they, alongside many Americans trying to make sense of a changing nineteenth-century world, negotiated and inscribed class and status difference. As the United States transformed into a more industrialized, urban nation in the mid-nineteenth century, many Americans looked to the country as a site of purity and authenticity, none more memorably than Henry David Thoreau in *Walden*. If Mary Brown of North Elba stood for antislavery, she also stood for the "rustic" country.[133]

All of this was again exposed when Mary Brown traveled to Concord in the spring of 1860 to attend a fund-raising party at the Alcotts.[134] A "rush" of people appeared in response to the news that Mary would be present, demonstrating the celebrity she possessed a full six months after Brown's execution. Louisa May Alcott wrote, "So many people cooly [sic] came who were not invited, and who had no business here. People sewed and jabbered till Mrs. Brown, with Watson Brown's widow and baby came; then a levee took place." She continued,

The preparations had been made for twenty at the utmost, so when forty souls with the usual complement of bodies appeared, we grew desperate, and our neat little supper turned into a regular "tea fight." A., C., B., and I rushed like comets to and fro trying to fill the multitude that would eat fast and drink like sponges. I filled a big plate with all I could lay hands on, and with two cups of tea, strong enough for a dozen, charged upon Mr. E. and Uncle S. [Emerson and Samuel May], telling them to eat, drink, and be merry, for a famine was at hand. They cuddled into a corner; and then, feeling that my mission was accomplished, I let the hungry *wait* and the thirsty *moan* for tea, while I picked out and helped the regular Antislavery set.[135]

Alcott resented those who had just shown up out of mere curiosity (rather than out of membership in the "regular Antislavery set"), but she, too, looked upon Mary as an object of interest. Her assessment of Mary paralleled Ellen Emerson's depiction of Annie: she looked to her as a symbol of the martyr Brown and of a life lived far from the refined society she knew in Concord. She described Mary as "a tall, stout woman, plain, but with a strong, good face." Mary possessed "a natural dignity that showed she was something better than a 'lady,'" though, Alcott added condescendingly, "she *did* drink out of her saucer and used the plainest speech."[136] Alcott would later show sympathy for her fictional Meg March when she allowed her rich friends to take her well beyond her comfort zone, but she did not have the same compassion for Mary Brown. Like Higginson and Spring, the Concord set looked to the Brown women's rustic characteristics as proof of both their noble ties and their lack of savoir faire.

Alcott applied this same odd blend of reverence and snobbery to Bell's nearly one-year-old son Freddy. Describing Freddy as "bright-eyed" and "handsome," the budding writer added, "He is named Frederick Watson Brown, after his murdered uncle and father, and is a fair, heroic-looking baby, with a fine head, and serious eyes that look about him as if saying, 'I am a Brown! Are these friends or enemies?'" Though posed in lighthearted fashion, her question was one that would earmark the Brown women for life. In the study with Bell and the baby, Alcott and a companion, she wrote, "worshipped . . . at the shrine of John Brown's grandson, kissing him as if he were a little saint, and feeling highly honored when he sucked our fingers, *or walked on us with his honest little red shoes, much the worse for wear.*"[137]

By the time of this Concord encounter, one Brown had fled the scene: Annie. It is hard to imagine the disorientation she must have felt as she

FIGURE 7.   Isabella "Bell" Thompson Brown and her son Freddy, July 15, 1860. Ella Thompson Towne Scrapbook, John Brown Family Collection, Huntington Library, San Marino, California. Reproduced by permission of The Huntington Library.

moved from the Kennedy farm to North Elba to Concord, where she was adorned in fine dresses purchased by others. Annie was overwhelmed by the juxtaposition of her months of sleeping without a pillow and playing watchdog, alongside this new life in refined society where she was expected to dress properly, not like an "outlaw girl." She felt misunderstood in Concord. Even Thoreau, who had compared Brown's gallows to Christ's cross, told her he would "have to bite a ten penny nail in two, before he can understand me," she recalled years later.[138] In the 1880s, she somewhat bitterly recalled, "They understood a good many languages and things but did not *understand me*."[139]

In Concord she found herself shopping for city dresses while haunted by memories of the past year. Her sense that stoic self-possession was expected from a Brown came up against the sixteen-year-old girl's debilitating grief. "The honor and glory that some saw in the work," she recalled later, "did not fill the aching void that was left in my heart, after losing so many loved ones and friends." Although she conceded that it may have been a "benefit" to be with other young people, school was difficult: "My memory was effected. . . . The harder I studied the less I seemed to know." She added that nothing could prevent her from "*thinking, all the time*" and dwelling on the "*terrible shock*" of Harpers Ferry.[140] In *The Past Is a Foreign Country*, David Lowenthal writes that "heightened recollections seem to bring the past not only to life, but into simultaneous existence with the present, making it appear closer than the present, which it both haunts and hypnotizes."[141] This was certainly true for Annie, whose recollections of Brown's raiders and their loss were ever present in Concord. Her grief was so intense that she later recalled she had locked "myself in my room and lay and roll on the floor in the agony of a tearless grief for hours at a time."[142] John Jr.'s wife Wealthy soon wrote to Ruth of her concern about Annie's "ill health," and that "she says she wishes she had never left home."[143]

Annie's trauma and anxiety were only compounded by new losses and shocks. The last of Brown's jailed raiders, Alfred Hazlett and Aaron Stevens, were due to hang on March 16, a few short weeks after her arrival in Concord. She received a final letter from Stevens in which he said he had been glad to "hear from you once more before I go to the land of the spirits."[144] And as she anticipated his hanging, Annie learned of another unexpected loss: that of Martha and her newborn daughter Olive. Reporting the deaths to James McKim, Bell stated simply, "Dear Sister Martha is taken from us and we are left quite alone, it is very lonely here now without her she was a dear good woman we shall miss her sadly."[145] Mary wrote that she had cared for Martha during four weeks of illness but that "her baby only lived two days & she gradualy sunk away with a raging fever that we never got the upper hands of. we done all we could for her but God see fit to take her." Lamenting briefly, she wrote, "We have been called upon to drink deep of the cup of affliction," but, she declared, "may thy will Oh Lord be done."[146] Such sentiments offered little comfort to Annie.

All of her emotions came to a head when, out of the blue, escaped raider Charles Tidd appeared in Concord.[147] "I do not know as I can describe my feelings on that day when I met Tidd at your house," she recalled years later to Sanborn. "It seemed to me that someone had come back to me from *my dead*, like one coming out of a night-mare, that I saw in him something real that I must grasp for fear it would escape me." They may have met more than once, enough to get those in Concord curious about the connection. "I know," she recalled to Sanborn, "your sister thought we were 'lovers,' so did Mrs. Emerson. I could not make her understand or comprehend such a friendship." But, she explained solemnly, "A soldier could understand the tie that bound us without an explanation."[148]

The reappearance of a fellow "soldier" and the further reminder that she was not "understood" in Concord society proved too much. Annie did not dare discuss her unhappiness with Sanborn or the Alcotts. Instead, she turned to Tidd, who arranged for her to visit his sister. "He knew," she stated, "I was . . . totally unfit to study and that I needed diversion more than school books."[149] Ultimately, Annie fled Concord for the safety of North Elba.[150] Writing to Mary Stearns following Annie's return, Ruth offered news of how Annie was bearing up. "She stait [sic] with us last night, and she seemed quite cheerful, and said she felt in better spirits than she had for some day."[151] Recalling her decision a year later, Annie wrote that she had left because "I thought it a harder task than my mind ought to bear, it was more than I ought to do."[152]

After Annie's departure Sarah stayed on and, by all accounts, flourished. After a brief trip to North Elba in the summer of 1860, she returned to Concord. Sanborn wrote to Mary, "We are glad to see her back again and so are her schoolmates. She says, she has had a good time, and did not want to leave here at all."[153] Mary wrote to Sarah shortly after that "I am glad you are well and are having a good time. I hope you will try to be good & I believe that you will. Mr. Sanborn writes very flattering accounts of you." She added, "I have got the old part of the house all plastered & finished so that we shall be very comfortable this winter & a room [done] off for you when you come home."[154] This letter is intriguing. Was Mary trying to entice Sarah to want to return to North Elba with the promise of her own room—something she could not expect in the confines of Brown poverty but had come to enjoy in Concord society? Was she apprehensive about Sarah's apparent embrace of Concord, a place that was so unlike North Elba? Had Sanborn's comment that Sarah had not wanted to leave offended her mother?

If Mary was sensitive to any of this, the events that followed would have furthered her feelings. The following spring not only Sarah but Annie returned to Concord. Annie likely felt that she had to prove that her courage had returned—that now it was something that she "ought to do." Mary, worried about the mounting cost, confided to Sanborn that "as I don't know anything about how much money there is for us or what the situation of it is I don't know whether she can return or not."[155] But more than this, Mary was concerned with how the girls' time would be spent. Abolitionists had again resumed debate about the Brown daughters. They were now insisting that Annie and Sarah study a subject that Mary felt her daughters had been studying perfectly well at North Elba (for free, no less): housekeeping.

In their original term in Concord, Annie and Sarah had undertaken a course of study that included English, music, and, to Sarah's delight, drawing. She had especially excelled at it, and this was a primary reason that Mary Brown worked for her to return to Concord. But she was soon confronted by those who did not feel that art was the only course of study lacking in North Elba. Rebecca Spring again chimed in and claimed a special knowledge of Brown and his desire that Annie and Sarah become "strong, intelligent, expert industrious Christian housekeepers." Brown likely intended for his wife to continue Sarah's training in housekeeping at home, recognizing that as Annie had kept house both at North Elba and for more than a dozen men at the Kennedy farmhouse, her training in that area was complete.

He likely meant "housekeeper" as a humble practice, not a course of study, but in the mid-nineteenth century, with social and household hierarchy in flux, housekeeping suddenly acquired new importance.[156] "Every thing is moving and changing," wrote Catharine Beecher in her famous treatise on homemaking, and she saw provision of detailed and standardized information about domesticity, from cooking to laundry to infant care, as central for this new realm.[157] Americans agreed, and her *Treatise on Domestic Economy* was reprinted almost yearly in the 1840s and 1850s.[158] Women such as Spring were well versed in Beecher's belief that domestic education belonged alongside other subjects such as mathematics and painting, and she pushed for Brown's daughters to have such training upon their return to Concord.[159] Writing to Sanborn, Mary argued that Sarah's desire and her own were for other studies. "If she returns I think that she had better not try to learn housework," she wrote. Aware that John Brown had stressed the importance of his daughters' learning "the music of the broom, wash-tub, needle spindle, loom, axe, syche, hoe, flail, etc.," she noted, "I feel all that you express of what her dear Father said." But, she added, "I feel that she can learn housework at a much less expence at home."[160]

Mary did not get her wish. By the time she wrote this, Annie and Sarah had returned to Concord. There, they boarded with the Alcotts, who apparently were deemed better than the "rustic" Mary to instruct her daughters in John Brown's ideal "housekeeping." Louisa May Alcott—who, though from a poor family was clearly of the respectable "Antislavery set"—was to be their model. Trading her fascination for irritation, Alcott noted in her diary that "John Brown's daughters came to board, and upset my plans of rest and writing. . . . I had my fit of woe up garret on the fat rag-bag, and then put my papers away, and fell to work at housekeeping."[161] The onetime housekeeper at the Kennedy farmhouse and her sister, long accustomed to chores at North Elba, could only fall to work alongside her. They likely knew that there was little to be learned from the "Antislavery set" about housekeeping that they did not already know, but they yielded to its need to educate Brown's daughters.

❧ Chapter 5

The Search for a New Life

As the Civil War raged, Mary gathered her youngest daughter and meager belongings. Despite Brown's final wish that she would always live in Essex County, she intended to leave their Adirondack home and Brown's grave behind. She left North Elba in a wagon driven by Lyman Epps, longtime family friend and one of the few remaining African American settlers from Gerrit Smith's land-grant settlement. Mary, nine-year-old Ellen, and Salmon's family first went to Iowa. They were soon joined by Sarah, now seventeen, and Annie, who had just returned from a second mission into the South. From Iowa they would travel two thousand miles by wagon on the overland trail to California. There, Mary told her daughters, they would create new lives and find better opportunities.

How had the Brown women arrived at this moment? Against the backdrop of the Civil War, Mary Brown had struggled to access her portion of the John Brown fund. She had contended with North Elba winters, the constraints of poverty and dependence upon abolitionist benefactors, and the departure of two sons and a daughter to new battlefields. Ultimately, she decided to put aside John Brown's jailhouse decree that she remain a permanent resident of Essex County to grasp for a better economic future in the West. In migrating, she also sought refuge from the curiosity and burdens associated with being both reviled and celebrated as John Brown's kin. None of this had proven possible at North Elba. Embracing Brown's motto of "Action, Action," she had taken the dramatic step of leaving for a new life.

The Browns hoped that the newness of California would offer them a chance to re-create themselves. And it did. But their new start was not un-complicated. As the broader world transformed during the war and beyond, Mary Brown and her daughters remained linked to the heady antislavery days of the 1850s. The more time that passed, the more fiercely Americans debated about John Brown. In California, the Brown women would find their livelihoods—and even their very lives—implicated in this complicated remembrance. Though they distanced themselves from the eastern sites of war, this offered little protection from the fierce contest over the man that one newspaper deemed the "frightener of the great state of Virginia."[1]

A New War against Slavery

The Browns had eagerly followed news of the Civil War's outbreak in April 1861 from North Elba. Mary, Annie, Sarah, and Ellen lived in the Brown home, while Ruth and Henry resided nearby with their children Johnny, Ella, Grace, and baby Dauphin, named for Henry's slain brother. Salmon, Abbie, and their daughter Cora also lived in the neighborhood. They may have talked about how others in the nation were finally matching the Browns' personal sacrifice as the numbers of dead fathers, husbands, and sons on Civil War battlefields mounted. Because of his Kansas gunshot wound, Henry Thompson was not eligible to enlist, while thirty-eight-year-old Jason and thirty-six-year-old Owen chose to remain in Ohio instead of fighting.[2] Two Brown sons, John Jr. and Salmon, enlisted in the Union army, perhaps seek-ing redemption for declining to serve at Harpers Ferry. Mary also regarded with fear the departure south of one more Brown: Annie.

From the war's outbreak, the Brown family culture of self-sacrifice domi-nated discussion of what the Browns owed this new cause. Although the war was initially waged to preserve the Union rather than to end slavery, John Jr. and Salmon regarded their participation as akin to fighting slavery. John Jr. wrote to Franklin Sanborn that he felt "to sustain the Government in the present war is to engage in a contest for the freedom of all."[3] Writing to George Stearns in April 1861, he confided, "I am now endeavoring to raise a company of Anti-Slavery men as volunteers, trusting that the time is not distant when we can act without being obliged to *fight* the *North* as well as South."[4] Salmon, too, looked to fight, perhaps prodded by a letter from Thomas Wentworth Higginson that described how he was raising a regi-ment of "men of anti-slavery principles."[5] Salmon recalled, "I felt it to be my duty to . . . fight for the principles that had cost my father and brothers their lives."[6] Salmon was commissioned a lieutenant and traveled with a local Plattsburgh regiment to Albany in early 1862.[7]

For a third time, Mary and the other Brown women watched as one of their own departed North Elba to fight on the antislavery battlefield. For once they did not sustain any losses, as almost as soon as Salmon reached Albany, he was dismissed. Some in his group were concerned that once they got into Virginia "it would be detrimental to the interest of the regiment . . . to be associated with a Son of John Brown."[8] Salmon was stung. Years later, he recalled, "I had been all thro the Border ruffian fights in Kansas and I felt hurt and humiliated that I should be unwelcome in a regiment which was ready enough to sing that my fathers body lay a mouldering in the grave but his soul was marching on."[9] John Jr., too, soon returned home.[10]

Annie also looked for a second tour of duty as an antislavery "soldier," yearning to again push the boundaries of women's activism and to claim a role in Brown family duty. In 1861 raider Barclay Coppoc wrote her of his work to free slaves in Missouri; his death a few months later in a train wreck may have encouraged her to do what she could to "take up arms" herself.[11] When Salmon departed, Annie despaired, "What a pity it is that I belong to the <u>weaker sex</u>, for if I were *only* a <u>man</u> then I could go to *war*."[12] By the summer of 1863, Annie realized that there was a way. She wrote to William Lloyd Garrison that she was "desirous of going South to Port Royal, Hilton Head, or elsewhere to engage in teaching 'Contrabands.'" She continued, "I have often thought of going before, and I beleive that climate would suit me. I could go for six months, and perhaps longer if I went soon."[13] At a convention in Philadelphia, she got her chance.[14] She wrote home of her intentions in the fall of 1863.

Mary Brown's response is one of just a handful of truly revealing letters that survive in her hand. From Fort Edward Institute, a boarding seminary where she and budding artist Sarah were now enrolled, Annie wrote home of her desire to teach, but Mary did not respond. (She would later acknowledge that the news had left her "allmost struck . . . dumb."[15]) Annie tried again. Finally, her mother responded with a lengthy letter confiding her fears and hopes. A typical Mary letter is short and matter-of-fact, reporting on news of home. She occasionally wrote letters of consolation full of religious rhetoric. And infrequently, she wrote letters in which she reported fondly on grandson Freddy. But it was rare for Mary to write as she did here: both in acknowledging her hesitation and in her warm assurance to Annie that she was "very near and dear to me wherever you are." Though she noted Annie's desire to work for "a great cause," she revealed her fear of losing another child.

"I was not prepared for it just now," she wrote. But she offered her prayer "that God's blessing may rest upon you in your undertakeing." As she had in the days surrounding Brown's capture and execution, Mary found meaning in the Brown family ideal of sacrifice for a cause. "If you feel it to be your duty we will all submit to it," she wrote, and implored Annie to "write very often all about every thing."[16]

In the winter of 1863 Annie set out to teach at Union-occupied Norfolk, Virginia, with at least one other teacher-recruit, Worcester Quaker Sarah E. Wall, under the auspices of the New England Freedmen's Aid Society or the National Freedmen's Relief Association of New York.[17] Before departing, she spent at least one night at the home of William Still, a prominent African American member of the Pennsylvania Antislavery Society. There she met fugitive slave John William Dungy; this meeting likely spurred her on in her commitment to travel south.[18] Mary had journeyed south in the wake of Brown's raid. Now, Annie entered Virginia, a keystone of the Confederacy that had formed partly in response to her father's actions at Harpers Ferry. The Union army had invaded and occupied the port city of Norfolk early in 1862, freeing approximately ten thousand slaves. Schools were opened to educate African American children by day and adults by night. Over fifteen hundred African American students in Norfolk were taught by some thirty teachers during the Civil War.[19]

In wartime Norfolk Annie faced many challenges. Teachers struggled to work without adequate materials or support: at one point during the war, one school in Norfolk had 457 students of all levels but only three teachers.[20] Teaching contraband slaves consisted not only of typical classroom teaching but of missionary work, housekeeping, and providing medical care.[21] Annie also likely witnessed much poverty, disease, and even death among the freedpeople. In the year in which Annie went to Norfolk, Virginia teacher H. S. Beals wrote, "I followed scores of children to their graves, who, but for cold and hunger, would have been here today."[22] In December 1863, by which time Annie was in Norfolk, another teacher wrote, "I can not tell you how busy I am. Those who are escaping bondage are pressing in in all directions. From one to two hundred arrive every few days, and it is a matter of no small moment to know where to shelter them." She added, "I see sights *often*, OFTEN, that make my heart ache, and which I have no power to relieve."[23] Dealing with these dire needs and the resulting emotions likely took over day-to-day life upon Annie's arrival.

Like her brother John Jr. in his first year as teacher, Annie may have found all of this overwhelming. A rare surviving letter hints that some challenge arose during her second Virginia sojourn. With evident pride, John Jr. wrote to her, "I am indeed truly glad that you have gone to teach *Contrabands* and especially that you have gone to *Virginia* for that purpose." Annie confided some kind of difficulty, but he admonished her to be patient, adding, "Don't let any temporary discouragement unnerve you." "As in the natural," he continued, "so in the world of the mind there are sun-shine and shade, one comes as the *necessary* complement and counterpart of the other. Bearing this always in mind you cannot get discouraged and fly the track."[24]

Even if she bore John Jr.'s advice in mind, nothing else about her life in Norfolk worked to reassure her. Historian Joe Richardson notes that many teachers had previous school experience, but even with this, they had "nothing that would prepare them for what they would endure in Virginia. They were in a war zone that could only be entered with a military pass. A Norfolk teacher 'heard distinctly all day . . . rapid and heavy cannonading,' while a Craney Island class was disturbed by the firing of gunboats." He adds that even after Confederate troops were defeated, "the teachers still had to contend with hostile local whites. When James F. Sisson went to church the first Sunday after his arrival, a pretty, well-dressed teenager stepped up and 'administered a dose of spit' upon him."[25]

Unlike many of her colleagues, Annie had already lived in integrated societies at North Elba and the Kennedy farmhouse, and she may have been stung by some of her fellow teachers' racism.[26] Or she may have felt as though she were back among Concord abolitionist society, since many other teachers came from middle-class backgrounds.[27] Her discomfort could have also stemmed from the rising racial tensions in Norfolk. The Union occupation did nothing to assuage and in fact greatly heightened white southerners' sense that their life was under attack. In the summer of 1863, a prominent doctor shot and killed a white former teacher from Vermont who was leading a new regiment of African American troops through a Norfolk street. Annie presumably arrived in town in the month following the doctor's execution, and the Richmond General Assembly declared him a martyr for the Confederacy the following March.[28]

Unlike her work at the Kennedy farm, Annie's time teaching "contrabands" remains shrouded in mystery, as little direct evidence of her experience is accessible today.[29] But in 1864 some Americans were aware that John Brown's daughter was teaching freedpeople. Reports circulated that she was teaching in a mansion-turned-schoolhouse that once belonged to the governor who had allowed her father's death sentence.[30] The *Sacramento Bee* reported, "Among the most singular of the mutations of fortune is the fact that a daughter of John Brown is now teaching a school for negro children in the old mansion of Henry A. Wise, in Virginia."[31] The *Indianapolis Daily State*

Sentinel more bluntly reported that "John Brown's daughter is teaching little niggers in Gov. Wise's house."[32] In actuality Annie, along with other teachers, had only visited the school at the Wise farm. While she was there, a guard had presented her with a brass curtain ring "to remember Gov Wise by."[33]

A Decision to Start a New Life

Mary Brown followed the news of the war with great interest. She saw it as validating Brown's mission. After hearing of a party that the Stearns had hosted to celebrate the Emancipation Proclamation and unveil a bust of John Brown, she wrote to Mary Stearns.[34] She noted that after she had read in the *Liberator* of the gathering of "some of the most noble souls that our country contains," her "soul leaped for joy." She made note of Stearns's participation in a delegation to request that Lincoln recruit African American soldiers, adding, "I am very much rejoiced that the collered people are allowed to fight. I feel that that is just as it should be." She concluded, "I feel that there is a great deal to be encouraged about, but God only knows where the end of this teriable affliction that is upon us."[35] Just as John Brown's epistles to his family had become increasingly polemical during the Kansas years, Mary Brown's letters now adopted a more political tone and a new sense of urgency.

Even as Mary continued to classify the Stearns and other abolitionists as friends, she grew increasingly unhappy in her dealings with them. After meeting with James Redpath, she wrote to her daughter-in-law. "You look in the Liberator," she instructed, and "you will see how unjustly the fund has been distributed."[36] In addition to her ire that Bell had been ignored, Mary was frustrated with her inability to access promised funds. Writing to Mary Stearns in late 1860, she noted that her "dear husband" had wanted the family to remain at North Elba. But, she stated bluntly, "if we do it is necessary to improve the place so that we can have some resource from it."[37] Over the next few years, her letters to the Stearns and to other Brown backers recorded mounting annoyance.[38]

Mary and other members of the Brown family had also grown increasingly sensitive to what one family acquaintance later described as the "curious stares and unwelcome gaze of the populace."[39] The Brown family's celebrity proved expensive, as they were called to host various visitors and drop-in company. Ruth wrote to Mary Stearns as early as April 1860, copying a letter from John Jr. that explained his family's mounting expenses. "Even before the demonstration at H.F our house has been like a well patronized Hotel," he had written to her, adding, "Very many coming to see us from motives for mere curiosity, such folks will say 'I heard a great deal about you, and I thought I'd like to see, and now I'm satisfied, but I should like to see your sharp rifle before I go away.'"[40]

By mid-war, Mary Brown's frustration drove her to action: westward migration. Many historians emphasize that the decision to migrate west was often a male decision; men, historian Richard White notes, were "the customary authority in these decisions."[41] Other scholars add that women often regretted being wrenched from the idealized "home" space they had created.[42] For Mary Brown it was quite the opposite: she weighed the risks and gains and determined that she and her daughters would create a new home instead of remaining where they were or moving closer to other Pennsylvania and Ohio relatives. She and son Salmon were drawn to the opportunities farmers would have in California, ones with which North Elba could never compete.[43] She confided to Owen in early 1864, "I very much regret that I ever spent a cent on that farm in North Elba."[44] In one of the more popular emigrant guidebooks, Lansford Hastings described the soil of California's valley as "vastly rich and productive," adding, "I venture nothing when I say, that it is not only not surpassed, but that it is not even equaled."[45] After nearly a decade of winters at North Elba, Mary Brown might have relished Hastings's description of the climate of western California as "that of perpetual spring."[46]

Salmon and Mary did not simply seek the opportunity for economic advantage; instead, they looked to the "new country" to make an altogether fresh start. "After my father John Brown was executed," Salmon later recalled, "We wanted to go away to a new country."[47] Writing of her decision to Mary Stearns, Mary Brown elaborated. "I have thought that perhaps I had better" leave North Elba for a western home, she reasoned, "as it would give Annie and Sarah a chance to do something for themselves in a new country that they cannot have here." The last of this phrase is especially striking, both a practical and emotional assessment of what would be denied her daughters if they stayed in the place where their father was buried. Perhaps reflecting on her own life of dependence, Mary added that her daughters had needed schooling to "prepare them to earn a liveing for themselves."[48] Mary regretted the need to leave John Brown's grave, but she felt almost compelled to leave.[49] Watson's widow Bell reported, "Mother Brown wrote that she could not resist the temptation."[50]

Thus in the midst of the Civil War, the North Elban Browns fled notoriety and looked to escape the dependency that had plagued Mary for decades. Salmon's family, Mary, and Ellen first took a train out to Cleveland, to visit with the families of John Jr., Jason, and Owen.[51] After visiting with the

Ohio Browns they continued west, arriving in early winter of 1863–1864 in Decorah, Iowa, where Sarah and Annie were to meet them. The winter they passed in Iowa was a hard one. Ellen was occasionally ill, and Mary reported "a great deal of sickness all about us."[52] Popular emigrant guides that spoke of California as "one of the most healthy portions of the world" likely confirmed her sense that the "new country" was the right place for the Brown family to start over.[53] As she prepared for spring travel, Mary also waited for the arrival of the Thompsons.[54]

Ruth and Henry Thompson never appeared. They found such comfort while visiting John Jr. and Wealthy that they decided to remain nearby in Put-in-Bay, a small island in Lake Erie. John Jr. and his family had moved there after his brief Civil War service, and they were soon joined by fugitive Owen. Though one side of the 1,382-acre island became a popular summer resort spot for the wealthy, John Jr. found much peace in the 10 acres he bought on the opposite shore. "The cultivation of grapes, and fruit of all kinds," Wealthy wrote to a relative, "is very profitable, as well as pleasant, business here. . . . John has found just the place he has always longed for, and is delighted with it."[55] John Jr. and Wealthy would spend the rest of their lives in this secluded spot. Though he would write countless letters to newspapers to answer his father's detractors, John Jr. saw his home as a refuge from a world that misunderstood him.[56] When Ruth and Henry arrived, they too found the place they had longed for.[57] With the exception of Jason, who lived in nearby Akron, all of John and Dianthe's children now lived on Put-in-Bay island, acting as what Wealthy would later call a "little colony."[58]

Even when the "little colony" on Put-in-Bay broke up, none of Dianthe's children ever lived near Mary or their half-siblings again.[59] Put-in-Bay proved a frustrating place to make a living, and the Thompsons left for better farming opportunities in Hickory Grove, Wisconsin, in 1872. Though they were close to some members of Henry's family, Ruth missed the "genuine love and sympathy" she had with her Brown kin. The Thompsons ultimately migrated once more, arriving in Pasadena, California, in the mid-1880s to join brothers Jason and Owen. The move to Pasadena, Ruth hoped, would bring all that she had loved about the "good society" of Put-in-Bay.[60] And it seemed to do so, offering her youngest daughter Mary access to education and securing her family in a Republican-dominated, temperance-minded community that offered sympathy and patronage to the children of John Brown. She and her brothers were especially aided by Horatio Nelson Rust, who had helped raise money for her father in the 1850s and who now worked for the Indian Bureau in California. Well-connected in Pasadena and beyond, he was ever willing to use those ties to aid the family of John Brown.[61] In part because of Rust, Ruth found a home where it was not only comfortable but beneficial to be a Brown. In the summer of 1886, Ruth, Henry, and her brothers were even paraded through the streets during a GAR gathering. When "John Brown's Body" played, Ruth wept, and she and her brothers wrote to the *Pasadena Union* to express their gratitude for such treatment.[62] Though poor and ever-reliant on charity, Ruth lived in peace in Pasadena until her death in 1904.[63]

Despite the distance, Ruth remained in contact with her sisters, but the years of separation took a toll. By the 1890s Wealthy, John Jr.'s wife, would profess not to even know the names of Salmon's, Annie's, and Ellen's children.[64] Initially, Mary Brown's decision to leave North Elba had caused some strain with her stepchildren, and this likely contributed to the drifting apart of the two sets of Browns. Writing to Henry and Ruth in 1862, John Jr. had outlined a different vision. He identified Put-in-Bay island as "where I intend to live and where I am trying and hoping to get those of our family together who want to live near each other and in the best place in *all* respects to make a home and acquire an independence & competence which I [never] saw or dreamed of seeing."[65] The language he employed made the recipient list for his invitation unclear. "Please say to Bell that I am trying to provide a good place for her and little Freddy—and for others of our family who want to leave North Elba & would be pleased with my enterprise," he instructed Ruth. He concluded with a reference to a phrase from Brown's jailhouse letters: "I am trying to 'gather the scattered remnants of our broke family' and build up our walls in a more congenial and less inhospitable region."[66] And Mary appears to have felt some unease. After reporting Bell's loneliness at North Elba, Mary wrote to Annie, "I shall ask her to come out here and live with us but I fear that she will not come or that Ruth and Henry will influence her to go where they are."[67]

The Westward Trek

In late April 1864 Mary and her three daughters traveled with Salmon, Abbie, and their two young daughters Cora and Minnie from Decorah to Council Bluffs, Iowa, to join a wagon train. In his guidebook, Lansford Hastings recorded his "high glee, jocular hilarity, and happy anticipation, as we thus started forward into the wild expanse, of the untrodden regions of the 'western world.'"[68] The Brown party, however, likely departed with mixed emotions: anticipation and excitement mingled with fear, uncertainty, and some touch of nostalgia. By the time they reached Council Bluffs, from where they would ferry across the Missouri River to begin the westward journey, Mary and son Salmon had already outfitted their group with three wagons, six Spanish merino sheep, a few cows, and all the necessary provisions for their trip.[69] Aware that other wagon trains had been disturbed by Native Americans as well as animals, they also packed weapons.[70] Salmon drove his family, Mary drove Annie, Sarah, and Ellen, and two hired men drove the third wagon and took charge of the sheep in exchange for bed and board.

Though the Brown women had been long accustomed to hard work and poor circumstances, the westward journey still proved difficult. Historians John Faragher and Christine Stansell summarily describe westward travel as "exhausting, toilsome, and often grueling."[71] Even before they set out, daughter Annie reported that Mary had worked alongside one of the hired men, digging to find a better source of water. Mary would be called upon to perform such tasks throughout the trek.[72] Annie, Sarah, and Ellen also assisted Abbie in minding her two young daughters. The youngest was just thirteen months, and Abbie occasionally roped her to the wagon wheel so she could not stray too far.[73]

Annie was more struck by the novelty and adventure than the drudgery and danger. At fifteen she had traveled to Maryland to live alongside Brown's raiders, at nineteen to Norfolk to teach former slaves, and now, at twenty, she anticipated a two-thousand-mile westward trek. Even though Annie had lived in unusual circumstances before, she was struck by their new lifestyle. "I have not been in a house but three or four times since we started and not to stay then," she wrote to her sister-in-law Bell, adding, "Just think of squatting on yoke-pads and on the ground or wagon tongues evenings instead of being in a house like you are!"[74] Arriving at Council Bluffs, she was likely greeted by the same scene that Harriet Loughary, a mother of six who traveled to Oregon in the same year, described: "Large numbers of emmigrant waggons are centering here, and in Council Bluffs. Rendezvousing and preparing for the march. The whole country is so dotted with tents and covered waggons, as to resemble an army in quarters, some going to the newly discovered Idaho gold mines, but mostly families on the way to Oregon and California."[75] Excitedly writing to Bell on May 21, 1864, Annie noted that they had been ferried across the river and would join a wagon train the following day. She closed with her hope that Bell would join them in "the 'Promised Land.'"[76] The next day the Browns started west, ferrying over the Missouri in the same place as Loughary had weeks prior. The trek that would take them well over four months was under way.

Safety was in numbers, and the Browns joined with a wagon train under the direction of a staunch Union supporter named Woodruff. Harriet Loughary reached Fort Laramie, just inside Dakota Territory, on June 8, 1864, likely about three weeks prior to the Browns. There, she reported hearing news of Union victories in the war. Her train celebrated by singing such songs as "The Star-Spangled Banner" and "Hang Jeff Davis in a Sour Apple Tree."[77] The Browns may have participated in similar celebrations, feeling that their cause was being furthered, even though they were far from the theaters of war.

From Fort Laramie the Browns intended to follow the westward trail to the South Pass and make their way through the Rocky Mountains. At some point, the Browns separated from Woodruff's train. But having heard tales of danger, they soon had second thoughts. Abbie recalled that the Browns had heard of several travelers who had been killed.[78] They might have been the same victims Harriet Loughary saw evidence of on her trip a few weeks earlier; her wagon train passed the grave of a man killed by Sioux, and attached to it was a note warning fellow travelers of the peril they faced.[79] Concerned, the Browns joined a wagon train from Indiana and journeyed onward toward the Rockies. Some of the members of the new train, Abbie recalled years later, "seemed to know who we were and were very friendly."[80] After joining up with another, larger train of eighty wagons, they encountered the Sioux. One day, their wagons were surrounded by what Abbie estimated as 250 Sioux, and she recounted that one man had even grabbed "Mr. Brown's sister's hair" in the course of riding in and out of the wagons. Eventually the train leader ordered the wagons to halt, and the men, Salmon included, drew their weapons. Seeing the guns, the Sioux rode away.[81]

As they continued across Dakota Territory and the eight-thousand-foot summit of the Rockies, another danger confronted the Browns. It proved far more personal than the disease and accidents that imperiled most travelers: Confederate loyalists enraged at the thought of Browns in their midst. Shortly after the Sioux had been driven away, the southern sympathies of the larger wagon train became apparent, and talk circulated of the famous Browns' kin among a group Annie described as "Tennessee rebels of the worst kind."[82] Some of Salmon's sheep were poisoned, and the Browns suspected that it had been intentional.[83] But the danger was even graver. One night, some men approached Salmon to report a plan to kill them all "for the part John Brown and his family had taken against the south at Harper's Ferry."[84]

In the middle of the plains, thousands of miles from North Elba, the Browns faced a weighty decision: to stay with the large party and risk the approach of an angry mob, or to strike out on their own and face whatever trouble they might encounter. The Browns chose the latter and attempted to outrun the eighty-wagon train. Stealing away, they drove through much of the night. "I had a feeling if they meant business they would try to overtake us," Abbie recalled, adding, "We left that night and traveled until four o'clock in the morning when going down a steep hill the front wagon tipped over."[85] Though Mary Brown had known many moments of fear in her life, she may have felt unprepared for this. Waiting for daylight to come so they could fix the wagon and continue, she surely wondered what would happen if their pursuers overtook them. The Browns spent a week racing for Camp Connor at Soda Springs in Idaho Territory. At one point, Abbie recalled, they turned and saw the large wagon train in pursuit of them, pulling over a hill in the distance. According to both Annie and Abbie, their party arrived mere hours before the pursuing train pulled in.[86] Union troops at Camp Connor forced the Confederate sympathizers to take a loyalty oath before sending them onward to Oregon Territory.

These happenings soon made papers in the East. After noting that Brown's family had left the East "to seek another and more eligible home in California," the *Boston Commonwealth* reported "a painful rumor, not yet fully confirmed, that after leaving Missouri, it having been ascertained that they were John Brown's family, they were pursued by Missouri guerrillas, captured, robbed and murdered."[87] Even relatives back east heard such reports. "Do you hear any thing from Mrs. Brown and Salmon?" Henry Thompson's mother inquired in a letter to her son. "When you write me tell me some say they were all killed others say they got safe to Cal."[88] The *Boston Commonwealth* soon retracted its report of the Browns' demise. The *Liberator* also posted the news and included a reprint of one of Annie's letters. "I wrote you last while at Soda Springs. I did not tell you the danger we were in, for I thought you would worry for nothing," she wrote to the Browns at Put-in-Bay, adding, "There was a train of Tennessee rebels of the worst kind got us into their company and were going to kill Salmon, and doubtless the rest of us."[89]

From Soda Springs the Browns, accompanied for at least part of the time by six soldiers, commenced the remainder of their trek. They went southwest into Nevada Territory and then approached the eastern slopes of the Sierra Nevada range. There their wagons were "hoisted up with ropes and chains, winches and pulleys, and then let down again in the same way." After this maneuver, historian Lillian Schlissel notes, there remained "another hundred miles through the twisting slopes of the mountains until the travelers saw the green color of the Sacramento valley."[90] Though many of the routes into California went through this valley to the city of Sacramento, the Browns went farther north, eventually camping at a place then called Battle Meadow.

While encamped, they became friends with Aurelius and Helen Brodt and decided to join with their wagon train, one bound for the small but bustling town of Red Bluff on the Sacramento River, about 130 miles north of modern-day Sacramento.[91]

Annie's account of what Abbie called "all our hairbreadth escapes" is almost shocking in its dismissal of the danger and hardships her party had faced.[92] After somewhat blithely describing their weeklong race to Camp Connor, Annie summed up their journey for Wealthy. "You will ask how I liked crossing the Plains," she wrote. "It will do for six months of one's life, but I should hate to waste another six months by doing it over again." Somewhat surprisingly—or not, given that Annie might have wanted to appear to be a strong soldier—she concluded, "We had a remarkably good time and for the most part enjoyed it, did not suffer privation as I had supposed we would; still I do not advise anyone to undertake the journey."[93] As for her new home, she withheld judgment, but she took note of the tall balsam and pine trees on the mountains; her fascination with the California landscape had begun.[94] Like John Jr., she would turn to it as a sanctuary, a refuge from the problems that she would face in the years to come.

A New Life in Red Bluff

Newspapers in Red Bluff, the Brown women's residence for the first six years of their tenure in California, proclaimed their arrival. The *Red Bluff Semi-Weekly Independent* announced that a "large Emigrant Train from the East, by the plains across, arrived in town this forenoon," adding that "among the number was the wife, son, and three daughters of John Brown, the hero of Harper's Ferry notoriety, and the frightener of the great state of Virginia."[95] The "notoriety" to which the *Independent* alluded would determine the course of their lives in California. Though in a "new country" with better opportunities, Mary Brown and her daughters were still poor. When they first arrived in Red Bluff, their surname evoked sympathy and community aid, allowing Mary to live securely and to re-create herself as an active member of the community for perhaps the first time in her life.

The Browns had arrived in Red Bluff at an important moment in its history.[96] Because of its location near the head of navigation on the Sacramento River, Red Bluff had quickly become a critical junction of supply for northern California mines.[97] The Tehama County seat since 1857, Red Bluff had its own flour mill, brewery, saloons, hotels, livery stables, brickyard, schools, and churches. An 1880 survey of Tehama County offered this description: "The streets were thronged with large mule-teams and extensive pack-trains;

steamers arrived almost daily; large numbers of people were constantly arriving to engage in business; buildings arose as if by magic; streets were laid out, a school-house was built, and Red Bluff became a prominent point upon the map of the State."[98] After her years at North Elba, Mary Brown was drawn to the bustling town. West promoter Samuel Bowles described Red Bluff in 1869 as "a central point of commerce for all northern California and southern Oregon." Bowles added that Red Bluff was also "the present home of the widow and daughters of the immortal John Brown. They straggled in here, weary and poor, from their overland journey, but found most hospitable greeting from the citizens and have secured a permanent home."[99]

This "most hospitable greeting" was not necessarily to be expected. The same sectional tensions existed that Mary had seen manifested in the Browns' chase across the prairie.[100] Though Confederate support was more concentrated in southern California, there was no small degree of southern support (as well as antipathy toward the Union) throughout the state. Lincoln had won California in 1860 only by a narrow margin. Historian Leonard Richards argues that some people had even wanted to remove California from the Union: though much of this sentiment was concentrated in the south, the most famous plot, one involving a takeover of Alcatraz and San Francisco, occurred in the north.[101] In short, California remained embattled.[102]

Though Red Bluff and northern California were not hotbeds of Confederate sentiment, they did have a strong Democratic presence prior to the Civil War. Red Bluff voters had favored northern Democratic presidential candidate Stephen Douglas in 1860, but its *Semi-Weekly Independent* emerged as staunchly pro-Union throughout the war. By 1864 the Democrat-leaning *Beacon* ceased publishing, and Tehama County settled into pro-Union majority sentiment.[103] The area's response to the death of Lincoln the year after the Brown women arrived was indicative of overall community sentiment. Resident Aurelius Brodt described how within three hours of the news of Lincoln's death, "stores & shops were closed—flags draped in mourning and hung at half mast." But he also alluded to a small Confederate population. "Some [Unionists] went up and down the streets," Brodt reported, "looking for Copperheads that dare express joy at the death of Lincoln, that they might hang them to the first tree."[104]

Despite the Confederate minority, when the Browns appeared in 1864, they were welcomed. Abbie Brown recalled that they arrived a "hungry, almost barefoot, ragged lot" but that the people of the town "came generously to our aid," providing groceries, shoes, cloth, and necessities.[105] An official fund-raising drive soon followed, as interested parties hoped to purchase a home for Mary and her family. The *Independent* reported, "A one dollar subscription has been started in Sacramento. . . . Every town in the State should send its mite to assist in this enterprise."[106] It later appealed, "The East educated his children, the West is called upon to provide a home for the widow and her youngest daughters." It continued, "We hope all true and loyal men will come forward with their contributions and place the widow and children of John Brown in a position where want will not intrude in the future as it has in the past. A home is their just due."[107]

These fund-raising efforts stemmed from sympathy evoked by the Brown women's surname; the sense that a home was "their just due" implies as much. Mary had little choice but to accept the charity. And though she may have been embarrassed by the publicity, a home of her own was appealing. Because they had raised money to provide it, Red Bluff citizens looked to it as more than just a private residence; it was deemed the "John Brown cottage." This was not the first time that Mary and her daughters would find charity and their celebrity interlinked: this had been one hallmark of the "John Brown Year." Nor would it be the last. Reports on the cottage fund and the Browns' whereabouts appeared back east. The *Boston Commonwealth,* for instance, told its readers of the fund and concluded, "Recent events have endeared the hero of Harper's Ferry even to the rough and uncouth Californians."[108] By February 1866 the fund-raisers could claim victory. Four lots on the southeast corner of Main and Willow streets were presented to Mary Brown, and a cottage was soon built and deeded to all four Brown women.[109]

By the time it was ready, Annie and Sarah were supplementing the family income. Soon after their arrival in Red Bluff, Annie and Sarah took teacher examinations at the local academy.[110] Six teaching certificates were awarded in 1866, and it is likely that two were to Annie and Sarah.[111] Both made their living as schoolteachers over the next few years.[112] Sarah taught in nearby Antelope Valley for at least one term, and she also advertised in the *Independent* her ability to do stamping and embroidery.[113] Annie also taught in multiple schools, including Oat Creek, a school for African American children. While teaching there she boarded with the family of an African American veteran from the Civil War.[114] The goodwill that was extended to John Brown's kin in Red Bluff, however, did not mean that the citizens there believed in the Browns' antiracist creed. The *Independent* dismissed reports that Annie was teaching at a "colored school in Red Bluff." The writer added indignantly, "The colored school that Miss Brown is engaged in is eight miles from Red Bluff, we do not know of a single colored child in Red Bluff."[115] Though this might have served as a warning as to the limits of Red Bluff's toleration, for their first few years the Browns remained contented there.

Mary and her daughters soon became involved in a local reform association. Similar opportunities had been available to her when she lived in such places as Hudson, Ohio, but there is no evidence that Mary (or Ruth, for that matter) belonged to any reform organizations prior to the war. At North Elba, the Browns were too isolated and poor to have participated in the traditional work associated with antislavery women. Now in Red Bluff, with two grown daughters teaching and Ellen attending school, Mary Brown surely felt her life dramatically altered. For the first time ever, her days were not occupied with minding children or managing a large family, and she was secure in her possession of a home. Perhaps this is why she only then became involved in reform activities. Or possibly—shrewdly pragmatic—she surveyed her new life thousands of miles from her abolitionist patrons and sought the kind of mutual aid available to her through association life. The fact that it was "mutual aid" may have given it a special appeal to a poor woman long dependent on charity. Whatever her reasoning, Mary Brown's involvement in the Independent Order of Good Templars was a notable occurrence.

The Independent Order of Good Templars was formed in the 1850s in upstate New York and was soon very popular in the United States, as well as internationally.[116] The Templars organized in California in 1854, and in 1860 a statewide Grand Lodge formed. For female members in California, dues were at least twenty-five cents per quarter; in addition, the Brown women would have paid an initiation fee of approximately fifty cents.[117] In joining the Templars, the Brown women pledged "total abstinence from all intoxicating liquors" and vowed to work toward complete prohibition of the manufacture and sale of liquor, the election of "good, honest men" to administer prohibition-minded laws, and "persistence in efforts to save individuals and communities from so direful a scourge, against all forms of opposition and difficulties, until our success is complete and universal."[118] The need for such vows appeared especially dire to temperance-minded Americans observing the saloon culture of California. At an 1866 meeting, the Brown women may well have heard a letter from organization leader G. B. Taylor read in which he referred to the "peculiarly perplexing character" of the work in California.[119]

Mary was drawn to the Good Templars' mission, perhaps because she shared reformers' fears about the "peculiarly perplexing character" of California or because she saw herself as carrying out her late husband's temperance sentiment.[120] Despite the notoriety associated with her surname, Mary chose to submit her name for membership and to risk being blackballed and rejected in a public ceremony. Her identity was not hidden: she was listed as one of the local chapter's founding members and as the "widow of John

Brown of Harper's Ferry notoriety."[121] The California bylaws demanded that Mary's name be submitted by another member, at which point she would be investigated and then voted on, with the very real possibility that she could be rejected by other members.[122] Not only Mary sought to join, but Annie, Sarah, and Ellen as well, despite the threat their notoriety might have posed in the balloting process. They were inducted knowing that at any time they could be fined, suspended, or expelled for violating the order's temperance laws or for being found guilty of anonymous accusations of "unworthy conduct."[123] Such trials did happen at the Red Bluff lodge, and Mary and her daughters acted in spite of them.[124]

The Good Templars' work with the sick also likely appealed to Mary Brown. Part of every meeting involved discussion of which if any members were ill, and each lodge had a visiting committee.[125] Leo McCoy, who moved to Red Bluff in 1872 and became keenly interested in the history of the Brown women, recalled that Mary was remembered as a "kindly woman" who "rendered much service to the families of Red Bluff in the way of nursing the sick."[126] As she had in the year after Brown's death, Mary sought a broader outlet for caring for others as a way to deal with the trials her life had held. Red Bluff seemed to offer her the perfect setting: an opportunity to live in her own home and to make her own decisions about how to be of use in the world. Though the way she had gotten this home signaled the extraordinary dimension of her life, what she and her daughters craved most was an ordinary existence. But this would never be the case.

"John Brown, the Horse Thief and Murderer"

In 1867 the Brown surname became embroiled in a newspaper war that would eventually drive the Browns from Red Bluff.[127] That spring E. J. Lewis and Ave Townsend launched the *Red Bluff Weekly Sentinel* with an attack on the Reconstruction government. The paper's second issue continued in this vein, addressing its ire at Radical Republicans—and John Brown. Linking local politician John Swett to so-called "Black Republicanism," the *Sentinel* proclaimed that Swett was "magnifying the virtues of old John Brown, the horse thief and murderer." The editors of the *Independent*, onetime promoter of the "John Brown Cottage" fund, rose to Brown's defense. "Such is the manner in which the refined and gentlemanly editor of the *Sentinel* refers to a man whose widow and orphans live in our midst, and apparently for no other reason than the malignant satisfaction," its editor wrote. "It is not enough they must bear their great grief as best they can, but an unfeeling wretch must mount the editorial tripod, and hurl an insult to his memory in their face."[128] The *Independent* later elaborated on how the insult had been "hurl[ed]": "whenever Mr Sentinel issued a paper that was well spiced with John Brown, he threw or caused to be thrown, the papers into the yard of the John Brown family."[129]

The Brown family had long endured attacks on John Brown, especially in the national press. But to have such attacks renewed in Mary's own community—and to have them so publicly debated where Ellen, now thirteen, attended school—was too much. On October 14, 1867, the *Sentinel* ran an advertisement that Salmon had written, perhaps at Mary's prodding. Though he professed to "car[e] less what Copperheads say," Salmon could not help but respond to the *Sentinel*'s accusation that his father was "a horse thief and a murderer." He lashed out. "For the benefit of those zealous seekers of notoriety who are too cowardly to earn it in a fair way," he wrote, "I will give $100 in gold coin for the family record of the writer of those articles in the *Sentinel*."[130] The Browns' connection to "the frightener of the great state of Virginia" had ceased to work in their favor. They decided to leave, and looked farther north in California for refuge.

In July 1870, Mary Brown sold for $285 the home that had been given to her by the citizens of Red Bluff and bought a house and an acre in Rohnerville.[131] Salmon purchased a home next door, in addition to a forty-acre sheep ranch in nearby Bridgeville.[132] Rohnerville was a small town near Eureka in the Eel River Valley. Like Red Bluff, the Humboldt Bay area was originally settled in the 1850s as outposts for gold-mining camps in northern California.[133] Humboldt County—with its 175 miles of ocean coast—was organized in 1853. As Humboldt Bay opened the way for shipments from San Francisco, it became a supply center for inland mining camps. Natural resources of pastureland and the redwood forests allowed new industries to develop after an initial gold rush, and it was these new opportunities, as well as potential safe haven, that likely drew Salmon and Mary's attention.[134] Though more isolated than Red Bluff, by 1869 Rohnerville was also on the rise.[135]

Despite these resources, access to the Browns' "new country" was quite difficult. Even today, Humboldt County remains isolated from other parts of California, though its "Lost Coast" has of late become popular with tourists. In her work on the history of southern Humboldt County, Mary Siler Anderson notes that even as travel developed, "overland travel was a laborious, uncomfortable business."[136] The Browns likely made their way on an overland route similar to one taken a few years prior by John Carr. Describing his 1866 journey, Carr recounted a mad adventure in which he packed all of his belongings—including four children—on mules and moved his family overland, crossing mountains and creeks, camping out nights, and dealing with the region's cold fog. He judged their trek a success, noting that the "children stood the trip in their boxes very well."[137]

When the Browns departed Red Bluff, they traveled with a recent addition to their clan. In 1869 Mary had watched as twenty-six-year-old Annie wed Samuel Adams.[138] Samuel had lived in Chicago and then Kansas before arriving in Red Bluff sometime soon after the Civil War. How Annie met Samuel is not clear, nor is what he thought of her link to John Brown.[139] Though women in the West did tend to marry later than their counterparts, it is hard to resist speculating that Brown's notoriety affected her marital prospects.[140] There is also no evidence of community reaction to her marriage, though in marrying someone from Chicago, she escaped the kind of furor that erupted when Jefferson Davis's daughter, Winnie, became engaged to a northerner.[141] With their wedding, Annie—like her own mother—became a stepmother, to Samuel's daughter Irona.[142] Samuel had gotten into some legal trouble after a bar fight in Red Bluff, and that, as well as the chance for him to open a new blacksmith shop in a growing area, led the pair to join Mary and her siblings in their move north.[143] Despite this indication that Samuel had a problem with alcohol, Annie began married life hopefully and happily.

She settled quickly into family life. Following her mother's pattern, she began a cycle of childbearing that would occupy her for nearly two decades. Sarah Wall, Annie's Norfolk roommate, noted that in the early years of their marriage, Annie "manifested so much joy in her children that I hoped the melancholy that tinged her early years was dispelled by the happiness of her domestic life."[144] Her first daughter was born a little over a year after her wedding and was named in her mother Mary's honor. Other children soon followed. Bertha was born in May 1872, John Archibald (nicknamed "Archie") in July 1873, Lolita in August 1874, Grace in May 1876, Samuel Francis in July 1877, Sarah in April 1880, Edith in March 1882, Landon Augustus (Gus) in July 1884, and, finally, Richard Louis in January 1887.[145]

The other Brown women followed patterns they had established in their Red Bluff home. Mary likely delivered many of Annie's children, as well as those born to others in the community.[146] Sarah continued to work as a teacher. At one point she moved in with Salmon and Abbie's family to serve as teacher to his children; like Annie and Samuel, they ultimately had ten.[147] Ellen finished her schooling and met Fortuna schoolteacher James Fablinger, and they married in January 1876 at the Methodist Episcopal Church in Rohnerville.[148] The Browns also experienced loss in this new place. Salmon and Abbie's daughter Cora, a toddler on the overland journey, died in 1878 after a horse-riding accident, and Annie as well as Ellen lost babies shortly after their births.[149]

FIGURE 8.   Sarah Brown in a photograph taken sometime in the 1870s or 1880s. Humboldt County Historical Society.

As in Red Bluff, Mary Brown continued to claim a new life for herself as a quiet worker. In November 1873 she wrote to a relative and explained her delay in responding to his correspondence: "Forgive my delay in not writing sooner," she wrote, explaining, "I have a good deal to do not for myself but for others."[150] As she had been glad to have "others for me to love and do for" in the months that followed Brown's raid on Harpers Ferry, Mary continued

Figure 9. Ellen Brown Fablinger in a photograph taken sometime in the 1870s or 1880s. Humboldt County Historical Society.

to adhere to her own brand of Brown's motto of "Action, Action" in making a new life for herself in Rohnerville.[151] Mary was still regarded by some in the community as a curiosity—one resident recalled how her mother, when a little girl, had been taken to peer in the windows of Mary's home to get a glimpse of "John Brown's widow"—but she was content enough with her life in Rohnerville to urge her stepchildren Jason and Ruth to move there.[152] Some of her solace may have come from her activities in the local Congregational church, to which Sarah, Ellen, and perhaps Annie also belonged.[153]

The Browns were still contacted by autograph seekers and those wanting to honor John Brown, including French writer Victor Hugo, who presented them with a medal to commemorate Brown.[154] In a letter to John Jr., Sarah referenced receiving letters from "all over the country," as well as many visitors.[155] But throughout the 1870s and in the decades that followed, she and her daughters became increasingly aware of the criticism directed toward John Brown and their own resulting notoriety. Because of this, some of the Browns grew increasingly uncomfortable with having their personal matters written about in the press. When Brown biographer James Redpath wrote letters seeking donations for them in 1871, Salmon and Sarah Brown joined together to rebuff him harshly.[156] They placed a letter in the *Humboldt Times*, informing the editors that they had been "startled and deeply chagrined" by this report of their poverty. They explained, "We take this method of saying to all whom it may concern that John Brown's family . . . are all well and are doing well, and wish to maintain decent self respect and merit the reputation of having ordinary sagacity, if possible."[157] But while they desired such privacy and "decent self respect," in the decades that followed the Browns also found themselves frequently caught up in public discussions of John Brown. But they would no longer be in Rohnerville.

In 1881 Mary Brown and two of her daughters, Sarah and Ellen, moved to Saratoga, a small town in the Santa Clara Valley near San Francisco. In a letter to John Jr., Sarah—who remained unmarried—explained that Rohnerville "was a very poor place for a woman to make anything as it had all run down and was very dull living there."[158] Ellen's husband, James, a schoolteacher in the area, was employed but could barely make enough to support his growing family. Even marriage did not lift Ellen from the Brown struggle with poverty. Saratoga, they all hoped, would finally offer a place where Mary's dream of a self-sustaining livelihood could be realized. Much of its initial gold rush–derived industry was gone, replaced by fruit production.[159] The Browns purchased a 160-acre ranch on a mountain overlooking the town after an exploratory trip by Sarah. They were drawn to the property in part for its isolation. Ellen had grown increasingly plagued by negative reports about John Brown, to the extent that she had to publicly deny claims that she had fought with a group of men who taunted her with a rendition of "John Brown's Body."[160] She would shy away from the public eye ever after, and her subsequent history is largely obscured from the public record.

Although onetime Confederate sympathizers in the area were at first hostile to the Browns, the newcomers soon found themselves welcomed in Saratoga.[161] As ever, this welcome was evident in charity to the Brown women—and as usual, they needed it. Though Sarah had initially referred to their mortgage there as being on "easy terms," the Browns faced a problem common to many others who arrived to take up fruit raising: it took at least five years before trees started to produce enough to make any kind of profit, and they never seemed to make enough money to live comfortably.[162] Sarah continued to be embarrassed by publicity that declared them impoverished— "it cut us very much," she wrote to John Jr.—but in the end she felt that she and her siblings ought to put aside their pride and accept the charity on Mary's behalf.[163] The Browns then busied themselves with trying to make their lands profitable and work off their debt, a task that would prove all-consuming.

❧ CHAPTER 6

Mary Brown's 1882 Tour and the Memory of Militant Abolitionism

Mary Brown received a surprise invitation to participate in a celebration of John Brown in Chicago in the summer of 1882. She made plans to travel there and beyond with her daughter Sarah's help.[1] Now in her mid-sixties, Mary saw this opportunity as fulfillment of her longtime wish to return east to see friends and family and to visit the graves of her lost ones. Newspapers took notice of her plans; Sarah's letter relaying Mary's acceptance of W. J. W. W. Washington's offer was reprinted in the *Chicago Tribune* and a number of other papers under the headline "John Brown's Widow to Come East."[2] The travel would have been impossible for someone of Mary's class status without patronage. R. L. Higgins, a Saratoga benefactor, wrote to Washington, equating charity to Brown's widow with a Civil War pension. "A monument to the old hero is due his memory," he wrote, arguing, "It is a debt all Americans owe." But, he added, "so also do we owe his widdow more than we shall ever be able to pay." Comparing what was due her to what had been raised for President James Garfield's widow, he continued, "can we not pause a moment to think of one who has not only given up husband but sons"?[3] Mary Brown soon set to packing, eager and perhaps a little nervous about returning east.

In his appeal Higgins focused on her family losses on behalf of antislavery, but others would focus on the deeds of her infamous husband and sons. Her trip occurred against a backdrop of heated debate about John Brown: who he had been, how he should be remembered, and how he was linked to the Civil War. As she traveled from Chicago to North Elba to Boston to Topeka, Mary Brown's presence was often used to convey different narratives about the past by Americans reckoning not only with the nation's past but with its present. She was a highly charged symbol, a stand-in for all kinds of other things on Americans' minds in the Gilded Age: race, reunification, Civil War memory, and the ongoing struggle for civil rights for African Americans. Her trip is a window into a critical period in the contest over how Brown, as well as the broader Civil War, was to be remembered.

Gracious yet silent, Mary in her position as a relic of the abolitionist agitator lent a solemn air to commemorations of John Brown throughout the East in the summer and fall of 1882. Her actions—as well as what she left undone and unsaid—reveal her continued reflection on her family's activism and her sense of what role "John Brown's widow" should play in memorialization. Revisiting family and John Brown sites, she relived her history, returning eagerly to places that she had left behind in her flight to California. She undertook a long journey, often alone, for the purposes of reuniting with family and staking some kind of claim on behalf of Brown's memory.

The Pottawatomie Revelations

Washington's invitation for Mary to travel to Chicago came at an important moment in the Brown women's lives, as they wrestled with new revelations of John Brown's participation in murder at Pottawatomie Creek in Kansas in May 1856. There, in the middle of the night, five proslavery settlers were lured from their beds and killed in gruesome fashion by a group of broadsword-wielding men. In the days and weeks that followed, the attack and its perpetrators were much-talked about in Kansas, where a Franklin County grand jury heard testimony about the matter, and the affair was also written about in eastern newspapers.[4] The New York Herald had detailed the grisly killings, even naming Brown as the culprit, but he had denied participation.[5] (In the most literal sense, he was correct: his sons and son-in-law did the killing as he watched.) Though Brown had been named in the Herald and in a congressional report investigating the Kansas violence, many still defended him as having played no part. All this changed in 1879 when James Townsley, a member of Brown's party in Kansas, published his claim that Brown had orchestrated the killings of the three Doyles, William Sherman, and Allen Wilkinson.[6] Others took up the fight, arguing over not just Brown's responsibility but over the nature of pre–Civil War Kansas and if that in any way excused what others classified as cold-blooded murder.

As they were far from the Kansas battlefield in the mid-1850s and the men confessed little upon their return, *what* the Brown women knew and *when* is unclear. It seems likely that Brown himself admitted nothing of his involvement to Mary beyond his initial letter that described the sack of Lawrence and casually mentioned being "accused" of the Pottawatomie crimes.[7] As participants, sons Owen, Oliver, and Frederick knew the truth. Oliver may have confided something prior to his death in 1859, but Owen lived far from Mary, Annie, Sarah, and Ellen and did not have much contact with them after their move west. Salmon, too, appears to have kept silent. Even Ruth—whose husband Henry was likely responsible for the deaths of two of the men—seems to have known little of what occurred. Historian Robert McGlone argues convincingly that the Brown sons were long affected by Kansas.[8] But Mary Brown was far from Kansas at the time, and John Brown was rarely home with her in the years that followed. When new evidence about the events at Pottawatomie emerged in the late 1870s, igniting renewed public debate about her husband's cause and actions, Mary herself may have been reeling from revelations she had not been previously been privy to, despite her family's direct involvement.

Mary had been long aware of a letter that Mahala Doyle, widow and mother to three of Brown's victims, had written Brown at the Charles Town jail. Doyle defended her family against the charge that they were slaveholders and detailed how Brown and his men had shot her husband and two sons "in cold blood." Mary may have identified with her emotions as Doyle outlined the loss of a husband and two sons, ages twenty and twenty-three, and described herself as "a poor disconsolate widow with helpless children."[9] As Brown's role at Pottawatomie was confirmed beyond reasonable doubt decades later, did her mind wander back to Doyle's widow?[10] Whatever her inner resolve, new revelations about Pottawatomie were on the minds of some of Brown's staunchest defenders during Mary Brown's three-month trek eastward that began in Chicago in late summer of 1882.

Chicago

Mary Brown came to realize how contested Brown's memory was in two large, widely covered Chicago gatherings and in the public responses to them. She may not have grasped the shadow that would loom over her trip at its inception, when all seemed auspicious. The Chicago picnic must have seemed to Mary as if it would be spectacular, worth all the trouble of a trip to the East (though given the availability of the railroad from San Francisco to Chicago, it was nothing compared to her 1864 trek west). She was told of Washington's plans for a procession of the GAR post of Chicago, of three bands set to provide music, and that a host of onetime abolitionist comrades would make appearances. Other announcements boasted the involvement of Frederick Douglass and General Grant, as well as two of her stepsons.[11]

If such descriptions had heightened her expectations of the trip, they were quickly dashed. The *Tribune* reported that at the picnic, held at Ogden Grove, "the widow of the grand old hero of Harper's Ferry was subjected to an indignity that should never have been imposed upon her." None of the famous invitees appeared, and it seems that Washington had either been overzealous or intentionally misrepresented the affair. Mary spent a good part of the day sitting in a beer hall—ironic given her family's temperance views. It is hard to know whether the resulting press stemmed from racism or from fact, but the *Tribune* and other papers condemned the celebration in no uncertain terms. "The idea of a John Brown Monumental Association," its article stated, "originated in the brain of a colored person named Washington, who has initials more numerous than ought to be here set forth, but which in nowise indicate the character of the man who wears them."[12]

If Mary Brown wrote back to California to lament the experience, none of the letters survive. She appears to have focused on moving forward as she had in 1859 and 1864, an admirable response, as she may have had every inclination to board a train bound back to San Francisco. But she had reason to remain. An African American committee joined with a group of white Chicagoans that included Judge James Bradwell, a well-known lawyer who had worked with his wife, Myra, to end Mary Lincoln's confinement in 1875, to plan a better event.[13] Two days after the picnic fiasco, the joint committee hosted an elaborate interracial gathering designed to stake Chicago's claim to part of John Brown's history and to how he—and the broad abolitionist movement, also under fire—should be remembered.[14]

There, Mary Brown made a second appearance before a Chicago public that eagerly used her presence to claim links to John Brown. Several speakers recounted how Chicagoan Allen Pinkerton helped raise money for John Brown to transport a group of fugitives to Canada.[15] Another woman recounted the times when Brown and Frederick Douglass had stayed at her house.[16] Additionally, John Brown was tied to the broader abolitionist past. Judge Bradwell was the first of many speakers that night to link Brown's raid with the end of slavery, reminding the audience that within ten years of Brown's raid, "there was not a slave within the border of the United States." Illinois State Attorney Mills also spoke at length to the gathered crowd. Referring to "noble men" such as Garrison and Emerson, Mills argued that Brown had "joined his heart and his hand with the movement of anti-slavery." Harpers Ferry, Mills concluded, made way for "Abraham Lincoln's bugle blast in 1861 [more] than a score of other influences." He then turned to Mary Brown, noting that she had "seen at last the fulfillment of your prophecy and toils," conflating her, the broad abolitionist movement, and the Union army. "Thanks to your own struggles, the valor of Northern soldiers, fighting on a thousand battlefields for a free nationality, and a guarding Providence," he concluded, "the slave is free and panoplied with honoring and honored citizenship."[17]

Rev. James Podd, the speaker who followed Mills, stands out. On her trip, Mary would hear upward of a dozen speeches like Mills's, but there was only one instance when a speech moved beyond celebrating the demise of slavery to make radical claims about contemporary race relations. Podd, originally from the West Indies, had been called as the pastor of a Chicago Baptist church in 1881.[18] Unlike so many others, he looked to Mary Brown's presence as a means to argue for civil rights, not just to celebrate slavery's demise.[19] He singled Brown out not just as part of the abolitionist continuum but as "one of the grandest heroes of the Western world."[20] Instead of lauding abolitionists for ending slavery, he noted that Brown "voluntarily died to end Caucasian crime and lust," arguing, "The savior of the Negro race was not Abraham Lincoln or Charles Sumner; it was John Brown. He was the true author of the civil rights bill, that magna charta of our liberties drafted by Sumner." Significantly, he added, "and let me say here, for the colored race, that we want this bill enforced."[21] The *Chicago Tribune* noted that "great applause" followed this demand.[22] With this Mary Brown heard the only specific demand for African American civil rights that would occur during her trip. She was then introduced to "a storm of cheering and applause."[23] Whether they cheered her, Podd's speech, or both is unclear.

Local newspapers immediately worked to undercut Podd's radical demand. The *Tribune* stressed that at the Farwell Hall gathering, "the two races mingled as brothers and sisters," adding that both Mills and Podd had "received the same unstinted applause," meaning that "no thought of race or color marred the harmony" of the occasion.[24] Chicago-area and other newspapers proclaimed that the Farwell Hall gathering—in contrast to the previous affair—had been an enthusiastic, well-attended, and well-executed event, one that fittingly closed with a rousing rendition of "John Brown's Body."[25] The following day, Mary Brown was offered one final salute by the city of Chicago. Expressing their "heartfelt sympathy and good wishes for your future welfare," the committees who had worked up the Farwell Hall reception along with a group of local women presented her with over two hundred dollars.[26]

After decades of curiosity, Mary was quite conscious of her actions being presented "to the world." The day before Washington's Monumental Association gathering, a *Chicago Tribune* reporter had reintroduced Mary Brown to the local population. Despite the frequency of such an occurrence and her real need, Mary Brown remained uncomfortable with the ways in which the Brown celebrity yielded tangible rewards. The reporter captured this discomfort. Mary responded hesitantly upon mention of the possibility of donations to herself: "'I feel just this way—if the American people are disposed to add anything to what I have in consideration of the sacrifices of my husband and myself, I—I—I will accept it, but I do not want it to go out that I am a beggar.'" The *Tribune* writer added, "As she uttered the word 'beggar' she gave way to tears, and upon overcoming her emotions she asked the reporter to be kind enough not to present her to the world as a mendicant, saying that the idea was perfectly abhorrent to her."[27]

Mary did not recount this charity when she wrote to her family back west. She offered few details of her doings and no commentary on the standout episodes of the "wretched failure" at Ogden Grove or Podd's speech. She did note the interracial nature of her reception. "I never saw such enthusiasm amongst blacks and white in my life," she wrote. And she saw the hand of providence in her trip, declaring in typical fashion, "the Lord is in it." Of her trip's effects upon her, she added, "I think I am growing young."[28] Perhaps after years of day-to-day struggle to eke out a living, she found this trip to the East to be refreshing. Or, after decades of seeing Brown debated and watching her family suffer or gain as a result, she felt liberated to be in the middle of the memory making, even if she was not actively shaping it.[29]

Not everyone was as enamored of Mary Brown as those who clamored to greet her in Chicago. Within a few weeks, an article entitled "A Georgia View of John Brown" appeared in the *Macon Telegraph*. It was then reprinted in papers throughout the country, including Boston, where Mary would soon arrive. Highlighting the supposed worst crimes of abolitionists—fanaticism and miscegenation—the piece argued that John Brown was "not a man of distinction" but instead "coveted notoriety" and was "a worse man than . . . even Grant." The paper then offered its rationale for this assessment: "John Brown was a thief, a murderer, and a miscegenationist." This latter charge— one effectively employed decades prior to stir up anti-abolition sentiment— was now directed at Brown. Then, turning its ire not just on Brown but on the movement as a whole, the article claimed that Brown was "apotheosized" in the North and that his raid, one "instigated by Henry Ward Beecher and the devil," had helped incite civil war. The author directed his venom directly at Mary Brown and her Chicago hosts. "Other men at the North," he continued, "have been marked with like notoriety without having divine honors paid to their memories, and without leaving behind them widows to be provided for by affectionate mixed-breed Chicago picnic fanatics."[30] Such critique of Brown was typically unstated, glossed over by characterizations of him as a horse thief or murderer, but here a response to his radical ideas about race rose to the surface. Its vehemence reveals how, two decades past Harpers Ferry, Brown could still inspire such a fierce response—one that Mary's daughters, far away in California, would not be able to escape in decades to come.

A Return to North Elba

When the "Georgia view" appeared in early September, Mary Brown was too preoccupied to pay it much attention. Reports had begun circulating in Chicago that her son Watson's body had been recovered. Mary had specially designed her trip to include visits to the graves of the six children she had lost in Richfield, Ohio, so thoughts of Watson and Oliver's still-missing remains had surely been on her mind. Though the *Boston Congregationalist* described it as "another strange chapter in the family of John Brown," many Americans unable to reclaim their loved ones' remains after the Civil War may have felt that this was not as odd as other Brown family sagas.[31]

Mary had few clues about Watson's remains over the years. In his work to gather material in 1859, James Redpath encountered a source who reported that the body of one of the Brown sons had been taken by students enrolled at a medical college in Winchester, Virginia.[32] In 1862 the *Liberator* confirmed this. Garrison ran the following rather grisly item: "The Winchester, Va., correspondent of the New York *World*, in a letter dated March 18th, says—'I visited the Medical College in this town where M.D.'s are furnished to the Southern Confederacy. Prominent among the objects in the museum was the body of John Brown's son—the integument taken off, and the muscles, veins and arteries all preserved, the top of the cranium sawn off, and the lips purposely distorted in disrespect."[33] But it was only in 1882 that the Browns learned that, during the tumultuous fight over Winchester in the war, Watson's body had been taken to a doctor's office in Martinsville, Indiana. The office belonged to Jarvis J. Johnson, a surgeon for the Indiana Twenty-Seventh Regiment, who had been put in charge of the Confederate hospital that was lodged in the Winchester Medical College.[34] There, Johnson had found the body marked with a sign.[35] Though relic hunters had carried away some fingers and toes, much of the body remained, and Johnson ultimately described it as "one of the most beautiful specimens I ever saw."[36] Johnson wrote to the *Chicago Tribune* stating that he had "often thought that if the mother was alive and wanted [the body] I would send it to her."[37]

John Jr. determined that he would go to Martinsville to investigate.[38] As a Brown, he quickly became an object of curiosity: word of his identity spread on the train on which he traveled, and curious passengers watched as he read a newspaper.[39] After meeting Johnson, John Jr. looked at the remains, at first unsure of which half brother he was seeing. A reporter observed his analysis of the body and then re-created it for an eager audience. "The lid was removed," he recounted, "and for a time not a word was spoken. It was a scene for a painter; but skillful indeed must have been the hand to portray the feeling, the intense interest, the suppressed anxiety depicted on every countenance."[40] After his close examination, John Jr. made arrangements for the body to be shipped to North Elba for a reburial set for mid-October.[41]

In the meantime Mary waited at Put-in-Bay, where she had been reunited with John Jr. and Wealthy, Ruth and Henry, Owen, and Jason for the first time since 1864. From her cryptic reassurance to Salmon that she met with a "warm reception" from his half siblings, one surmises that Mary was at least a little nervous about the Brown reunion.[42] Perhaps time and the errand to which they all attended softened any hard feelings. Ruth described her happiness at recovering "our brother who had stood in a medical college to be gazed at by strangers for more than twenty years."[43] Mary Brown, too, drew solace from her chance to put at least one of her sons slain at Harpers Ferry to a proper rest. "The country is all awake to the fact that one of John Browns Sons Should have been kept amongst them for over twenty years, but I think that there is a wise Providence in it I cannot comprehend," she wrote to Salmon, exclaiming, "Oh I am so thankful that God has spared my life to see this time."[44]

After passing a few weeks reacquainting herself with her stepchildren, she departed for North Elba ahead of the others. She first traveled to Richfield, Ohio, where she visited the graves of the four children she had lost suddenly in the 1840s. After that, she traveled on to Meadville, Pennsylvania, where she visited with Day relatives. John Jr. met her there, and they traveled onward to North Elba, arriving on October 11, 1882, less than two months after she had departed from California.[45] Aided by abolitionist fund-raising, Ruth and Owen met them at North Elba.[46] There, Mary and her stepchildren, joined by Watson's widow Isabella and a group of abolitionists, planned to rebury what the *Los Angeles Times* labeled "the sacred remains."[47]

Watson was buried across from the North Elba farmhouse adjacent to his father's grave site. The *New York Evening Post* reported, "Of all the strange and romantic incidents in the career of John Brown and his family, one of the strangest was the burial yesterday in this mountain."[48] As at Brown's funeral, neither Mary nor Ruth spoke, though an 1856 letter from Watson to Mary Brown was read in her honor.[49] John Jr. and Owen spoke, as did Franklin Sanborn. At the close of the service, Ruth and her North Elba neighbors the Epps family sang "The Sweet By and By."[50] She reflected on their connection to a then-distant past, recalling, "The whole thing from beginning to end is like a romance."[51] She was not the only one to offer such a characterization.

Some reporters played up the "romance" of the day in order to foster sectional reconciliation. Rather than focusing on Mary's response or Watson's abolitionist identity, many newspapers highlighted John Jr.'s reading of a letter from a South Carolina man who had been with Watson Brown when he died. They used the letter and John Jr.'s response to it to host an impromptu reunion of North and South at Watson's grave. The South Carolinian, a man named Tayleure, reported Watson's dying belief that he had acted on behalf of "duty," and then added, "'I am a South Carolinian, and at the time of the raid was very deeply imbued with the prejudices of my State; but the sincerity, calm courage, and devotion to duty which your father and his followers then manifested impressed me very profoundly.'"[52] After John Jr. read this letter, he offered a "brief and earnest reply," reassuring the man that he had his—and the Browns'—sympathy and respect. Bluntly, he then added, "My father, brother, and comrades who fell at Harpers Ferry did not hate the people of the South. . . . Hoping at some time to offer a fraternal hand to you, who gave a cup of water to my dying brother when you deemed him an enemy, I remain, yours, for the rights of all."[53]

Though coverage of Watson's reburial was out of Mary's control, her desire to undertake the journey (and the real courage it required) comes through clearly. Whatever meaning others ascribed to her trip and to this burial, it appears to have been a difficult experience for Mary. Though she had in Chicago declared herself "growing young," burying one of her sons took a toll. Shortly afterward John Jr. wrote to Sanborn to confide that age was "beginning to show its effects with her."[54]

Boston

A few days after the funeral for Watson, Mary Brown departed North Elba for a final time. As she rode a train south and east toward Boston, she likely recalled other visits, foremost the one in the days following Brown's capture. Now, instead of Higginson, her escort and companion was Franklin

Sanborn.[55] Mary's visit afforded Bostonian abolitionists (African American as well as white) an occasion to gather together and commemorate their shared antislavery past. Previous gatherings had been held in Chicago in 1874 and in Philadelphia in 1875, and to some degree the gathering in Boston mirrored these. As Julie Roy Jeffrey has chronicled, such gatherings became especially important to abolitionists who were self-conscious of their shrinking numbers and of their marginalization as misguided and fanatical, incidental or downright unhelpful.[56] Mary's visit allowed Boston's abolitionist remnant to both celebrate its past and to claim its worth in the face of such attacks as "A Georgia View of John Brown." As at Chicago, Mary would not speak in public but instead serve as a symbol of the abolitionist past.

Outside Boston she met with old abolitionist friends. Sanborn had long stayed in touch with the Browns. He was especially eager to host Mary now, as he was hard at work on a volume about Brown that would appear in 1885. (To this end, he was avidly tracking down answers about Pottawatomie.) While in Concord she may have also visited with the Emersons and Alcotts. Finally, she spent a day at the home of Mary Stearns, who like Sanborn had long kept in touch with her family and remained active in working to shape Brown memory.[57]

On October 26, 1882, Mary traveled to Boston to make her first appearance at a reception that functioned as an abolitionist reunion. Members of the Garrison family appeared, as did Franklin Sanborn, Elizur Wright, Samuel Sewall, and countless others. As abolitionists memorialized Brown and their movement, Boston newspapers took over the task that had once occupied Boston and Concord abolitionists: scrutinizing Mary's every action and overall appearance to discern her linkage to "their" John Brown. The *Boston Daily Advertiser* reported, for instance, that at one meeting Mary "received her friends sitting, she was dressed simply in black, with a white lace about her throat and a black shawl draped about her shoulders." Her face was "seamed with many deep lines that grief and hard encounters with the world have engraven there." It concluded, "Her face carries a story, and did not we know what it was, something of it, the torture, the struggle, the heroism, the suffering, might easily be guessed."[58] The *Boston Journal* declared the sad tones of her voice in keeping with her experience, concluding, "as she sat with the group of old-time and sympathetic friends with a simplicity that was the outcome of a resigned strength, it was not hard to imagine that John Brown's sturdy spirit and exaltation of purpose must have owed much to her sustaining force of character."[59] In 1860 her "simplicity" had sometimes been viewed negatively, but here it was highlighted as proof of her "strength."

FIGURE 10. Mary Brown in 1882, the year of her cross-country journey. Boyd Stutler Collection, West Virginia State Archives.

Mary Brown was next hosted by two separate constituencies, the New England Women's Club and Boston's African American community. The New England Women's Club had been founded by Julia Ward Howe and other prominent women in 1868. Speakers on various subjects, from literature to art to suffrage to poverty, had long been a part of the club, along with receptions for prominent visitors.[60] For Mary's visit, they gathered in their typical spot on Park Street. Other famous figures in attendance included Sanborn, Lucy Stone, and Frank Garrison. Howe opened the meeting, and the *Boston Journal* reported that she "bespoke the interest of all present in the widow of the man who so firmly stood to the front of duty, conscience, and obligation." After a poetry reading Lucy Stone rose and spoke. Doubtless, Mary recalled the first time she had heard Stone speak while at Ruggles's water cure in 1849. The *Journal* reported that "all had opportunity for interchange of greetings while cups of chocolate were served."[61] Mary Brown—surrounded by so many who had known her husband and in the midst of prominent members of Boston society—must have thought back to other area receptions she had attended. If she drank out of her saucer this time, it was not noted.

Before she departed Boston, Mary was also feted by Boston's African American community in a church that the *Boston Daily Advertiser* reported was "completely filled."[62] Renowned African American abolitionist Lewis Hayden presided, and Mary Brown sat alongside his wife on the platform. Prayer, music, poems, and reminiscences made up the bulk of the evening, followed by addresses by former slave and writer William Wells Brown and Thomas Thomas, a longtime acquaintance of Mary's. Both Brown and Thomas described Brown's contribution to emancipation, and the *Daily Advertiser* noted, "At the conclusion of these exercises all present were given an opportunity to shake hands with the venerable lady, who was visibly affected by the warmth and sincerity of the reception."[63] The *Boston Journal* summarized the evening as "a beautiful testimonial of the love and reverence in which they hold the memory of the brave man" who died for freedom.[64] If the African American community used Mary's visit to make demands for contemporary rights as Podd had in Chicago, this fact was not reported. Neither was Mary's meeting with the widow of African American raider William Leeman, which was apparently orchestrated by Wendell Phillips.[65]

On the whole Boston abolitionists seemed eager to use Mary's visit to celebrate their past triumph of ending slavery but not to advocate for present civil rights issues. As in 1859, a committee was formed to oversee both fund-raising efforts and the disbursement of funds to Mary Brown.[66] At one such fund-raiser attendees were treated to a suffrage sketch by Amy Talbot Dunn entitled "Zekle's Wife."[67] A second event featured pieces by Julia Ward Howe, Mrs. George Henschel, Madame Madeline Schiller, Oliver Wendell Holmes, and J. J. Hayes. The most intriguing performance of the evening was a reading from "Brother Anderson's Sermon," which the paper described as "a negro dialect sketch." The sketch, included in *Shoemaker's Best Selections for Readings and Recitations* in 1880, features the possibly illiterate

"Brother Anderson" demonstrating the "noisy ways" and "passion" of African Americans in the midst of another man's sermon recommending "them to cultivate intelligence as well as passion."[68] The *Daily Advertiser* noted that the reading "convulsed the audience," but it seems an odd piece to be read at an occasion marking Brown.[69] While "Zekle's Wife" may have been used to work for contemporary reform, "Brother Anderson's Sermon" asked nothing radical on behalf of African Americans. In this way, the radicalism of Brown's demands on race matters was again glossed over.

Topeka

While in Chicago, Mary Brown had received a message from Franklin Adams, secretary of the Kansas State Historical Society. On behalf of the KSHS and the "people of Kansas," Adams extended Mary a "cordial invitation" to visit on her way home.[70] Mary accepted his invitation, and she was promised a reception as well as an escort to whatever sites she wished. Unlike Boston and Concord, which Mary had frequented in 1860, she had never been to Kansas. She may have wanted to see the places where her sons and husband had fought on the antislavery battlefield and to see the Browns' relatives, the Adairs, who lived in Osawatomie. She may have also hoped to take a stand on behalf of Brown in a geographic place closer to Pottawatomie Creek. Though not granted a public platform, perhaps she took comfort from the knowledge that her presence was being used to celebrate a Kansas past that highlighted her husband as a hero.

The Brown family was already acquainted with Franklin Adams through correspondence. They knew him to be a man interested in upholding Brown's reputation. Because of this, they had donated materials to the Kansas State Historical Society late in 1881.[71] Though she "part[ed] with them with tears," Mary had been glad to send KSHS some Brown papers, letters, and even relics.[72] Among the items were a host of letters from the era of "Bleeding Kansas," a photograph, a piece of the rock near Brown's grave site at North Elba, a lock of his hair, and a piece of the gallows on which he had been hanged.[73]

Adams knew that people in Kansas, like those throughout the country, remained fascinated by John Brown.[74] And like other Americans, Kansans were not of one mind about John Brown; it may have been the site of the most contentious fight about Brown's legacy. Debate there was fueled by the new revelations about Pottawatomie, as well as by the broader question of whether Brown had been important or irrelevant to Kansas.[75] Powerful players in Kansas's territorial history and contemporary public life chose sides, with some free-state fighters such as Adams supporting a heroic vision of

Brown while others vehemently disagreed, disputing the character and sig-
nificance of "Osawatomie Brown." In 1880, two years prior to Mary's visit,
free-state fighter George W. Brown had described John Brown's territorial
violence as counterproductive. He argued that the "real" heroes of Kansas
history were nonviolent free-state fighters, not those of the John Brown
variety, and he condemned the "horrible murders on the Pottawatomie,"
saying that they only incited further violence.[76] Charles and Sara Robinson
would propagate this vision of John Brown in the 1890s and far beyond.[77]
At the moment of Mary Brown's visit in 1882, Adams saw an opportunity to
use KSHS collections and its institutional structure to advocate for Brown's
nobility and importance to Kansas history, as well as to quell seemingly endless discussion of Pottawatomie.[78] Adams likely thought that Mary's presence
would be an asset in his fight to present the "truth" about Brown.[79] (He had
assiduously cultivated a relationship with Mary Stearns as well.[80])

Despite Adams's careful orchestration of her visit, Mary Brown's willingness to go to Kansas seems brave, given the contentious ongoing debate
about her husband. But its vociferousness was largely patched over during
the course of her visit. The word "Pottawatomie" was never uttered, nor
were radical claims concerning Kansas's new African American population
put forth. Instead, Mary Brown's presence was used to hark back to and celebrate the abolitionist past and to claim an important place in it for Kansas.
Her husband's radical stance on race and embrace of violent means were
muted in order to draw more people into embracing Mary and John Brown
as Kansas folk heroes of a sort.

On November 12, 1882, the *Topeka Daily Capital* reported Mary Brown's
arrival, noting that plans had been made for a "royal reception" to honor the
widow of "the man who struck the first blow for the abolition of slavery in
America."[81] Under the headline of "Osawatomie's Widow," the *Daily Kansas
State Journal* implored Topeka residents to turn out to show "her the love and
regard with which Kansans cherish the memory of her husband."[82] Various
committees were appointed to oversee aspects of the planning, ranging from
the reception to music to decorations. Outgoing Kansas governor John St.
John was tapped to preside, music was planned, and Brown comrades such as
August Bondi and Luke Parsons were specially invited to share their reminiscences.[83] The *Daily Kansas State Journal* confidently proclaimed that "every
preparation has been made to make this affair a success." It also made Mary's
position there clear: "Gov. St. John will preside at the reception, while a reception committee of representative ladies of Topeka will take possession of
Mrs. Brown, and see that all who desire will get a glimpse of the noble wife
of the late champion of freedom."[84]

The reception was held three days later, on November 15, 1882, and, as the event unfolded, the paper's phrase "take possession" seemed prescient. Mary Brown was not to be given an opportunity to offer her own interpretation of Brown, the war, or the present state of things in Kansas; instead, her presence was used to assert a particular narrative about Brown and Kansas.

The reception took place in a hall located in the old Senate chamber in the State House that was described by one paper as "usually dingy" but "appropriately decorated for the occasion by the committee of arrangements, with whom the work of preparations had evidently been a labor of love," for the hall now "presented a brilliant and highly attractive appearance."[85] Decorations included a portrait of John Brown surrounded by battle flags of Kansas, two sabers, and relics that included one of Brown's pikes, a piece of wood from the gallows, and a piece of rock from near his North Elba grave. The latter pair had special meaning to Mary, as they came from her donations.[86] Beside Governor St. John, speakers were to include KSHS president T. Dwight Thatcher, Senator Preston Plumb, August Bondi (who would recount battles at Osawatomie and Lawrence), and Adams himself, who held the "unbroken attention of the audience for some time" as he spoke about the relics and his reminiscences of Brown.[87] Musical entertainment by a Topeka male quartet and an African American cornet band, a laudatory poem by Joseph Waters, and performances of "The Star-Spangled Banner" and "John Brown's Body" by the local GAR would round out the night.[88] As at other locations, funds were also solicited on Mary's behalf. The audience—a large gathering composed of both whites and African Americans—was to hear in the evening's speeches a carefully orchestrated set of presentations designed to celebrate Kansas history and progress alongside Brown's noble role in that history. Mary Brown's presence was used to stake a claim to both. "To many even of those who revere the memory of her husband," Adams would soon report to Mary Stearns, "she must seem almost as one suddenly come down from those years of terrible struggle which her husband inaugurated, for the freedom of the slave."[89]

Governor St. John opened the night by introducing Mary as "the widow of the man who did more than any other to render the name of Kansas immortal."[90] The *Daily Kansas State Journal* reported the cheers that followed this introduction.[91] In his speech Thatcher, too, worked to make sure the audience knew that Kansas had been integral to Brown's history and vice versa. Looking to Mary, he described Kansas as "scene of one of her husband's greatest struggles" and reminded them of the loss of Frederick and of her endurance of "great privations" so that Brown could continue his fight. Senator Plumb, too, asserted both the importance of Kansas and Brown:

"The history of the struggle for freedom could never be written except it should include the history of Kansas," he stated, "and the history of Kansas could not be written, except it included that of John Brown who gave to Kansas and the world that heritage of freedom of which we are so proud and for which the world is so grateful."[92] Its present "wondrous prosperity," he concluded, had grown from the Free State struggle.[93]

St. John, in his lengthy speech, highlighted how Brown had been assessed in the decades after his work in Kansas. "When the husband of her to whom we gladly extend our heartiest greeting to-night," he stated, "fearlessly gave his life as a sacrifice for principle he was branded as a 'fanatic,' and shunned by moral cowards: politicians were afraid he would ruin the party. The country was full of such characters as Peter and Judas."[94] But times had changed, he asserted optimistically. Using John Brown to celebrate present-day modernity and liberality, St. John told the gathered crowd that he appreciated the honor of presiding at the meeting. "Twenty years ago," he noted, "there were but few, if any, places in the west where a meeting like this could, or at least would have been held; and very rarely was a man found then who would have cared to have presided over its deliberations."[95]

In celebrating Kansas liberality, St. John overlooked a significant and ongoing social issue of which many in the crowd were aware. In the late 1870s and early 1880s, more than fifteen thousand African Americans had migrated to Kansas from the South. They were known as the Exodusters, and white Kansans' response to them had been markedly mixed.[96] As the number of African Americans in the state and in its capital had grown, prejudice against them had become more marked. This was not particularly surprising, given that many Free State fighters in the 1850s had been less than enlightened on issues of race, wanting to block slavery from Kansas to avoid competing with African American laborers and white slave-owners.[97] The local newspaper debated African American character, and, as historian Robert Athearn had noted, "some Kansans, who earlier had talked in lofty terms about helping to solve a great national problem, were on the verge of panic."[98] This panic may have cost St. John. Just a week before he presided over Mary Brown's reception, he had been defeated in his bid to be a third-term governor. His defeat by George W. Glick, who would become Kansas's first Democratic governor, can also be traced to St. John's pro-temperance position and the entrance of a third-party candidate into the race, but his welcoming stance toward the Exodusters probably also worked against him.[99]

Though she was doubtless unaware of the intricacies of Kansas politics, Mary Brown knew of the influx of Exodusters into Kansas. Her eldest stepson, John Jr., had written letters in support of the Exodusters, and he frequently remarked in correspondence about their plight.[100] She may have been struck by the similarities between anti-Exoduster prejudice and the intolerance shown to her former North Elba neighbors. But despite the fact that St. John must have been thinking about his political capital, no one at the Topeka reception mentioned the Exoduster controversy, skipping over it in order to declare how much progress Kansas (and perhaps the nation) had made. As in Boston, the end of slavery and Brown's role in it was celebrated, not the status of African American civil rights. St. John, determined to celebrate this meeting as a hallmark of progress, closed by introducing Mary as "the widow of the man who had done more to make Kansas a free state than all men living or dead."[101] Notably, it was the freedom of Kansas—not that of slaves—that he feted. Glorifying John Brown, he placed questions about race and emancipation firmly in the past, not the present—and the past was long over.

Whatever Mary's thoughts, one Topeka paper called it "one of the most memorable gatherings ever held in this city."[102] Two days after Mary Brown's departure from Topeka, Adams wrote to Mary Stearns to report on the "cordial reception."[103] He enclosed news clippings and reported that Mary Brown had lived up to her husband's reputation, being "such a one as we might have expected to find as the relic of the rugged hero of Black Jack, Osawatomie, and Harper's Ferry." Her visit to Kansas and beyond had served his purpose: it, he continued, "has in no small measure increased the interest in John Brown and will help towards whatever may be contemplated to be done in his memory."[104] KSHS president Thatcher declared her to possess "the soul of truthfulness" and "an unworldly air, as of one who had dwelt among high and eternal verities. John Brown's gravity and devotion to duty were admirably reflected in his widow."[105]

After Mary departed Topeka she went on to Osawatomie, where she was met by the Adairs, relatives who had assisted her sons when they were in Kansas in the 1850s and with whom the family had long corresponded. After what she described as "a very pleasant time" there, she embarked on the trip back to California.[106] After taking a train to San Francisco, she visited overnight with Sarah—now living in San Francisco because of her work at the U.S. Mint there—and then returned to the Fablingers in Saratoga.[107] "I shall remember my visit to Kansas with a great deal of pleasure," she noted, adding that "the kind friends" that she had met in Topeka would never be forgotten.[108] In addition to the "kind friends," Mary also derived much comfort from being reunited with her scattered family.[109] Writing to Franklin Sanborn of her days in Kansas, she referred to having a "pleasant time," adding that she had seen "a great many friends and some relatives" and that she had "heard a great many things about the early history of Kanses."[110]

The Passing of Widow Brown

Following her time there, two articles appeared in the *Topeka Daily Capital* that intended to focus on Mary Brown's unique history. Writer Elizabeth Spring was critical that the speeches in Topeka "singularly failed, by even so much as one timely and appreciative phrase, to recognize her own individual heroism and devotion not to the father of her children alone, but also to the cause for which he gave his life."[111] Brown's story, she argued, did not just demonstrate his own nobility or the role of Kansas in ending slavery but "strongly testifies to the high courage, fidelity and patience" of his wife. "She never failed, never faltered, never counseled any compromise with wrong for peace or comfort's sake," Spring continued, "and that the strange, rugged old crusader loved her, in his angular and undemonstrative but no less sincere and exalting fashion, we may be quite sure."

Ironically, though she intended to highlight Mary, Spring ended up focusing on John Brown. Like others, she cast Mary as his ever-faithful, ever-dutiful partner. "If he could be heard from beyond the stars," Spring closed, "we may be certain that his encomium of this white-haired and steadfast partner of his struggles and troubles would be not less grateful and emphatic than that which Mohammed passed upon the wife who married him in his obscurity and clung to him so loyally: 'By God, there can never be a better woman! She believed in me when men despised me; she relieved my wants when I was poor and persecuted by the world. Of such stuff the saints are made.'"[112] In 1859 it had been important to abolitionists to present Mary Brown in this fashion, and over the decades, Brown defenders continued to use—and need—Mary as a symbol of his nobility. By 1882 Spring also looked to defend Brown against charges that he had been harsh and unfeeling in private life as well as at Pottawatomie. Highlighting his marriage, Spring argued that though Brown was "undemonstrative," his love (and perhaps purity) was real.

Newspapers throughout the country reported Mary Brown's passing a little over a year after her momentous trip. After returning to California, she visited Annie and Salmon and their families. In the summer of 1883, she and the Fablingers gave up hope for productivity from their mountaintop ranch. They sold it and moved down into the valley in Saratoga.[113] Late that year Mary became ill, likely with some kind of liver or kidney cancer, though Ruth felt that the "terrible strain" of the trip was also a factor.[114] In order to get better medical care, Mary soon moved to San Francisco, where daughter Sarah had secured work at the mint. Writing to John Jr. on February 25, 1884, Sarah declared herself "wholly occupied" with Mary's care. She added, "Mother is still with us, but just hangs between life and death. A few days will tell how it will turn with her."[115]

And a few days did. Mary died on February 29, 1884, a month and a half before her sixty-eighth birthday. After her body was laid out in the parlor of youngest Brown daughter Ellen's home, a funeral was held in the Saratoga Congregational Church.[116] The Reverend W. H. Cross preached a sermon based on a biblical text from Matthew that read "Well done, thou good and faithful servant . . . enter thou into the joy of the Lord."[117] He also eulogized Mary Brown, noting how she had endured despite difficult circumstances and poverty. He closed his sermon by saying, simply, "Truly it can be said of her, 'Well done, good and faithful servant.'"[118] Obituaries for Mary Brown appeared in newspapers all over the country, all alluding to her symbolic status as a link to antebellum history. Her death, the *San Francisco Call* noted, "will recall to the memory of a great portion of the world some of the exciting scenes of over a quarter of a century ago."[119] Even in death Mary Brown was presented as a relic of John Brown.

This depiction overlooked an important fact: that in the decades after Harpers Ferry, Mary Brown created a new life for herself, one founded on her identity as Brown's widow but also one that she defined for herself. Brown used his jailhouse letters to explain himself, but Mary did little of this. Instead, it is her series of actions—from her flight to the water cure to her pursuit of a new life in California—that speak to her interior sensibility. Though some abolitionists had cast her in roles ranging from dutiful widow to placid, dull spouse, the Mary Brown who emerges from the historical record was none of these things. In her actions after 1859, she proved her belief in self-sacrifice and her desire to have "others to live for."

Mary Brown was unlike some other contemporary widows of famous figures. Elizabeth Bacon Custer gave lectures, made appearances, and wrote letters to the editor in a self-conscious attempt to ensure that her husband was idealized after his death at Little Bighorn. In 1885, she even wrote an autobiography, *Boots and Saddles*. Her work was such that biographer Shirley Leckie classifies her as one of Custer's "major interpreters."[120] After Jefferson Davis's death, his widow Varina Davis completed and arranged for the publication of his memoir. In what she called her "sacred task," she worked to defend his life and work for the Confederacy—and her own.[121] Mary Brown never seems to have entertained the thought of writing something for public consumption. Her former acquaintance Rebecca Spring wrote a memoir in which she highlighted her connection to John Brown.[122] But then Spring was highly literate and well educated.

With rare exceptions, in the years after she moved to California Mary Brown chose to confine her action to the private sphere. The actions that she failed to take are revealing. Mary did not use her 1882 trip as any kind of public stage from which to claim her own interpretation of John Brown. At her first stop in Chicago, she celebrated what she called "a growing interest in the John Brown feeling that no tide can stop," but she did not work to actively shape or direct whatever she perceived the "John Brown feeling" to be.[123] In this, she was unlike some of her children, especially stepson John Jr. and daughter Annie, who reached out to the press and a potential public audience with increasing frequency to defend their father in the 1880s and 1890s. She also did not use her 1882 trip to repudiate the reconciliationist bent of the country, as Frederick Douglass had done the previous year in a speech at Storer College in Harpers Ferry. Like some she had met on her trip east, Mary Brown did not envision a place for herself as a civil rights activist in the post–Civil War world. She never spoke out in public about race relations after the end of slavery, and whatever her private feelings were about race matters prior to her 1884 death, they remain unknown.

✄ CHAPTER 7

Annie Brown Adams, the Last Survivor

In 1892 Franklin Sanborn wrote to enlist one-time Kennedy farm housekeeper Annie's aid. Annie now lived in a remote area along northern California's coast, raising a family and struggling to get by. Sanborn had been in frequent contact with her, always seeking to acquire new Brown-related information while offering occasional assistance. Now, he turned to Annie for help. A schemer named Richard Howard had recently claimed celebrity as the sole survivor of Brown's raid. In reality, the few raiders who had escaped were by this point dead; Howard's boast was an utter fabrication. Sanborn knew this. More important, he knew that Annie could prove it. Shortly thereafter, she wrote a scathing letter to the *Boston Transcript*. "I was my father's housekeeper at Kennedy Farm," she stated, "and know that this man Howard was not there." She then vehemently declared, "Since Owen Brown's death [in 1889], I am the only person who can honestly claim to be 'the last survivor.'"[1] In private correspondence, she described Howard as "a *fraud* and a humbug," adding, "This man seems to have studied his lesson well, but [he] neglected to make the acquaintance of the housekeepers at Kennedy Farmhouse, one of them still survives, and is certain that he was *not there*."[2]

Though outlandish, this incident was emblematic of many themes of Annie's adult life. Grappling with her own role as housekeeper to Brown's doomed raiders, Annie continued to define herself by her link to antislavery violence. She felt almost assaulted by the broader culture's turn-of-the-century consensus that Brown was a fanatic or worse, and she struggled to protect her children from their family connection. At the same time, she did not distance herself from the Brown name, unlike her younger sisters Sarah and Ellen. Throughout the late nineteenth and early twentieth century, Annie continued to correspond and interact with Brown biographers and the public realm of Brown memory, hoping to correct the errors she saw in the world's interpretation of her father. She hoped to claim her rightful place as the "last survivor" of Brown's raid, to finally get credit for Brown's dependence on her to keep watch at the Kennedy farmhouse.

Brown's Memory at the Turn of the Century

Publicity seeker Richard Howard chose an odd moment to connect himself to John Brown, as he did so against the backdrop of what Paul Shackel has termed "the national rejection of abolitionist ideals."[3] Onetime AASS lecturer Aaron Powell reminded a crowd a decade prior that a "spirit of oppression and race-prejudice" remained despite the abolition of slavery.[4] But even if abolitionists had wanted to fight "race-prejudice," their dwindling number would have been unable to stem the tide of what David Blight has famously characterized as the "reconciliationist" bent of the country. Between 1880 and 1915, Blight convincingly argues, Americans created a national consensus to "divert their eyes" from the fact that slavery and race had been at the core of the Civil War.[5] By 1915, the "dominant mode" of Civil War memory was rooted in sectional reconciliation, one forged by mutual sanctioning of Jim Crow. In remembering the war, Americans highlighted soldier bravery on both sides and buried mention of slavery, race, and emancipation—all the things with which John Brown was associated.[6] As Mary's 1882 trip had predicted, near the turn of the century only a few lone whites and African Americans continued to celebrate Brown's radical agenda: his commitment to racial equality.[7]

Still, unlike abolitionists such as Garrison, Brown was not simply marginalized and written out from popular memory. In part this was because he had too many advocates: well into the twentieth century men who had fought with Brown tried to preserve a heroic vision of him. His detractors were equally strident. As an 1899 biographer noted, Brown remained "written about much . . . and for the most part fiercely."[8] Brown loomed large in such periodicals as the *Century, New England Magazine, Midland Monthly, Outlook,* and the *Nation.* Some of these were liberal publications, but Brown garnered attention even in local newspapers from Boston to St. Louis to Los

Angeles. Despite the whitewashing of Civil War memory, Brown remained a captivating figure. Article after article appeared in the 1890s. Some of the pieces were blatantly polemical; others conveyed simple fascination, almost removing him from the contested narrative of the Civil War. By those who lauded him or even expressed ambiguity, Brown was increasingly portrayed as a man of courage: his radical ideas on race were written out, and he was recalled as someone who had acted, perhaps misguidedly, on principle.[9]

In this coverage and apart from it, American newspapers of the time frequently referenced the Brown children. Particularly after sons Jason and Owen moved atop a mountain outside Pasadena in southern California, their home became a site of pilgrimage for Brown supporters and curious tourists.[10] Some reporters looked to interview the children for clues to Brown's character; one such interview with John Brown Jr. was titled "The Soul of John Brown."[11] In addition, Brown's children were called upon to offer clues to his character and were looked to as possessing the courageous "fire" that had once burned inside him. Frequently, pieces about Brown's children were surprisingly sympathetic, especially when those children faced loss. This was especially true for Annie, who, of her siblings, endured the severest poverty, compounded by devastation from fires and earthquakes. The *Salt Lake City Weekly Tribune* once related its opinion that John Brown was a treasonous fanatic. But, its writer added, "at the same time his performance was one of the opening acts in that tragedy which had to be . . . and the modest grandeur but absolute courage with which he met death were enough to kindle admiration in the hearts of the men who executed him." Though dismissive of Brown's motivation, the paper highlighted both his courage and his link to the "tragedy" of the Civil War in its plea for assistance for Annie, whom it described as "a daughter of his, with her little children," who was "suffering for bread."[12] Perhaps because Americans seeking reconciliation had become so inclined to recognize soldier valor, John Brown's actions became enmeshed in that valor, one that could be admired even if it was thought misguided. Or perhaps an opposite instinct was at work. Perhaps even while sectional reconciliation was occurring, Americans needed to remember the tumultuous 1850s that had led to the Civil War, and John Brown stood in as a highly charged symbol of this "submerged" memory.[13]

Brown's children chronicled popular memory of their father and felt each slight. All sought refuge from a hostile world. Eldest son John Jr. lived out the remainder of his life on Put-in-Bay island, while youngest sibling Ellen shrank away from criticism of the father she barely remembered. Old and ailing, Salmon Brown would ultimately take his own life. Ruth's family and brothers Jason and Owen sought solace in the Pasadena Republican-leaning community that took some pride in hosting Brown's children. Annie would seek—but never find—a similar refuge inside and outside her home in northern California.

Annie's life after her departure from Red Bluff to Humboldt County was often overshadowed by her connection to John Brown. She was not unique among her siblings. Without exception, all of Brown's children had adult lives that were much affected by their surname. As had been the case for the Browns in the immediate aftermath of Harpers Ferry and in Red Bluff, this was not always unfortunate. Sympathetic communities and individuals continued to send money to Brown's sons and, especially, to his daughters in the years after Mary Brown's death. Daughters Ruth and Annie remained especially dependent upon charity, though all of Brown's children accepted aid at one time or another. Some unknown patron (likely the abolitionist Horatio Rust) even secured a position for Sarah in the U.S. Mint in San Francisco.[14]

But the family connection also overshadowed their lives in negative ways. The Brown children's poverty was paraded before curious Americans in the press, and they occasionally squabbled with each other about the propriety of such revelations of need.[15] They also contended about disposal of the few Brown relics and materials that they still held.[16] All of Brown's children grappled with their involvement in his antislavery work, and Brown sons John Jr. and Salmon remained especially prickly regarding their lack of participation at Harpers Ferry.[17] Annie and Ruth both suffered from nervous conditions that seem to have stemmed from their ties to Harpers Ferry—and for Ruth, from Henry's actions in Kansas.[18] And negative public opinion about Brown cut all of them, to the point that youngest daughters Ellen and Sarah strove to dismiss their connection to Brown.[19] The fact that some of the Brown siblings' descendants were taught not to acknowledge their link to him—or not even told of it at all!—offers further proof of how difficult it was living with the Brown surname in the late nineteenth and early twentieth century.[20]

Among the history of all the siblings, the story of Annie's adult life is an especially poignant narrative of the costs of being a Brown and a participant in his antislavery violence. In some ways it is also a cautionary tale about the ways in which Brown's most radical ideals could and did become muted in the late nineteenth century, even among his most fervent supporters. First and foremost, it is a story of isolation, both literal and figurative. Annie's flight to California's Lost Coast cut her off from community with any Brown kin, and a bad marriage and poverty limited her options even further. From the 1880s on, Annie mostly remained distant from the rest of the Browns. In 1895, funded by an abolitionist sympathizer, she would travel to visit Ruth, Sarah, and Ellen.[21] But as Annie grew more determined to have her position as "eyewitness" to Brown's raid validated, she offended the older faction of Brown siblings as well as her younger sisters, further severing her connections to those best positioned to understand her experience.[22]

Hope for a Backwoods Refuge

In the late 1880s, Annie and Samuel left Rohnerville, where they had been living since they departed Red Bluff in the late 1860s. Her sisters Sarah and Ellen had relocated to Saratoga with their mother in 1881, and Salmon's family had moved to Oregon. In a letter to an abolitionist patron, Annie announced her upcoming move to Petrolia, a smaller, more remote town in the Mattole River Valley about forty miles from her current home. Even after the oil boom that had led to its founding had waned, the population of the Mattole River Valley had continued to grow, and by 1875 Petrolia and the surrounding valley were supporting cattle ranches and farms and a population of close to five hundred people.[23] Annie hoped it would offer a new start for her family; by this time, her seven girls and boys ranged from eighteen-year-old Mary Vivian to one-year-old Richard.[24] She described Petrolia as "a wild back-wooding place, where the girls and boys can have a good chance to develop their energies and their muscles."[25]

Despite the advent of a stagecoach line to and from nearby Eureka, in the early 1870s Petrolia's isolation was striking. Even today, one road leads in and out of town, and a few days of poor weather can make travel treacherous.[26] A year after her arrival, Annie admitted, "We are almost like the Swiss Family Robinson, only we are not quite on an island, and do have communication with the outside world once in a long while."[27] On her trip from Rohnerville to Petrolia, Annie and her family got forewarning of both its beauty and isolation. They likely traveled over a road that had only recently been carved out of Humboldt County's mountains, valleys, and forests. It winds through a small section of the California redwoods and along the Pacific Coast, the latter just five miles before Petrolia, and the view is breathtaking.[28] Journalist Katherine Mayo would later describe it as "so beautiful as fairly to seem unreal." She added, "The Browns were ever pioneers and lovers of Nature undisturbed, but this one has exceeded them all, and certainly has found at once the farthest and the finest refuge that the continent affords."[29]

The setting did not bring the peace that Annie desired. In Petrolia as in Rohnerville, Annie's life remained dominated by "family cares" and the ever-present perils of poverty.[30] "The poorest days I ever saw at North Elba, we lived luxuriously beside of what I do now," she confided.[31] The year after her move, Annie apologized for a delay in responding to a letter. She reminded her correspondent that her time was limited because of her children—and her class status. "Two days after writing you, another little one was added to my family, and a year ago another still, making seven now living," she wrote. "And as I do not keep any servants, except my own two hands, and do all my work with the help of my children, I am kept so busy that I find it hard work to get time to even write a letter."[32] Annie's life, like her mother's, was dominated by childbearing, child rearing, and poverty. Perhaps even more so than for her mother, the circumstances of her marriage added to her challenges.

By the time of their move to Petrolia, Annie's life with Samuel had unraveled. The early happiness that she had experienced with him seems to have evaporated, replaced by a blend of anxiety and cynicism—both apparently justified. She had bargained that the move would allow her husband to "get better of his rheumatism, so he will be able to work at least part of the time."[33] Samuel had also promised that he "would *behave* like a man and *live* like one" there.[34] She hoped that Petrolia was remote enough that he would be removed from the temptations of saloons, which she termed "men's dens."[35] His alcoholism was so severe that, despite the distance between the sisters, all were aware of it.[36] Ruth noted how she wished that Annie "had married a good and noble man as I have got" and how her life "might have been a happy one."[37] Sarah was even more severe, describing Samuel as a "naturally low, vicious person further embittered by drink." "You can picture what a home is with such a person for the head," she added caustically.[38]

Not only did the isolation of Petrolia not afford Annie the reprieve she sought; it may have made matters worse. In 1894, she confided that although the high waters of winter kept Samuel from venturing to town to drink, "he just sits and smokes and growls and snarls all the time."[39] Though mortified, she was driven to seek help. Once she turned to Ruth's Pasadena benefactor Horatio Rust in real desperation. Samuel had been secretly trying to secure money from relatives in Chicago, and Annie feared he would use the money for no good. Additionally, Annie confided that his mind had grown "weaker" and that he was prone to fits of rage. She continued, "I think it will finally end in our being obliged to have him placed in an insane asylum," as when he was mad

he attempts to take the lives of whoever is the victim of his displeasure and threatens that he will kill us when we are asleep. . . . He is entirely out of money now, so he keeps sober, but we never know when to expect an outbreak. He has been very quiet and well behaved since the boys came back. God only knows how long it will last. He usually fights and abuses them shamefully, for all they do here on the place, but is now letting them put in the crops without any trouble. I think he has some scheme or project in view in connection with the money he expects, that is keeping him so docile.

She then implored, "I thought you, perhaps, might be able *to think a way, out of this affair*, so that it might be *done quietly*." Forebodingly, she added, "Please keep this where it can be used in evidence if it is needed, as no one knows what may happen here any day."[40]

Annie's life in the 1890s was a far cry from what she might have expected in the heady days of 1859, when she lived among Brown's raiders. Romanticizing Annie's experience, Ruth once stated that Annie had gone there to follow her "first lover," likely referring to Henry's brother Dauphin.[41] Then, she became the only Brown to travel south during the Civil War. Surely she had imagined extraordinary happenings would also follow her travel out west—not the ordinary life she now led. Like many nineteenth-century women, a cycle of childbearing and lack of real options constrained her choices in the face of a bad marriage. Poverty perhaps more than anything gave her daily life its shape. While that was familiar from her childhood, now it was not tinged with nobility. More than anything, her need defined her relationship to the outside world—need for assistance with her mundane present, and more and more, need for recognition for her extraordinary past. She felt perpetually slighted in regard to both.

Various groups and individuals raised money for Annie and her siblings throughout the nineteenth century and into the twentieth century. Abolitionists and aficionados offered personal patronage: Horatio Rust offered much assistance to Ruth, Jason, and Owen in southern California, while Franklin Sanborn continued to raise funds and maintain contact with all of Brown's children. A renewed Brown fund in the late nineteenth century assisted many of them, Annie included. Other local charitable groups responded to various circumstances—a fire at Annie Brown's home in the 1890s and a 1906 earthquake, for example—and raised money.[42] But as time passed, Annie not infrequently expressed her expectation that she deserved more. "Ever since John Brown's death, there have been parties raising money on one pretext or another for John Brown's poor family. The poor family have never received but a small amount of what has been claimed to have been raised, who does get it, is one of the unsolvable mysteries," Annie wrote with some bitterness in 1892.[43]

It is hard not to feel sympathy for Annie, trapped in a perilous life and suffering from the knowledge that her father was viewed negatively by many in the United States. But empathy cannot alter the hard truth about where her bitterness was sometimes directed. Annie sometimes aimed her ire at African Americans, who she did not feel had done enough to repay the debt they owed to her father and his family. This flew in the face of fact. Many African Americans, despite their own financial struggles, had rallied behind the Browns and sent money to Annie, Ruth, and other Brown siblings throughout the decades after Brown's raid. Regardless, Annie chronicled her belief that African Americans had not properly supported her over the years, and her attitude hardened as the years passed.[44]

In 1897 Annie was called to account for not acknowledging contributions from African Americans, and she responded in a letter that was reprinted in the African American newspaper the *Conservator*. Her letter was addressed to Ida B. Wells-Barnett, who had written the year previously to tell her that hearing about her "misfortune has caused thousands of our race who love the memory of your martyred father to sympathize with you and lend a helping hand in your hour of need." "We cannot do very much but what we attempt is most gratefully done," she added.[45] Donations had been gathered and sent, but they went unacknowledged by Annie.[46] Annie explained her overdue response by referencing her nervous condition and confusion over a list of contributors, and she defensively added that she would have written a "courteous answer" to any letter. She noted, "I am very much pleased to note the progress your people have made. It is truly wonderful, the stride they have made since the days when I used to teach 'contrabands' at Norfolk, Virginia, during the war." Her salutation is especially striking. As she had in the heady days of 1859–60, she signed her letter, "Yours for the right."[47]

By the time she penned this letter, much of Annie's earlier extraordinary attitudes about race—all those lessons from the Brown antislavery culture—appear to have been erased, replaced by some grudging resentment.[48] Annie was not the only Brown to espouse racially conservative positions.[49] She and some of her siblings, like most Americans, held conservative, racist beliefs in the late nineteenth century, the height of lynching and imposition of Jim Crow.[50] Annie's resentment also stemmed from her sense that her own work and her father's was being unacknowledged in the world at large. But some of her beliefs are startling in their echo of modern race-based resentments. In one letter recounting her situation, she described her eight children and their disadvantageous position. She noted, "They have had *very little* school and advantages, except what I could find time to teach them. The school is three miles from here, with an unbridged river between us and it. So they can only attend a short time during the middle of the summer." She then added, "If they were Indians or Negroes the Government would provide a school and the Missionary

Society send a missionary to care for the poor little heathen. But they are only the grandchildren of a man who was to some think foolish enough to try to do all he could for others."[51] Like many people, Annie was able to hold two incongruent beliefs simultaneously. She could exhibit the kind of prejudice her father advocated against while maintaining that his sacrifices on behalf of his beliefs were not being properly recognized by the world at large.

A Relic of John Brown's Raid

Reflecting on the American penchant for fascination with Brown and his family, Annie described her era as "an age that is addicted to unlimited curiosity about others private affairs, to an unseemly extent."[52] Isolated in Petrolia, Annie was somewhat protected from the deluge of periodicals dissecting and debating the life and legacy of John Brown. But she could not block them out completely—nor did she want to. No matter how hard she tried, she could not escape her memories of the past; her involvement in Brown's raid almost haunted her. Writing a letter on September 29, 1896, she noted, "Thirty-seven years ago this day Martha and I left the Kennedy farmhouse."[53] Other letters refer to her "bad mental state"—one usually connected to her memory of Brown.[54] Despite the pain it brought her, Annie felt increasingly compelled to participate in the public conversation about John Brown. In *Memory, War, and Trauma*, Nigel Hunt describes what he calls a "traumatic response." This manifests itself differently for different people; Annie matches his description of how, for some, "the memories of the event are overwhelming and continuous." Though his book is largely about trauma from modern war, Hunt's description of how trauma survivors, like all humans, are "compelled to narrate" is helpful in understanding Annie's need to talk about and claim her experiences even when doing so caused her anxiety.[55] Even if she had wanted to block out her past, she literally was compelled to recall it, by would-be biographers to organizers of the 1893 World's Fair who contacted her because of her link to Brown and her special knowledge of his raiders.

By her own choice, she also worked to commemorate Brown properly within her own household.[56] To Franklin Sanborn, she described how ideas about Brown hardened in California. Onetime governor of Kansas Charles Robinson, she wrote, "colored the ideas and opinions of the people on the Pacific Coast about John Brown." Because of this, she added, "My children have to squirm and get excused . . . from reciting that lesson."[57] Her very youngest child might have been exposed to Woodrow Wilson's popular 1902 textbook, *A History of the American People*. Wilson referred to Brown as a "mad fanatic" and "a blind and maddened crusader" and to Harpers Ferry as a "sinister thing."[58] Modern Brown family lore relates that Annie habitually scrawled "this is not true" in her grandchildren's textbooks.[59] To counter the lies she saw in popular opinion, Annie created a small library of her own. She obtained copies of Harriet Beecher Stowe's novels *Uncle Tom's Cabin* (1852) and *Dred* (1856), for, she said, "they were the best works I know of to help them understand the situation of this country under the slavery rule."[60] Writing to request a copy of raider Osborne Anderson's memoir, she stated, "I wish it for my children to read when they are old enough to understand it. I have tried to keep a collection of the best things that have been written about the affair for them."[61] Annie even sought to write accounts of Brown for her children as well as others, hoping to "try in a measure to contrast a little if possible the bad impression made on them, by what is said in the common school histories of 'John Brown's Raid.'"[62]

Even kindly intended accounts of Brown sometimes caused Annie pain. Her children once stumbled upon Frederick Douglass's account of his visit to the Browns and his description of their poverty. Balking at a portrayal of her family as too poor to afford even a tablecloth (as well as perpetually irate that Douglass had, in her mind, abandoned his promise to Brown), Annie informed her children that "there was *not* a *word* of *truth* in the statement."[63] At that point, her children refused to continue reading. Incidents such as that, as well as their discomfort in school, led Annie to "shut the past away."[64] But no matter how she tried, Annie could not manage this, in part because she saw herself as the keeper of her father's memory. A onetime caretaker at the Kennedy farmhouse, she was now a housekeeper in the nation at large, trying to make sure that the story of militant abolitionism did not get swept under the rug.

Annie was frequently contacted by Brown biographers and scholars who hoped to tap into her memories of Brown's raiders. Biographers courted her for assistance with their works, while aficionados and compatriots cultivated relationships with her and her siblings.[65] To say that Annie was courted is no understatement. Alexander Ross, a Canadian physician and abolitionist working on a book about his relationship to John Brown and about Brown's raiders, made a habit of sending Annie gifts; Annie promised in return to "redeem" her "promise" to write about the raiders.[66] In their works, biographers acknowledged the payoff from their careful courtship. In his 1885 *Life and Letters*, Sanborn remarked that the Brown children had "placed without reserve their papers in my hand."[67] Within the circle of Brown scholars there was also frequent jockeying for position as writers tried to secure previously unused materials and competed over who was closer to the Browns.[68] Sanborn and Richard Hinton were ever-attentive to the fact that the Brown daughters might possess hitherto unrevealed resources and looked to borrow family papers, sometimes neglecting to return them. Sanborn once denied Hinton's request to borrow some of his materials, perhaps inadvertently revealing his desire not to let anything that was solely his slip into Hinton's grasp. "Such materials as I have has [*sic*] chiefly come to me from the Brown family, from whom you also, I think, have received material,—much of it probably the same as mine."[69] Throughout the 1890s and early twentieth century, Annie wrote to Sanborn as well as Richard Hinton to try to reclaim papers. Her frustration came through on occasion, such as when she wrote to Hinton, "If it is not possible for you to find the letters, you can at least be polite enough to write and say so, and not treat the matter with the utter contempt you have hitherto done." She then stormed, "I frequently see and read articles in magazines and papers written by you, so I know that you are still alive, even if you do ignore my existence."[70] Annie's distrust of Hinton seems well-founded. In 1900 he advised another Brown biographer that Annie could be turned to for information but that she, like her siblings, would "have to be carefully worked."[71]

Whether they feuded or collaborated, all recognized the special value that the Brown siblings held for their work.[72] Because of her presence at the Kennedy farmhouse, Annie's expertise was particularly sought. She might have resented the intrusiveness, but instead it quickly became a cherished component of her identity. Writing to Alexander Ross's son, she reminded him that she had information about John Brown, "not the one the world knew, but my father, as I knew him."[73] Her boast was somewhat justified by the number of Brown writers who sought information from her. Thomas Featherstonhaugh also looked to secure Annie's expertise for a book on Brown's men, and he saw his access to her as a coup. In his *John Brown's Men*, he noted, "I may here remark that almost all of the little details of the life at the farm and much of the personal matter concerning the men are from the pen of Mrs. Adams in letters to me and have not been published before."[74] Featherstonhaugh also looked to Annie to accomplish a grimmer task. Sometime prior to 1899, the bodies of eight of Brown's raiders—including her brother Oliver—were supposedly unearthed about a half mile away from Harpers Ferry along the Shenandoah River.[75] All that had been found along the banks of the river were the large bones from the bodies of the eight men, so identification of Oliver per se was impossible.[76] Alongside the bones, however, were the remains of some woolen fabric. Annie's knowledge of some "large blanket-shawls" that "had been sent to the Kennedy farm as a present to the band from Philadelphia" confirmed that the bones were Brown's men.[77] Featherstonhaugh made arrangements to bury the eight sets of bones in a single casket at North Elba alongside the bodies of John Brown and

Watson.[78] He published an article about the "final burial of the followers of John Brown" a few years later.[79] In it, he included a drawing. It features five of Brown's raiders in a circle; in the middle is an image of Annie. She must have been gratified to be recognized by Featherstonhaugh for her role in Brown's raid. What is most striking about the image is the youth of Brown's men in comparison to the depiction of the middle-aged "Mrs. Annie Brown Adams." It is a poignant reminder of the sacrifices made by young men like Oliver Brown and Aaron Stephens for a cause (and by a means) that they believed was worth the loss of their life—and the way that the loss of the young men haunted the elder Annie Brown Adams.

FIGURE 11. Annie Brown Adams, ca. 1895. Library of Congress.

FIGURE 12.   Annie Brown Adams pictured at the center of raiders Oliver Brown, Watson Brown, John Henry Kagi, Jeremiah Anderson, and Aaron Stevens. This image was included in an article about the 1899 reburial of Oliver and other raiders, though the article itself neglected to mention Annie or her involvement in Brown's raid. Thomas Featherstonhaugh, "The Final Burial of the Followers of John Brown," *New England Magazine*, April 1901.

Of the Brown sisters, Annie put the most effort into her contacts with the biographers. She frequently reminded them that she, unlike some other Browns, was an *expert* and *eyewitness* to events at the Kennedy farm. Writing to Sanborn, for instance, she reminded, "Your acquaintances with the persons was very slight, some of them you never saw, while I was on the most intimate terms with a good many of them and had an 'every day' acquaintance with most of them."[80] With the past often lurking in her present, Annie expressed surprise, even offense, when she was not consulted. She chronicled various slights and was frequently irked by the appearance of articles showcasing her brother Salmon (or John, or Jason, or Owen) or even her sister Sarah as "the last Brown." To Richard Hinton, she petulantly stated, "It always seemed a little queer to me that so many persons have attempted to publish books or articles on John Brown without consulting me just a *little*."[81] To Annie, such consultation demonstrated that she belonged in an exclusive circle along-side the Brown biographers and abolitionists. She craved proof that others remembered her role in Brown's raid. Over the years, she came to consider Alexander Ross a friend, in large part because he continually wrote to her for her expertise about Brown's men (and sent presents). To Ross, she extended what she felt was the ultimate accolade. "I was with my father until two weeks before that Affair. . . . I had supposed until recently that my brother Owen and my self were the only now living survivors of that little band, but it seems that you too belonged to *our* Company."[82] Once again, Annie asserted that her role as housekeeper granted her a place in the history of violent abolitionism. Inviting Ross into "*our* Company," she indicated that he, like herself, could properly claim and comment on the history of radical abolitionism.

Always, she was concerned that Brown be placed before the world in what she described to Ross as his "*true* light," and she was increasingly bold about it.[83] For instance, she let Franklin Sanborn, her onetime schoolteacher in Concord, know of her disappointment in his *Life and Letters*. She wrote to Ross of her desire that Sanborn "do a better job" in his next work but that he was hard to convince and "set in his ways." She tried anyway. Of his second volume, she wrote, "I have supplied him with some materials for it, as I am anxious to have him do better work on that."[84] That she was truly "anxious" for this is clear: she wrote countless letters in which she, like some of her brothers, went through new works on Brown and even manuscript proofs to identify errors in fact and interpretation. Annie was desperate for some-one to do "better work." What did "better work" mean? For one, it meant avoiding matters that were meant merely to tantalize public appetites about Brown. Annie recoiled from sensationalism, certain that writers should focus on "better material" such as how Brown fit into abolitionist history and to highlight how he had fought selflessly for a righteous cause. Just as she had corrected her children's textbooks, she looked to right the view of the public at large. She wanted Brown and his men to be remembered as noble sol-diers—and her own work held up as worthy and deserving of soldier status.

In 1893 Americans celebrated the World's Fair in Chicago, and relic collector Frank Logan planned an exhibit to highlight Brown alongside Abraham Lincoln, hoping to use regard for the latter to increase appreciation of the former.[85] As abolitionists had during Mary's eastern tour, Logan linked Brown with the wider trajectory of slavery's abolition. A. J. Holmes, a former Iowa congressman who had recently purchased the engine house where Brown was captured, concocted a competing plan to display it at the fair.[86] Immediately after the Civil War, it had been a tourist attraction of sorts; "John Brown's Fort" had been painted on one side. But as Jim Crow took hold, the relic became less popular. Holmes now hoped its presence could turn the tide of public sentiment. Some, including Rust, were skeptical, while others were impressed by its potential as a "museum of abolition relics."[87] Hoping to cash in on public curiosity, Holmes further proposed that they attract crowds by manning the fort with living relics: Brown's grandchildren. The 1893 World's Fair would feature other live relics—so-called "primitive" people—but these were the only American "relics" invited to pose.[88] Holmes wrote to Brown's oldest daughters Annie and Ruth, offering to pay their children to come to Chicago to pose at the fort and sell admission tickets. Once again, the extraordinary dimension of Annie's life was offering a way out of ordinary poverty.

Annie found the offer tempting, as did her oldest son and daughter, who, she said, "thought it would be a nice chance to see something of the world and the World's Fair."[89] She worried, though, about Holmes's motivation.[90] Annie's reasoning stemmed from her discomfort with *becoming* a relic, an object of curiosity to fairgoers. This uneasiness outweighed both her desire to have a hand in how her father was commemorated and her wish for her children to enjoy an unexpected opportunity. Ultimately, she turned down Holmes's proposal.[91] Annie astutely summarized the Browns' particular brand of celebrity as well as the family's continued discomfort with it. "My work like that of the rest was a free will offering, not something to boast of or exhibit myself for," she explained, adding, "I may be a relic of John Brown's raid on Harper's Ferry, but I do not want to be placed on exhibition with other relics and curios, as such. . . . Nothing could tempt me to exhibit myself in a public place, and I do not feel right about the children going there for that purpose."[92]

Shortly after the John Brown fort debacle, she wrote to Franklin Sanborn. "I am not aspiring to any literary fame," she wrote, but "I must do something to pay some bills . . . and as I get so many applications from different persons to write for *nothing*, I thought there was no harm in my trying to make some of my writing pay some of my debts." With a shrewd sense of her celebrity value, she added that as she had few other resources, she could offer this to "the relic hunters."[93] She also seems to have earnestly wanted to write; it offered her a chance to get "the truth" out about John Brown.[94] Annie sent out a variety of her own manuscripts to periodicals as varied as *Cosmopolitan*, *Youth's Companion*, and some California magazines. Writing to Alexander Ross in 1894, she referred to a sketch she had written and sent to an eastern paper that had said they would pay if they liked it. "I have been waiting to hear from them, so I might ask you to congratulate me for having earned a few dollars to help myself, so far in vain," she confided.[95] She never was able to solicit Ross's felicitations, as nothing she wrote ever appeared in print.

Why this was so is complicated. Sometimes she took a long time to write a manuscript—and sometimes she never completed it because of the "nervous state" (as she described it) produced in her by her work at remembering the past.[96] Writing to Richard Hinton in 1895, she described the niche that she saw her work as filling—and the reason for its delay. She referred to Frank Stearns's memoir of his abolitionist father, noting, "Mr. Frank Stearns mentions the dearth of real incidents in the lives that have been written of father, that go to show the real man. This is the deficiency that I have always felt . . . and thought if I could have the leisure time at my disposal, I might supply." Again, she felt that she could make Americans understand the "real man" John Brown if only she could overcome the writer's block that her "*overstrained* nerves" induced, particularly when she revisited her past.[97] She also worried about the saturated market, wondering if too many books had already been written about John Brown. She remained convinced that she could do a better job than others had in telling Brown's story, but over the years had given away most of her papers and memories and allowed her father to become a "much worn subject."[98]

"And There Were None"

Annie's hope was again renewed in the early 1900s, when Oswald Garrison Villard, grandson of the famous abolitionist, planned "a thoroughly sympathetic yet discriminating view of Brown's life."[99] Despite Villard's relationship to the pacifist Garrison, Annie hoped that he would right the historical record on John Brown. Though she made room for men like Villard's grandfather in her story of how slavery was destroyed, she described two "types" of abolitionists—Garrisonian pacifists and the Brown counterpart—and then asked, rhetorically, which type Villard would prefer to have on his side when faced with a "man-eating tiger." The answer was obvious: "Moral suasion and non resistance are excellent doctrines to preach in times of peace," she wrote. "But often in troublous times, someone, has to fight for peace—and fight hard too, and then endure the remarks that are made by the carpet knights and quill-drivers, who were not in the fray, but staid peacefully at home enjoying the after benefits derived from other's exertions."[100] In her mid-sixties, Annie worried that she was running out of time to advocate for a "man-eating tiger" such as her father, and she hoped the well-known Villard would be able to do so on her behalf.

Like others before him, Villard hoped to unearth new Brown materials. It was in part to this end that he enlisted the aid of Katherine Mayo, an intrepid journalist who had been writing for the *New York Evening Post* since the 1890s.[101] In 1908, Villard dispatched her throughout the country to interview those who had known Brown, including his surviving sons Salmon and Jason, son-in-law Henry Thompson, and Brown's three daughters with Mary. Invested in Villard's success, Mayo journeyed on trains and stagecoaches, in urban and remote areas, seeking anecdotes of John Brown and any materials that might have been previously overlooked. Well-educated and cosmopolitan, Mayo was fascinated by the group she dubbed the "sturdy children of John Brown."[102] Like Rebecca Spring in 1859, she was struck both by their link to Brown and their distinction from herself. Between June and November of 1908, she visited Annie, Sarah, Ellen, and Henry Thompson and his daughter Mary, along with countless others, including Spring herself. All but Ellen provided her with lengthy interviews. Recounting her dismissal by Ellen, Mayo wrote to Villard, "I could cheerfully have Pottawatomied her on the spot, with all the paternal calm & godly satisfaction."[103]

In Pasadena she courted widower Henry Thompson and his school-teacher daughter Mary. Reflecting the longtime American penchant to see Brown kin, at first Mayo could barely get past her luck at being in the same room with someone so close to Brown's history. She exclaimed to Villard, "There is Mr Thompson *a Pottawatomie participant!*" Mayo was unsure of what details she would get out of Salmon, so she was bent on securing information from Henry: "H. Thompson is right here," she wrote excitedly, "and—I don't want to brag but I *think* I'll fetch him." Seizing on Mary's poverty, Mayo plotted:

My plan is, to get to know Mary T. as well as I can, in the next 3 or 4 days. I am going to take it for granted that you would think a little money well invested in this, & take her on one or two excursions. She has never been *to a single "sight"* around here—never had the price of a ticket *anywhere* to spare—& she looks *hungry* when you say Mt Lowe or Catalina Island. I'm going to take her to Mt Lowe tomorrow & somewhere else on Sunday—& it will cost quite a little bit—& by

Monday—I'm going to produce Townsley's statement & ask them to correct it—& I think they will do it. Also—Robinson. Wont that be worth it?[104]

Ultimately, Mayo would declare the courtship worth all her time and trouble, when one morning Mary revealed to her that one of the Pottawatomie victims, Doyle, had been shot after he was killed with broadswords. "Even F.B.S. [Sanborn], (unless Salmon has told him) does not know that, I think," Mayo wrote triumphantly.[105]

When Mayo arrived at Annie's door in 1908 after a wild adventure taking the stagecoach along the Mattole Road, she hoped for further revelations. Chronicling Annie's circumstances, Mayo exclaimed, "Oh, but the *slackness* and the *poverty*, the *needless* poverty there! The 'parlour' door hanging on one hinge. The dust, the litter, and acres—hundreds of acres of ground—*rich* ground, not so much as a tomato plant growing in it."[106] As she entered the dilapidated house, Mayo informed Villard, she was greeted by a pair of eyes that "blazed with pleasurable excitement" at the chance to speak of John Brown.[107] Annie's lack of success in publishing any memoirs, the dwindling circle of "survivors," and the continuing difficulties of her life made her especially eager to have the company of the young and vibrant Mayo.[108]

Like many before her, Mayo relied on Annie to verify classic John Brown stories such as Brown's request that John Jr. flog him rather than vice versa in midst of a punishment and the Brown family "compact" to fight slavery.[109] Annie complied. But after years of playing frustrated witness to eager biographers, Mayo soon declared Annie's usefulness to have come to an end. Mayo reported to Villard, "Under the small hours that night I hugged the kitchen stove, for I was frozen, and pumped Annie, who answered willingly, and like a good, clear witness," adding, "but who has already told all she means. Next morning early she was ready to begin again. Meantime, she had got out her papers—and there were none."[110] Mayo departed shortly thereafter, leaving Annie to write to Villard, "Miss Mayo made us a flying call. She did not stay long enough to do any good work. I like her very much and was sorry I could not have seen her longer. . . . If there is any further information that you wish, ask questions and I will try to answer them, as well as I can."[111]

Though many reviewers would praise the work that Oswald Garrison Villard would later call "the only first-class job I have ever done," Annie was disappointed in it.[112] Despite her efforts, his treatment of Pottawatomie, which he referred to as a "terrible violation of the statute and the moral law," pained her.[113] Her brother Salmon—also interviewed by Mayo—complained to Sanborn about the "snare" that Villard had set for him.[114] Sanborn made his disappointment known publicly, writing that the Brown children felt ill-used.[115] With the appearance of Hill Peebles Wilson's scathing indictment of Brown in 1913, Annie and her siblings were again enraged.[116] None of the Brown children would live to see the harsh criticisms published by Robert Penn Warren and James Malin a few decades later, though one Brown granddaughter would later sue Warner Brothers over its portrayal of Brown in the movie *Santa Fe Trail* (1940).[117]

In the decade after Villard's biography was published, Annie's remaining siblings died one by one. Owen, John Jr., and Ruth were long dead by the time it appeared, and her brothers Jason and Salmon died in 1912 and 1919, respectively.[118] Annie also outlived her younger sisters Sarah and Ellen. Sarah had lost her job at the San Francisco mint after Democrat Grover Cleveland's election in 1884, and she returned to the Saratoga area where she combined teaching music and art with orchard work and volunteer tutoring of Japanese immigrants. She had remained close to Ellen's family, one ultimately consisting of seven daughters and a son. Like all her sisters, Ellen remained poor throughout her life, constantly struggling to make orchard work supplement James Fablinger's pay as a teacher.[119] Brown's youngest daughters Sarah and Ellen died in the summer of 1916. Each suffered from cancer, and Ellen died a month after Sarah's passing.[120] The sisters were buried next to Mary Brown in Madronia Cemetery in Saratoga.

After Samuel's death in 1914, Annie lived alone for the first time in her life.[121] Within a few years of becoming a widow, she moved to nearby Holmes Flat, California, to live close to her daughter Bertha's family.[122] During these years, Annie spent a lot of time with her grandchildren, especially Bertha's youngest daughter Alice, who had the daily task of helping her grandmother button her shoes. One morning, Alice recalls, she found Annie with "tears in her eyes." Even at this point in her life, Annie continued to read and "correct" scholarship on Brown, and she had again been disappointed by something she had read. It was not an interpretation of Brown that had so upset her; instead it was a reference to the Brown family's poverty. "The book," her granddaughter Alice recalls, "said John Brown's family lived on Johnny Cake and honey. She had drawn red lines through it and in the margin listed all of the things they did have." She added, "I'm sure she loved her father and was defending him."[123]

Annie died on October 3, 1926, just thirteen days before she would have marked the sixty-seventh anniversary of Brown's raid at Harpers Ferry and her own work at the Kennedy farmhouse.[124] She was buried at a small cemetery in Rohnerville.[125] Many newspapers carried accounts of the death of "John's Brown Daughter."[126] The *Los Angeles Times* opened its article, "Another link of pre–Civil War days has been severed with the death of Annie Brown Adams, last surviving member of the family of John Brown of Harper's Ferry fame." At long last, Annie likely would have been gratified by the *Times*'s recognition of her "spectacular, tragic girlhood" and her role at the Kennedy farmhouse.[127]

Epilogue

The Last Echo from John Brown's Grave

> My work like that of the rest was a freewill offering,
> not something to boast of or exhibit myself for. I may
> be a relic of John Brown's raid on Harper's Ferry, but
> I do not want to be placed on exhibition with other
> relics and curios, as such.
>
> —Annie Brown Adams, 1892

A piece in the *Hartford Courant* a few weeks after Annie's death reveals Americans' continued fascination with John Brown and their resulting interest in his kin. The article opened by stating that Annie, the "only surviving child of John Brown," had died. Her death, it continued, "recalls the colorful career of the Torrington-born abolitionist whose ill-fated Ferry adventure hurried on the Civil War and caused him to be immortalized in song, legend and history."[1] Its headline is striking, given the place of Brown's family in post–Civil War America: "Last Echo from John Brown's Grave: Death of Daughter, Who Guarded Torrington Native as He Prepared for Raid, Revives Question Whether Abolitionist Was Martyr or Villain." Annie's life, like those of her mother and siblings, was shaped by the family's radical antislavery creed, from an antebellum participation in Brown's mission to the particular brand of celebrity that the Brown lineage granted to his kin in post–Civil War America. During their lifetime, the Brown women were well known. Whether famous or infamous, they were frequently highlighted by the press. This culminated in 1882 when Mary was paraded in front of crowds from Chicago to Topeka to Boston and used to stake claims to particular histories of the antislavery movement.

The response to Annie's death marked a "last echo" not just from Brown's grave but for the Brown women's renown. Despite their celebrity then— and the continued fame of John Brown—at present the Brown women's history is little known, even among Civil War buffs or Brown aficionados. Even Annie is rarely mentioned in the narrative of Brown's raid, apart from the aside that she was Brown's "housekeeper."[2] Annie's grave site is not designated as any kind of historic place; in fact, until recent work by Brown descendant Alice Keesey Mecoy, it was even difficult to find. In Saratoga, visitors do occasionally come to the Madronia Cemetery to see the graves of Mary, Sarah, Ellen, and Jean Libby and local historians have worked tirelessly to recover their lives there.[3] In Pasadena, some residents celebrate their link to Owen Brown, but Ruth's presence is rarely mentioned. Despite the fact that a treacherous hike is required to reach it, Owen's grave atop a mountain still draws visitors. Ruth's grave, though in good shape, is not visited or marked with any kind of distinction.

Recently, at the bicentennial of Brown's birth and the sesquicentennial of his raid, the Brown women garnered some limited attention. Alice Keesey Mecoy, great-great granddaughter of Annie Brown, appeared at the 150th anniversary conference at Harpers Ferry in October 2009; she blogs about her experience of researching her family history.[4] In upstate New York, Adirondack historian and author Sandra Weber performs "Times of Trouble," a musical program depicting the lives of Mary and John Brown, while Peggy Eyres penned the song "Mary Brown, Abolitionist" for a 1997 CD celebrating Adirondack life and history.[5] Greg Artzner and Terry Leonino, the musical duo Magpie, released a CD of music to commemorate Brown's story that includes a cover of Peggy Eyres's song about Mary and an original song about Annie's experience at the Kennedy farm.[6] Magpie also performs *Sword of the Spirit*, a one-act play featuring John and Mary Brown.[7] In their play, Mary Brown is eloquently expressive and ever faithful, a true believer in Brown's cause. A final contemporary depiction of the Brown women comes from a 2009 performance by the Kansas City Lyric Opera of *John Brown*. It is an opera written by Kirke Mechem Jr., son of a past director of the Kansas State Historical Society.[8] Mechem takes creative license with the Brown women's story, transporting Annie and Martha—along with Frederick Douglass—to Kansas, where Annie appears as a grown woman supporting her father in his work there as well as at Harpers Ferry.[9] All of these presentations highlight the Brown women's bravery and belief in the antislavery cause, and they represent commendable efforts to get the Brown women's story out to the American public. While true to varying degrees, they are also uncomplicated, unlike the account I hope that I have provided here.

With this book, I have aimed to recapture the experiences of the Brown women, both their involvement in Brown's antislavery work and their lives outside of it. Frustratingly little can be found about certain periods and elements of their lives. However extraordinary their connection to Brown's antislavery activism rendered their lives, they also remained ordinary, removed from both record keeping and record making. But for their soldiering in his "army," the lives that the Brown women led would have been confined to the ordinary realm of domestic life. Thinking about her connections to Brown's raiders, Annie once proclaimed to Franklin Sanborn that "a soldier could understand the tie that bound us without explanation."[10] The Brown women were also bound by their antislavery activism—and more than that, by their ties to John Brown. Perhaps they felt that only another Brown could truly understand their atypical experience and place in American life, before and after Brown's raid. Each of their lives blended typical female life with extraordinary happenings, perhaps most notably with daughter Annie's participation in the Harpers Ferry raid.

Brown's raid ultimately brought on sectional breakdown, the Civil War, and the demise of American slavery. Forever after, the war and Brown's raid were indelibly linked, most visibly in the mural by John Steuart Curry that hangs in the Kansas Statehouse. For many Americans, to grapple with John Brown was to wrestle with the ultimate meaning of the Civil War. Americans understood the post–Harpers Ferry Brown women through the lens of a changing and contested memory of John Brown. As ever, the rendering of the past served the present. Americans angry about the causes and consequences of the Civil War, particularly those linked to the four million slaves that the war freed, lashed out at the Brown women. Pro-Confederate groups chased them across the prairie on their westward trek, while an 1882 Georgia newspaper dismissed Mary Brown as the wife of a thief and miscegenationist. Admirers, on the other hand, sanitized Brown's memory in the late nineteenth century. Those who appeared to laud him in Topeka and Boston in 1882 rarely alluded to Brown's radical stance on race; instead, they remembered him as a critical link in the battle to end slavery and as a courageous warrior, and his children were commended for their links to him. Whether Brown's children embraced their heritage or attempted to flee it, they never escaped the shadow of their father.

In telling the story of the Brown women, I have tried, as Annie once chided Alexander Ross, to place them before the world in their "true light." The complicated picture that emerges from this might not please everyone, especially the most fervent of Brown's admirers, but I have tried to be faithful to what I know as well as what I cannot know from the evidence that is left of their lives, ideas, and experiences. Their devotion to Brown's cause is not as simplistic as abolitionists in 1859—and Brown supporters in decades hence—have depicted it. But in their post–Harpers Ferry lives, Mary and Ruth worked, each in her own way, to uphold Brown's memory. Notably, neither they nor Annie worked in what we might call civil rights efforts after emancipation.[11] Most Americans did not notice this because the narrowed vision matched their own.

Regardless, the cost of the women's participation in Brown's antislavery work was high. Perhaps the Browns would have been poor regardless of John Brown's choices and notoriety, but the loss of husband and sons for her to depend on made Mary Brown's economic straits even harder. For the Browns who participated in his violence, Annie included, there appears to have been a psychological cost as well. Only Henry Thompson, secure in his domestic life with Ruth, seems to have escaped the frantic search for refuge that marked John Jr., Jason, and Owen's lives in the decades after 1859.[12] The "ties that bound" the Brown women were multifaceted: a need to defend their father against attacks on his legacy, a link to charity from the outside world, and, for Annie especially, a never-ending struggle to discern what it had all meant.

✣ Acknowledgments

I first became interested in the women of John Brown's family in 2005 when I read a biography of the radical icon and wondered about the experiences of his female kin. Uncovering their story and seeking its intersection with American memory of radical antislavery has engaged my deepest intellectual passion. It has also brought me into contact with numerous individuals to whom I am indebted. It is with much gratitude that I acknowledge the individuals and institutions that helped shape this work.

At Cornell University Press, Michael McGandy worked diligently to shepherd this book through to publication. Sarah Grossman offered assistance and was ever ready to answer my pesky questions about images and other production matters. Manuscript editor Susan Specter oversaw the final stages of publication and provided helpful guidance. Copyeditor Glenn Novak sharpened my prose and helped to further clarify my ideas. I owe special thanks to the press's anonymous reader and to reader Evan Carton for helpful suggestions on the manuscript and for the time and care that each gave it. Their suggestions and questions, along with those of Michael, Susan, and Glenn, have made this a much better work.

I also thank Wendy Gamber for her steady counsel and support. Her generous feedback has helped throughout the writing of this book. Steve Stowe has also been a critical reader, ever ready to ask astute questions as well as to share my fascination with modern memory of the Civil War. Nicole Etcheson has been an invaluable mentor and role model as well as an astute reader. I owe her tremendous thanks. Ed Linenthal offered helpful insight into violence, trauma, and memory. At Indiana I also benefited from the knowledge and advice of Konstantin Dierks, Ellen Dwyer, Sarah Knott, Deidre Lynch, and Jim Madison. I had the opportunity while at Indiana to work at the *Journal of American History.* Susan Armeny, Steve Andrews, Deneise Hueston, Nancy Croker, and my fellow EAs made my three years working there a pleasure, intellectually and otherwise. I also thank Leslie Brown, Jerry Cooper, Louis Gerteis, Chuck Korr, and Laura Westhoff for their mentoring at the University of Missouri–St. Louis. Steve Aylward, Joan Bugnitz, Miles Grier, Frank Kovarik, Steve Missey, Dan Monahan, Rich Moran, Peggy Pride, and Terry Quinn were generous and inspiring colleagues at St. Louis University High School.

I appreciate the writers, historians, and scholars who have offered feedback, advice, and invaluable information during my research for this book. As he worked on *Midnight Rising,* Tony Horwitz exchanged ideas and information with me about Annie Brown. I appreciate materials that he sent, feedback that he offered, and the opportunities that he provided to have exchanges with someone else who was elbow-deep in Brown sources and Annie's story. I owe special thanks to W. Caleb McDaniel for suggestions on an early draft of chapters 3 and 4. I am also grateful to Greg Artzer, David Blight, Ronald Butchart, Mary Chiao, Louis DeCaro Jr., Paul Finkelman, Blake Gilpin, Julie Holcomb, Andrew Kahrl, Carol Lasser, Jean Libby, Robert McGlone, Alice Keesey Mecoy, Sandra Petrulionis, David Reynolds, Peggy Russo, John Stauffer, and LeeAnn Whites for feedback, advice, and fruitful leads. Through Jean Libby I made the acquaintance of Alice Cook Hunt, who lived with her grandmother Annie Brown Adams until Annie's death in 1926, when Alice was ten. Alice wrote out two reminiscences and mailed them to me, an extraordinarily generous act for someone she had never personally met. In the early stages of my research I attended a weeklong seminar on biography and women's history at Radcliffe. I thank Nancy Cott and Megan Marshall for facilitating the seminar and my writing workshop, respectively. I received helpful feedback from Carol Faulkner, Lori Ginzberg, Melanie Gustafson, Hélène Quanquin, Jennifer Ross-Nazzal, Carolyn Stefanco, Laura Wexler, and Sharon Wood. For feedback on conference presentations I am indebted to Janet Beck, Victoria Bynum, Evan Carton, Nicole Etcheson, Lynne Getz, Julie Holcomb, Julie Roy Jeffrey, Bruce Laurie, Brian McKnight, and Stephen Towne. Colleagues at Appalachian State University provided valuable feedback on my final chapter. I owe particular debts to Michael

Behrent, Judkin Browning, Alima Bucciantini, Andrea Burns, Lynne Getz, Ralph Lentz, Myra Pennell, Sheila Phipps, and Neva Specht; to James Puffer for last-minute editorial assistance; and to the wonderful students I taught there, particularly those who enrolled in my course on John Brown and continually challenged me to think about my sources and Brown's relevance to modern America and Americans. I thank my new colleagues at Eastern Illinois University for their warm welcome and support for my research.

Archivists and librarians assisted me in gathering materials about the Brown women, both onsite and from afar. I am grateful to the distance education librarians and interlibrary loan staff at Indiana University and to Diana Johnson at Appalachian State University for procuring materials. My research on the Brown women took me all over the country, from upstate New York to Southern California. At the Huntington Library I thank Meredith Berbee, Peter Blodgett, Lita Garcia, Juan Gomez, Susi Krasnoo, Diana Pam, and especially Olga Tsapina, who worked to help secure the three images from the Ella Towne Thompson scrapbook that appear in this book. At the Massachusetts Historical Society I thank Anne Bentley, Peter Drummey, Elaine Grublin, and Conrad Wright. Gwen Mayer was a great source of help during my visit to the Hudson Library and Historical Society. Virgil Dean and the staff of the Kansas State Historical Society made a few days there highly productive. Virgil provided context for Mary Brown's visit to Topeka in 1882 as I prepared an article on the topic, and he and the press's two anonymous readers offered helpful feedback that allowed me to sharpen my argument about Mary Brown's appearance there. I am grateful to *Kansas History* for allowing me to reprint portions of that article in chapter 6. Linda DeLong at the Humboldt County Historical Society, April Hope Halberstadt at the Saratoga History Museum, Laura Walker Cooskey at the Mattole Valley Historical Society, and Jean Libby made my trip to northern California very fruitful. Curt Hanson at the University of North Dakota and Jean Martello at the St. Lawrence County Historical Society helped me track down copies of relatively obscure letters by Ruth Brown Thompson. Constance Maroli-Skocay at the Concord Free Public Library helped me find materials relating to the Brown daughters' time in Concord. Additionally, I appreciate assistance from the reference and archival staffs at the Bancroft Library, Boston Public Library, Chicago Historical Society, Columbia University, Cornell University, Houghton Library, Ohio Historical Society, Pasadena History Museum, Smith College Archives, Stanford University Archives, SUNY–Plattsburgh's Special Collections, and West Virginia State Archives. For permission to quote from their manuscript collections I thank the Boston Public Library, Chicago Historical Society, Concord Free Public

Library, Huntington Library, Massachusetts Historical Society, Ohio Historical Society, and Stanford University Archives.

I was financially assisted in both my research and writing by a number of institutions. I thank the History Department and College of Arts and Sciences at Indiana University for their support for both research and writing. A short-term research fellowship from the Massachusetts Historical Society inaugurated my research on the Brown women, while funding from the Gilder Lehrman Foundation facilitated my use of the phenomenal Oswald Garrison Villard Manuscripts at Columbia. A one-month fellowship at the Huntington Library enabled me to make use of Brown family and California history resources and to finish writing the dissertation that became this book in the loveliest setting that a historian could imagine. A one-year writing fellowship from the Charlotte Newcombe Foundation allowed me time to think through questions related to Brown's use of violent means. A new faculty research fellowship from Appalachian State University allowed me to do further research on the Brown children and to place them in a broader context.

Well before the time that I was actively studying the Brown women, good teachers inspired me to pursue historical study. I thank high school teachers Larry Marsh and Doug Lane for introducing me to scholarly pursuit of history (and literature) and for being role models of engaged teachers and learners. In our present era in which teachers are under attack from many quarters, it is especially important to me to recognize their role in shaping my ideas about the past—and about what my own future could be. I am ever grateful for my undergraduate experience at Knox College. Penny Gold first introduced me to women's history, while Rich Christen oversaw my training in history education. I cannot sufficiently express my gratitude to Rodney Davis and George Steckley. I spent many afternoons working in George Steckley's office in Old Main, adding records to his Admiralty Court database and providing other research assistance. It is clear to me now that it was this experience that made me eager to have my own set of historical questions to answer (not to mention my own microfilm reader). I am still trying to develop a library research assignment that has the same rigor and long-term effects as the one employed by Rodney Davis in his upper-level courses. He, too, schooled me in the art of being a historian in course work and in his hiring of me as a research assistant for a Lincoln papers transcription project the summer after I graduated. Both of them exhibited generosity, high standards, and an engagement with teaching that made an indelible impression on me.

Last but certainly not least, I thank my family and good friends. My parents, Jim and Kay Laughlin, have consistently offered help in ways large and small. Our early vacations to Springfield, Illinois, and Mansfield, Missouri, surely instilled a love of nineteenth-century America in me. Since we were little, my brother David has been one of my best friends, and now that we are grown-ups I appreciate the friendship that he and his wife, Rachel, offer. I am also grateful to Jo and Bob Freese, Glen and Laura Owens, Jay and Karen Sadlon, Bill and Stephanie Schultz, Jared Schultz, and to all four of my grandparents: William and Kathryn Owens and Kevin and Dorothy Laughlin. Shannon Smith, Laura Burt, Erin Crawford, Karen Dunak, Christine Dunn, Katie Fitzpatrick, Debbie Kraus, and Neva Specht have enriched my life with their friendship. In addition, Karen and Shannon read countless drafts of chapters and offered invaluable critique and encouragement.

My grandfather William Howard Owens died when I was a college freshman, but I still hear him telling me to go at it with gusto. Every child should have such a supporter. My grandfather did not live long enough to meet the two men who share the name William in my present life, though I will always fervently wish that he had. My husband Bill gave me the book that sparked my interest in the Brown women, and he has put up with them (as well as me) for the last eight years. His love, encouragement, and steady calm ground me. I foolishly thought that I could finish this manuscript in the first months after our son Henry William arrived in May 2010. As I write this more than two and a half years later, I am delighted by all the ways he has disrupted my work. His wholehearted embrace of the world and his curiosity inspire me, and I am very grateful for the little world that the three of us share.

❧ Notes

The following abbreviations have been used in the notes:

BFC	Brown Family Collection, Huntington Library, San Marino, CA
BGC	Brown-Gee Collection, Hudson Library and Historical Society, Hudson, OH
BPL	Anti-Slavery Manuscripts, Boston Public Library
CC-SUNY	Edwin N. Cotter Jr. Collection on John Brown, 2002.1, Special Collections, Feinberg Library, SUNY–Plattsburgh
CFPL	William Monroe Special Collections, Concord Free Public Library, Concord, MA
CHS	John Brown Collection, Chicago Historical Society
ELDR	James William Eldridge Papers, 1797–1902, Huntington Library, San Marino, CA
GLC	Gilder Lehrman Collection, on deposit at the New-York Historical Society
HLHS	Houghton Library and Historical Society, Hudson, OH
HUNT	Huntington Library, San Marino, CA
JBJR	John Brown Jr. Papers (microfilm), Ohio Historical Society, Columbus
KSHS	Kansas State Historical Society, Topeka
KTO	John Brown Collection (Kansas State Historical Society), Kansas Territorial Online, http://www.territorialkansasonline.org/~imlskto/cgi-bin/index.php
LoC	Manuscripts Division, Library of Congress

MAY	Samuel J. May Anti-Slavery Manuscript Collection, #4601, Division of Rare Books and Manuscripts, Cornell University Library, Ithaca, NY
MHS	Massachusetts Historical Society, Boston
OGL	Orin G. Libby Papers, Elwyn B. Robinson Department of Special Collections, Chester Fritz Library, University of North Dakota, Grand Forks
OGV	John Brown (Oswald Garrison Villard) Manuscripts, Columbia University, Rare Books and Manuscripts Library, New York
RUST	Horatio Nelson Rust Papers, 1799–1906, mss RU 1–1231, Huntington Library, San Marino, CA
S/AC	Slavery/Antislavery Collection, Sophia Smith Collection, Smith College Archives, Northampton, MA
SFP	Stevens Family Papers, 1770–1911, Ms. N-966, Massachusetts Historical Society, Boston
SLCHS	St. Lawrence County Historical Society, Canton, NY
SPRING	M0541, Rebecca Spring Papers, ca. 1830–1900, Department of Special Collections and University Archives, Stanford University Libraries, Palo Alto, CA
STUT	Boyd Blynn Stutler Collection of John Brown Papers, 1821–1961, microfilm, West Virginia State Archives, Charleston
STUTDB	John Brown/Boyd B. Stutler Collection Database, West Virginia Memory Project, West Virginia State Archives, http://www.wvculture.org/history/wvmemory/jbdetail.aspx?Type=Text&Id=712
SYKES	Velma West Sykes Collection of John Brown Papers, 1832–1964, microfilm, Kansas State Historical Society, Topeka

Introduction

1. Ruth Brown Thompson to John Brown, February 20, 1858, in Franklin Sanborn, *Life and Letters of John Brown, Liberator of Kansas, and Martyr of Virginia*, 3rd ed. (Concord, MA: Franklin Sanborn, 1910), 442.

2. Watson Brown to Bell Brown, September 8, 1859, in Sanborn, *Life and Letters*, 542.

3. Louisa May Alcott to Anna Alcott Pratt, [May 27], 1860, in *The Selected Letters of Louisa May Alcott*, ed. Joel Myerson, Daniel Shealy, and Madeleine B. Stern (Boston: Little, Brown, 1987), 55.

4. Thomas Wentworth Higginson, as quoted in James Redpath, *The Public Life of Capt. John Brown, with an Auto-Biography of His Childhood and Youth* (Boston: Thayer and Eldridge, 1860), 66.

5. Ellen Brown to John Brown, November 1859, in *Echoes of Harper's Ferry*, ed. James Redpath (Boston: Thayer and Eldridge, 1860), 428.

6. "Speech by Ralph Waldo Emerson," in Redpath, *Echoes of Harper's Ferry*, 121. On the widespread belief that women were thought more naturally led by the heart—and thus more sympathetic—see Karen Halttunen, *Confidence Men and Painted Women: A Study of Middle-Class Culture in America, 1830–1870* (New Haven, CT: Yale University Press, 1982), esp. chap. 3.

7. Richard Henry Dana, "How We Met John Brown," *Atlantic Monthly*, July 1871, 5.

8. One of the few scholarly pieces to look at Brown's family is Robert E. McGlone, "Rescripting a Troubled Past: John Brown's Family and the Harpers Ferry Conspiracy," *Journal of American History* 75, no. 4 (1989): 1179–1200. Perhaps understandably, McGlone is most interested in the Brown sons, particularly in parsing out how they built memories of the past steeped in guilt over their nonparticipation at Harpers Ferry. Two other exceptions are Paul Finkelman, "Manufacturing Martyrdom: The Antislavery Response to John Brown's Raid," in *His Soul Goes Marching On: Responses to John Brown and the Harpers Ferry Raid*, ed. Paul Finkelman (Charlottesville: University of Virginia Press, 1995); and Wendy Hamand Venet, "'Cry Aloud and Spare Not': Northern Antislavery Women and John Brown's Raid," ibid.

9. Since 2002, six new biographical treatments of Brown have appeared: Louis A. DeCaro Jr., *"Fire from the Midst of You": A Religious Life of John Brown* (New York: NYU Press, 2002); John Stauffer, *The Black Hearts of Men: Radical Abolitionists and the Transformation of Race* (Cambridge, MA: Harvard University Press, 2002); David Reynolds, *John Brown, Abolitionist: The Man Who Killed Slavery, Sparked the Civil War, and Seeded Civil Rights* (New York: Alfred A. Knopf, 2005); Evan Carton, *Patriotic Treason: John Brown and the Soul of America* (New York: Simon & Schuster, 2006); Robert E. McGlone, *John Brown's War against Slavery* (Cambridge: Cambridge University Press, 2009); and Tony Horwitz, *Midnight Rising: John Brown and the Raid That Sparked the Civil War* (New York: Henry Holt, 2011). In addition, four documentary readers, two anthologies, and countless articles have been published.

10. I believe that physical depictions of Mary Brown have unfairly influenced how she is portrayed by Brown scholars. In his *John Brown: The Making of a*

Martyr, Brown detractor Robert Penn Warren built on the tradition of citing Mary's physical features and her reticence as proof of her inner inferiority. After telling the story of Brown's marriage proposal, Warren wrote that "beneath a certain awkwardness was a great physical vigor, and the embarrassed silences cover a profound, unquestioning devotion to the hard responsibilities of her life. She was ignorant, but possessed a primitive stoicism which meant an efficient if sometimes uncomprehending adaptability to fact." He also described Mary in the 1850s: "The raw-boned, silent girl, who had left the spinning in John Brown's house to take up the more arduous business of being his helpmate, was now a woman, worn by the hard experiences of her life. Still awkward, still ignorant, but competent and stoic." This notion of Mary as "stoic," less than bright, and "primitive" shows up in more-recent biographies of Brown. Stephen Oates quoted Warren directly in his biography, and he, David Reynolds, and Evan Carton classify Mary as a "follower" of John Brown. All of them focus on Mary's physical features: Reynolds notes that Mary was "dour-faced" and "persevering," while Oates and Louis DeCaro Jr. repeat the typical description of her as big-boned. Robert Penn Warren, *John Brown: The Making of a Martyr* (Nashville, TN: Payson and Clark, 1929), 29, 127; Stephen Oates, *To Purge This Land with Blood: A Biography of John Brown* (New York: Harper & Row, 1971), 26; Carton, *Patriotic Treason*, 164; Reynolds, *John Brown, Abolitionist*, 50, 126; DeCaro, *"Fire from the Midst of You,"* 84.

11. Franklin Sanborn to George Stearns, Amos Lawrence, and other subscribers to the John Brown fund, August 25, 1857, STUT, reel 1. Italics mine.

12. This characterization of the Brown women's role stems from conversation with historian LeeAnn Whites. In her work, she argues that in 1850s and Civil War Missouri, for instance, women's labor in supplying men was essential—not peripheral—to the war effort. See LeeAnn Whites, "Forty Shirts and a Wagonload of Wheat: Women, the Domestic Supply Line, and the Civil War on the Western Border," *Journal of the Civil War Era* 1 (March 2011): 56–78; and LeeAnn Whites and Alecia P. Long, eds., *Occupied Women: Gender, Military Occupation, and the American Civil War* (Baton Rouge: LSU Press, 2009).

13. See Julie Roy Jeffrey, *The Great Silent Army of Abolitionism: Ordinary Women in the Antislavery Movement* (Chapel Hill: University of North Carolina Press, 1998). The Brown women's experience challenges a historiographical approach to abolitionism (and the larger Civil War) that is often dominated by a "separate spheres" mentality. Brown scholarship, on the other hand, is dominated by discussions of (masculine) violence. The experience of the Brown women straddles this divide. Key recent scholarship on women and antislavery includes Carol Faulkner, "The Root of the Evil: Free Produce and Radical Antislavery, 1820–1860," *Journal of the Early Republic* 27, no. 3 (2007): 377–405; Jeffrey, *Great Silent Army*; Alison Portnoy, *Their Right to Speak: Women's Activism in the Indian and Slave Debates* (Cambridge, MA: Harvard University Press, 2005); Stacey Robertson, *Hearts Beating for Liberty: Women Abolitionists in the Old Northwest* (Chapel Hill: University of North Carolina Press, 2010); Beth Salerno, *Sister Societies: Women's Antislavery Organizations in Antebellum America* (DeKalb: Northern Illinois University, 2005); Jean Fagan Yellin and John C. Van Horne, eds., *The Abolitionist Sisterhood: Women's Political Culture in Antebellum America* (Ithaca, NY: Cornell University Press, 1994). On women

and violence, see Margaret Hope Bacon, "By Moral Force Alone: The Antislavery Women and Nonresistance," in Yellin and Van Horne, *Abolitionist Sisterhood*, 275–97; Jeffrey, *Great Silent Army*, chap. 5; Kristin Tegtmeier Oertel, *Bleeding Borders: Race, Gender, and Violence in Pre–Civil War Kansas* (Baton Rouge: LSU Press, 2009); and Wendy Hamand Venet, *Neither Ballots nor Bullets: Women Abolitionists and the Civil War* (Charlottesville: University of Virginia Press, 1991).

14. Julie Roy Jeffrey notes that women in Hudson, OH, sent some objects to the Boston and Philadelphia antislavery fairs in the late 1830s and early 1840s, so it is possible that Mary and Ruth did this. See Jeffrey, *Great Silent Army*, 111. Jeffrey's work is about so-called "ordinary" (and ofttimes rural and midwestern) women, she also highlights class issues at work. See also Jeffrey, "'Stranger, Buy . . . Lest Our Mission Fail': The Complex Culture of Women's Abolitionist Fairs," *American Nineteenth Century History* 4, no. 1 (2003): 1–24. On women's antislavery activism in Ohio, see Robertson, *Hearts Beating for Liberty*.

15. For "peculiarly woman's cause," see Frederick Douglass, *Life and Times of Frederick Douglass* (Hartford, CT: Park Publishing Co., 1882), 551, accessed at http:// books.google.com/books?id=EQmknGd90hUC. Much of the work on female antislavery also emphasizes nineteenth-century female abolitionists' beliefs in what Julie Roy Jeffrey describes as "women's special duty" to end slavery. The Brown women seem not to have had this same belief, perhaps because John Brown himself emphasized the ideal of (human) sympathy for all in his family, male and female. Jeffrey, *Great Silent Army*, 36; Julie Roy Jeffrey, "The Liberty Women of Boston: Evangelicalism and Antislavery Politics," *New England Quarterly* 85 (March 2012): 38–77; and Salerno, *Sister Societies*, 6.

16. This is not to say that other women did not also chafe against gender constraints, just that the Brown women did not seem to turn rhetoric on its head in order to make women special agents of antislavery the way that some others did. On hot water, see Ruth Brown Thompson in Sanborn, *Life and Letters*, 132; on her plea to be involved, see Ruth Brown Thompson to John Brown, February 20, 1858, in ibid., 442.

17. John Brown to "my dear wife and children," January 30, 1858, ibid., 441.

18. Brown's letters—part of what Paul Finkelman credits with his "manufacturing" of martyrdom—were reprinted in one of James Redpath's memorial volumes as well as in newspapers in the days surrounding his execution. Redpath, *Echoes of Harper's Ferry*, 387–433; Finkelman, "Manufacturing Martyrdom."

19. John Brown Jr. to Franklin Sanborn, June 11, 1882, HM 3621, HUNT. Reproduced by permission of the Huntington Library.

20. Finkelman, "Manufacturing Martyrdom."

21. In part, the Brown fame arose from the antebellum public sphere's "emerging" culture of celebrity. Advancements in print culture, the mass publication of memoirs and biographies, and urbanization (among other factors) created a relish for sensationalism. Accordingly, the Brown name offered Mary and her daughters what Pierre Bourdieu has labeled "symbolic capital," that is, the "prestige and renown attached to a family and a name" that was "readily convertible back into economic capital." For the Browns, their symbolic status brought much-needed "economic capital." David Haven Blake, *Walt Whitman and the Culture of American*

Celebrity (New Haven, CT: Yale University Press, 2006), 41–48; Pierre Bourdieu, "Structures, Habitus, Power: Basis for a Theory of Symbolic Power," in *Culture/Power/History: A Reader in Contemporary Social Theory*, ed. Nicholas B. Dirks, Geoff Eley, and Sherry B. Ortner (Princeton, NJ: Princeton University Press, 1994), 174. See also Thomas N. Baker, *Sentiment and Celebrity: Nathaniel Parker Willis and the Trials of Literary Fame* (New York: Oxford University Press, 1999); Leo Braudy, *The Frenzy of Renown: Fame and Its History* (New York: Oxford University Press, 1986); and Joy Kasson, *Buffalo Bill's Wild West: Celebrity, Memory, and Popular History* (New York: Hill & Wang, 2000.

22. Higginson, as quoted in Redpath, *Public Life of Capt. John Brown*, 60–72; Theodore Tilton, "A Personal Interview with Captain Brown's Wife," *Independent*, November 17, 1859.

23. *Red Bluff (CA) Semi-Weekly Independent*, October 3, 1864, as quoted in "John Brown's family in Tehama County," typescript manuscript, SYKES.

24. Brian Jordan argues that Union veteran amputees became "living monuments," that their bodies themselves became "obvious sites for remembering the war." This idea of bodies themselves as "obvious sites for remembering the war" is very useful to me in thinking about Brown's children. Though quite different from his wounded Union veterans, they were equally recognizable, especially for Brown supporters and those looking to uphold an emancipationist memory of the war. Brian Jordan, "Living Monuments: Union Veteran Amputees and the Embodied Memory of the Civil War," *Civil War History* 57 (June 2011): 121, 122.

25. In an article on the 1876 Centennial Exhibition, Susanna Gold describes memory as "more a reflection of the present needs of the community than of real events." The "function" of memory, she adds, "is not to chronicle the past but to communicate ideas about it." Susanna W. Gold, "'Fighting It Over Again': The Battle of Gettysburg at the 1876 Centennial Exhibition," *Civil War History* 54 (September 2008): 278.

26. I use the terms "memory making" and "memory" to describe what was in reality not one memory but a contest over how Brown and the abolitionists would be remembered. To indicate this contested—and continually constructed—nature, I could instead use the plural and refer to "memories" of the Civil War, Harpers Ferry, and John Brown. While I think the plural is helpful in terms of stressing the subjective nature of historical memory and the multiplicity of "truths" put forward about Brown and the Civil War era, it misses the contested nature of historical memory—that historical actors do not see themselves as putting forward one of many possible memories, but the truth about the past. This would certainly prove true for Brown's children, as well as abolitionists. See David Thelen, ed., *Memory and American History* (Bloomington: Indiana University Press, 1990); Jay Winter, *Remembering War: The Great War between Memory and History in the Twentieth Century* (New Haven, CT: Yale University Press, 2006), introduction.

27. On the broad shift in memory, see David Blight, *Race and Reunion: The Civil War in American Memory* (Cambridge, MA: Belknap Press of Harvard University Press, 2001). Recent works have complicated Blight's thesis, identifying groups or subjects that kept debate about or emancipationist narratives of the "won cause" at the forefront. John Neff suggests the need to temper the idea that a sentiment

of reconciliation dominated white American memory. He argues that while the reunion movement was "genuine and real," it was "not the sole response to the war." Importantly, commemoration of the dead "remained the polestar of sometimes bitter memory." John Neff, *Honoring the Civil War Dead: Commemoration and the Problem of Reconciliation* (Lawrence: University Press of Kansas, 2005). See also William A. Blair, *Cities of the Dead: Contesting the Memory of the Civil War in the South, 1865–1914* (Chapel Hill: University of North Carolina Press, 2004); Barbara A. Gannon, *The Won Cause: Black and White Comradeship in the Grand Army of the Republic* (Chapel Hill: University of North Carolina Press, 2011); M. Keith Harris, "Slavery, Emancipation, and Veterans of the Union Cause: Commemorating Freedom in the Era of Reconciliation, 1885–1915," *Civil War History* 53 (September 2007): 264–90; Jordan, "Living Monuments"; and Joan Waugh, *U.S. Grant: American Hero, American Myth* (Chapel Hill: University of North Carolina Press, 2009).

28. As Barbara Taylor has dryly noted, biography can be a "controversial enterprise for historians." Taylor, "Separation of Soul: Solitude, Biography, History," *American Historical Review* 114 (June 2009): 641. It is telling of both biography's importance and its odd position within the academy that the *American Historical Review* published a roundtable entitled "Historians and Biography" in the summer of 2009. For examples of critique of biography, see Barbara Tuchman, "Biography as a Prism in History," in *Telling Lives: The Biographer's Art*, ed. Marc Pachter (Philadelphia: University of Pennsylvania Press, 1981), 145; and Lori Ginzberg, "The Pleasures (and Dangers) of Biography," *Journal of Women's History* 19, no. 3 (2007): 205–6.

29. Alice Kessler-Harris, "Why Biography?" *American Historical Review* 114 (June 2009): 630, 626.

30. Of the approximately 400 letters written to the Brown women, 256 were written by John Brown (66 to Mary only; 44 to Ruth and Henry; and the rest to some combination of Mary and his children), 44 were written by one of the Brown sons or daughters-in-law, 14 by one of Brown's raiders (12 addressed to Annie and 2 to Mary), 30 by abolitionists ranging from Lydia Maria Child to William Lloyd Garrison, and 4 were letters from Henry Thompson to Ruth. The rest are from various Brown family members. Of 301 letters total written by the Brown women, 65 were written by Mary Brown (dating 1848–82, with the bulk dated prior to 1865); 92 were written by Ruth Brown Thompson (dating 1853–1902, and pretty evenly divided among the decades); and 116 were written by Annie Brown Adams (dating 1858–1914, with the bulk of the letters from the 1880s and 1890s). There are also very few letters by Brown's two youngest daughters. I have only 19 written by Sarah Brown and 9 by Ellen Brown Fablinger.

31. Jean Strouse, "Semiprivate Lives," in *Studies in Biography*, ed. Daniel Aaron (Cambridge, MA: Harvard University Press, 1978), 113–31.

32. The exception is the "Brown Family Collection" at the Huntington Library in San Marino, CA, which contains a number of letters and other materials, many of which had been compiled into a scrapbook by Ruth Brown Thompson's daughter Ella Thompson Towne.

33. Robert McGlone has called this process "rescripting." McGlone, "Rescripting a Troubled Past."

34. Jeremy D. Popkin, *History, Historians, and Autobiography* (Chicago: University of Chicago Press, 2005), 23.

35. The existence of family letters does not in itself ever guarantee a complete picture of the past, of course. As Martha Hodes has recently noted in *The Sea Captain's Wife*, family letters "are nonetheless peculiar historical documents that must also be read for what is evaded or unspoken." She adds, "People's lives, and the ways in which they remember and record those lives, can never be perfect reflections of one another. The act of recounting always involves the selection of observations, the editing of emotions, even the omission of entire experiences." Martha Hodes, *The Sea Captain's Wife: A True Story of Love, Race, and War in the Nineteenth Century* (New York: W. W. Norton, 2006), 28–29.

36. The sources for Ruth and Annie's lives are relatively plentiful. A collection of letters written by Annie in the last decades of the nineteenth century are contained in the Gilder Lehrman Collection, while letters from and about Ruth as well as other materials related to her life in Southern California are held by the Huntington Library in several collections. Additionally, I was lucky enough to find a few letters from the 1870s in a small Wisconsin historical society. For Sarah and Ellen, the sources are thinner, though they as well as Annie and Ruth are well represented in the Oswald Garrison Villard collection of manuscripts and materials relating to his 1910 biography of Brown, now housed at Columbia University's rare book and manuscript library.

1. The Brown Family's Antislavery Culture, 1831–49

1. John Brown Jr. as quoted by Franklin Sanborn, "John Brown's Family Compact," *Nation*, December 25, 1890, p. 500. This account is quoted verbatim in Oswald Garrison Villard, *John Brown: A Biography Fifty Years After* (Boston: Houghton Mifflin, 1910), 45–46.

2. Three recent biographies make use of this dramatic moment. See Carton, *Patriotic Treason*, 87; Horwitz, *Midnight Rising*, 25–26; Reynolds, *John Brown, Abolitionist*, 65.

3. In an important article on the Brown family memory, Robert McGlone offers a long critique of the story and asserts that the Brown siblings reworked the past to provide themselves with "morally ambiguous and psychologically self-affirming roles." McGlone blames Sanborn for the invention of the oath to counter a flood of anti-Brown writing in the 1880s. McGlone, "Rescripting a Troubled Past," 1196.

4. See, for example, Carton, *Patriotic Treason*, 87.

5. Two female journalists attempted biographies of Mary Brown in the mid-twentieth century, though neither found a publisher. See Velma West Sykes, "Widowed by the Gallows," typed manuscript, folder 1, box 2, Velma West Sykes Papers, 1820–1975, LoC; and Grace Goulder Izant, "John Brown's Wives," typescript manuscript, folder 7, box 2, series 3, BGC. Other recent works on Mary Brown and the Brown family include Jean Libby, "John Brown's Family and Their California Refuge," *Californians* 7, no. 1 (1989): 14–23; Damon Nalty, *The Browns of Madronia* (Saratoga, CA: Saratoga Historical Foundation, 1995); and Daniel Rosenberg, *Mary*

Brown: From Harpers Ferry to California (Occasional Paper no. 17, American Institute for Marxist Studies, 1975).

6. Katherine Mayo, notes on interview with Sarah Brown, September 16–20, 1908, folder "Brown, Miss Sarah," box 6, OGV.

7. Clarence Gee notes from Boyd Stutler's John Brown scrapbook, from *Maine Republican* (Portland), December 1884 (signed by M.E.B.), folder 5, box 8, series 2, BGC. There are conflicting reports of Mary's age at the time of her marriage to John Brown, with some biographers describing her as sixteen at the time of their marriage. I believe the confusion stems from the fact that she was sixteen when she moved into his household but turned seventeen in April 1833, a few months prior to their marriage. Her tombstone lists her birth year as 1816, and I have found no convincing evidence that it is wrong.

8. Though Dianthe deserves further treatment, this book is largely confined to the years after which the movement for immediate emancipation burgeoned in the United States—and perhaps in the Brown household, though John Brown Jr. would recall his mother Dianthe feeding a fugitive slave in the 1820s. John Brown Jr., reminiscence, in Sanborn, *Life and Letters*, 35. For information about Dianthe see ibid., 17, 33–38; and Grace Goulder Izant, *Hudson's Heritage: A Chronology of the Founding and Flowering of the Village of Hudson, Ohio* (Kent, OH: Kent State University Press, 1985), 125. Some Brown biographers have made much of Dianthe's supposed bouts of mental illness. See Oates, *To Purge This Land with Blood*, 23; DeCaro, *"Fire from the Midst of You,"* 69–70; and Reynolds, *John Brown, Abolitionist*, 38.

9. Izant, *Hudson's Heritage*, 125.

10. John Brown to Henry Stearns, autobiographical letter dated July 15, 1857, in *John Brown: The Making of a Revolutionary; the Story of John Brown in His Own Words and the Words of Those Who Knew Him,* ed. Louis Ruchames (New York: Grosset & Dunlap, 1969), 48. In an account as much constructed as real, he added that she was "remarkably plain," using this to highlight these other qualities.

11. In a recollection given to Franklin Sanborn in 1882, Milton Lusk recalled his falling out with John Brown: the "austere" Brown had objected to his Sunday visits to his sister and mother when they worked for Brown. Milton Lusk, reminiscence, in Sanborn, *Life and Letters*, 33, 34.

12. For a description of New Richmond, see Oates, *To Purge This Land with Blood*, 19–22.

13. John Brown to Owen Brown (father), August 11, 1832, typescript copy, SYKES. Such deathbed scenes were not uncommon. Abraham Lincoln had been called to his mother's bedside before her death when he was ten, as had his future wife Mary Todd been called to her mother's deathbed. See David Herbert Donald, *Lincoln* (New York: Simon & Schuster, 1995), 26.

14. See Izant, *Hudson's Heritage*, 128–29.

15. Catherine Clinton, *Mrs. Lincoln: A Life* (New York: HarperCollins, 2009), 12.

16. For "urgent practical needs," see Ronald White, *A. Lincoln* (New York: Random House, 2009), 28. In the absence of courtship letters or declarations of love, Brown biographers have made much of the tale of Brown's proposal to the teenage girl. Like Dianthe, Mary offers the modern reader no letters or records that attest to

their courtship. In the early twentieth century, one of the youngest Brown children, Sarah, recounted the story of her father's proposal: "J.B. approved of her—perhaps saw the staying power in her—& one day gave her a letter offering marriage. She was so overcome that she dared not read it, but took it to bed that night & slept with it under her pillow. Next morning she found courage to read it. When she went down to the spring for water, for the house, J.B. followed her & she gave him her answer there." It would not be surprising if Brown proposed with a letter, but the more important detail is how the story was used. As he did with Dianthe in his 1857 autobiographical letter, John Brown may have used the story to highlight Mary's "plain" qualities and her devotion. But according to her daughter Sarah, it was a story that later in her life Mary would repeat frequently, with pleasure. Katherine Mayo, notes, talks with Sarah Brown, September 16–20, 1908, folder "Brown, Miss Sarah," box 6, OGV. Many scholars and Brown aficionados have used the proposal story to highlight how Mary was a "follower" of John Brown. See Villard, *John Brown*, 24–25; Sykes, "Widowed by the Gallows," chap. 1; Carton, *Patriotic Treason*, 71; and Oates, *To Purge This Land with Blood*, 26.

17. Such quick replacement was also common. Within a year of Lincoln's mother's death, his father, Thomas, married Sarah Bush Johnston, a woman with three of her own children. Lincoln's future wife, Mary Todd, had to welcome new stepmother Elizabeth Humphreys just seventeen months after her mother's death. Donald, *Lincoln*, 26–28; Clinton, *Mrs. Lincoln*, 12–13.

18. For "singularly unsuccessful," see Jean H. Baker, *Mary Todd Lincoln: A Biography* (New York: W. W. Norton, 1987), 29; for "healing," see White, *A. Lincoln*, 28.

19. Particularly in the years immediately following their marriage, it is hard to discern how close Mary was to her stepchildren: there was clearly some strain with Ruth at times, and Wealthy, John Jr.'s wife, would much later claim that Mary had not been affectionate toward any of the children. Sarah Brown would counter her, claiming, "The elder children were always devoted to her—She made them a good step-mother." Katherine Mayo, notes on interview with Mrs. John Brown Jr. [Wealthy Brown], November 30–December 3, 1908, folder "Brown, Mr. and Mrs. John Jr.," box 6, OGV; Mayo, notes on talks with Sarah Brown, September 16–20, 1908, folder "Brown, Miss Sarah," box 6, OGV.

20. Paul Finkelman describes him as "almost cruel to his children," and Bertram Wyatt-Brown also highlights his lack of tenderness and embrace of corporal punishment. David Reynolds titles one chapter "The Patriarch," while John Stauffer describes him as a "rigid domestic patriarch." Paul Finkelman and Peggy Russo, eds., *Terrible Swift Sword: The Legacy of John Brown* (Athens: Ohio University Press, 2005), xxvii; Bertram Wyatt-Brown, "'A Volcano beneath a Mountain of Snow': John Brown and the Problem of Interpretation," in Finkelman, *His Soul Goes Marching On*, 17; Reynolds, *John Brown, Abolitionist,* chap. 4; Stauffer, *Black Hearts of Men*, 91.

21. On the growth of a more affective ideal of fatherhood, see Steven Mintz, *Huck's Raft: A History of American Childhood* (Cambridge, MA: Belknap Press of Harvard University Press, 2004).

22. For "little chick," see John Brown to Mary Brown, March 7, 184[4], in *Meteor of War: The John Brown Story*, ed. John Stauffer and Zoe Trodd (New York: Brandywine Press, 2004), 50.

23. Salmon Brown, "My Father, John Brown: By Salmon Brown, the Only Survivor of Twenty Children," *Outlook*, January 25, 1913, pp. 212–13. The *Outlook*, as other periodicals at the time did, ignored the fact that three Brown daughters—Annie, Sarah, and Ellen—were yet alive.

24. Annie Brown Adams to Garibaldi Ross, December 15, 1887, 3007.17, GLC.

25. Almost without exception, John Brown is remembered as good in the sickroom. See Ruth Brown Thompson as quoted in Villard, *John Brown*, 20; Salmon Brown, "My Father, John Brown," 215.

26. John Brown to wife and children, November 26, 1838, STUT, reel 1.

27. John Stauffer is critical of Brown's corporal punishment, noting that Brown shut his eyes to the fact that it was the same "brute force" that slave owners relied on. Stauffer, *Black Hearts of Men*, 91.

28. Ruth Brown Thompson, quoted in Sanborn, *Life and Letters*, 93.

29. Annie Brown, statement written for Franklin Sanborn, November 1886, typescript copy, folder 8, box 46, CHS.

30. Stephen M. Frank, *Life with Father: Parenthood and Masculinity in the Nineteenth-Century American North* (Baltimore: Johns Hopkins University Press, 1998), 140.

31. John Brown to Henry Stearns, July 15, 1857, in Sanborn, *Life and Letters*, 12–17.

32. John Brown to Mary Brown, February 1842, STUT, reel 1. Though it is often overlooked, Brown's ideas about parenting and discipline were dynamic. His second-youngest daughter, Sarah, enjoyed drawing, and she once colored a face on the wall of the Brown home. When questioned, she professed ignorance; at this, she reported that Brown "looked her through, with solemn, piercing eyes, then said, very slowly, and gently, but with terrible solemnity: 'If you did it, you *would* know.'" "That," she added, "closed the incident. One of the older children, in such a case, would have been severely whipped." Mayo, notes on talks with Sarah Brown, September 16–20, 1908, folder "Brown, Miss Sarah," box 6, OGV.

33. John Brown to Mary Brown, August 22, 1850, box 7, ELDR. Reproduced by permission of the Huntington Library.

34. Horwitz, *Midnight Rising*, 9.

35. As recent biographer David Reynolds notes, words such as "Puritan" and "Calvinist" were and are often applied to John Brown. Unlike many other reformers, Reynolds notes, Brown "never surrendered the Calvinistic doctrines—predestination, total depravity, God's sovereignty, and so forth—he had learned from his parents." Reynolds, *John Brown, Abolitionist*, esp. 25. The only full treatment of Brown as a religious figure comes in DeCaro's *"Fire from the Midst of You."* DeCaro contends that Brown's faith was rooted in both the Old and New Testaments—and argues that this New Testament side of Brown has frequently been overlooked by other biographers.

36. Jon Butler, *Awash in a Sea of Faith: Christianizing the American People* (Cambridge, MA: Harvard University Press, 1990), 225. On the rise of immediate abolitionism and antebellum antislavery, see Robert H. Abzug, *Cosmos Crumbling: American Reform and the Religious Imagination* (New York: Oxford University Press,

1994); Paul Goodman, *Of One Blood: Abolitionism and the Origins of Racial Equality* (Berkeley: University of California Press, 1998); James B. Stewart, *Holy Warriors: The Abolitionists and American Slavery* (New York: Hill & Wang, 1976); and Ronald Walters, *The Antislavery Appeal: American Abolitionism after 1830* (Baltimore: Johns Hopkins University Press, 1978). On antebellum religion, see Mark Noll, *America's God: From Jonathan Edwards to Abraham Lincoln* (New York: Oxford University Press, 2002).

37. Leo P. Hirrel, *Children of Wrath: New School Calvinism and Antebellum Reform* (Lexington: University Press of Kentucky, 1998), 2. According to Sylvia Hoffert's recent biography, Jane Grey Swisshelm appears to have had a similar faith to Brown. Her reform impulse came, Hoffert argues, not from the Second Great Awakening but from her family's Scotch-Irish Calvinism. Grant Wacker argues that in the years after the Revolution, many Americans "drifted away" from Congregational (Puritan) beliefs. I like his use of the phrase "drifted away," as it does not imply a wholesale back-turning, allowing for how men such as John Brown and Lyman Beecher continued to be influenced by the old forms of faith as well as by the new. Sylvia Hoffert, *Jane Grey Swisshelm: An Unconventional Life, 1815–1884* (Chapel Hill: University of North Carolina Press, 2004), esp. chap. 1, "That Olde-Time Religion"; Grant Wacker, "Religion in Nineteenth-Century America," in *Religion in American Life: A Short History*, ed. Jon Butler, Grant Wacker, and Randall Ballmer (New York: Oxford University Press, 2003), 180.

38. Ruth Brown Thompson in Sanborn, *Life and Letters*, 38–39.

39. Sykes, "Widowed by the Gallows," chap. 5, pp. 8–9, in Sykes Papers, LoC.

40. A year before they moved to North Elba, Mary and Ruth had proposed that they furnish the parlor of their Springfield, Massachusetts, home. Brown opposed their choice, encouraging them to instead save the money to buy clothing for the community in North Elba; all agreed that this was the right course. Ruth Brown Thompson in Sanborn, *Life and Letters*, 100.

41. Salmon Brown recalled Brown's "sense of equity" as one of his most "striking characteristics." Salmon Brown, "My Father, John Brown," 212.

42. Douglass, *Life and Times of Frederick Douglass*, 287.

43. Douglass's use of "odd" makes me think that at least part of his notice was about gender, not just class. Frederick Douglass, "John Brown," speech at Storer College, May 30, 1881, in Ruchames, *John Brown*, 292.

44. Early scholarship on abolitionism focused intensively on the AASS, the figure of Garrison, and elite New England abolitionists. In recent years, antislavery scholars have pushed for inclusion of a broader abolitionist community, one that includes women, ordinary people, and African Americans—as well as those working prior to 1831—in the story of American antislavery. See, for example, Yellin and Van Horne, *Abolitionist Sisterhood*; Richard S. Newman, *The Transformation of American Abolitionism: Fighting Slavery in the Early Republic* (Chapel Hill: University of North Carolina Press, 2002); and John Stauffer and Timothy Patrick McCarthy, eds., *Prophets of Protest: Reconsiderations of American Abolitionism* (New York: New Press, 2006). At the same time, new and quite helpful reconsiderations of famous Garrisonians—from Lucretia Mott to Parker Pillsbury—are ongoing. See Stacey M. Robertson, *Parker Pillsbury: Radical Abolitionist, Male Feminist* (Ithaca,

NY: Cornell University Press, 2000); and Carol Faulkner, *Lucretia Mott's Heresy: Abolition and Women's Rights in Nineteenth-Century America* (Philadelphia: University of Pennsylvania Press, 2011).

45. William Lloyd Garrison, "To the Public," *Liberator*, January 1, 1831, accessed at http://www.pbs.org/wgbh/aia/part4/4h2928t.html.

46. On the rise of Garrisonian abolitionism, see Stewart, *Holy Warriors*; Walters, *Antislavery Appeal.*

47. Brown recalled this story in his 1857 autobiographical letter to young Henry Stearns. There is some debate about its authenticity, though it certainly demonstrates that in 1857 Brown saw his entire life as centering on the development of his antislavery belief. For discussion of it as an "aphoristic memory," see McGlone, *John Brown's War against Slavery*, 53–55.

48. There is some dispute about how early John Brown first saw copies of Garrison's newspaper. David Reynolds reports that he saw it as early as 1831 or 1832, while Stephen Oates and Evan Carton date it later, as 1833 or 1834. Reynolds, *John Brown, Abolitionist*, 51; Oates, *To Purge This Land with Blood*, 30; Carton, *Patriotic Treason*, 73.

49. See, for example, Carton, *Patriotic Treason*, 81–83; Reynolds, *John Brown, Abolitionist*, 62–65; and Stauffer, *Black Hearts of Men*, 118–19.

50. John Brown to Frederick Brown, November 21, 1834, in Sanborn, *Life and Letters*, 40–41. In this particular letter the "practical" plans involved founding a school for African Americans and somehow adopting a slave into the Brown family, and he specifically mentioned that he had "consulted the feelings of my wife and my three boys."

51. Ruth Brown Thompson, "Reminiscences of John Brown, of Kansas and Harper's Ferry," typescript dated December 2, 1882, RU 369, box 1, RUST. Reproduced by permission of the Huntington Library. In Sanborn's *Life and Letters*, John Jr. recounts a similar, though seemingly different, episode where Brown arose in a joint church meeting to protest segregation in seating of African Americans. "He then invited the colored people to occupy his slip," John Jr. recalled, adding, "The blacks accepted, and all of our family took their vacated seats. This was a bomb-shell, and the Holy Spirit in the hearts of Pastor Burritt and Deacon Beach at once gave up his place to another tenant. Next day father received a call from the Deacons to admonish him and 'labor' with him." It seems likely that Ruth's and John Jr.'s memories were different accounts of the same event; as a note to John Jr.'s account, Sanborn remarked, "A shorter account of this affair, as remembered by Ruth Thompson, has already been given," and the version from her memoir appears previously in his work. Although technically this calls into question the precise accuracy of each account, I look to them both as demonstrating the same thing: the power of this early antislavery lesson—this action—on Brown's children. John Brown Jr., reminiscence, in Sanborn, *Life and Letters*, 52; Sanborn, ibid., 53; Ruth Brown Thompson, reminiscence, ibid., 37.

52. Ruth recalled that after this episode, "the whole church was 'down on him.'" Ruth Brown Thompson, "Reminiscences of John Brown, of Kansas and Harper's Ferry," typescript dated December 2, 1882, RU 369, box 1, RUST. Reproduced by permission of the Huntington Library. See also John Brown Jr. reminiscence in Sanborn, *Life and Letters*, 53.

53. John Brown to "my Dear Wife and Children," April 27, 1840, box 7, ELDR. Reproduced by permission of the Huntington Library.

54. John Stauffer argues that Brown "embraced feminism" and was willing to blur lines of gender, though without the same intensity as he approached race. But, Stauffer concedes, Brown was a "rigid patriarch" in practice. Stauffer, *Black Hearts of Men*, 209, 233.

55. Brown's beliefs and resulting relationships with African Americans, Reynolds argues, were "as earth-shaking in [their] implications as Harpers Ferry was in fact." Reynolds, *John Brown, Abolitionist*, 129.

56. Some scholars assert that John Brown was unusual—even unique—for his ability to transcend race. John Stauffer puts Brown into a group of "radical abolitionists" who, he argues, rejected racial (and gender) conventions and sought instead to adopt a "black heart." Stauffer, *Black Hearts of Men*, 6.

57. See Chris Dixon, *Perfecting the Family: Antislavery Marriages in Nineteenth-Century America* (Amherst: University of Massachusetts Press, 1998), 7.

58. In her excellent treatment of Parker Pillsbury, Stacey Robertson argues that his commitment to this was such that he "subverted traditional notions of manly strength and self-control to construct a vision of manhood that rejected male dominance." She notes that it was hard for Pillsbury to create a "completely egalitarian household"—but vouches for his sincerity in the attempt. Chris Dixon also details how many radical abolitionists looked "to place reciprocal affection, not power, at the heart of marriage." There never seems to have been any notion that John Brown had such radical ideals—and he was never accused, as Dixon's radicals were, of trying to "undermine the entire social order" with his progressive gender ideals, though one critic in 1882 would label him a "thief, a murderer, and a miscegenationist." Robertson, *Parker Pillsbury*, 3, 46; Dixon, *Perfecting the Family*, x, xi; "A Georgia View of John Brown," *Boston Daily Advertiser*, September 14, 1882, p. 8.

59. To some of her father's biographers, Annie Brown Adams recalled that her father "was strong for women's rights and women's suffrage." This seems a late-in-life skewing of Brown's actual beliefs, offered as further proof of his nobility by a daughter who was frustrated by the way his reputation was being tarnished. Stephen Oates offers this valuable evenhanded assessment: "Annie Brown Adams later claimed that Abby Kelly and Lucretia Mott both had influenced Brown and that he had been an *advocate* of woman suffrage and women's rights. I could find no corroboratory evidence of this." And, tellingly, Annie also offered this statement to Horatio Nelson Rust in 1895 about her parents' interactions: "I said to [Brown], 'I have often wondered how you two such positive characters, persons who were each so determined to have their own way in every thing, as you and mother are, managed to get along without quarreling.' 'Oh, I never quarreled with your mother; when she gets in my way or does not agree with me, I just shove her on one side,' waving his hand to illustrate it, 'and go right along about my business,' he said with a little laugh." Annie quoted in Villard, *John Brown*, 50; Stauffer, *Black Hearts of Men*, 232; Oates, *To Purge This Land with Blood*, 372n14; Annie Brown Adams, Account of the Raid on Harpers Ferry, 1895, RU 283, box 3, RUST. Reproduced by permission of the Huntington Library.

60. In her biography of Harriet Tubman, Catherine Clinton offers the intriguing opinion that Brown referred to Tubman as "Captain" because of the limitations he had in views of women. See Catherine Clinton, *Harriet Tubman: The Road to Freedom* (New York: Little, Brown, 2004), chap. 9.

61. It had begun to admit females along with male students in the 1840s, and perhaps this, along with the school's antislavery leanings, was what led to Ruth's attendance. With the later exception of her youngest sisters, she and John Jr. were the only Brown children to leave home to receive schooling, perhaps so that they could secure employment as teachers. For more information on the school, see Tina Stewart Brakebill, *"Circumstances Are Destiny": An Antebellum Woman's Struggle to Define Sphere* (Kent, OH: Kent State University Press, 2006), 11–14.

62. John Brown to Ruth Brown, September 1, 1847, in Sanborn, *Life and Letters*, 38.

63. Brown, a nonconformist in many ways, may have been influenced by the nineteenth-century ideology that has been described as "separate spheres," that is, public versus private, one for men and the other for women. On separate spheres ideology and challenges to this characterization, see Linda Kerber, "Separate Spheres, Female Worlds, Woman's Place," *Journal of American History* 75 (June 1988): 9–39; and Carol Lasser, "Beyond Separate Spheres: The Power of Public Opinion," *Journal of the Early Republic* 21 (Spring 2001): 115–23.

64. On religious tensions between John Brown and his sons, see also DeCaro, *"Fire from the Midst of You,"* 207–10.

65. Villard, *John Brown*, 20. Villard continues, "'And that was perfectly true' is Salmon Brown's confirmation of the remark."

66. John Brown to John Brown Jr., January 18, 1841, MIC 50, JBJR.

67. Higginson as quoted in Redpath, *Public Life of Capt. John Brown*, 68.

68. In the early nineteenth century, scholars concur that new romantic ideals of companionate marriage and marital choice emerged and that marriage became "a union of love, based on the attraction of opposites." E. Anthony Rotundo, *American Manhood: Transformations in Masculinity from the Revolution to the Modern Era* (New York: Basic Books, 1993), 4.

69. There is some debate about the date of this letter. In their collections, Ruchames lists it as 1846 without comment, but Stauffer says it is likely 1847 and DeCaro likely 1846. My hunch is that it is 1846—that the family was still separated (in 1847 Mary Brown was also in Springfield, where the letter is written from), and in 1846 Mary might have just confided her pregnancy with Sarah. Ruchames, *John Brown*, 65–66; Stauffer and Trodd, *Meteor of War*, 49; DeCaro, *John Brown*, 126.

70. John Brown to Mary Brown, March 7, 184[4], in Stauffer and Trodd, *Meteor of War*, 49–50.

71. John Brown to Henry Stearns, July 15, 1857, in Sanborn, *Life and Letters*, 17.

72. For a sense of how much Mary was in charge of while Brown was away, see John Brown to Mary Brown, November 23, 1845, box 7, ELDR; John Brown to Mary Brown, June 29, 1846, ibid.; John Brown to Mary Brown, October 19, 1846, ibid.; John Brown to Mary Brown, January 8, 1847, ibid.

73. Mary Brown had thirteen children in an age in which marital fertility was on the decline. In *Intimate Matters*, John D. Emilio and Estelle Friedman note that

in the nineteenth century, married couples exercised increasing control over their fertility: while on average, couples in 1800 had 7 children, by 1850 the number had dropped to 5.42. John D. Emilio and Estelle Friedman, *Intimate Matters: A History of Sexuality in America* (New York: Harper & Row, 1988), 56, 58. On the family in the nineteenth century and its transition (what has been called the emergence of the "modern" family), see Stephanie Coontz, *The Way We Never Were: American Families and the Nostalgia Press* (New York: Basic Books, 2000); and Steven Mintz and Susan Kellogg, *Domestic Revolutions: A Social History of American Family Life* (New York: Free Press, 1989).

74. The looming presence and experience of death and loss often led to transformations. See Nicholas Marshall, "'In the Midst of Life We Are in Death': Affliction and Religion in Antebellum New York," in *Mortal Remains: Death in Early America*, ed. Nancy Isenberg and Andrew Burstein (Philadelphia: University of Pennsylvania Press, 2002), 181–84.

75. Clarence Gee notes from Boyd Stutler's John Brown scrapbook, from *Maine Republican* (Portland), December 1884, signed by M.E.B., folder 5, box 8, series 2, BGC.

76. John Brown to John Brown Jr., September 25, 1843, in Stauffer and Trodd, *Meteor of War*, 47.

77. John Brown to John Brown Jr., September 25, 1843, in Sanborn, *Life and Letters*, 58. This was not an uncommon description of death. Nicholas Marshall describes a similar story to Sarah's death, and he takes the family's view of death as leading to a better world as proof of a lessening of predestination orthodoxy. Marshall, "'In the Midst of Life We Are in Death,'" 178–80.

78. Judith Walzer Leavitt refers to "the shadow the women carried throughout their married lives, the frequency and the tragedy of infant and child mortality" and "a possible death sentence with every pregnancy," as even by the early twentieth century a woman had a one-in-thirty chance over the span of her life of dying in childbirth. Though Leavitt's women write candidly about their fears, I found no such writing by Mary Brown or any of her daughters. Judith Walzer Leavitt, *Brought to Bed: Childbearing in America, 1750 to 1950* (New York: Oxford University Press, 1986), 18, 20, 25.

79. Clarence Gee notes from Boyd Stutler's John Brown scrapbook, from *Maine Republican* (Portland), December 1884 (signed by M.E.B.), folder 5, box 8, series 2, BGC. In hindsight, she maintained that "even in these trials God upheld me."

80. John Brown to John Brown Jr., January 11, 1844, in Sanborn, *Life and Letters*, 59.

81. See Oates, *To Purge This Land with Blood*, 54–59.

82. There were opportunities available to women to join reform societies for temperance and antislavery in Akron and beyond, but it seems as if Mary—preoccupied with so many children, household chores, Brown's absences, and little money for organizational dues—would have been unable to take advantage of this even if she had so desired. In her new book on abolitionist women in the Old Northwest, Stacey Robertson highlights the involvement of women—many with middle-class backgrounds that enabled such activity—in Ohio in antislavery work; see Robertson, *Hearts Beating for Liberty*. See also Bertram Wyatt-Brown, "Abolition and Antislavery in Hudson and Cleveland: Contrasts in Reform Styles," in *Cleveland: A*

Tradition of Reform, ed. David D. Van Tassel and John J. Grabowski (Kent, OH: Kent State University Press, 1986), 92–112; and Kathleen L. Endres, *Akron's "Better Half": Women's Clubs and the Humanization of the City, 1825–1925* (Akron, OH: University of Akron Press, 2006).

83. Beecher quoted in Susan Strasser, *Never Done: A History of American Housework* (New York: Pantheon, 1982), 105.

84. In 1910, Oswald Garrison Villard was one of the first to fault Ruth: though he did not name Ruth, he wrote of Amelia's death as occurring after being "accidentally scalded through the carelessness of an elder sister." Many biographers have followed his lead. Stephen Oates referred to the incident as a "calamity" due to "some carelessness on Ruth's part." David Reynolds refers to "a household accident caused by Ruth." Villard, *John Brown*, 35; Oates, *To Purge This Land with Blood*, 55; Reynolds, *John Brown, Abolitionist*, 81. In his recent biography, Evan Carton avoided assigning blame. Carton, *Patriotic Treason*, 106.

85. John Brown to wife and children, November 8, 1846, in Stauffer and Trodd, *Meteor of War*, 52.

86. John Brown to Ruth Brown, January 5, 1847, and January 6, 1847, in Ruchames, *John Brown*, 66.

87. John Brown to Mary Brown, November 29, 1846, in Sanborn, *Life and Letters*, 142.

88. Ibid.

89. John Stauffer argues convincingly that Brown's personal tragedies—combined with events in the country, beginning with Lovejoy's death in 1837—led to a transformation in his religious vision and his drive to halt slavery. They made Brown "want to replace his existing world with his millennial and perfectionist vision." Stauffer, *Black Hearts of Men*, 119.

90. Ibid., 157.

91. In *Life and Letters of John Brown*, Franklin Sanborn wrote that Mary had been an "invalid" before leaving Springfield in 1849, and in a letter of September 1, 1847, John Brown wrote Ruth of Mary's "bilious fever" after the move to Springfield from Akron. It seems probable that some of Mary's illnesses were pregnancy related. See Sanborn, *Life and Letters*, 105; John Brown to Ruth Brown, September 1, 1847, in Sanborn, *Life and Letters*, 145. On the way that pregnancy could "maim for life," see Leavitt, *Brought to Bed*, 28. Antislavery activist Angelina Grimké, for one, had lifelong complications and illnesses relating to one pregnancy. On this, see Mark Perry, *Lift Up Thy Voice: The Grimké Family's Journey from Slaveholders to Civil Rights Leaders* (New York: Viking, 2003), 189–90.

92. John Brown to Owen Brown, January 16, 1848, in Sanborn, *Life and Letters*, 24.

93. Judith Walzer Leavitt describes the nineteenth century as a period of great transition from home to hospital for childbirth: by the 1930s, physicians and hospitals would replace midwives and homes as the primary location and tenders to childbirth. A physician may have been available in the Hudson area and likely Akron, and Mary's births may have been tended to by women in the area—maybe Ruth and other relatives. In one early episode, Ruth recalled John Brown tending his family when they were ill with scarlet fever, and how neighbors criticized him for not calling a physician—so clearly they were available. There is also a story of John Brown,

while en route to fetch a doctor for a sick Dianthe, stopping to apprehend a thief. See Leavitt, *Brought to Bed*; Sanborn, *Life and Letters*, 94–95; James Foreman to James Redpath, December 28, 1859, in Ruchames, *John Brown*, 171–76.

94. Ruth Brown Thompson, as quoted in Sanborn, *Life and Letters*, 44. Ruth's recollection of this event, both that in Sanborn's biography and in the longer version contained in the Rust papers at the Huntington Library, focuses almost entirely on her father's grief.

95. Dana, "How We Met John Brown," 5, 6, 7.

96. Susan Cayleff, *Wash and Be Healed: The Water-Cure Movement and Women's Health* (Philadelphia: Temple University Press, 1987), 3.

97. "Wash and be healed" was the motto of the popular *Water-Cure Journal.* Jane B. Donegan, *"Hydropathic Highway to Health": Women and Water-Cure in Antebellum America* (New York: Greenwood, 1986), 20. Susan Cayleff identifies water cures as "a vital link in the national reform network" and notes that the therapy "adopted into its tenets the beliefs promulgated in the vegetarian, physical education, temperance, and dress-reform movements." Cayleff, *Wash and Be Healed*, 139.

98. On Garrison, see Harriet Alonso, *Growing Up Abolitionist: The Story of the Garrison Children* (Amherst: University of Massachusetts Press, 2002), 58–59.

99. Clarence Gee, "Dr. David Ruggles' Water-Cure Establishment," typescript notes on an 1847 advertisement from the *North Star*, folder 7, box 8, series 2, BGC; Cayleff, *Wash and Be Healed*, 80; Graham Russell Gao Hodges, *David Ruggles: A Radical Black Abolitionist and the Underground Railroad in New York City* (Chapel Hill: University of North Carolina Press, 2010). There is also mention of David Ruggles and his water cure in Northampton in issues of the *Water-Cure Journal* dated November 15, 1846; February 15, 1847; April 15, 1847; July 1, 1847; October 1, 1848; November 1, 1848; and February 1, 1849.

100. "Northampton Water Cure Establishments," November 1, 1848, *Water-Cure Journal.*

101. For instance, right around the time of Mary's departure, Jason wrote to John Jr., "I was very much pleased with your letter and the Water Cure Book you sent . . . me. I have always had a great faith in the the [*sic*] free use of the sparkling waters. I read both through almost without laying them down the arguments were so good in favor of Water. If you will give the publisher of the Water Cure Journal a dollar and send it to us a year, when I see you I will be a paying you well for it." Jason Brown to John Brown Jr., August 17, 1849, MIC 50, JBJR.

102. "Water cure establishments are springing up all over the land, & I hope ere long, there may be one, to which the poor can have access. At present the expensiveness of board & treatment, cuts them off from the benefit of water cure establishments, while their prejudices, strengthened by their ignorance, prevents them from using it in the simplest cases at home." Sarah Grimké to Elizabeth Pease, April 18, 1848, folder 574, BMS Am 1906, Houghton Library, Cambridge, MA.

103. Cayleff, *Wash and Be Healed*, 86; Hodges, *David Ruggles*, 188; Mary Brown to John Brown Jr., November 8, 1847, Stutler Collection, reel 2.

104. John Brown Jr. to John Brown, September 18, 1849, MIC 50, JBJR.

105. Mary Brown to John and Wealthy Brown, September 11, 1849, MIC 50, JBJR.

106. She added, "Say to him I should like a letter from him & that if I should not leave here befor his return I want him to come this way & see me." Mary Brown to John Brown Jr., September 25, 1849, MIC 50, JBJR.

107. Ruth Brown to Mary Brown, September 7, 1849, John Brown Collection, KSHS.

108. Ruth Brown to Mary Brown, October 31, 1849, folder 3, box 2, series 3, BGC.

109. Ruth Brown to Mary Brown, September 7, 1849, John Brown Collection, KSHS.

110. Cayleff, *Wash and Be Healed*, 141.

111. Donegan, *"Hydropathic Highways to Health,"* 104. Some scholars assert that at the water cures women received birth control advice as well. See ibid., 109n87; Cayleff, *Wash and Be Healed*, 157, 195n52.

112. In a letter to Garrison and reprinted in the *Liberator*, Samuel May Jr. referred to how in the week following November 5, 1849, Lucy Stone had speaking engagements in Hampshire County, where Northampton is located. In a second letter, written the following week, he mentioned Stone's address to a Northampton audience. Samuel May Jr. to William Lloyd Garrison, November 5, 1849, reprinted in the *Liberator*, November 9, 1849; Samuel May Jr. to William Lloyd Garrison, November 12, 1849, ibid., November 16, 1849.

113. Though Stone was nominally an antislavery lecturer, by November 1849 her lectures were increasingly focused on woman's rights. In February of 1850 petitions on behalf of woman suffrage were submitted to the Massachusetts legislature, including ones from over half of the towns where Stone had lectured. It appears that she only started gathering signatures after her appearance at the Northampton water cure, so Mary Brown likely had no chance to sign one, but the coming battle likely influenced Stone's discussion that day. For information on this, see Joelle Million, *Woman's Voice, Woman's Place: Lucy Stone and the Birth of the Woman's Rights Movement* (Westport, CT: Praeger, 2003), 100–103.

114. This describes a resolution offered by Stone at a quarterly meeting of the Worcester County South Division Anti-Slavery Society at Millville and Blackstone, MA, October 27–28, 1849. *Liberator*, November 9, 1849.

115. For "good meetings," see Samuel May Jr. to William Lloyd Garrison, November 12, 1849, reprinted in the *Liberator*, November 16, 1849. On the opposition that Stone faced while lecturing, see Alice Stone Blackwell, *Lucy Stone Blackwell: Pioneer of Woman's Rights* (1930; Charlottesville: University Press of Virginia, 2000), 76–83; and Andrea Moore Kerr, *Lucy Stone: Speaking Out for Equality* (New Brunswick, NJ: Rutgers University Press, 1992), 54. An episode where someone had thrown a hymnbook at Stone had been reported in the *Liberator* on July 14, 1848, so it is possible that Mary had even heard of opposition to Stone beforehand.

116. Mary Brown to John Brown Jr., November 8, 1849, STUT, reel 2. This was misdated as 1847, but a copy in the Edwin Cotter collection corroborates that the correct date is in fact 1849. See Mary Brown to John Brown Jr., November 8, 1849, typed copy of original owned by Boyd Stutler, CC-SUNY. Thanks to Caleb McDaniel for directing me to this letter.

117. Ruth Brown to Wealthy Brown, March 10, 1850, excerpted in Katherine Mayo notes, folder J.B. First Days in Charlestown Jail, box 4, OGV. Ruth was not issuing her stepmother a compliment, though she added that "I have no difficulty with her." It appears that part of the "large" feelings showed in Mary's chastising of her stepson Owen about his religious skepticism.

118. Villard, *John Brown*, 24–25.

2. North Elba, Kansas, and Violent Antislavery

1. In Richard Hinton, *John Brown and His Men, with Some Account of the Roads They Travelled to Reach Harper's Ferry* (New York: Funk & Wagnalls, 1894), 444.

2. Hinton, *John Brown and His Men*, 17.

3. Ruth Brown Thompson in Sanborn, *Life and Letters*, 99.

4. Ruth Brown Thompson, "Reminiscences of John Brown, of Kansas and Harper's Ferry," typescript dated December 2, 1882, RU 369, box 1, RUST. Reproduced by permission of the Huntington Library.

5. Ruth Brown Thompson to Wealthy Hotchkiss Brown, September 27, 1852, MIC 50, JBJR.

6. Henry and Ruth Thompson to John Jr. and Wealthy Brown, May 7, 1854, MIC 50, JBJR.

7. In *The Black Hearts of Men*, John Stauffer highlighted North Elba as Brown's choice of where he most wished to be in the 1850s, asserting that even when he traveled far from it, it was North Elba that he saw as home and where he forged close friendships with African Americans. Stauffer, *Black Hearts of Men*, 173.

8. Ruth Brown Thompson, "Reminiscences of John Brown, of Kansas and Harper's Ferry," typescript dated December 2, 1882, RU 369, box 1, RUST. Reproduced by permission of the Huntington Library.

9. The two best resources about North Elba come from the works of local historian Mary MacKenzie and the archival collection of Edwin Cotter, longtime superintendent of the John Brown Farm outside modern Lake Placid. MacKenzie's writings are compiled in *The Plains of Abraham: A History of North Elba and Lake Placid—Collected Writings of Mary MacKenzie*, ed. Lee Manchester (Utica, NY: Nicholas Burns Publishing, 2007). Cotter's papers are housed in special collections at SUNY–Plattsburgh, and they include a host of materials related to North Elba. A few articles also offer information, including Amy Godine, "Home Truth: The Saga of African-Americans in the Adirondack Past," *Adirondack Life* (January/February 1994): 46–64.

10. 1855 State Census of North Elba, folder 140, box 12, CC-SUNY.

11. Lyman Epps Jr. claimed, "I remember as John Brown was about to leave for the South, he wanted my Father to go with him, but my Mother pleaded with my Father not to go, as she had several little children, and without means to live on. She explained to Mr. Brown, and he being a man of most tender heart, could not bear to have my Father leave us. My Father was most anxious to follow this most noble hearted man, so my Mother finally consented if they could get her $200 for the childrens keep, but at that time it could not be done." Lyman Epps to O. G. Libby, August 4, 1938, folder 133, box 11, CC-SUNY.

12. Edwin Cotter, notes, "Miscellaneous Blacks in Gerrit Smith Colony at North Elba," folder 136, box 11, CC-SUNY.

13. Salmon Brown as quoted in the *Adirondack Daily Enterprise*, May 1913, notes on "Black families of North Elba," folder 136, box 11, CC-SUNY.

14. In her reminiscence, Ruth referred to him as "Cyrus Thomas."

15. Ruth Brown Thompson, quoted in Sanborn, *Life and Letters*, 100.

16. Dana, "How We Met John Brown," *Atlantic Monthly*, July 1871, 6, 1.

17. Bruce Laurie, *Beyond Garrison: Antislavery and Social Reform* (New York: Cambridge University Press, 2005), 233.

18. Reynolds, *John Brown, Abolitionist*, 121. On antislavery violence, see Stanley Harrold, "John Brown's Forerunners: Slave Rescue Attempts and the Abolitionists, 1841–1851," *Radical History Review* 55 (1993): 104–5; Stanley Harrold and John McKivigan, eds., *Antislavery Violence: Sectional, Racial, and Cultural Conflict in Antebellum America* (Knoxville: University of Tennessee Press, 1999); and Jeffery S. Rossbach, *Ambivalent Conspirators: John Brown, the Secret Six, and a Theory of Slave Violence* (Philadelphia: University of Pennsylvania Press, 1982).

19. John Brown to Mary Brown, November 28, 1850, in Sanborn, *Life and Letters*, 106.

20. John Brown to Mary Brown, January 17, 1851, ibid., 132.

21. Reynolds, *John Brown, Abolitionist*, 121.

22. Ruth Brown Thompson in Sanborn, *Life and Letters*, 131.

23. Ibid.

24. It is clear that Ruth took a lot of pride in Cyrus. For example, she once wrote to Wealthy describing Annie and Sarah's schooling and berry picking and added, "Cyrus is doing great buisness by way of farming" and that he had wheat, oats, potatoes, turnips, etc. Ruth Brown to Wealthy Brown, August 6, 1850, MIC 50, JBJR.

25. Ruth Brown Thompson in Sanborn, *Life and Letters*, 132.

26. For more on the Thompsons, see Mary MacKenzie, "The Thompson Clan: Sharing John Brown's Dream," in MacKenzie, *Plains of Abraham*, 97–106.

27. Ruth Brown to Wealthy Brown, March 10, 1850, MIC 50, JBJR. Her close relationship to her brothers also comes through in Ruth's letters about her courtship. See, for example, Jason Brown to Ruth Brown Thompson, November 1, 1850, 6348.01, GLC; John Brown Jr. to Ruth Brown Thompson, February 23, 1851, 4463.05, ibid.

28. Ruth Brown to Wealthy Brown, August 6, 1850, MIC 50, JBJR.

29. Ibid.

30. In his work on the Hutchinson Family Singers, Scott Gac relates a similar gap between mother and daughter: Abby Hutchinson, born the same year as Ruth, attended the Milford Female Seminary, something her mother Polly never could have done. Scott Gac, *Singing for Freedom: The Hutchinson Family Singers and the Nineteenth-Century Culture of Antebellum Reform* (New Haven, CT: Yale University Press, 2007), 122.

31. Brakebill, *"Circumstances are Destiny,"* 43. Celestia Rice Colby was acquainted with John Jr. (and likely Ruth) at the Grand River Institute in Ashtabula County, Ohio. Brakebill suggests that the GRI exposed Colby to "radical speakers and ideas," but there is no record from Ruth's letters of influence her education had on her.

32. Carroll Smith-Rosenberg, "The Female World of Love and Ritual," *Signs* 1, no. 1 (1975): 1–29.

33. Ruth Brown to Wealthy Brown, March 10, 1850, MIC 50, JBJR. Ruth added that it would "cut me to the heart" when Owen received a letter from John Jr. and she did not get one from Wealthy. Somehow Mary was embroiled in the middle of this, though the exact circumstances are unclear. Ruth Brown Thompson to "Dear Brother and Sister," August 13, 1851, MIC 50, JBJR.

34. Ruth Brown to John Jr. and Wealthy Brown, May 23, 1850, MIC 50, JBJR.

35. Ruth Brown Thompson to Wealthy Brown, September 27, 1852, MIC 50, JBJR.

36. John Jr. and Wealthy's son, John Brown III, was mentally disabled and lived with them for the remainder of his life. They had one additional child, Edith, who was not born until 1866. Ruth and Henry's son John Henry Thompson was born at North Elba in 1852. See Ruth Brown Thompson to John and Wealthy Brown, October 25, 1852, MIC 50, JBJR; Ruth and Henry Thompson to John and Wealthy Brown, February 1, 1853, ibid.; Ruth Brown Thompson to John Brown Jr., September 1, 1858, ibid.

37. Ruth Brown to Wealthy Brown, April [16], 1852, MIC 50, JBJR.

38. To John Jr., John Brown wrote, "Ruth was married in Sept. & I think has done well." John Brown to John Brown Jr., November 4, 1850, MIC 50, JBJR.

39. Ruth Brown Thompson to "Dear Brother and Sister," August 13, 1851, MIC 50, JBJR.

40. John Brown to Ruth and Henry Thompson, January 23, 1852, in Sanborn, *Life and Letters*, 148.

41. For the best example, see Ruth Brown Thompson to "my dear brother" [John Brown Jr.], April 19, 1853, MIC 50, JBJR. This exchange did not seem to dampen the friendship between the Thompsons and John Jr. and Wealthy; Ruth and Henry made the long and costly journey to Ohio to pay them a visit the spring after she wrote this letter.

42. John Brown to Ruth Brown Thompson, August 10, 1852, in Sanborn, *Life and Letters*, 151.

43. For Brown's response, see John Brown to Ruth and Henry Thompson, June 30, 1853, ibid., 110.

44. Ruth and Henry Thompson to John Jr. and Wealthy Brown, February 1, 1853, MIC 50, JBJR.

45. For the report about the sons driving cattle, see Villard, *John Brown*, 75. On the trip of the Brown women, see John Brown to John Brown Jr., March 24, 1851, MIC 50, JBJR.

46. Mary had two more children in Akron. Though she would return to North Elba in the mid-1850s, she would never give birth there. She had no recorded pregnancies after 1854, when she was thirty-seven years old. This is earlier than many women at the time ceased childbearing, though it is hard to tell if this came from any efforts on Mary's part or Brown's lengthy absences between 1854 and 1859.

47. John Brown to children [John Jr. and Wealthy Brown], May 14, 1852, in Sanborn, *Life and Letters*, 149.

48. John Brown to John Brown Jr., July 20, 1852, ibid., 150.

49. John Brown to Ruth Brown Thompson, August 10, 1852, ibid., 151.

50. See John Brown to Ruth and Henry Thompson, January 25, 1854, ibid., 155, for a reference to Mary not being in as good health as when Ruth had visited; see John Brown to John Brown Jr., February 9, 1854, ibid., 156, for a reference to Mary being ill and his hopes she would be better again.

51. "We have a new daughter now Five days old," Brown wrote on September 30, 1854, adding, "Mother & child, are both doing well to appearance." John Brown to children, September 30, 1854, in *A John Brown Reader: The Story of John Brown in His Own Words, in the Words of Those Who Knew Him, and in the Poetry and Prose of the Literary Heritage,* ed. Louis Ruchames (New York: Abelard-Schuman, 1959), 94.

52. Thanks to Carol Faulkner for raising this idea in response to a paper that I presented at the Berkshire Conference on Women's History in June 2008.

53. There is evidence that Brown planned this return to North Elba for several years. See John Brown to Mary Brown, December 27, 1852, in Sanborn, *Life and Letters,* 108–9; John Brown to Ruth and Henry Thompson, April 6, 1853, ibid., 109; John Brown to children, May 10, 1853, STUT, reel 1. For his request that North Elba's African American population be consulted, see John Brown to Ruth and Henry Thompson, September 30, 1854, in Stauffer and Trodd, *Meteor of War,* 81. In his letter to Mary, he noted that their "old neighbors" seemed to "wish them back," but it is unclear if he was asking Mary's opinion about the matter.

54. Ruth Brown Thompson to Mary Brown, November 15, 1854, folder 14, box 1, John Brown Collection, KSHS.

55. For background on sectional conflict in the 1850s and the coming of the Civil War, see Shearer Davis Bowman, *At the Precipice: Americans North and South during the Secession Crisis* (Chapel Hill: University of North Carolina Press, 2010); Stanley Harrold, *Border War: Fighting over Slavery before the Civil War* (Chapel Hill: University of North Carolina Press, 2010); Michael Holt, *The Fate of Their Country: Politicians, Slavery Extension, and the Coming of the Civil War* (New York: Hill & Wang, 2004); Bruce Levine, *Half Slave and Half Free: The Roots of Civil War* (New York: Hill & Wang, 1992); Michael Morrison, *Slavery and the American West: The Eclipse of Manifest Destiny and the Coming of the Civil War* (Chapel Hill: University of North Carolina Press, 1997); Elizabeth Varon, *Disunion! The Coming of the American Civil War, 1789–1859* (Chapel Hill: University of North Carolina Press, 2008); and Steven E. Woodworth, *Manifest Destinies: America's Westward Expansion and the Road to Civil War* (New York: Alfred A. Knopf, 2010).

56. Nicole Etcheson, *Bleeding Kansas: Contested Liberty in the Civil War Era* (Topeka: University Press of Kansas, 2004), esp. 5–8.

57. That said, it was not uncontroversial when the New England Emigrant Aid Company, led by Eli Thayer, armed settlers. See Etcheson, *Bleeding Kansas,* 37.

58. John Brown Jr. to John Brown, May 20, 1855, in Stauffer and Trodd, *Meteor of War,* 82.

59. Ibid., 82–83.

60. Jason Brown to "Dear Mother, Brothers, and Sisters," July 22, 1855, Ella Thompson Towne scrapbook, BFC. Reproduced by permission of the Huntington Library. On the death of Austin and his burial in Missouri, see Jason Brown to

Owen Brown Sr., June 14, 1855, folder 15, box 1, series 1, BGC. On John Brown's effort to dig up Austin and rebury him in free land, see John Brown to Owen Brown, October 19, 1855, typescript, folder 5, ibid.

61. John Brown Jr. to John Brown, May 24, 1855, in Stauffer and Trodd, *Meteor of War*, 83. The date is different because the second was a postscript to the first.

62. Oliver Brown to "Brother and Sister," August 8, 1855, in Ella Thompson Towne scrapbook, BFC. Reproduced by permission of the Huntington Library. Though Oliver's letter was addressed to Ruth and Henry, he presumably expected them to share it with Mary.

63. John Brown to John Brown Jr., August 21, 1854, in Stauffer and Trodd, *Meteor of War*, 80. Emphasis in original.

64. John Brown to Ruth and Henry Thompson, September 30, 1854, ibid., 81. Many historians cite this and other such letters as proof of Brown's sense of African Americans' equality. It is striking that Brown modeled his consultation with the African Americans. Much as he had made a point to seat all at his table, he modeled his belief that the North Elba population should be consulted. He apparently did not find it necessary to model consulting his wife.

65. John Brown to Ruth and Henry Thompson, November 2, 1854, ibid., 82.

66. On John Brown and the Kansas violence, see Carton, *Patriotic Treason*, 167–220; DeCaro, *"Fire from the Midst of You,"* 216–36; Albert J. von Frank, "John Brown, James Redpath, and the Idea of Revolution," *Civil War History* 52, no. 2 (2006): 142–60; Karl Gridley, "'Willing to Die for the Cause of Freedom in Kansas': Free State Emigration, John Brown, and the Rise of Militant Abolitionism in the Kansas Territory," in Stauffer and McCarthy, *Prophets of Protest*, 147–64; Oates, *To Purge This Land with Blood*, 97–177; and Reynolds, *John Brown, Abolitionist*, 138–205.

67. Many men went to Kansas without their wives, sometimes because of the reluctance of the women. See Nicole Etcheson, "'Labouring for the Freedom of the Territory': Free-State Kansas Women in the 1850s," *Kansas History* 21 (Spring 1998): 71–74.

68. Ruth Brown Thompson in Sanborn, *Life and Letters*, 105.

69. Born in 1856, Ella Thompson Towne remembered (or claimed to) John Brown saying goodbye before leaving for Kansas or Harpers Ferry, and she recalled playing much with aunt Ellen. "Ellen and I were great 'pals,'" she recalled. See Ella Thompson Towne to the Owen Brown Family Reunion, "Recollections of North Elba, New York," May 27, 1932, typescript copy by Gee, folder 1, box 2, series 2, BGC.

70. Mary Brown to John Brown, May 20, 1856, typescript copy, SYKES.

71. Frederick Brown to "dear brother and all," September 12, 1855, Ella Thompson Towne scrapbook, BFC. Reproduced by permission of the Huntington Library.

72. John Brown to wife and children, November 23, 1855, in Sanborn, *Life and Letters*, 205. According to Salmon, Mary especially was lonely there, which is understandable since Ruth was more immersed in the local community and had many of the Thompson kind around. In a letter to North Elba, Salmon referred to how Ruth had written "that Mother and Wat felt quite lonesome," but he did not offer much sympathy, adding, "that is not any thing more than they might expect. They both volenteered to go to that cold and miserable land and I know of no plan but

to wind it through for a while any way." Salmon Brown to "Dear Mother, Brothers and Sisters," August 16, 1855, MS05–0027, STUTDB, http://www.wvculture.org/history/wvmemory/jbdetail.aspx?Type=Text&Id=712.

73. Oliver Brown to Mary Brown, August 8, 1855, in Sanborn, *Life and Letters*, 198; John Brown Jr. to Mary Brown, September 16, 1855, in Villard, *John Brown*, 92.

74. John Brown to wife and children, October 13, 1855, in Sanborn, *Life and Letters*, 201.

75. John Brown to "Dear Wife [Mary Brown] & Children every one," December 16, 1855, folder 15, box 1, KTO, http://www.territorialkansasonline.org/~imlskto/cgi-bin/index.php?SCREEN=show_document&document_id=102547.

76. Nicole Etcheson, Lynne Getz, and Kristin Tegtmeier Oertel have detailed the hardships that women faced on the Kansas frontier. In addition to dealing with their primitive surroundings, women struggled with their inability to create the type of home that was idealized by middle-class culture. Etcheson, *Bleeding Kansas*, 40; Etcheson, "'Labouring for the Cause of Freedom'"; Lynne Getz, "Partners in Motion: Gender, Migration, and Reform in Antebellum Ohio and Kansas," *Frontiers* 27, no. 2 (2006): 102–35; and Oertel, *Bleeding Borders*.

77. Wealthy Brown to Watson Brown, September 16, 1855, in Villard, *John Brown*, 92.

78. Ellen Sherbondy Brown to Mary Brown, November 25, 1855, ibid., 112. John Jr.'s wife Wealthy soon added, "Our men have so much *war* and *elections* to attend to that it seems as though we were a great while getting into a house." Wealthy Brown to Mary Brown, January 6, 1856, ibid., 127.

79. Wealthy Brown to "friend Louisa" [Louisa Barber], March 23, 1856, STUT, reel 2.

80. Both Etcheson and Oertel describe how some women in Kansas became combatants themselves. See Oertel, *Bleeding Borders*, 80; and Etcheson, *Bleeding Kansas*, 83.

81. John Brown to wife and children, June 1856, in Sanborn, *Life and Letters*, 238.

82. Ibid., 240.

83. Jason Brown to "Dear Brother, Sister, and all Dear Friends at home," 1856, handwritten copy by Katherine Mayo, folder "Brown, Jason," box 2, OGV.

84. John Brown to wife and children, September 7, 1856, in Sanborn, *Life and Letters*, 317.

85. Ibid., 318.

86. John Brown Jr. to "John Brown & brothers," September 8, 1856, in Sanborn, *Life and Letters*, 325.

87. Owen Brown to Mary Brown, August 27, [1856], http://www.kansasmemory.org/item/4300.

88. John Brown to wife and children, April 7, 1856, http://www.kansasmemory.org/item/4263.

89. John Brown to wife and children, February 1, 1856, http://www.kansasmemory.org/item/4257.

90. Henry Thompson to Ruth Brown Thompson, May 1856, typescript copy, SYKES.

91. Ruth Brown Thompson to "My Dear & Much-Loved Husband," June 10, 1856, Ella Thompson Towne scrapbook, BFC. Apparently Ruth was waiting on Henry to name the new baby, for she added, "I will send you a little of her hair. You must tell me what to call her." Additionally, this letter contains a passage that perhaps hints at tension between Ruth and Mary: "My health is middling good, but I have not dared to attempt to write since the first letter I wrote you since I was sick, for I made my eyes very weak writing too soon, and I got a scolding for it." Reproduced by permission of the Huntington Library.

92. Sanborn, *Life and Letters*, 3.

93. Franklin Sanborn, *Recollections of Seventy Years* (New York: R. G. Badger, 1909), vol. 1, 126.

94. Ibid., 1:129.

95. Henry Thompson and Ruth Brown Thompson to John Brown, April 21, 1858, http://www.kansasmemory.org/item/4827.

96. Sanborn, *Recollections of Seventy Years*, 1:126.

97. John Brown to Mary Brown, September 13, 1858, STUT, reel 1.

98. On the fund-raising he was beginning for his family, see "Letter re. subscription to support his family," July 27, 1857, STUT, reel 1; Franklin Sanborn to George Stearns, August 25, 1857, ibid. Brown made Mary aware of his efforts, writing to her in late 1858 that he was "doing all in my power to make you comfortable." John Brown to wife and children, December 2, 1858, ibid.

99. John Brown to Franklin Sanborn, May 15, 1857, ibid.

100. In an 1857 speech to potential backers, Brown had referenced all the sacrifices his sons had made in Kansas, though he did not specifically mention the home-front sacrifices occurring at North Elba. See John Brown, "An Idea of Things in Kansas" (1857), in *John Brown's Raid on Harpers Ferry: A Brief History with Documents*, ed. Jonathan Earle (Boston: Bedford / St. Martin's, 2008), 59–62.

101. Franklin Sanborn to George Stearns, Amos Lawrence, and other fund subscribers, August 25, 1857, STUT, reel 1.

102. John Brown to Franklin Sanborn, May 15, 1857, STUT, reel 1.

103. In Hinton, *John Brown and His Men*, 444.

104. Sanborn, *Life and Letters*, 498–99.

105. Annie Brown to John Brown Jr., December 15, 1858, MIC 50, JBJR. For the letter describing the trip to the mountain, a party that included Watson and his wife Isabella (Bell), Salmon and his fiancée Abbie Hinckley, William Thompson (who would be one of Brown's raiders), and an African American man, see Annie Brown to John Brown Jr., July 19, 1857, ibid.

3. Annie Brown, Soldier

1. Sanborn, *Life and Letters*, 531.

2. When older biographies mentioned the girls' presence, discussion quickly moved into the melodramatic: "Mere girls, they had old heads upon their shoulders. They filled their arduous posts well and bravely, and fully won the respect of the hardy men," Oswald Garrison Villard wrote solemnly in 1910. Velma West Sykes, a mid-twentieth-century journalist, reported that it was the presence of "two attractive girls in the farmhouse—one a virgin and the other the bride of Oliver Brown" that

"served to increase the irritability of these lusty young men for action" and caused Brown to push up the date of his attack. Villard, *John Brown*, 405; Velma West Sykes, "Daughter Helped John Brown Keep Plot Secret," *Kansas City Times*, October 17, 1967, folder 6: Annie Brown Adams, box 2, series 2, BGC.

3. Ruth Brown to Wealthy Hotchkiss Brown, August 6, 1850, JBJR. For a discussion of the nineteenth-century use of the phrase "going to housekeeping," see Hodes, *Sea Captain's Wife*, esp. 60, 94, 207.

4. On such rhetoric and female reform work, see Andrea M. Atkin, "'When Pincushions Are Periodicals': Women's Work, Race, and Material Objects in Female Abolitionism," *ATQ* 11, no. 2 (1997): 93–113; Lori Ginzberg, *Women and the Work of Benevolence: Morality, Politics, and Class in the Nineteenth-Century United States* (New Haven, CT: Yale University Press, 1990); Jeffrey, *Great Silent Army*; Jeffrey, "'Stranger, Buy . . . Lest Our Mission Fail.'"

5. Annie referred to herself in this way in her 1886 statement written for Franklin Sanborn.

6. Reynolds, *John Brown, Abolitionist*, 28.

7. On the Secret Six, see Rossbach, *Ambivalent Conspirators*.

8. Biographer Kate Clifford Larson describes Tubman as "a fixture in his plans until nearly the end." Larson, *Bound for the Promised Land: Harriet Tubman, Portrait of an American Hero* (New York: Ballantine, 2004), 161. See also Clinton, *Harriet Tubman*, esp. chap. 9.

9. Mary Brown appears to have written her husband a letter stating that his sons desired to give up war after their experiences in Kansas; Brown's letter to her of March 31, 1857, refers to the "resolution of the boys to 'learn and practice war no more.'" Of all the letters written by Mary Brown that have since gone missing, this one might be the biggest loss. It is impossible without her original letter to understand the context for their sons' request—and what it meant that they appear to have come to Mary Brown to speak on their behalf. John Brown to Mary Brown, March 31, 1857, in Sanborn, *Life and Letters*, 388.

10. David Reynolds wrongly dismisses Jason as "timid," as the Browns did not think of him in this way. The family seemed to put Jason into his own category and to take seriously his aversion to violence. Reynolds, *John Brown, Abolitionist*, 293.

11. John Brown to Ruth Brown Thompson, January 30, 1858, in Sanborn, *Life and Letters*, 441.

12. Ruth Brown Thompson to John Brown, February 20, 1858, ibid., 442.

13. Ibid. David Reynolds, for instance, writes that "all the wives in the family, including John Brown's Mary, had considered antislavery violence mistaken ever since the death of Frederick and the insanity of John Brown Jr. in 1856." Reynolds, *John Brown, Abolitionist*, 293. I have not been able to find anything on record where a Brown woman condemned antislavery violence on principle or confessed apprehensions after the events of Kansas.

14. "I. Smith" [John Brown] to Mary, July 5, 1859, in Velma West Sykes, "A Biography of Mrs. John Brown," typescript MSS, chap. 8, p. 1, folder 1, box 2, Sykes Papers, LoC.

15. No responding letter from Mary has been found, nor is there evidence of any such letter. Especially given her passive-aggressive dealings with Brown when

she went to Ruggles's water cure against his wishes, it seems utterly reasonable that Mary did not write a direct response to Brown's request. The few pieces of other evidence that exist—including a statement from Annie Brown, and claims from abolitionists after Harpers Ferry—are too clouded by the writers' agendas to accept without further corroboration. In 1886 Annie gave a statement that she had protected her father from knowing the "real truth" about Mary's absence as proof that Mary objected to Brown's mission, and she also claimed that her mother had tried to block her leaving for Maryland. In an 1895 recollection for Horatio Nelson Rust, Annie did not mention any sabotage, merely noting that "Mother did not wish to go" and that Martha went in her place. Some scholars accept Annie's 1886 statement as proof that Mary did not support Brown. But even if Mary wanted herself and her fifteen-year-old daughter to remain at home, this does not mean she completely disapproved of Brown's mission. Robert McGlone argues that, since Kansas, Mary had believed that antislavery violence was not the right method. He wrote of her "unspoken opposition to the enterprise that had become his obsession." But how can an opposition that was "unspoken" be corroborated? In looking at her later life, Annie seems here to have been swayed by extreme loyalty to her father's memory to recast the past. By 1886, she was impoverished, isolated, and had felt for a long time that no one really understood her experience—her mother included. Annie Brown Adams, statement written for Franklin Sanborn, November 1886, CHS; Annie Brown Adams, Account of Raid on Harpers Ferry, 1895, RU 283, box 3, RUST (reproduced by permission of the Huntington Library); McGlone, "Rescripting a Troubled Past," 1189.

16. I owe thanks to Caleb McDaniel for feedback on an early draft for helping to clarify this point.

17. Mary D. Smith to "dear husband," June 29, 1859, no. 175, Ferdinand Dreer Papers, Historical Society of Pennsylvania, Philadelphia. Thanks to Louis DeCaro Jr. for directing me to this letter.

18. "I. Smith" [John Brown] to Mary, July 5, 1859, in Velma West Sykes, "A Biography of Mrs. John Brown," typescript MSS, chap. 8, p. 1, folder 1, box 2, Sykes Papers, LoC.

19. John Brown to Mary Brown, August 11, 1859, HM 15207, HUNT. Reproduced by permission of the Huntington Library.

20. Most firsthand information does come from various accounts written by Annie decades later for Franklin Sanborn, Alexander Ross, Thomas Featherstonhaugh, and Horatio Nelson Rust, all of whom hoped to use her accounts (and did) in their own writing. All appear in the footnotes that follow. One final firsthand account was provided by Osborne Anderson, a raider who escaped. For general information and background about the Kennedy farmhouse and the raid, I have relied on Carton, *Patriotic Treason*, 277–323; DeCaro, *"Fire from the Midst of You,"* 237–63; DeCaro, *John Brown*, 70–89; Horwitz, *Midnight Rising*, 97–126; McGlone, *John Brown's War against Slavery*, 246–306; Oates, *To Purge This Land with Blood*, 253–310; Reynolds, *John Brown, Abolitionist*, 288–333; and Stauffer, *Black Hearts of Men*, 236–61.

21. Annie Brown Adams, Account of Raid on Harpers Ferry, 1895, RU 283, box 3, RUST. Reproduced by permission of the Huntington Library.

22. Katherine Mayo, typewritten notes from interview with Annie about the Kennedy farm, folder "Adams, Annie Brown," box 1A, OGV.

23. Ibid.

24. Thomas Featherstonhaugh, *John Brown's Men; the Lives of Those Killed at Harpers Ferry, with a Supplementary Bibliography of John Brown*. Southern History Association, October 1899, 6.

25. Osborne Anderson, "A Voice from Harper's Ferry: A Narrative of Events at Harper's Ferry; with Incidents Prior and Subsequent to Its Capture by Captain Brown and His Men" (Boston, 1861), in *Black Voices from Harpers Ferry*, ed. Jean Libby (Palo Alto, CA, 1979), 24; Annie Brown Adams to Garibaldi Ross, December 15, 1887, in Stauffer and Trodd, *Meteor of War*, 106.

26. Mrs. Huffmaster once commented, "Your men folks has a right smart lot of shirts." Annie Brown Adams to Garibaldi Ross, December 15, 1887, in Stauffer and Trodd, *Meteor of War*, 106.

27. Annie Brown Adams, Memories of Kennedy Farm, etc., 3007.49, GLC.

28. Annie Brown Adams, "Tobacco," 1895, RU 286, box 3, RUST. Reproduced by permission of the Huntington Library.

29. Anderson, "Voice from Harper's Ferry," 25.

30. Annie Brown Adams recollections in Villard, *John Brown*, 418.

31. Cook had been sent to live in Harpers Ferry the previous year to scout and lived in town with his local wife, so he was not as accustomed to the loft escape. He would later come under attack for his supposed disloyalty to Brown and the raiders after a confession in the Charles Town jail.

32. Annie Brown Adams, statement written for Franklin Sanborn, November 1886, CHS.

33. Ibid.

34. Annie Brown Adams, Account of Raid on Harpers Ferry, 1895, RU 283, box 3, RUST. Reproduced by permission of the Huntington Library.

35. Annie Brown Adams recollections in Villard, *John Brown*, 419.

36. Annie Brown Adams, Account of Raid on Harpers Ferry, 1895, RU 283, box 3, RUST. Reproduced by permission of the Huntington Library.

37. Annie Brown Adams, statement written for Franklin Sanborn, November 1886, CHS.

38. Annie Brown Adams, Memories of Kennedy Farm, etc., 3007.49, GLC.

39. Annie Brown Adams, statement written for Franklin Sanborn, November 1886, CHS. She was not the only Brown to be so troubled. Writing to Mary shortly after their arrival, Martha stated, "Oliver says he must confess that he told you a few lies when he was at home. But he says you must excuse him on the ground that it was a necessity." Martha Brown to "Mother" [Mary Brown], September 18, 1859, folder 11, box 46, CHS.

40. Annie Brown Adams to Garibaldi Ross, December 15, 1887, in Stauffer and Trodd, *Meteor of War*, 106.

41. Annie Brown Adams, statement written for Franklin Sanborn, November 1886, CHS.

42. Annie Brown Adams to Garibaldi Ross, December 15, 1887, in Stauffer and Trodd, *Meteor of War*, 105.

43. Annie Brown Adams, statement written for Franklin Sanborn, November 1886, CHS.

44. Redpath, *Public Life of Capt. John Brown*, 242.

45. Anderson, "Voice from Harper's Ferry," 25.

46. Ibid.

47. Annie Brown Adams, Account of Raid on Harpers Ferry, 1895, RU 283, box 3, RUST. Reproduced by permission of the Huntington Library.

48. Carton, *Patriotic Treason*, 284–85.

49. Watson Brown to Bell Brown, September–October 1859, in Sanborn, *Life and Letters*, 549.

50. Oliver Brown to "Mother, Brother, and Sisters," September 9, 1859, in Sanborn, *Life and Letters*, 547.

51. Jeremiah Anderson to "dear brother," September 28, 1859, box 1, ELDR. Reproduced by permission of the Huntington Library.

52. Annie Brown Adams, statement written for Franklin Sanborn, November 1886, CHS.

53. Edwin Coppoc to Mary Brown, November 1859, typescript copy from *New York Illustrated News*, December 24, 1859, in folder 4, box 1, series 3, BGC; Barclay Coppoc to Annie Brown, January 13, 1860, typed extracts, folder 8, box 46, CHS.

54. Annie Brown Adams to Richard Hinton, May 23, 1893, folder "Adams, Annie Brown," box 1A, OGV.

55. Anderson, "Voice from Harper's Ferry," 23–24.

56. Salmon Brown, "My Father, John Brown," in Ruchames, *John Brown*, 195.

57. Katherine Mayo, Kennedy Farm Notes, folder "Adams, Annie Brown," box 1A, OGV.

58. Featherstonhaugh, *John Brown's Men*.

59. She and Martha later subscribed to *Banner of Light*, a periodical that contained verse and stories as well as reports of people's encounters with the spirit world. In part they might have done this at Oliver Brown's request: according to Annie, he promised to try to contact them through its columns if he were killed. Annie Brown Adams, Account of Raid on Harpers Ferry, 1895, RU 283, box 3, RUST. Reproduced by permission of the Huntington Library.

60. Annie Brown to Thomas Wentworth Higginson, November 28, 1859, Mss. E.5.1 p. 128, BPL. Courtesy of the Trustees of the Boston Public Library/ Rare Books. By this time, Brown was imprisoned and was not so open-minded, instead writing Brown-of-old letters in which he proclaimed her need to become a Christian. Of this, she wrote to Higginson, "I am sorry that I cannot do as he wishes."

61. Annie Brown to Aaron D. Stevens, January 9, 1860, folder Stevens family, January 7–19, 1860, SFP.

62. In notes compiled by Katherine Mayo, there are indications that only some of the men (Stevens, Kagi, Jeremiah Anderson, and the Browns and Thompsons) knew the full plan; others thought it would be like the raids in Missouri. See "Raiders Foreknowledge of the Plan," folder "Adams, Annie Brown," box 1A, OGV. Owen confirmed this in a statement to Franklin Sanborn in the 1880s. See Owen Brown, in Sanborn, *Life and Letters*, 541–42.

63. "Raiders Foreknowledge of the Plan," folder "Adams, Annie Brown," box 1A, OGV; Statement of Annie Brown for Franklin Sanborn, November 1886, CHS.

64. Owen Brown, in Sanborn, *Life and Letters*, 542.

65. John Brown advised the men to have as little communication with the outside world as possible to avoid attracting unnecessary attention. That said, I do not want to overstate the degree to which communication was cut off. It is clear that letters went out from—and likely into—the farmhouse quite frequently, and in a September 9 letter to his family Oliver Brown implored, "Please, all write." John Brown to Wife and Children, August 16, 1859, STUT, reel 1; Oliver Brown to Mother, Brother, and Sisters, September 9, 1859, in Sanborn, *Life and Letters*, 547.

66. They appear to have left September 29, 1859. Jeremiah Anderson to "dear brother," September 28, 1859, box 1, ELDR. Reproduced by permission of the Huntington Library.

67. Annie Brown Adams, Account of Raid on Harpers Ferry, 1895, RU 283, box 3, RUST. Reproduced by permission of the Huntington Library.

68. John Brown to Wife and Children, October 1, 1859, in Sanborn, *Life and Letters*, 550.

69. Oliver Brown to Martha, October 9, 1859, typescript copy, folder 12, box 1, series 3, BGC.

70. Stauffer, *Black Hearts of Men*, 237. For many years few if any slaves were thought to have joined Brown, but some scholars offer compelling arguments that Harpers Ferry's African American population was much more active. See Hannah Geffert and Jean Libby, "Regional Black Involvement in John Brown's Raid on Harpers Ferry," in Stauffer and McCarthy, *Prophets of Protest*, 165, 167; DeCaro, *John Brown*, esp. 70–89; and Libby, *Black Voices from Harpers Ferry*.

71. In addition, the others killed were John H. Kagi, Stewart Taylor, William H. Leeman, Lewis S. Leary, and Dangerfield Newby.

72. In addition to Owen, the escapees were Charles P. Tidd, Barclay Coppoc, Francis J. Merriam, and Osborne P. Anderson. John E. Cook and Alfred Hazlett fled but were later caught. Merriam, the grandson of wealthy Boston abolitionist Francis Jackson, was the only raider with direct ties to the elite abolitionist community.

73. The *Boston Evening Courier*, for instance, reported on October 17 that an "insurrection" had "broken out at Harper's Ferry, where an armed band of abolitionists have full possession of the government arsenal." *Boston Evening Courier*, October 17, 1859.

74. See Finkelman, "Manufacturing Martyrdom," in Finkelman, *His Soul Goes Marching On*, 41–66.

75. John Brown to Mrs. George L. Stearns, November 29, 1859, 5925.01, GLC.

76. See Venet, "'Cry Aloud and Spare Not,'" esp. 102–3.

77. Ibid., Child quoted p. 100. On abolitionist reaction to John Brown's raid, see William Henry, "Hero, Martyr, Madman: Representations of John Brown in the Poetry of the John Brown Year, 1859–1860," in Russo and Finkelman, *Terrible Swift*

Sword, 141–61; Stauffer, *Black Hearts of Men*, 236–81; and Venet, *Neither Ballots nor Bullets*, 21–22.

78. Lydia Maria Child to Anne Warren Weston, November 28, 1859, Mss. A.5.1 no. 79, BPL. Courtesy of the Trustees of the Boston Public Library/Rare Books.

79. Child to [Anne Warren Weston?], December 22, 1859, Mss. A.5.1. no. 82, BPL. Courtesy of the Trustees of the Boston Public Library/Rare Books.

80. Lydia Maria Child to Rebecca Spring, November 18, 1859, folder 22, box 1, SPRING. Courtesy of the Department of Special Collections and University Archives, Stanford University Libraries.

81. Child's and Spring's reactions to Brown were nothing if not sentimental, keyed to the emotional sensibility that middle-class and elite women valued. On how sentimentalism was a means for middle-class Americans to assert their sincerity and authenticity, see Halttunen, *Confidence Men and Painted Women*, 153.

82. Lou V. Chapin, "The Last Days of Old John Brown," *Overland Monthly and Out West Magazine* 33 (April 1899), 326. The reports offered by Annie and Ruth differ somewhat. Ruth's account highlights Martha as the bearer of the news, while Annie's highlights her role in reading out loud. I think I have pieced it together correctly: that Martha brought the news to Ruth and Henry, who then sent word to the Brown home, where Annie read the news aloud to a gathered group.

83. Katherine Mayo notes, "Life at Kennedy Farm," folder "Adams, Annie Brown," box 1A, OGV.

84. Chapin, "Last Days of Old John Brown," 326.

85. "John Brown's Interview with Senator Mason, Congressman Vallandigham and others, October 18, 1859," in Stauffer and Trodd, *Meteor of War*, 125.

86. Quoted in Carton, *Patriotic Treason*, 325. Carton does not identify the particular speaker.

87. On Brown's trial, a bizarre production, see Brian McGinty, *John Brown's Trial* (Cambridge, MA: Harvard University Press, 2009); and Robert McGlone, "John Brown, Henry Wise, and the Politics of Insanity," in Finkelman, *His Soul Goes Marching On*, 213–52.

88. John Brown to "My Dear Wife and Children," October 31, 1859, in Sanborn, *Life and Letters*, 579–80.

89. Ellen Brown to John Brown, November 9, 1859, in Redpath, *Echoes of Harper's Ferry*, 428.

90. Annie Brown to John Brown, November 9, 1859, ibid.

91. After she had fled to the woods at the Kennedy farmhouse, only Watson had understood "the mood that prompted it and had been a great help to me in talking and advising me how to overcome those feelings and moods years before I ever went down there." Statement of Annie Brown for Franklin Sanborn, November 1886, CHS.

92. Annie Brown to Thomas Wentworth Higginson, December 4, 1859, typescript copy, folder "Adams, Annie Brown," box 1A, OGV; Brown to Thomas Wentworth Higginson, January 17, 1860, Mss. E.5.1 p. 159, BPL (courtesy of the Department of Special Collections and University Archives, Stanford University Libraries). Such letters would continue: in 1861, she ended a letter to James McKim

by writing "Fremont and Freedom." Annie Brown to Mr. McKim, October 14, 1861, MAY. Courtesy of the Division of Rare and Manuscript Collections, Cornell University Library.

93. Annie Brown to Thomas Wentworth Higginson, December 4, 1859, typescript copy, folder "Adams, Annie Brown," box 1A, OGV.

94. Higginson in Redpath, *Public Life of Capt. John Brown*, 67.

95. Annie Brown to Aaron Stevens, December 27, 1859, folder Dec. 26–31, 1859, SFP.

96. A. D. Stevens to "my dear sister," March 1, 1860, 3007.2, GLC.

97. Chapin, "Last Days of Old John Brown," 326.

98. Ibid., 328.

99. Esther Salaman notes that memories of events can "come back involuntarily, bring with them strong emotions, and give a sensation of living in a past moment." Esther Salaman, "A Collection of Moments," in *Memory Observed: Remembering in Natural Contexts*, ed. Ulric Neisser (San Francisco: W. H. Freeman and Co., 1982), 63.

100. Literature on trauma, history, and memory is useful to understanding Annie's mind-set. Elizabeth Snyder Hook notes a "link between catastrophic events (whether of natural origin or human design) and the survivor's struggle to bear witness." She adds, "In order for survivors of trauma to make sense of their experiences, they must accommodate the traumatic incident into their current concept of self and into the ever-emerging text of their personal life histories. The path to such integration, Pierre Janet concludes, is language: the conversion of traumatic memory into narrative memory." Elizabeth Snyder Hook, "Awakening from War: History, Trauma, and Testimony in Heinrich Böll," in *The Work of Memory: New Directions in the Study of German Society and Culture*, ed. Alon Confino and Peter Fritzsche (Champaign: University of Illinois, 2002), 136–37, 140. Other helpful works on trauma and memory include Cathy Caruth, *Unclaimed Experience: Trauma, Narrative, and History* (Baltimore: Johns Hopkins University Press, 1996); and Michael S. Roth, *The Ironist's Cage: Memory, Trauma, and the Construction of History* (New York: Columbia University Press, 1995).

101. For the only mention of Annie, see testimony of John C. Unseld, January 5, 1860, in *Invasion at Harper's Ferry* (Washington, DC: Government Printing Office, 1860), 4.

102. In her insistence that her 1859 housekeeping be recognized, Annie challenged Brown's chroniclers to include a woman in the tale of radical, and violent, antislavery. Her challenge still stands. Despite all the scholarship on antislavery violence and on Brown's raid, both remain very "male" stories, with female abolitionists such as Lydia Maria Child only appearing to swoon over Brown as he awaited execution. Julie Roy Jeffrey asserts that some early abolitionist memoirs helped erase radical women out of antislavery's history, and I am inclined to think the same things happened to violent antislavery agitators. The Browns are left out of many abolitionist reunions of the 1880s and 1890s, and even the 1882 commemorations of Brown across the country only employed Mary Brown as a prop. Julie Roy Jeffrey, *Abolitionists Remember: Antislavery Autobiographies and the Unfinished Work of Emancipation* (Chapel Hill: University of North Carolina Press, 2008), 19.

4. Newfound Celebrity in the John Brown Year

1. Tilden G. Edelstein, *Strange Enthusiasm: A Life of Thomas Wentworth Higginson* (New Haven, CT: Yale University Press, 1968), 228; Carton, *Patriotic Treason*, 324; Oates, *To Purge This Land with Blood*, 336; Rossbach, *Ambivalent Conspirators*, 223–24.

2. Higginson in Redpath, *Public Life of Capt. John Brown*, 65.

3. Higginson to mother, November 5, 1859, no. 647, series 2, Letters and Journals of Thomas Wentworth Higginson, BMS Am 784, Houghton Library, Cambridge, MA.

4. Details of the trip home taken from Clarence Gee, "John Brown's Remains after the Execution at Charlestown, VA.," typed notes, box 9, series 1, BGC; Robert Gordon, "A Mournful Trip," *Adirondack Life*, January/February 1984, 16–32; Mary Hannah Field, "A Brave Life," *Overland Monthly*, October 1885, 360–37; typed notes: editorial from the *Daily Cleveland Herald*, December 3, 1859, folder "J.B. Funeral and Burial," box 3, OGV; Rebecca Hemphill to Oswald Garrison Villard, February 26, 1908, ibid.; *The Anti-Slavery History of the John-Brown Year* (New York: American Anti-Slavery Society, 1861); "The Burial of John Brown," *New York Weekly Tribune*, December 17, 1859; and "On the Trail of John Brown: What Mary Brown Saw," www.adkhistorycenter.org/jbweb/intro.html.

5. *Anti-Slavery History of the John-Brown Year*, 130–31.

6. For these particular details see "On the Trail of John Brown: What Mary Brown Saw," www.adkhistorycenter.org/jbweb/intro.html.

7. *Anti-Slavery History of the John-Brown Year*, 132. The identity of the author of the AASS booklet is not clear. Wendell Phillips was on the executive committee that ended its term in May 1860 and likely contributed to this part.

8. "The Burial of John Brown," *New York Weekly Tribune*, December 17, 1859. For another description, see Field, "Brave Life."

9. Lydia Maria Child to Fanny Kemble, January 1860, STUT, reel 2. Some of this pity and sympathy was also directed at Brown's jailed raiders. Rebecca Spring to Aaron Stevens, February 13, 1860, folder 14, box 1, SPRING (courtesy of the Department of Special Collections and University Archives, Stanford University Libraries); and Rebecca Spring to Aaron Stevens, January 24, 1860; folder Jan. 23–31, 1860, SFP.

10. Elizabeth Clark, "'The Sacred Rights of the Weak': Pain, Sympathy, and the Culture of Individual Rights in Antebellum America," *Journal of American History* 82 (September 1995): 463–93.

11. And even during the war, the popularity of Alexander Gardner's exhibit of war photos—including those of the dead—would point to Americans' need to "see" the suffering occurring on their behalf. On death and its meaning during the war, see Drew Faust, *This Republic of Suffering: Death and the American Civil War* (New York: Random House, 2008).

12. Thomas Wentworth Higginson to Annie and Sarah Brown, November 4, 1859, typescript copy, SYKES.

13. I gleaned the details, dates, and itineraries of Mary's travels from the following: Ruth Brown Thompson to Thomas Wentworth Higginson, November 14, 1859, Ms. E.5.1 p. 93, BPL; Mary Brown to Higginson, November 15, 1859, Ms. E.51.1

p. 94, ibid.; John Brown to James Miller McKim, November 25, 1859, Ms. 895, ibid.; Anne Brown to Higginson, November 28, 1859, Ms. E.5.1 p. 128, ibid.; George Sennott to Higginson, November 5, 1859, Ms. E.51.1 p. 72, ibid.; Field, "Brave Life"; Higginson to Annie and Sarah Brown, November 4, 1859, typescript copy, SYKES; J. Miller McKim to William Lloyd Garrison, November 25, 1859, ibid.; Higginson, "A Visit to John Brown's Household in 1859," in *Contemporaries* (Boston: Houghton Mifflin, 1899), 219–43; J. M. McKim to John Brown, November 22, 1859, box 6, OGV; John Brown to Mary Brown, November 26 [27?], 1859, in Stauffer and Trodd, *Meteor of War*, 153–54.

14. Higginson, in Redpath, *Public Life of Capt. John Brown*, 65.

15. While abolition was a "sacred vocation," it was also an adventure. Sarah McKim would later write to Mary that she and her husband "often talk of your interesting visit to us, and our melancholy but exciting journey to Harpers Ferry." Higginson clearly relished his novel trek to and from North Elba. He wrote to Annie and Sarah upon his and Mary's arrival in Boston of a seeming lark they had had involving the pair "walking into Jay village with her and a broken-down buggy." Donald Matthews, "Abolition as a Sacred Vocation," in *Antislavery Reconsidered: New Perspectives on the Abolitionists*, ed. Lewis Perry and Michael Fellman (Baton Rouge: LSU Press, 1979); Sarah McKim to Mary Brown, December 2, 1860, copy, folder "Brown, Mrs. John and Family," box 6, OGV; Thomas Wentworth Higginson to Annie and Sarah Brown, November 4, 1859, typescript copy, SYKES.

16. Thomas Wentworth Higginson to Annie and Sarah Brown, November 4, 1859, typescript copy, SYKES.

17. Franklin Sanborn to Salmon Brown, November 5, 1859, box 53, ELDR. Reproduced by permission of the Huntington Library.

18. Thomas Wentworth Higginson to Annie and Sarah Brown, November 4, 1859, typescript copy, SYKES.

19. George Sennott to Thomas Wentworth Higginson, November 5, 1859, Ms. E.51.1 p. 72, BPL. Courtesy of the Trustees of the Boston Public Library/Rare Books.

20. John Brown to Thomas Wentworth Higginson, November 4, 1859, in Stauffer and Trodd, *Meteor of War*, 139.

21. Richard D. Webb, *The Life and Letters of Captain John Brown, Who Was Executed at Charlestown, Va., December 2, 1859, for an Armed Attack upon American Slavery; with Notices of Some of His Confederates, 1861* (London: Smith Elder and Co., 1861), iii.

22. John Brown to wife and children, November 8, 1859, in Sanborn, *Life and Letters*, 586.

23. Ibid., 586. For recent interpretations of Brown's "no," see Reynolds, *John Brown, Abolitionist*, 389; Carton, *Patriotic Treason*, 328.

24. Marie Marino Mullaney, "Feminism, Utopianism, and Domesticity: The Case of Rebecca Buffum Spring, 1811–1911," in *A New Jersey Anthology*, ed. Maxine N. Lurie (New Brunswick, NJ: Rutgers University Press, 2002), 164. Spring's unpublished memoir offers a chronicle of her travels and friendships with famous Americans and Europeans. See Rebecca Spring, "Auld Acquaintances," unpublished manuscript typescript, HM 46944, HUNT. Reproduced by permission of the Huntington Library.

25. Spring, "Auld Acquaintances," 25.

26. As Marie Mullaney dryly notes, "they were not the sort of people one would typically associate with utopian communal schemes. Wealthy, Yankee, white, Republican, Protestant, and self-indulgent, theirs was a life of breeding, gentility, and comfort." Mullaney, "Feminism, Utopianism, and Domesticity," 172.

27. A classic example comes in a story of her visit to a famous woman's home in Edinburgh, Scotland. She recalled, "As I was not strong, the carriage came for me early. I was sorry to leave the agreeable company, but Margaret consoled me afterwards, by telling me that when I left the room De Quincy asked: 'Who is that lady with the charming manners?'" Spring, "Auld Acquaintances," 33–34.

28. Rebecca Buffum Spring, "A Visit to John Brown in 1859," in *Virtuous Lives: Four Quaker Sisters Remember Family Life, Abolitionism, and Women's Suffrage*, ed. Lucille Salitant and Eve Lewis Perera (New York: Continuum, 1994), 121.

29. Ibid., 122.

30. Chapin, "Last Days of Old John Brown," 330.

31. Ibid. As Nan Enstad has argued, Mary here used a declaration of fashion to make a rather serious stand. Though Enstad's argument is based around conscious commodity *consumption*, Mary Brown's choice *not* to be such a consumer seems similar in its political meaning. See Nan Enstad, *Ladies of Labor, Girls of Adventure: Working Women, Popular Culture, and Labor Politics at the Turn of the Century* (New York: Columbia University Press, 1999).

32. Rebecca Spring to Judge Parker, 1859, folder "Spring, Mrs. R. B.," box 16, OGV.

33. Katherine Mayo, interview with Mrs. Rebecca Spring, September 1908, ibid.

34. Mary Brown to John Brown, November 13, 1859, in Redpath, *Echoes of Harper's Ferry*, 427.

35. Ibid.

36. Mary Brown to John Brown, November [29?], 1859, ibid., 428.

37. John Brown to Mary Brown, November 21, 1859, in Sanborn, *Life and Letters*, 595.

38. John Brown to Mary, November 26 [27?], 1859, in Stauffer and Trodd, *Meteor of War*, 154.

39. On McKim, see Ira V. Brown, "Miller McKim and Pennsylvania Abolitionism," *Pennsylvania History* 30 (January 1963): 56–72. On Wendell Phillips see James Brewer Stewart, *Wendell Phillips: Liberty's Hero* (Baton Rouge: LSU Press, 1986). Visit details taken from *New York Times*, December 3, 1859, news clipping, Franklin Benjamin Sanborn Scrapbook, vol 1., STUT, reel 5; James Miller McKim, "Our Philadelphia Correspondence," *National Anti-Slavery Standard*, December 3, 1859; Redpath, *Public Life of Capt. John Brown*; article about visit of John and Mary Brown, *Boston Evening Courier*, December 3, 1859; "The Tragedy in Virginia—the Arrival of Mrs. Brown," *Liberator*, December 9, 1859; *Anti-Slavery History of the John-Brown Year*.

40. Benjamin H. Smith Jr. to Benjamin H. Smith Sr., December 1, 1859, Benjamin H. Smith Papers, 1859–65, HUNT. Reproduced by permission of the Huntington Library.

41. The *Liberator*, for instance, prefaced its report with "if we may believe Capt. Avis." *Liberator*, December 9, 1859.

42. Redpath, *Public Life of Capt. John Brown*, 390.

43. Ibid., 390–91.

44. Article about visit of John and Mary Brown, *Boston Evening Courier*, December 3, 1859.

45. Redpath, *Public Life of Capt. John Brown*, 390.

46. For example, under the headline of "Last Hours of Capt. Brown" were: "Interview between Brown and his wife" and "Mrs. Brown searched for weapons or poison." *Boston Herald* news clipping, Sanborn Scrapbook 1, STUT, reel 5.

47. Tilton, "Personal Interview with Captain Brown's Wife." For a concise summary of the insanity issue see McGlone, "John Brown, Henry Wise, and the Politics of Insanity," in Finkelman and Russo, *His Soul Goes Marching On*, 213–52; Wyatt-Brown, "'A Volcano beneath a Mountain of Snow,'" ibid., 10–38.

48. Tilton, "Personal Interview with Captain Brown's Wife."

49. McKim, "Our Philadelphia Correspondence."

50. "The Tragedy in Virginia—the Arrival of Mrs. Brown," *Liberator*, December 9, 1859.

51. Katherine Mayo, notes on Interview with Miss Annie Miller, March 20, 1908, folder Harper's Ferry Raid, box 9, OGV. Annie Miller was the hotel owner's daughter.

52. Article about visit of John and Mary Brown, *Boston Evening Courier*, December 3, 1859. Other accounts reversed this and had John Brown losing composure. The *Courier*'s report concluded with the Browns' farewell: "The parting, especially on his part, exhibited a composure, either feigned or real, that was surprising."

53. Mary Brown to Gov. Wise, November 21, 1859, typescript copy, SYKES. Others were also working on her behalf. See J. Miller McKim to Francis Beacon, November 22, 1859, typescript copy, ibid.

54. Henry Wise to Mary Brown, November 26, 1859, Ms. B.1.6 vol. 7, no. 78, BPL. Courtesy of the Trustees of the Boston Public Library/Rare Books.

55. Gary Laderman, *The Sacred Remains: American Attitudes toward Death, 1799–1883* (New Haven, CT: Yale University Press, 1996). On desecration to corpses, see also Michael Sappol, *A Traffic of Dead Bodies: Anatomy and Embodied Social Identity in Nineteenth-Century America* (Princeton, NJ: Princeton University Press, 2002); and Franny Nudelman, *John Brown's Body: Slavery, Violence, and the Culture of War* (Chapel Hill: University of North Carolina Press, 2004), esp. chap. 2.

56. *Anti-Slavery History of the John-Brown Year*, 130; DeCaro, *"Fire from the Midst of You,"* 266.

57. Annie Brown to Rebecca Spring, May 29, 1860, folder "Spring, Mrs. R. B.," box 16, OGV.

58. Finkelman, "Manufacturing Martyrdom," in *His Soul Goes Marching On*, 47.

59. Ibid. 46–47.

60. Thomas Wentworth Higginson to Salmon Brown, December 2, 1859, RU 93, box 1, RUST. Reproduced by permission of the Huntington Library.

61. Quoted in Finkelman, "Manufacturing Martyrdom," 49.

62. Ruth Brown Thompson to Thomas Wentworth Higginson, December 27, 1859, Ms. E.5.1 p. 151, BPL. Courtesy of the Trustees of the Boston Public Library/ Rare Books. For another description see Joshua Young, "The Funeral of John Brown," *New England Magazine*, April 1904, 229–43.

63. Wendell Phillips, "Burial of John Brown," in Ruchames, *John Brown*, 268.

64. *Anti-Slavery History of the John-Brown Year*, 131.

65. Mary Brown to Mary Stearns, January 7, 1863, STUT, reel 2. And this circle grew: Freddy, Bell and Watson's son, was a favorite, and soon after Brown's funeral, Salmon welcomed a daughter. Annie Brown to James McKim, October 14, 1861, MAY (courtesy of the Division of Rare and Manuscript Collections, Cornell University Library); Annie Brown to Thomas Wentworth Higginson, January 17, 1860, Ms. E.5.1 p. 159, BPL (courtesy of the Trustees of the Boston Public Library/ Rare Books).

66. Ruth Brown Thompson to Mary Stearns, January 17, 1860, STUT, reel 2. For contact between Owen and the North Elba Browns, see Owen Brown to Martha Brown and Annie Brown, November 27, 1859, RU 324, box 1, RUST; and Martha Brown to "My Dear Friends O.X. & C.P.T." [Owen Brown and Charles Tidd], December 21, 1859, Ella Thompson Towne Scrapbook, BFC.

67. Knowing this would be the case, Brown had used his prison letters to solicit aid for his family. John Brown to Thaddeus Hyatt, November 27, 1859, in Sanborn, *Life and Letters*, 606; John Brown to "My Dear Friend E.B.," November 1, 1859, ibid., 583.

68. Article about visit of John and Mary Brown, *Boston Evening Courier*, December 3, 1859.

69. Article about visit of John and Mary Brown, *Boston Morning Journal*, December 3, 1859.

70. See Ruth Brown Thompson to Lydia Maria Child, April 9, 1860, STUT, reel 2. On the kiss legend, see Finkelman, "Manufacturing Martyrdom," 51–53.

71. Richard Hinton to "dear bereaved friends" [Brown family], December 23, 1859, box 27, ELDR. Reproduced by permission of the Huntington Library.

72. Writing to the Stearns, Mary encouraged them to visit. Seconding her stepmother, Ruth wrote to Mary Stearns, "*We all want you to come.*" Mary Brown to George and Mary Stearns, December 27, 1859, typescript copy, folder 3, box 2, series 3, BGC; Ruth Brown Thompson to Mary Stearns, December 26, 1859, STUT, reel 2.

73. Ruth Brown Thompson to Mary Stearns, January 17, 1860, STUT, reel 2.

74. Annie Brown to Wendell Phillips, December 13, 1859, folder 316, Wendell Phillips Papers, series 2, BMS Am 1953, Houghton Library, Cambridge, MA.

75. The Brown sons made their way from Ohio, relying on provisions from the John Brown fund and other donations. Once they reached North Elba, they realized that they did not have enough money to return home and again solicited donations. See Ruth Brown Thompson to Mrs. Stearns, April 22, 1860, STUT, reel 2; John Brown Jr. to George Stearns, June 30, 1860, typescript copy, folder 12, box 4, series 3, BGC; John Brown Jr. to Marcus and Rebecca Spring, May 2, 1860, box 6, OGV; John Brown Jr. to George Stearns, June 30, 1860, folder North Elba Celebrations, box 13, ibid.; Wealthy Brown to Ruth Brown Thompson, March 27, 1860, 6348.02, GLC.

76. For this quote and information about the gathering, see "Celebration at North Elba," *Liberator*, July 27, 1860.

77. Merrill Peterson, *John Brown: The Legend Revisited* (Charlottesville: University of Virginia Press, 2002), 36. Others wrote to request permission to visit. Horatio Rust, for instance, wrote to Mary Brown in 1863, stating, "I would very much like to visit your place the home of Him who's memory I can hold dear and in respect some time perhaps I may do so I am anxious to visit the Grave." Horatio Rust to Mary Brown, June 27, 1863, STUT, reel 3.

78. Ruth Brown Thompson to Thomas Wentworth Higginson, November 14, 1859 Ms. E.5.1 p. 93, BPL. Courtesy of the Trustees of the Boston Public Library/ Rare Books.

79. Annie Brown to J. Miller McKim, December 27, 1859, MAY. She continued, "Some have said to me that they envied me my situation. I believe that if they would stop and ask themselves if they were willing to part with their Father and two Brothers (three Brothers, I should have said, for one had to be sacrificed on the *bloody altar* of Kansas) and have one Brother made an outlaw with a price upon his head, and be robbed of the dearest friends they *ever* possest they would not make such an idle wish." Courtesy of the Division of Rare and Manuscript Collections, Cornell University Library.

80. Horatio Nelson Rust to Mary, December [21?], 1859, folder 3, box 2, Sykes Papers, LoC.

81. Mary Brown to J. Miller McKim, January 10, 1860, typescript copy, folder 3, box 2, series 3, BGC.

82. Mary Brown to Sarah Brown, November 11, 1860, folder 3, box 2, Sykes Papers, LoC.

83. Appeal for Aid to John Brown Family, Circular to Rev. John Carpenter, November 28, 1859, box 9, series 1, BGC.

84. Many later meetings held to commemorate Brown's execution doubled as fund-raisers for the families of Brown and the other slain and jailed raiders. African American groups also raised money for the Brown family. O.V. and others to John Brown, November 17, 1859, in Redpath, *Echoes of Harper's Ferry*, 391. On African American contributions, see also Benjamin Quarles, *Allies for Freedom: Blacks and John Brown* (New York: Oxford University Press, 1974).

85. Ralph Waldo Emerson, Speech delivered at Tremont Temple, November 18, 1859, in Redpath, *Echoes of Harper's Ferry*, 71.

86. Thaddeus Hyatt in Redpath, *Echoes of Harper's Ferry*, 390–91. He obscured from historical memory the fact that three of the four Brown sons still living had not participated.

87. "The John Brown Fund," *Chatham (Ontario) Planet*, September 13, 1860, typescript notes, box 9, series 1, BGC.

88. Thomas Wentworth Higginson to mother, November 22, 1859, no. 648, series 2, Higginson Letters and Journals, BMS Am 784, Houghton Library, Cambridge, MA.

89. On the fund for Garrison, see Alonso, *Growing Up Abolitionist*, 231–32. The money from the original John Brown Fund was divided as follows: Mary, Annie, Sarah, and Ellen collectively received $2,250, John Brown Jr. $1,000; Mary Ann Thompson (widow of William Thompson) $500, Owen Brown $400, Jason Brown

$300, Salmon Brown $200, Ruth Brown Thompson $200, Barclay Coppoc $50, the Boston Committee $100, and "other colored sufferers" $350. "The John Brown Fund," *Chatham (Ontario) Planet*, September 13, 1860, typescript notes, box 9, series 1, BGC. It is noteworthy that the Brown sons received funds even though they were not publicly mentioned much. It is likely that the "other colored sufferers" were the families of the African American raiders. In this and in other activities, money was raised for the families of the other raiders, too. Mary Leary, widow of raider Lewis Leary, wrote to James Redpath, for instance, to thank him for the book and "also for the efforts that you have made in my behalf," efforts that apparently involved helping her raise money to purchase a home. See Mary S. Leary to James Redpath, February 2, 1861, typescript copy, SYKES.

90. Mary Brown to Samuel E. Sewall, February 13, 1861, STUT, reel 2.

91. Mary Brown to George Stearns, June 23, 1861, in Sykes manuscript, chap. 13, folder 1, box 2, Sykes Papers, LoC.

92. Mary Brown to Franklin Sanborn, August 6, 1861, folder 1080, Phillips Papers, series 2, BMS Am 1953, Houghton Library, Cambridge, MA.

93. See, for example, Mary Brown to editors of the *New York Tribune*, February 14, 1860, folder 12, box 46, CHS.

94. See Lydia Maria Child to James Redpath, November 28, 1859, STUT, reel 2; James Redpath to Aaron Stevens, December 21, 1859, SFP. On Child, see Carolyn Karcher, *The First Woman in the Republic: A Cultural Biography of Lydia Maria Child* (Durham, NC: Duke University Press, 1994), 427.

95. Mary to J. Miller McKim, March 6, 1860, typescript copy, folder 3, box 2, series 3, BGC.

96. Paul Finkelman writes that Phillips and Stearns persuaded Mary to go with Redpath but acknowledges that the situation is a bit unclear. See Finkelman, "Manufacturing Martyrdom," in *His Soul Goes Marching On*, 55. McKim apparently thought poorly of Redpath, who he thought had been untruthful in some instance. Mary Brown to J. Miller McKim, March 6, 1860, typescript copy, folder 3, box 2, series 3, BGC.

97. Lydia Maria Child to Chapman, January 1, 1860, Ms. A.5.1 no. 87, BPL. Courtesy of the Trustees of the Boston Public Library/Rare Books.

98. Lydia Maria Child to "niece Mary," December 2, 1859, STUT, reel 2.

99. Lydia Maria Child, in *Correspondence between Lydia Maria Child, and Gov. Wise and Mrs. Mason, of Virginia* (New York: American Anti-Slavery Society, 1860), 13; Lydia Maria Child to "niece Mary," December 2, 1859, STUT, reel 2.

100. *The Public Life of Capt. John Brown* was published "with the sanction and approval of the family of Captain Brown," as attested to by letters from both Mary and Salmon. Redpath, *Public Life of Capt. John Brown*, 5.

101. Annie Brown to J. Miller McKim, December 27, 1859, MAY. Courtesy of the Division of Rare and Manuscript Collections, Cornell University Library.

102. Mary A. Brown to Herman L. Vaill, December 29, 1859, folder 10, box 8, series 2, BGC.

103. Mary Brown to J. Miller McKim, March 6, 1860, typescript copy, folder 3, box 2, series 3, BGC. She explained the circumstances: "I was at first myself in favour of Mrs Childs writing the life of my dear husband but after hearing what

Mr Philipps Mr Sterns & Mrs Childs & others said about it I altered my mind about it."

104. John Brown to Mary Brown, November 16, 1859, in Sanborn, *Life and Letters*, 592. This letter was widely publicized, appearing in the *National Anti-Slavery Standard* the day after Brown's execution.

105. John Brown to Rebecca Spring, November 24, 1859, in Sanborn, *Life and Letters*, 599.

106. Ibid.

107. These offers are mentioned in Rebecca Spring to Thomas Wentworth Higginson, February 10, 1860, Ms. E.5.1 p. 181, BPL. Additionally, in the fall of 1859 a George W. Hall of Ballston Spa, New York, and a Tiffany Waterford had "proposed to educate the three youngest children of John Brown, & I so wrote Mrs Child." Bullard had been in correspondence with Lydia Maria Child about this matter. Mary Brown to Edward Fitch Bullard, January 24, 1860, handwritten copy, MAY.

108. Rebecca Spring to Mary Brown, December 1, 1859, STUT, reel 3.

109. Notably, Wright would go on to marry one of Garrison's sons, another way that Eagleswood seems connected to the Garrisonian faction. On Eagleswood, see Gerda Lerner, *The Grimké Sisters from South Carolina: Rebels against Slavery* (Boston: Houghton Mifflin, 1967), esp. 328–40.

110. Mullaney, "Feminism, Utopianism, and Domesticity," 171.

111. Emphasis in the original. Rebecca Spring to Thomas Wentworth Higginson, January 19, 1860, Ms. E.5.1 p. 164, BPL. Courtesy of the Trustees of the Boston Public Library/Rare Books.

112. Lerner, *Grimké Sisters*, 329.

113. Though later manual labor and technical education would be used to inscribe class (and race) difference and status, Weld seems to have believed that such education would create class harmony and allow classical education to be available to a large group of society. See Stephen P. Rice, "Hand and Heart: The Manual Labor School Movement," in Rice, *Minding the Machine: Languages of Class in Early Industrial America* (Berkeley: University of California Press, 2004), 69–95.

114. Lydia Maria Child to Edward Fitch Bullard, December 19, 1859, typescript copy, folder 3, box 2, series 3, BGC.

115. Rebecca Spring to Thomas Wentworth Higginson, January 30, 1860, Ms. E.5.1 p. 172, BPL. Courtesy of the Trustees of the Boston Public Library/Rare Books. In his biography of his father, Frank Stearns gives his father George Stearns much of the credit. Frank Preston Stearns, *The Life and Public Services of George Luther Stearns* (Philadelphia: J. B. Lippincott, 1907), 199.

116. Rebecca Spring to Thomas Wentworth Higginson, February 10, 1860, Ms. E.5.1 p. 181, BPL. Courtesy of the Trustees of the Boston Public Library/Rare Books.

117. Child wrote, "I heard a report that she had been advised to place her daughters at Concord, because there were too many fashionable city girls at Eagleswood; but who gave the advice, I know not." Lydia Maria Child to Rebecca Spring, March 19, 1860, folder 22, box 1, SPRING. Courtesy of the Department of Special Collections and University Archives, Stanford University Libraries.

118. Mary Brown to J. Miller McKim, March 6, 1860, typescript copy, folder 3, box 2, series 3, BGC.

119. Mary Brown to Edward Fitch Bullard, January 24, 1860, handwritten copy, MAY. Courtesy of the Division of Rare and Manuscript Collections, Cornell University Library.

120. Petrulionis traces an active antislavery movement there throughout the 1850s. They were also caught up in the intrigue of having their own Franklin Sanborn implicated. Sandra Harbert Petrulionis, *To Set This World Right: The Antislavery Movement in Thoreau's Concord* (Ithaca, NY: Cornell University Press, 2006), esp. 139.

121. Mary Brown to J. Miller McKim, March 6, 1860, typescript copy, folder 3, box 2, series 3, BGC.

122. Martha Brown to J. Miller McKim, January 31, 1860, MAY. Courtesy of the Division of Rare and Manuscript Collections, Cornell University Library.

123. Katherine Mayo notes, Interview with Rebecca Spring, Los Angeles, September 1908, folder "Spring, Rebecca," box 16, OGV. Spring seemed especially hardened by the passing of time: she added that Mary was "no help to her husband; merely, no hindrance. She took care of the family. She was good for that." By 1908, Spring had experienced her own reversal of fortune: she still took pride in being genteel, but she also lived in some want in Los Angeles. This in turn may have made her even more determined to distinguish herself from Mary Brown. See Rebecca Spring to Arthur Loring MacKaye, February 23, 1896, HM 46955, HUNT; Spring to MacKaye, April 2, 1896, HM 46956, ibid.; Spring to MacKaye, 1896, HM46957, ibid.; Spring to MacKaye, October 3, [1897], HM 46959, ibid.; and Spring to MacKaye, July 15, 1908, HM 46962, ibid.

124. Receipts for Brown, Sarah and Anna (1860–61), folder 15, series 2, Franklin Benjamin Sanborn Papers, 1845–1936, CFPL; Franklin Sanborn to Thomas Wentworth Higginson, February 24, 1860, Ms. E.5.1 pt. 2 p. 199, BPL. Receipts indicate that money was donated for them that year from money received from Gerrit Smith ($15), J. R. [Manley] ($30.25), and W. Phillips ($30), in addition to whatever the Stearnses and Sanborns might have offered. For information about Sanborn's school, see Kenneth Walter Cameron, "Sanborn's Preparatory School in Concord (1855–1863)," *American Renaissance Literary Report* 3 (1989): 34–84; and Petrulionis, *To Set This World Right*, esp. chap. 4.

125. Catalogue of the teachers and pupils of the Concord School, 1858–1859 (1859), William Ellery Channing and F. B. Sanborn, Collection of materials issued by or relating to the Concord School, Concord, Massachusetts, 1855–1862, CFPL. Sarah became an accomplished artist, and the Saratoga Historical Foundation in California has several pieces of her artwork, including charcoal portraits of her mother and bearded father. A picture of them hanging in the museum can be found at   http://www.alliesforfreedom.org/John_Brown_Family_History_Gallery.html. On Sarah Brown as an artist, see April Hope Halberstadt, "Sarah Brown, Artist and Abolitionist," July 2006, http://www.saratogahistory.com/History/sarah_brown.htm.

126. Sarah Brown, "A Reminiscence: School Days at Concord, Mass.," in *After Harper's Ferry: John Brown's Widow—Her Family and the Saratoga Years* (Saratoga, CA: Saratoga Historical Foundation, 1964).

127. Louisa May Alcott that night received congratulations on having a story published in the *Atlantic Monthly*. Anne B. Adams, "Some Pleasant Recollections of Concord People," in "Three Contemporary Accounts of Louisa May Alcott, with Glimpses of Other Concord Notables," ed. Joel Myerson and Daniel Shealy, *New England Quarterly* 59 (March 1986): 117.

128. Ellen Emerson to [John Haven Emerson], February 22, 1860, in *The Letters of Ellen Tucker Emerson*, vol. 1, ed. Edith E. W. Gregg (Kent, OH: Kent State University Press, 1982), 211. Mary Ryan notes that the farm family functioned for urban middle-class aspirants "more as an idyll of the past than as a contemporary reality." Mary Ryan, *The Empire of the Mother: American Writing about Domesticity, 1830–1860* (New York: Haworth Press, 1982), 98.

129. Ellen Emerson to [John Haven Emerson], February 22, 1860, in *Letters of Ellen Tucker Emerson*, vol. 1, 211. Emphasis mine. It was not just the Emerson women who had this concern. See Franklin Sanborn to Theodore Parker, quoted in Petrulionis, *To Set This World Right*, 146. Higginson, in Redpath, *Public Life of Capt. John Brown*, 70.

130. John Russell Bartlett, *Dictionary of Americanisms: A Glossary of Words and Phrases Usually Regarded as Peculiar to the U.S.*, 1st ed. (New York: Bartlett and Welford, 1848), iii, 86, 94.

131. Katherine Mayo interview with Thomas Wentworth Higginson, December 26, 1907, folder "Higginson, T. W.," box 9, OGV.

132. Lawrence J. Friedman, *Gregarious Saints: Self and Community in American Abolitionism, 1830–1870* (Cambridge: Cambridge University Press, 1982), 46. Julie Roy Jeffrey has exposed how women's antislavery fairs revealed a similar tension, with self-consciously "genteel" abolitionists proclaiming a "reverence for the simple life" without really understanding country life. She attributes this in part to an "uneasy positioning" of reform movements such as antislavery "within a middle-class, market-driven, consumer society." Words such as "simple" and "rustic"—used to describe Mary Brown in 1859 and to describe the Brown women throughout the nineteenth century—were shorthand for all these divisions. Jeffrey, "'Stranger, Buy . . . Lest Our Mission Fail,'" 4.

133. She was not the only famous abolitionist to have this connection. The *Boston Transcript* would portray the well-known antebellum antislavery quartet the Hutchinson Family Singers as "genuine children of the rugged New Hampshire soil." The only female of their group, Abby, would be portrayed in similar fashion: simple, candid, and genuine, all attributes to which many reformers aspired. *Boston Transcript*, May 9, 1885, as quoted in Gac, *Singing for Freedom*, 70; Gac, *Singing for Freedom*, 197.

134. After the Concord party, Mary journeyed on to Boston. Franklin Sanborn to Wendell Phillips, May 22, 1860, folder 1080, Wendell Phillips Papers, series 2, BMS Am 1953, Houghton Library, Cambridge, MA.

135. Louisa May Alcott to Anna Alcott Pratt, [May 27], 1860, in *Selected Letters of Louisa May Alcott*, edited by Joel Myerson, Daniel Shealy, and Madeleine B. Stern (Boston: Little, Brown, 1987), 54–55.

136. Ibid., 55.

137. Ibid. Emphasis in original.

138. Annie Brown Adams to A. M. Ross, July 31, 1887, 3007.15, GLC.

139. Annie Brown Adams to A. M. Ross, December 28, 1887, 3007.18, GLC.

140. Ibid. Emphasis in original.

141. David Lowenthal, *The Past Is a Foreign Country* (Cambridge: Cambridge University Press, 1985), 203.

142. Annie Brown Adams to A. M. Ross, December 28, 1887, 3007.18, GLC.

143. Wealthy Brown to Ruth Brown Thompson, March 27, 1860, 6348.02, GLC.

144. Aaron Stevens to Annie Brown, March 1, 1860, typed copy, folder 8, box 46, CHS.

145. Bell Brown to James Miller McKim, March 6, 1860, MAY. Courtesy of the Division of Rare and Manuscript Collections, Cornell University Library.

146. Mary Brown to J. Miller McKim, March 6, 1860, typescript copy, folder 3, box 2, series 3, BGC.

147. During their visit, he spoke to her of the impending hangings and, perhaps even harder for her to grapple with, cast blame on her father for the losses. Statement of Annie Brown written for Franklin Sanborn, November 1886, CHS.

148. Ibid.

149. Tidd suggested that Annie visit his sister, and she did so. Brown solidarity seems to have faltered as some of the older Brown children felt that their stepmother was not showing Annie enough sympathy. Ruth confided to Mary Stearns, "The first time I saw her after the dreadful news reached us, I was *alarmed* at her appearance, and talked with Mother about her, but she never seemed to understand Annie's case." Apparently Mary Stearns intervened; Ruth later wrote that her mother seemed to better understand "now, since reading your kind and tender letter." Ruth continued, "Thanks for your kindness to Annie. She is very dear to me, and to see her suffering under this soul crushing sorrow, touches my heart deeply." Ruth Brown Thompson to Mary Stearns, April 22, 1860, STUT, reel 2. John Jr. also wrote to Mary Stearns. With less-than-veiled criticism of his stepmother, he continued, "Will you, dear Mrs Stearns who so quickly read her heart be to her a *Spiritual* Mother. 'Tis not every Natural Mother who is by nature qualified to fill such a place. I feel that *you* are." John Brown Jr. to Mary Stearns, May 1, 1860, ibid.

150. There is little evidence of how her mother responded, if she saw Annie's behavior as out of line or if she was offended by Mary Stearns's intervention. To James McKim the following December, she simply noted, tersely, "Annie & Ellen send their love. Annie went to Concord to attend School but was obliged to come home & has not been able to return." Mary Brown to J. Miller McKim, December 9, 1860, typescript copy, folder 3, box 2, series 3, BGC.

151. Ruth Brown Thompson to Mrs. Stearns, April 22, 1860, STUT, reel 2.

152. Annie Brown to Mr. McKim, October 14, 1861, MAY. Courtesy of the Division of Rare and Manuscript Collections, Cornell University Library.

153. Franklin Sanborn to Mary Brown, September 5, 1860, folder 3, box 2, Sykes Papers, LoC.

154. Mary Brown to Sarah Brown, November 11, 1860, folder 3, box 2, Sykes Papers, LoC.

155. Mary Brown to Franklin Sanborn, August 6, 1861, folder 1080, Phillips Papers, series 2, Houghton Library, Cambridge, MA.

156. Wendy Gamber refers to the mid-nineteenth century as the golden age of the home. Gamber, *The Boardinghouse in Nineteenth-Century America* (Baltimore: Johns

Hopkins University Press, 2007), 2. In a time of anxiety about the new social order, the home became "a locus of conflict, a thing to be struggled over and for," and abolitionists took part. Amy Schrager Lang, *The Syntax of Class: Writing Inequality in Nineteenth-Century America* (Princeton, NJ: Princeton University Press, 2003), 129. See also Laurie Ousley, "The Business of Housekeeping: The Mistress, the Domestic Worker, and the Construction of Class," *Legacy: A Journal of American Women Writers* 23, no. 2 (2006): 132–47.

157. Catharine Beecher, *A Treatise on Domestic Economy, for the Use of Young Ladies at Home, and at School*, rev. ed. (Boston: Thomas H. Webb, 1843), 40.

158. Kathryn Kish Sklar, *Catharine Beecher: A Study in American Domesticity* (New York: W. W. Norton, 1976), 151. Sklar explains Beecher's beliefs that the home was a "vehicle for national unity" and that her book functioned as a mechanism "to shape a coherent ideology of domesticity that would answer the needs of American democracy." Ibid., 158.

159. John Brown to Rebecca Spring, November 24, 1859, in Sanborn, *Life and Letters*, 599.

160. Mary Brown to Franklin Sanborn, August 6, 1861, folder 1080, Phillips Papers, series 2, Houghton Library, Cambridge, MA.

161. Louisa May Alcott, in *The Journals of Louisa May Alcott*, ed. Joel Myerson and Daniel Shealy (Boston: Little, Brown, 1989), 105.

5. The Search for a New Life

1. *Red Bluff Semi-Weekly Independent*, October 3, 1864, as quoted in "John Brown's family in Tehama County," typescript manuscript, SYKES.

2. The information on Henry Thompson comes from Clarence Gee, notes taken from records at the Courthouse in Elizabethtown, NY, folder 10, box 4, series 3, BGC. I would speculate that Owen did not enlist because of disability, as well as because of the danger posed to him because he was technically still a fugitive. Jason's reasoning is less clear.

3. John Brown Jr. to [Franklin Sanborn], July 29, 1861, STUT, reel 2. For more information see John Brown Jr. to George Stearns, August 9, 1861, Stearns Papers, KSHS; John Brown Jr. to George Stearns, September 23, 1861, ibid.; Wealthy Brown to "Uncle Jerry," January 8, 1862, folder 2b, box 3, Brown-Clark Collection, HLHS.

4. John Brown Jr. to George Stearns, April 29, 1861, Stearns Papers, KSHS.

5. Thomas Wentworth Higginson to Salmon Brown, November 1, 1861, box 26, ELDR. Reproduced by permission of the Huntington Library.

6. Fred Lockley, Draft story on Salmon Brown interview, 1916, MS13–0019, STUTDB, http://www.wvculture.org/HiStory/wvmemory/jbdetail.aspx?Type=Text&Id=1438.

7. Salmon Brown to Fred Lockley, August 14, 1914, MS05–0050, STUTDB, http://www.wvculture.org/HiStory/wvmemory/jbdetail.aspx?Type=Text&Id=735.

8. Salmon Brown to Lockley, August 14, 1914.

9. Salmon Brown as quoted in Fred Lockley, Draft story on Salmon Brown interview, 1916.

10. John Jr. apparently left the army because of illness. John Brown Jr. to Jason Brown, March 25, 1862, box 7, ELDR. Reproduced by permission of the Huntington Library.

11. Barclay Coppoc to Annie Brown, March 14, 1861, typed extracts, folder 8, box 46, CHS. The familial affection that had existed at the Kennedy farm continued in these letters. Tidd closed one letter by entreating Annie, "Remember me ever as your brother." Charles Plummer Tidd to Annie Brown, March 21, 1861, RU 250, box 1, RUST. Reproduced by permission of the Huntington Library. On Coppoc, see Benjamin F. Gue, "Iowans in John Brown's Raid," *American Historical Magazine* 1, no. 2 (1906): 161; Horwitz, *Midnight Rising*, epilogue; and Jeanette Mather Lord, "John Brown: They Had a Concern," *West Virginia History* 20 (April 1959): 163–83.

12. Annie Brown to Richard Hinton, February 16 and 23, 1862, box 1, ELDR. The italic type indicates something Annie had underlined in the original, while the double underscore is something that she underlined twice. Reproduced by permission of the Huntington Library.

13. Annie Brown to William Lloyd Garrison, June 9, 1863, STUT, reel 2. For reference to her teaching, see Annie Brown Adams to Alexander M. Ross, April 13, 1879, 3007.8, GLC; Sarah E. Wall to "dear friend," December 7, 1884, folder 2.28, John Brown Papers, KSHS; and Annie Brown Adams to Ida B. Wells-Barnett, June 7, 1897, published in the *Conservator*, June 19, 1897, Horatio Rust Scrapbook of Clippings, 1882–1902, RU 371, RUST. I have also pieced together the (still sketchy) details of Annie's teaching from Rosenberg, "Mary Brown"; Boyd Stutler, "Annie and Sarah Brown in School, and as Teachers," typescript notes, STUT, reel 6; and Peterson, *John Brown: The Legend Revisited*, 38.

14. Sarah E. Wall to "dear friend," December 7, 1884, folder 2.28, John Brown Papers, KSHS.

15. Mary Brown to Annie Brown, December 3, 1863, RU 322, box 1, RUST. Reproduced by permission of the Huntington Library.

16. Ibid.

17. Sarah E. Wall reported, "She and I occupied the same room for two months in Norfolk, Va, in the winter of '63–4. . . . We met in Phila. at a convention, and both having a desire to do something for the freedmen, we were brought together by Mrs. Sarah R. May of Leicester, & went from there to Norfolk." Sarah E. Wall to "dear friend," December 7, 1884, folder 2.28, John Brown Papers, KSHS. According to Ronald Butchart, whose Freedmen's Teachers Project has uncovered an amazing amount of data on teachers in freedpeople's schools between 1861 and 1876, Sarah R. May was active in two societies that sponsored teachers, the Leicester Freeman's Aid Society and the larger New England Freedman's Aid Society, with which it merged in 1866. My sincere thanks to Ron for providing information on Sarah Wall from his database of teachers and for his suggestions and ideas about Annie's teaching career. For more, see Ronald E. Butchart, *Schooling the Freed People: Teaching, Learning, and the Struggle for Black Freedom, 1861–1876* (Chapel Hill: University of North Carolina Press, 2010).

18. William Still, *The Underground Railroad* (Philadelphia: Porter and Coates, 1872), 542, 541. On Still's narrative, see Jeffrey, *Abolitionists Remember*, esp. 61–91.

19. Thomas C. Parramore with Peter C. Stewart and Tommy L. Bogger, *Norfolk: The First Four Centuries* (Charlottesville: University Press of Virginia, 1994), 217.

20. Joe M. Richardson, *Christian Reconstruction: The American Missionary Association and Southern Blacks, 1861–1890* (Athens: University of Georgia Press, 1986), 13.

21. Nina Silber, "A Compound of Wonderful Potency: Women Teachers of the North in the Civil War South," in *The War Was You and Me: Civilians in the American Civil War*, ed. Joan E. Cashin (Princeton, NJ: Princeton University Press, 2002), 36.

22. H. S. Beals to S. S. Jocelyn, September 7, 1863, from the American Missionary Association files, as quoted in Richardson, *Christian Reconstruction*, 57.

23. Letter from Miss E. James, December 19, 1863, from *American Missionary* 8 (February 1864), p. 36, in folder 84, box 7, CC-SUNY.

24. John Brown Jr. to Annie Brown, January 10, 1864, box 7, ELDR. Perhaps nostalgic of his own days as a teacher (and glossing over his own difficulties!), John Jr. wrote, "Have you not found your sphere? That of teacher I know by experience, to be the most congenial of all others to me. It is satisfactory, glorious—heavenly." Reproduced by permission of the Huntington Library.

25. Richardson, *Christian Reconstruction*, 11.

26. Ronald Butchart notes that northern teachers were not universally abolitionist or equality-minded in their outlooks. Moreover, he writes, "There was no necessary relationship between embracing the abolition of slavery and working affirmatively to assure that legal emancipation would be followed by political and economic emancipation." Butchart, *Schooling the Freed People*, xiii.

27. Silber, "Compound of Wonderful Potency," 37. Ronald Butchart points out that contrary to our stereotype, not all of the teachers were relatively affluent. Butchart, *Schooling the Freed People*, xv.

28. Parramore, *Norfolk*, 210, 220–21; Sarah E. Wall to "dear friend," December 7, 1884, folder 2.28, John Brown Papers, KSHS.

29. From a few scattered references, it is clear that Annie wrote to her family at North Elba and frequently to her sister-in-law Bell about her experiences, but very little of the correspondence has been located. In upward of one hundred surviving letters, only two reference her teaching. In one is the curt statement that in "the winter of 1863–4 I taught in contraband schools in Norfolk and Portsmouth, Va., attending sunday school in Gov. Wise's mansion at his plantation with Elizabeth [Dour]. We little knew what changes a few years may bring forth." Annie Brown Adams to Alexander M. Ross, April 13, 1879, 3007.8, GLC.

30. The conversion of Henry Wise's house to a school came much to the glee of abolitionist-minded teachers. One, a Rev. W. S. Bell, had a letter published in the *American Missionary* in which he wrote, "We have organized an interesting school in the dining-room of the Wise house. A negro school in Gov. Wise's house! Here, where treason was talked over, and toasts drank to the success of the traitors, we every day hear sung the famous John Brown song. We lack one thing; the young folks very much want to see the likeness of the old hero. Can't some kind friend send us one to be *hung* on the wall of our school room?" Rev. W. S. Bell, December 7, 1864, in *American Missionary* 8 (February 1864): 37.

31. *Sacramento Bee*, May 8, 1865, p. 1. The story that she had taught school in his house was widely reprinted, while other newspapers printed denials. On the controversy see Peterson, *John Brown: The Legend Revisited*, 38.

32. *Indianapolis Daily State Sentinel*, March 14, 1864, p. 2.

33. Bell Thompson Brown to Ruth and Henry Thompson, January 3, 1864, folder 5, box 1, CC-SUNY. Bell referred to receiving a "long letter from Annie last week, she was in Norfolk Virginia enjoying herself finely."

34. Charles Heller, *Portrait of an Abolitionist: A Biography of George Luther Stearns* (Westport, CT: Greenwood Press, 1996), 142.

35. Mary Brown to Mary Stearns, March 3, 1863, STUT, reel 2.

36. Mary Brown to Bell and Freddy, September 27, 1862, typescript copy, folder 3, box 2, series 3, BGC. On Redpath's connection to this Haytian Relief fund (a second fund that followed the original John Brown Fund), see John McKivigan, *Forgotten Firebrand: James Redpath and the Making of Nineteenth-Century America* (Ithaca, NY: Cornell University Press, 2008), esp. 70–79.

37. Mary Brown to George and Mary Stearns, October 21, 1860, quoted in Velma West Sykes, "A Biography of Mrs. John Brown," chap. 13, pp. 5–6, folder 1, box 2, Sykes Papers, LoC.

38. Mary Brown to George Stearns, August 13, 1861, Stearns Papers, KSHS; Mary Brown to George Stearns, May 14, 1862, ibid.; Mary Brown to Samuel Sewell, February 13, 1861, typescript copy, SYKES.

39. W. D. Sherwood to Clarence Gee, January 27, 1927, folder 5, box 8, series 2, BGC.

40. Ruth Brown Thompson to Mary Stearns, April 22, 1860, STUT, reel 2.

41. Richard White, *"It's Your Misfortune and None of My Own": A History of the American West* (Norman: University of Oklahoma Press, 1991), 209. The Browns migrated in the heyday of travel on the overland trails: between 1841 and 1867, 350,000 Americans traveled by wagon to Oregon and California. Julie Roy Jeffrey, *Frontier Women: "Civilizing" the West? 1840–1880*, rev. ed. (New York: Hill & Wang, 1998), 3.

42. Lillian Schlissel argues that diaries offer "eloquent records that leave-taking was a painful and agonizing time." Schlissel, *Women's Diaries of the Westward Journey*, 3rd rev. ed. (New York: Schocken Books, 2004), 28.

43. Watson Brown had apparently considered going to California in the years prior to Harpers Ferry. During the war, the Browns were again drawn by glowing tales from a neighbor, a relative of Salmon's wife Abbie. Watson Brown to "dear brothers," October 24, 1858, BFC; Lockley, Draft story on Salmon Brown interview, 1916; "Across the Plains in the Early 60's, as Told by One Who Participated in the Stirring Events of That Adventurous Western Era," memoir by Abbie Brown, reprinted in the *Lake Placid (NY) News*, September 29, 1916, typescript copy by Clarence Gee, folder 10, box 2, series 3, BGC.

44. Mary Brown to Owen Brown, January 31, 1864, folder [9?], box 8, series 2, BGC.

45. Lansford W. Hastings, *The Emigrants' Guide to Oregon and California* (1845) (Princeton, NJ: Princeton University Press, 1932), 81.

46. Ibid., 82.

47. Lockley, Draft story on Salmon Brown interview, 1916.

48. Mary Brown to Mary Stearns, August 4, 1863, MS04–0079, STUTDB, http://www.wvculture.org/HiStory/wvmemory/jbdetail.aspx?Type=Text&Id= 682.

49. She hoped abolitionists would tend it, inquiring, "I Should like to know what My Dear husbands friends intend to do about removeing [sic] his remains or what they would advise to be done in case we all leave this Country." Mary Brown to Mary Stearns, August 4, 1863, MS04–0079, STUTDB, http://www.wvculture.org/HiStory/wvmemory/jbdetail.aspx?Type=Text&Id=682. In later years, Kate Field, a wealthy woman with transcendentalist ties, sought to purchase the home and grave site to restore its condition. Field even proposed that after the purchase, Mary Brown be resettled there (apparently without any consultation of Mary!) Kate Field to William Claflin, Gov. of Mass., September 7, 1869, typescript copy from original in Rutherford B. Hayes Library, folder 5, box 4, series 3, BGC. For background, see Lillian Whiting, *Kate Field: A Record* (Boston: Little, Brown, 1889).

50. Bell Thompson Brown to Henry and Ruth Thompson, April 3, 1864, folder 5, box 1, CC-SUNY.

51. To get ready to go, to make the overland journey, and to survive until the first harvest once out west, Richard White estimates, a family needed between $750 and $1,500. White, *"It's Your Misfortune and None of My Own,"* 185.

52. Mary Brown to Owen Brown, January 31, 1864, folder [9?], box 8, series 2, BGC.

53. Hastings, *Emigrants' Guide to Oregon and California*, 85.

54. Mary Brown to Annie Brown, December 3, 1863, RU 322, box 1, RUST. Reproduced by permission of the Huntington Library.

55. Wealthy Brown to "Uncle Jerry," January 17, 1863, folder 2b, box 3, Brown-Clark Collection, HLHS. By 1865 Put-in-Bay was producing grapes and wine to be exported via Detroit. Charles Frohman, *Put-in-Bay: Its History* (Columbus: Ohio Historical Society, 1971), 55.

56. Interviewed in 1889, John Jr. confirmed his delight: "I lead a peaceful life here, with only the gay summer butterfly guests flitting across my solitude." John Brown Jr. as quoted in Frohman, *Put-in-Bay*, 53.

57. John Brown Jr. to "my dear friend" [Franklin Sanborn], April 17, 1864, STUT, reel 2. See also Ella Thompson Towne to the Owen Brown Family Reunion, "Recollections of North Elba, New York," May 27, 1932, typescript copy by Clarence Gee, folder 1, box 2, series 2, BGC. On Ruth's desire to live close to her siblings, see also Ruth Brown Thompson to Wealthy Brown, August 15, 1860, folder 367, box 36, CC-SUNY.

58. Wealthy Brown to "Uncle Jerry," April 28, 1872, folder 2b, box 3, Brown-Clark Collection, HLHS.

59. See John Brown Jr. to Jeremiah Root Brown and family, April 28, 1872, folder 2B, box 3, Brown-Clark Collection, HLHS. On the Thompsons' life in Wisconsin, see also Wealthy Brown to "Uncle Jerry," January 4, 1874, ibid.; and Ruth Brown Thompson to Nellie Baynton, December 7, 1873, Miscellaneous Correspondence, 1818–1952, SLCHS.

60. Ruth Brown Thompson to Nellie Baynton, December 7, 1873, Miscellaneous Correspondence, 1818–1952, SLCHS.

61. Soon after their arrival, Rust spearheaded a fund-raising drive to help Ruth and Henry buy a home, writing to Franklin Sanborn and Mary Stearns as well as newspapers throughout the country. The editor of the *Chicago Inter-Ocean* sent Rust a letter listing his donors and requesting receipts for each donor, signed "by one or other of the daughters, as a memento of John Brown etc." He added that "printed receipts would do, if it would save tiresome writing-closing 'daughter of John Brown of Ossawatomie Kansas.'" Though Ruth and her family never escaped an ever-looming threat of poverty, to some extent Rust's efforts were successful, and his efforts to keep them and her brothers out of need would continue until (and beyond) Ruth's death in 1904. Writing to him from Redondo Beach after he helped fund her trip there in 1891, Ruth exclaimed, "My heart is *full* of gratitude to you, my dear kind friend, for your efforts in our behalf." Jonathan Plummer to Horatio Rust, March 5, 1890, RU 170, box 2, RUST; Ruth Brown Thompson to Horatio Rust, September 12, 1891, RU 356, ibid. Reproduced by permission of the Huntington Library. For his contact with Sanborn and Mary Stearns, who declined to contribute because of her own economic straits, see Franklin Sanborn to Horatio Rust, March 7, 1887, RU 217, box 1, ibid.; Mary Stearns to Horatio Rust, May 31, 1887, RU 237, ibid.; Mary Stearns to Horatio Rust, June 21, 1889, RU 238, ibid.; Franklin Sanborn to Horatio Rust, December 16, 1889, RU 218, ibid.; F. G. Adams to Horatio Rust, December 17, 1889, RU 4, ibid. On Rust, see Jane Apostol, "Horatio Nelson Rust: Abolitionist, Archaeologist, Indian Agent," *California History* (Winter 1979–80): 304–15.

62. *Pasadena Union*, as quoted in Hiram Reid, *History of Pasadena. . . .* (Pasadena, CA: Pasadena History Co., 1895), 321; "Neighborhood News," *Los Angeles Times*, August 19, 1886.

63. For more on Ruth's life in Pasadena, see Bonnie Laughlin-Schultz, "'Could I Not Do Something for the Cause?' The Brown Women, Antislavery Reform, and Memory of Militant Abolitionism" (PhD diss., Indiana University, 2009), chap. 7; Bonnie Laughlin-Schultz, "John Brown's Children in Southern California," unpublished mss.

64. Wealthy Brown to Richard Hinton, December 11, 1892, box 8, ELDR. Reproduced by permission of the Huntington Library.

65. John Brown Jr. to Henry and Ruth Thompson, October 15, 1862, box 7, ELDR. Reproduced by permission of the Huntington Library. Jason also appears to have strongly desired the family to live close together, and there is some sense that her stepchildren thought Mary had erred by going west. See Jason Brown to Salmon Brown, February 21, 1860, ibid.; Jason Brown to "dear brother," December 3, 1863, ibid.

66. John Brown Jr. to Henry and Ruth, October 15, 1862, ELDR. Reproduced by permission of the Huntington Library.

67. She continued, "I hope not it is no place for poor Bell if she would get evry thing into money and come out here and buy sheep she could have a good liveing from the interest." Mary Brown to Annie Brown, December 3, 1863, RU 322, box 1, RUST. Reproduced by permission of the Huntington Library.

68. Hastings, *Emigrants' Guide to Oregon and California*, 6.

69. I have mapped the route I believe they took from various Brown sources as well as from the emigrant guidebooks, others' accounts of 1864 journeys, and secondary scholarship on the westward journey.

70. Hastings urged that emigrants bring "good gun" powder and lead, as well as pistols and ammunition. Hastings, *Emigrants' Guide to Oregon and California*, 143.

71. Johnny Faragher and Christine Stansell, "Women and Their Families on the Overland Trail to California and Oregon, 1842–1867," *Feminist Studies* 2, nos. 2–3 (1975): 150.

72. Annie Brown to Isabella Thompson Brown, May 15, 1864, in copies of Annie Brown letters, Lydia Brown Crothers to the Owen Brown Family Reunion, 1930, folder 9, box 8, series 2, BGC.

73. "Across the Plains in the Early 60's," memoir by Abbie Brown, BGC. On "benign neglect" of children on the journey, see Schlissel, *Women's Diaries of the Westward Journey*, 49.

74. Annie Brown to Isabella (Bell) Thompson Brown, May 15, 1864, copy enclosed in Lydia Brown Crothers to the Owen Brown Family Reunion, 1930, folder 9, box 8, series 2, BGC. A few years after she had been widowed, Bell married another Brown cousin, and Lydia was their child. She played a large role in maintaining contact with the broad Owen Brown family, and many of her letters are included in the Brown-Gee, Brown-Clark, and Brown Family reunion papers at Hudson Library and Historical Society.

75. Harriet A. Loughary, "Travels and Incidents" (1864), in *Covered Wagon Women: Diaries and Letters from the Western Trails, 1840–1890*, ed. Kenneth L. Holmes, vol. 8, *1862–1865* (Spokane, WA: Arthur H. Clark Co., 1989), 121.

76. Annie Brown to Isabella Thompson Brown, May 15, 1864, in copies of Annie Brown letters, Lydia Brown Crothers to the Owen Brown Family Reunion, 1930, folder 9, box 8, series 2, BGC.

77. Loughary, "Travels and Incidents," 134.

78. "Across the Plains in the Early 60's," memoir by Abbie Brown, BGC.

79. Loughary, "Travels and Incidents," 136. See also White, *"It's Your Misfortune and None of My Own,"* 199; Schlissel, *Women's Diaries of the Westward Journey*, 118, 119.

80. "Across the Plains in the Early 60's," memoir by Abbie Brown, BGC.

81. Though the Browns extended empathy to African Americans, Abbie did not exhibit the same attitude in her recollection to Native Americans. "I will never forget if I live a thousand years," she recalled, "how they looked with their heads all lowered and their horrible naked brown shoulders shining in the sun. They were huge powerful specimens of Indians and looked cruel as death."

82. Annie Brown to Bell Thompson Brown, October 9, 1864, in Ella Thompson Towne, "Letters Tell Story of John Brown's Widow's Trip across Continent," *Lake Placid (NY) News*, November 24, 1939, p. 6, in folder 9, box 8, series 2, BGC. See also Annie Brown to "My Very Dear Sister," October 9, 1864, reprinted in the *Liberator*, November 25, 1864.

83. Annie Brown to "My Very Dear Sister," October 9, 1864, reprinted in the *Liberator*, November 25, 1864.

84. Salmon Brown as quoted in Rosenberg, "Mary Brown," 22.

85. Abbie Brown, "Across the Plains in the Early 60's," BGC. Abbie left out the fact that they were accompanied by a smaller contingent of Union wagons, or at least this is what Annie Brown wrote to the relatives at Put-in-Bay shortly after their arrival. Annie Brown to "My Very Dear Sister," October 9, 1864, in *Liberator*, November 25, 1864.

86. Details from "Across the Plains in the Early 60's," memoir by Abbie Brown, BGC; Annie Brown to Isabella Thompson Brown, May 15, 1864; Annie Brown to "My Very Dear Sister," October 9, 1864, in *Liberator*, November 25, 1864.

87. Editorializing, the paper continued, "Nothing could be more natural than, once known to the Missourians of the guerilla order, they should be thus victimized." *Boston Commonwealth*, September 23, 1864, copy in Ella Thompson Towne Scrapbook, BFC. Reproduced by permission of the Huntington Library.

88. Jane Thompson to Henry Thompson and family, January 11, 1865, folder 5, box 1, CC-SUNY.

89. Annie Brown to "My Very Dear Sister," October 9, 1864, reprinted in the *Liberator*, November 25, 1864.

90. Schlissel, *Women's Diaries of the Westward Journey*, 27.

91. Leo McCoy, "California History of the Family of John Brown," STUTDB, http://www.wvculture.org/HiStory/wvmemory/jbdetail.aspx?Type=Text&Id=2381. Helen Brodt was an artist who would ultimately paint a portrait of John Brown from Mary Brown's daguerreotypes. She would be one of Mary's first California friends. Ethel Brodt Wilson (daughter), quoted in Harry Noyes Pratt, "A Woman Pioneer on Lassen's Peak," *Overland Monthly and Out West Magazine*, vol. 82 (November 1924), 488.

92. "Across the Plains in the Early 60's," memoir by Abbie Brown, BGC.

93. Annie Brown to "My Very Dear Sister," October 9, 1864, reprinted in the *Liberator*, November 25, 1864.

94. Ibid.

95. *Red Bluff Semi-Weekly Independent*, October 3, 1864, as quoted in "John Brown's family in Tehama County," typescript manuscript, SYKES.

96. On the history of Red Bluff, see Edward Galland Zelinsky and Nancy Olmsted, "Upriver Boats: When Red Bluff Was the Head of Navigation," *California History* 64 (Spring 1985), 86–117; and E. J. Lewis, *Tehama County, California, Illustrations Descriptive of Its Scenery . . . with Historical Sketch of the County* (San Francisco: Elliot and Moore, 1880).

97. As a result, between 1853 and 1860 its size had doubled, from 1,000 to 2,000. Lewis, *Tehama County*, 19.

98. Ibid.

99. Samuel Bowles, *Our New West—Records of Travel between the Mississippi River and the Pacific Ocean* (Hartford, CT: Hartford Publishing Co., 1869), 171.

100. William Deverell, "Thoughts from the Farther West: Mormons, California, and the Civil War," *Journal of Mormon History* 34, no. 2 (2008): 6. See also Leonard L. Richards, *The California Gold Rush and the Coming of the Civil War* (New York: Alfred A. Knopf, 2007); and Ronald C. Woolsey, "The Politics of the Lost Cause: 'Secesh-

ers' and Democrats in Southern California during the Civil War," *California History* 69 (Winter 1990–91): 372–83.

101. Richards, *California Gold Rush and the Coming of the Civil War*, 230–31.

102. Debate remains heated about the extent of pro-Confederate leanings and activity in California. See Robert J. Chandler, "An Uncertain Influence: The Role of the Federal Government in California, 1846–1880," *California History* 81, nos. 3–4 (2003): 224–71; Laurence Fletcher Talbott, "California Secessionist Support of the Southern Confederacy: The Struggle, 1861–1865" (PhD diss., Union Institute, 1995); and Steven E. Sodergren, "Exercising Restraint: Military Responses to Southern Sentiments in California during the Civil War," *Military History of the West* 37 (2007): 1–27.

103. See Wilbert Phay, "John Brown's Family in Red Bluff, 1864–1870" (MA thesis, Chico State College, 1986); Lewis, *Tehama County*, esp. 101–4.

104. Aurelius H. Brodt to Mrs. Daniel Brodt, April 24, 1865, STUT, reel 2.

105. "Across the Plains in the Early 60's," memoir by Abbie Brown, BGC.

106. *Red Bluff Weekly Independent*, April 13, 1865, as quoted in Rosenberg, "Mary Brown," 26. Citizens throughout northern California founded branches of the John Brown Cottage fund; Sacramento sent $350 to the Red Bluff committee. Another appeal of the *Independent* read, "If every man, woman and child in California who has hummed 'John Brown's Body Lies a Moulding in the Grave' will throw in a dime, his family will have a home.'" See Clarence Gee / Boyd Stutler, "California History of the JB family," typescript copy, SYKES; *Independent*, undated and January 1866, as quoted in Phay, "John Brown's Family in Red Bluff," 26, 31.

107. *Red Bluff Semi-Weekly Independent*, June 5, 1865, quoted in Leo McCoy, "California History of the John Brown Family"; Rosenberg, "Mary Brown," 26–27; Phay, "John Brown's Family in Red Bluff," 31.

108. *Boston Commonwealth*, April 22, 1865, as quoted in Clarence Gee / Boyd Stutler, "Overland Journey of the Brown Family, 1863–1864," typescript notes, folder 9, box 8, series 2, BGC.

109. For this information, see Phay, "John Brown's Family in Red Bluff," 31; Leo McCoy, "California History of the John Brown family." Mary faced one final obstacle before she could claim she owned her cottage outright. A local woman named Amanda Hoag sued Mary, claiming prior possession of the lots. Wilbert Phay suggests that Hoag's motivation was political; she supposedly raised her flag to celebrate Lincoln's assassination and hated John Brown. Her lawsuit was dismissed the following month. See Rosenberg, "Mary Brown," 27; and Phay, "John Brown's Family in Red Bluff," 33.

110. In her letters to her sister-in-laws Wealthy and Isabella, Annie confided their plans upon arrival: Mary and Ellen (now age ten) would live in town, while she and Sarah would move out into the country and take posts as teachers. Salmon and his family had already moved out into the country, where Salmon began to build up a sheep herd. Annie Brown to Bell Thompson Brown, October 9, 1864, in Ella Thompson Towne, "Letters Tell Story of John Brown's Widow's Trip across Continent," *Lake Placid News,* November 24, 1939, p. 6, folder 9, box 8, series 2, BGC; Annie Brown to Wealthy Brown, October 9, 1864, *Liberator*, November 25,

1864; Salmon Brown notice in *Red Bluff Independent*, May 25, 1865, as quoted in Phay, "John Brown's Family in Red Bluff," 25.

111. Lewis, *Tehama County*, 75. For a broad survey, see E. S. Campbell, comp., "Historical Review of the Public Schools of Tehama County, from the Year 1853 to the Year 1880," ibid., 74–77.

112. Pay in the Red Bluff schools peaked in 1867–68, when Annie and Sarah would have averaged upward of $70 a month (including board) for the six months that school was in session. In the following two school years, pay fell to between $62 and $65. Lewis, *Tehama County*, 76.

113. "Significant Historical Objects and Sites Surrounding the Cinderella Motel, Red Bluff," folder 5, box 8, series 2, BGC; Phay, "John Brown's Family in Red Bluff," 27.

114. As best as can be ascertained, Annie taught there in 1867–68 and possibly 1868–69. See Lewis, *Tehama County*, 75; Golden Anniversary edition of the *Red Bluff Daily News*, November 21, 1935; "John Brown's family in Tehama County," typescript copy, SYKES.

115. *Red Bluff Independent*, June 20, 1866, as quoted in Phay, "John Brown's Family in Red Bluff," 28.

116. At the order's peak in 1868, it had over two hundred thousand members in North America, and by 1873 there were lodges on six continents and millions of members. David M. Fahey, *Temperance and Racism: John Bull, Johnny Reb, and the Good Templars* (Lexington: University Press of Kentucky, 1996), 12. On the Templars in California, see Gilman M. Ostrander, *The Prohibition Movement in California, 1848–1933*, University of California Publications in History, vol. 57 (Berkeley: University of California Press, 1957), esp. 23–36. The fact that they accepted both male and female members and allowed for women to serve on committees and in leadership roles made them immediately popular with women, who "had responded to the temperance pledge in greater numbers and with more enthusiasm than men." Ian Tyrell, *Woman's World, Woman's Empire: The Woman's Christian Temperance Union in International Perspective* (Chapel Hill: University of North Carolina Press, 1991), 17.

117. The dues for men were much higher, $1.50 per quarter, and additional dues were required from both sexes for advancement in rank. Independent Order of Good Templars, Grand Lodge of California, *Constitution and By-laws of the Grand Lodge* (San Francisco: Francis, Valentine & Co., Printers, 1866), 18, 28. The dues are notably low in comparison to another organization that Mary Brown would come into contact with in 1882, the New England Woman's Club: in 1881, their entrance fee was $5 and their annual fee $10. See Jennie June Croly, *The History of the Woman's Club in America* (New York: Henry G. Allen & Co., 1898), 45.

118. Good Templars' Platform, adopted 1859, in Independent Order of Good Templars, Grand Lodge of California, *Constitution and By-laws of the Grand Lodge* (Sacramento: Russell & Winterburn, 1867), 39.

119. *Proceedings of the Seventh Annual Session of the Grand Lodge of the Independent Order of Good Templars, Held at Sacramento, September 1866* (Sacramento: Russell & Winterburn, Printers, Union Book and Job Office, 1866), 10.

120. It is notable that *all* the Browns—with the possible exception of Salmon Brown—became active in temperance work in the years and decades after the

Civil War. John Jr. repeatedly refused to sell his grapes for wine making. Ruth, too, would attend WCTU meetings in Pasadena in the latter part of the nineteenth century, and she and her brothers Owen and Jason would be inducted into the local chapter.

121. Lewis, *Tehama County*, 91. Ellen Brown appears listed as a member. Annie and Sarah are listed as "Worthy Vice Templars." The Red Bluff Lodge was organized in October 1865 by a Rev. A. C. McDougal in the local Presbyterian church. The Red Bluff Lodge is identified as no. 192, with meetings on Friday nights, in *The Illustrated Fraternal Directory Including Educational Institutions of the Pacific Coast. . . .* (San Francisco: Bancroft Co., 1889), 321.

122. *Constitution and By-laws of the Grand Lodge* (1866), 16–17.

123. The constitution and bylaws contain an explanation of this lengthy and potentially costly trial process, but it is clear that the Brown women could have been accused of "unworthy conduct" by an unknown and protected accuser. See article 10, section 1, *Constitution and By-laws of the Grand Lodge* (1866), 22–23. On the protection of accusers, see also article 9, "Divulging Private Matters," ibid., 30. For the restrictions on discussion, see article 10, section 1, ibid.

124. In the year the Red Bluff lodge was organized, the yearly report mentioned three suspensions and two expulsions. The report from the next year identified 194 members, five suspensions, and three expulsions. See *Proceedings of the Seventh Annual Session of the Grand Lodge of the Independent Order of Good Templars, Held at Sacramento, September 1866* (Sacramento: Russell & Winterburn, Printers, Union Book and Job Office, 1866), 50; *Proceedings of the Eighth Annual Session of the Grand Lodge of the Independent Order of Good Templars, Held at Sacramento, September 1867* (Sacramento: Russell & Winterburn, Printers, Union Book and Job Office, 1867), 58.

125. See order of business, *Constitution and By-laws of the Grand Lodge* (1866), 36; *Constitution and By-laws of the Grand Lodge* (1867), 29.

126. Leo L. McCoy to Boyd Stutler, October 26, 1930, STUTDB, http://www.wvculture.org/HiStory/wvmemory/jbdetail.aspx?Type Text&Id=2381. Other reports confirm this. See Mary Fablinger to Velma West Sykes, February 20, 1964, folder 4, box 1, Sykes Papers, LoC; Samuel Bowles, *Our New West—Records of Travel between the Mississippi River and the Pacific Ocean* (Hartford, CT: Hartford Publishing Co., 1869), 171.

127. For a history of the newspaper war between the *Independent* and the *Sentinel*, see Lewis, *Tehama County*, 101–2. Lewis was connected with the *Sentinel*, but nonetheless he offers a useful overview.

128. *Red Bluff Independent*, as quoted in Phay, "John Brown's Family in Red Bluff," 40.

129. *Red Bluff Independent*, October 2, 1867, quoted in Phay, "John Brown's Family in Red Bluff," 41.

130. *Red Bluff Sentinel*, October 24, 1867, quoted in Phay, "John Brown's Family in Red Bluff," 41. He added, "Mr. Writer doubtless considers himself a brave man, will he be so kind as to present his name in person. I can be found at my ranch five miles south of Tehama."

131. Phay, "John Brown's Family in Red Bluff," 44.

132. Rosenberg, "Mary Brown," 29.

133. These and other details in this paragraph from "The Town Named after Henry Rohner," author unknown, http://sunnyfortuna.com/history/rohnerville/index.htm.

134. *Memorial and Biographical History of Northern California.* . . . (Chicago: Lewis Publishing Co., 1891), 142. See also A. T. Hawley, *The Climate, Resources and Advantages of Humboldt County, Cal., Described in a Series of Letters to the* San Francisco Daily Evening Bulletin (Eureka, CA: *Daily and Weekly Humboldt Times*, J. E. Wyman & Son publishers, 1879), 21.

135. It had been established in 1859, the year of Brown's death. By 1870 the rising population (now at 250 in the town itself) supported two hotels, a drugstore, a saloon, three blacksmith shops, various other shops, a doctor, and three churches. By the end of the decade, it possessed an additional schoolhouse, a Congregational church, various fraternal organizations, and other comforts. Hawley, *Climate, Resources and Advantages of Humboldt County.*

136. Mary Siler Anderson, *Backwoods Chronicle: A History of Southern Humboldt, 1849–1920* (Redway, CA: Southern Humboldt County Press, 1985), 19.

137. John Carr, *Pioneer Days in California: Historical and Personal Sketches* (Eureka, CA: Times Publishing Co., 1891), 409–10. He noted that there was a stage line between Hydesville and Eureka, but it seems most likely that their overland trek followed the road that is now State Road 36 between Red Bluff and Hydesville. Even in his description of a 1915 trek from San Francisco to Eureka, Rev. William Rader noted the difficulty—and beauty—of the trip in the "untrodden wilds" of Humboldt County. At one point while driving along the Eel River he described "descend[ing] upon a crooked road with breathless interest, if not fear—possibly the most thrilling and crooked road in all the world." Rader as quoted in Leigh H. Irvine, *History of Humboldt County, California, with Biographical Sketches.* . . . (Los Angeles: Historic Record Co., 1915), 98, 123.

138. Copy of marriage certificate, November 29, 1869, Annie Brown Adams binder, Mattole Valley Historical Society, Petrolia, CA.

139. Mary A. Woodworth to Horatio Rust, Mary 10, 1897, RU 257, box 4, RUST. Reproduced by permission of the Huntington Library. Woodworth was a sister of Samuel. For more information on Samuel, see Edwin Cotter, unpublished manuscript, pp. 24–32, CC-SUNY. Cotter's manuscript cites family tradition that the pair met while Samuel was making a trip across the Plains, but I have seen no corroborating evidence for this.

140. Joan M. Jensen and Darlis S. Miller, "The Gentle Tamers Revisited: New Approaches to the History of Women in the American West," in *Women and Gender in the American West,* ed. Mary Ann Irwin and James F. Brooks (Albuquerque: University of New Mexico Press, 2004), 19, 20.

141. Joan E. Cashin, *First Lady of the Confederacy: Varina Davis's Civil War* (Cambridge, MA: Belknap Press of Harvard University Press, 2006), 246–48, 260–73, esp. 271.

142. According to Edwin Cotter, Samuel had been married when he lived in Kansas, and his first child, Irona Sierraville Adams, was born there in 1861. Cotter then has him coming to California and having a second child, Grant, before his wife died. I have seen no evidence of Grant in any of Annie's family records, though it

is clear that Irona was part of her life. Edwin Cotter, unpublished manuscript, pp. 24–25, CC-SUNY.

143. In their move, Samuel was escaping notoriety (and potential persecution) from a bar fight. Reports from the *Red Bluff Independent* show that Samuel Adams in July 1869 had shot and wounded a James McTurk over an election bet that Adams lost. The charges against Adams were dismissed by a Justice Supan, who had previously dismissed charges against another person who had shot McTurk. See *Red Bluff Independent*, July 8, 1869, September 11, 1869, and September 16, 1869, quoted in Phay, "John Brown's Family in Red Bluff," 42.

144. Sarah E. Wall to "dear friend," December 7, 1884, folder 2.28, John Brown Papers, KSHS.

145. All information from Genealogy, folder 6: Annie Brown Adams, box 2, series 2, BGC. Other sources from the Mattole Valley Historical Society confirm this.

146. In addition, Mary delivered babies to other families. Mrs. Aletta Lea to Mrs. Freda Heyne Madsen, Eureka, 1962, in Josephine Brizzard Appleton, "The Browns of Rohnerville, 1870–1881," *Humboldt Historical Society Newsletter* (November–December 1965), box 10, series 2, BGC.

147. On Sarah, see Mary Brown to Ruth Brown Thompson, July 26, 1875, typescript copy, folder 3, box 2, series 3, BGC. For Salmon and Abbie's children, see Clarence Gee, Genealogy Notes on Salmon Brown, folder 5, box 2, series 2, ibid.

148. Appleton, "Browns of Rohnerville."

149. Annie's daughter Lolita died a month after her birth, and a few years later, Annie lost another daughter, one-year-old Grace. See Clarence Gee, Genealogy Notes on Annie Brown Adams, folder 5, box 2, series 2, BGC.

150. Mary Stearns to Jeremiah Brown, November 21, 1873, folder 41, box 1, series 1, BGC.

151. Mary Brown to Mary Stearns, January 7, 1863, STUT, reel 2.

152. Letter from Geraldine to author, Arcata, 1965, in Appleton, "Browns of Rohnerville"; Mary Stearns to Jeremiah Brown, November 21, 1873, folder 41, box 1, series 1, BGC; Mary Brown to Jason and Ellen Brown, January 15, 1873, 8261, GLC; Mary Brown to Ruth Brown Thompson, July 26, 1875, typescript copy, folder 3, box 2, series 3, BGC.

153. Mary Brown to Jason and Ellen Brown, January 15, 1873, 8261, GLC.

154. Regarding the medal, see John Brown Jr. to William Lloyd Garrison, September 12, 1878, Ms. A.1.2 v. 40, BPL; Seymour Hirsh, "Servile Insurrection and John Brown's Body in Europe," *Journal of American History* 80 (September 1993): 499–524. For an example of continued autograph seeking, see Jason Brown to W. W. Crannell, March 4, 1874, STUT, reel 2; Ruth Brown Thompson to W. W. Crannell, March 14, 1875, ibid. The story of Owen Brown's escape was also featured in the *Atlantic Monthly* in 1874, and the *Nation* and other periodicals continued to run stories about the Brown family.

155. Sarah Brown to John Brown Jr., May 4, 1881, folder 23, series 3, Sanborn Papers, CFPL. Quoted by permission of the Concord Free Public Library.

156. James Redpath to unknown party, March 13, 1871, STUT, reel 3.

157. *Humboldt Times*, May 27, 1871, quoted in Andrew Genzoli, "Rohnerville was Friendly to John Brown's Widow," untitled news clipping, September 26, 1977, John Brown Family Folder, Humboldt County Historical Society, Eureka, CA.

158. Sarah Brown to John Brown Jr., May 1, 1881, folder 23, series 3, Sanborn Papers, CFPL. Quoted by permission of the Concord Free Public Library.

159. Apricots, prunes, grapes, oranges, lemons, cherries, and olives filled the valley, turning it into "one vast orchard," and by virtue of the railroad, Santa Clara County became an important supplier of fruit to all points east. Eugene T. Sawyer, *History of Santa Clara County, California* (Los Angeles: Historic Record Co., 1922), reprint by San Jose Historical Museum Association, 139. See also Florence Cunningham, *Saratoga's First Hundred Years*, ed. Frances L. Fox (Fresno, CA: Valley Publishers, 1967), esp. 22–28, 125–30.

160. Rumor had it that Ellen had thrown dirt in the face of the singing men and threatened another offender with a revolver. Though Ellen denied these reports, she declared to reporter Leroy Gates that she would "take an insult from no man" and interjected her defenses of her father throughout the interview. Leroy Gates, "John Brown's Widow: She Is Visited by a Correspondent of the *Inter Ocean* at Her California Home: A Sketch of Her Appearance, and Her Reminiscences of Her Famous Husband," *Daily Inter Ocean*, April 6, 1881. This article apparently was reprinted across the country. See, for example, *San Francisco Chronicle*, April 15, 1881; and *Wisconsin State Register*, June 18, 1881.

161. See Nalty, *Browns of Madronia*, 7–8; R. V. Garrod, *Saratoga Story* (Saratoga, CA: Saratoga Historical Foundation, 1961), 23; Cunningham, *Saratoga's First Hundred Years*, 132–33; and typed notes on news clipping, Sam Hanson, "Threats, Then Friends, for John Brown's People," *Los Gatos Daily Times*, March 26, 1953, folder 5, box 8, series 2, BGC.

162. Sarah Brown to John Brown Jr., May 1, 1881, folder 23, series 3, Sanborn Papers, CFPL. Quoted by permission of the Concord Free Public Library. The Browns put down $200 (out of $1,850), owed $500 soon after, and then three more yearly installments until it was all paid off. A friend to the Browns, R. L. Higgins, worked with the editor of the *San Francisco Mercury*, J. J. Owen, to raise funds. According to local historian Damon Nalty, Mary Brown received the title to 160 acres on May 21, 1881. Nalty, *Browns of Madronia*, 21. For mentions of fund-raising, see Horatio Nelson Rust to Franklin G. Adams, December 3, 1880, Personal Papers, folder 23, box 2, John Brown Papers, KSHS; W. Edicott Jr. to F. B. Sanborn, May 2, 1881, Papers, folder 25, ibid.; Franklin Sanborn to Henry Villard, June 28, 1882, folder 2, box 1A, OGV; *San Jose Mercury*, March 30, 1881; ibid., April 7, 1881; and Nalty, *Browns of Madronia*, 14–21.

163. Sarah Brown to John Brown Jr., May 1, 1881, folder 23, series 3, Sanborn Papers, CFPL. Quoted by permission of the Concord Free Public Library.

6. Mary Brown's 1882 Tour

1. Sarah Brown to John Brown Jr., August 11, 1882, enclosed in John Brown Jr. to [Franklin Sanborn?], August 22, 1882, STUT, reel 2.

2. *New York Times*, August 7, 1882; *Chicago Tribune*, August 5, 1882.

3. R. L. Higgins to W. J. W. W. Washington, August 12, 1882, folder 26, box 2, John Brown Papers, KSHS. Higgins also asked that his letter be forwarded to Sanborn, hoping that funds would also be raised in the East.

4. Some of the grand jury's testimony can be found at Kansas Territorial Online. For an account that describes seeing "Old Man Brown" in a wagon, see Amos Hall et al., Testimony taken before the grand jury investigating the Pottawatomie murders, KTO, territorialkansasonline.org/~imlskto/cgi-bin/index.php?SCREEN=show_document&SCREEN_FROM=border&document_id=102379&FROM_PAGE=&topic_id=70.

5. *New York Herald*, June 8, 1856, in Stauffer and Trodd, *Meteor of War*, 91, 92. For a reference to Brown as the "leader" and holder of a "bloody dagger," see *New York Herald*, June 10, 1856, ibid., 93.

6. James Townsley, "The Pottawatomie Killings: It Is Established beyond Controversy That John Brown Was the Leader," *Paola (KS) Republican Citizen*, December 20, 1879, p. 5. For background, see Peterson, *John Brown: The Legend Revisited*, esp. 60–70; Julie Courtwright, "'A Goblin That Drives Her Insane': Sara Robinson and the History Wars of Kansas, 1894–1911," *Kansas History* 25 (Summer 2002): 102–23; and Etcheson, *Bleeding Kansas*, 107–11. For an assessment of the accuracy of the accounts given in 1879 and beyond, see McGlone, *John Brown's War against Slavery*, 88–91.

7. John Brown to wife and children, June 1856, in Stauffer and Trodd, *Meteor of War*, 85.

8. McGlone, "Rescripting a Troubled Past"; McGlone, *John Brown's War against Slavery*, 128–34.

9. Mahala Doyle to John Brown, reprinted in the *New York Express*, November 20, 1859, in Stauffer and Trodd, *Meteor of War*, 88; Mahala Doyle to John Brown, November 20, 1859, GLC, http://www.gilderlehrman.org/sites/default/files/swf/jbrown/index.php.

10. It was not only Mary who recalled Mrs. Doyle. David Utter, a Chicago minister who published an attack on Brown in the *North American Review* in 1883, advertised for her, and other pro- and anti-Brown factions sought her out. See H. L. Cargill to Hon. A. A. Lawrence, April 19, 1885, folder "Items removed from Amos Lawrence volume, pp. 150–158," John Brown Collection, 1861–1918, MHS; Maggie Moore on behalf of Mahala Doyle to Amos Lawrence, May 26, 1885, ibid.

11. "John Brown. Yesterday's Celebration Proves a Wretched Failure. The Widow of the Old Hero Dragged around the Grounds. None of the Advertised Speakers Puts in an Appearance," *Chicago Tribune*, August 24, 1882.

12. Ibid. The *Tribune* then offered disparaging descriptions of the African Americans in attendance. "After casting about for some time a kind of meal was prepared for the lady, and she was placed in the beer-saloon adjoining the park to wait for it. In the meantime about four hundred people, the majority of whom were colored, had assembled at the grove, and were devoting their time to the absorption of beer." After Mary's meal, the reporter continued, "she was literally dragged through a mob of people of all colors and stations, most of whom were called away from the beerstands to shake her by the hand." The failure of Washington's picnic was reported in other cities. "The Proposed John Brown Monument," *Boston Daily Advertiser*, August 24, 1882; "John Brown's Monument Not Marching On," *Los Angeles Times*,

August 25, 1882; "A Disgraceful Failure," *Cincinnati Daily Gazette*, August 24, 1882; *Macon Weekly Telegraph*, August 26, 1882.

13. James Wilson Pierce, *Photographic History of the World's Fair and Sketch of the City of Chicago* (Baltimore: R. H. Woodward and Co., 1893), 104.

14. *Chicago Tribune*, August 25, 1882. The *New York Times* also reported on this. *New York Times*, August 26, 1882.

15. "Osawatomie Brown—His Widow Warmly Welcomed," *Chicago Daily News*, September 1, 1882.

16. *Chicago Daily Inter Ocean*, September 1, 1882.

17. "John Brown. Chicago Pays a Sympathetic Tribute to the Memory of the Martyr," *Chicago Tribune*, September 1, 1882.

18. For background on Podd, see William J. Simmons, "Rev. James Alfred Dunn Podd," in *Men of Mark: Eminent, Progressive, and Rising* (Cleveland: George M. Rewell and Co., 1887), 252–56.

19. On a long tradition of African American admiration for John Brown, see Reynolds, *John Brown, Abolitionist*, 488–99. In his important new work on Brown memory, Blake Gilpin argues that between 1859 and 1920, both whites and African Americans interested in reform used John Brown, but that they drew "different lessons from his radical project of freedom," with African Americans acknowledging Brown as a "violent *and* heroic liberator," while whites portrayed him solely as man of ideals. R. Blakeslee Gilpin, *John Brown Lives! America's Long Reckoning with Violence, Equality, and Change* (Chapel Hill: University of North Carolina Press, 2011), 56.

20. *Chicago Daily Inter Ocean*, September 1, 1882.

21. "Osawatomie Brown—His Widow Warmly Welcomed," *Chicago Daily News*, September 1, 1882.

22. "John Brown. Chicago Pays a Sympathetic Tribute to the Memory of the Martyr," *Chicago Tribune*, September 1, 1882.

23. "Osawatomie Brown—His Widow Warmly Welcomed," *Chicago Daily News*, September 1, 1882; "John Brown. Chicago Pays a Sympathetic Tribute to the Memory of the Martyr," *Chicago Tribune*, September 1, 1882.

24. "Mrs. John Brown. Wind-Up of the Reception Ceremonies," *Chicago Tribune*, September 2, 1882.

25. "Osawatomie Brown—His Widow Warmly Welcomed," *Chicago Daily News*, September 1, 1882. See also "John Brown. Chicago Pays a Sympathetic Tribute to the Memory of the Martyr," *Chicago Tribune*, September 1, 1882; *Chicago Daily Inter Ocean*, September 1, 1882; and *Chicago Times*, September 1, 1882. As with the failed picnic, reports on this gathering appeared in newspapers throughout the country. See *Boston Daily Advertiser*, September 1, 1882; *Boston Congregationalist*, September 13, 1882, p. 3; "Helping John Brown's Widow," *Boston Journal*, September 1, 1882; *New York Times*, September 1, 1882; *New York Times*, September 5, 1882; *Los Angeles Times*, September 3, 1882.

26. "Mrs. John Brown. Wind-Up of the Reception Ceremonies," *Chicago Tribune*, September 2, 1882.

27. *Chicago Tribune*, August 22, 1882.

28. Mary Brown to Salmon Brown, September 7, 1882, box 7, ELDR. Reproduced by permission of the Huntington Library.

29. In a letter to her niece the spring after her trip, Mary referenced "looking over my letters" in a way that made her interest in the John Brown past apparent. Mary Brown to Lucy Brown Clark, March 15, 1883, holograph copy, folder 13, box 1, series 1, BGC.

30. "A Georgia View of John Brown," *Boston Daily Advertiser* (reprinted from *Macon Telegraph*), September 14, 1882, p. 8. At the same time, a positive—if fictitious— story was also reprinted in the national press. It was an interview with James Williams, who claimed he was the African American baby that Brown had stooped to kiss en route to execution. This event did not occur. Details even in Williams's account prove it false, as he reported that Brown made a speech (he did not) and that the crowd cried (there was no crowd, just servicemen). After originating in the *Louisville Commercial*, the story appeared in at least two papers, the *Chicago Tribune* (August 30, 1882) and the *New York Times* (August 27, 1882).

31. "John Brown's Son," *Boston Congregationalist*, October 25, 1882, p. 10. For ongoing postwar efforts to identify and rebury the dead, particularly as performed by women in cemeteries, see Faust, *This Republic of Suffering*, 233–49.

32. Redpath, *Public Life of Capt. John Brown*, 405–6.

33. "The Body of John Brown's Son," *Liberator*, March 28, 1862, p. 51. Mary received a letter the following year that implied that Watson's remains had been buried by the Tenth Maine Regiment during the war, and she may have believed this, but her response to the body's recovery makes it seem as though she doubted this report, at least by 1882. Horatio N. Rust to Mary Brown, January 27, 1863, folder 106, box 9, CC-SUNY.

34. "John Brown's Sons. The Skeleton of One Said to Be in a Doctor's Office in Martinsville, Ind.," *Chicago Tribune*, September 6, 1882.

35. A. W. Macy, "Buried after Twenty-Three Years: A Sequel to the Fight at Harper's Ferry," folder 2, box 6, series 1, BGC.

36. Jarvis J. Johnson to editor of *Chicago Tribune*, August 27, 1882, MIC 50, JBJR.

37. "John Brown's Sons. The Skeleton of One Said to Be in a Doctor's Office in Martinsville, Ind.," *Chicago Tribune*, September 6, 1882. Apparently it had been known in Martinsville that Johnson had the body in a box in his office for years and that he used it to illustrate anatomy. "His Body's A'Mouldering: One of Old John Brown's Sons Identifies a Brother's Body; a Complete History of the Body Now in the Possession of a Martinsville Physician," *Indianapolis Journal*, September 11, 1882.

38. H. A. Parker to Jarvis J. Johnson, September 2, 1882, MIC 50, JBJR; H. A. Parker to John Brown Jr., September 2, 1882, ibid.; Jarvis J. Johnson to John Brown Jr., September 4, 1882, ibid.; Jarvis J. Johnson to John Brown Jr., September 5, 1882, typescript copy, folder 11, box 1, series 3, BGC (this letter was also published in *Indianapolis Journal*, September 9, 1882).

39. "His Body's A'Mouldering," *Indianapolis Journal*, September 11, 1882.

40. A. W. Macy, "Buried after Twenty-Three Years: A Sequel to the Fight at Harper's Ferry," folder 2, box 6, series 1, BGC.

41. Ibid.

42. Mary Brown to Salmon Brown, September 7, 1882, box 7, ELDR. Reproduced by permission of the Huntington Library.

43. Ruth Brown Thompson to Thomas Featherstonhaugh, postscript added October 7, 1896, in letter of October 6, 1896, folder 18, box 6, OGL.

44. Mary Brown to Salmon and Family, September 16, 1882, typescript copy from *Collector* magazine, June 1930, folder 5, box 8, series 2, BGC.

45. These details from Mary Brown to Salmon and Family, September 16, 1882, ibid.; Franklin Sanborn to [F. G. Adams], October 12, 1882, "Manuscripts, Vol. 10 Letters (correspondence received), Jan. 1882–Aug. 1883," Records of the Kansas State Historical Society, Correspondence Received, February 1881–August 1883, KSHS.

46. John Brown Jr. to Franklin Sanborn, November 4, 1883, STUT, reel 2.

47. "Events at Home: The Remains of Ossawatomie Brown's Son," *Los Angeles Times*, September 10, 1882.

48. "John Brown's Son. His Burial at North Elba Twenty-Three Years after His Death at Harpers Ferry" (reprinted from the *New York Evening Post*), *Chicago Tribune*, October 19, 1882. For coverage outside of Chicago, see "John Brown's Son," *Boston Congregationalist*, October 25, 1882; *New York Times*, September 9, 1882; *New York Times*, September 10, 1882; and *Los Angeles Times*, September 10, 1882.

49. It apparently was one that Mary Brown had donated to the Kansas State Historical Society, which sent a copy in honor of the occasion.

50. Ruth Brown Thompson to Thomas Featherstonhaugh, October 6, 1896, folder 18, box 6, OGL. Following the burial, Ruth kept in touch with the Epps family. Lyman Epps Jr. to Ruth Brown Thompson, 1885, reprinted in "Lyman Epps to Reach Century Mark Tuesday," *Mirror of the Adirondacks*, vol. 36, no. 7, news clipping, Ella Thompson Towne Scrapbook, BFC.

51. Ruth Brown Thompson to Thomas Featherstonhaugh, October 6, 1896, folder 18, box 6, OGL.

52. Of the Civil War, he added, "'The War, in which I took part on the Southern side, eradicated many errors of political opinion, and gave growth to many established truths not then recognized. I have for my own part no regrets for my humble share in the revolt; but I have now to say that I firmly believe the War was ordained of God for the extermination of slavery, and that your father was an elected instrument for the commencement of that good work.'" "John Brown's Son. His Burial at North Elba Twenty-Three Years after His Death at Harpers Ferry" (reprinted from the *New York Evening Post*), *Chicago Tribune*, October 19, 1882.

53. Ibid. Nina Silber notes another "romance of reunion" from the northern perspective—the idealization of marriage between a northern man and a southern woman. Nina Silber, *The Romance of Reunion: Northerners and the South, 1865–1900* (Chapel Hill: University of North Carolina Press, 1995).

54. John Brown Jr. to Franklin Sanborn, October 27, 1882, HM 3622, HUNT. Reproduced by permission of the Huntington Library.

55. Sanborn noted on October 25 that Mary Brown was with him and had been there since the eighteenth, and that her Boston receptions would start the following day. F. B. Sanborn to F. G. Adams, October 25, 1882, "Manuscripts, Vol. 10 Letters (correspondence received), Jan. 1882–Aug. 1883," Records of the Kansas State Historical Society, KSHS.

56. Jeffrey, *Abolitionists Remember*, 161, 164, 198–201, 162.

57. For Mary's schedule, see "John Brown's Widow," *Boston Journal*, October 26, 1882. For the report on Mary Stearns's "kindness," see Ruth Brown Thompson to Mary Stearns, March 22, 1887, Stearns Papers, KSHS.

58. "John Brown's Widow. A Reception in Her Honor on the Back Bay—Meeting of the Committee on the Fund," *Boston Daily Advertiser*, October 27, 1882, p. 8.

59. "John Brown's Widow in Boston," *Boston Journal*, October 27, 1882.

60. Mary Brown's visit is included in a long list of receptions for a host of women, ranging from Lucy Stone to a friend of Florence Nightingale. The annual dues surely made it a more elite club than Mary Brown's Red Bluff Good Templars. In 1881 the fee for life membership was raised to $100, and an entrance fee of $5 was added to a $10 annual fee. Julia A. Sprague, compiler, *History of the New England Women's Club, from 1868 to 1893* (Boston: Lee and Shepard Publishers, 1894), 44, 3; Croly, *History of the Woman's Club in America*, 45.

61. "The Widow of John Brown. Reception at the Woman's Club," *Boston Journal*, October 28, 1882.

62. *Boston Daily Advertiser*, October 31, 1882, p. 8. The *Boston Journal* numbered the crowd at six hundred. "Mrs. John Brown's Reception by the Colored People of Boston," *Boston Journal*, October 31, 1882.

63. *Boston Daily Advertiser*, October 31, 1882, p. 8.

64. "Mrs. John Brown's Reception by the Colored People of Boston," *Boston Journal*, October 31, 1882.

65. On this visit, see Scott Wolfe to Edwin Cotter, October 4, 1988, folder 287, box 25, CC-SUNY. Wolfe's letter refers to an original letter of Mrs. S. H. Brann to John Brown Jr., September 6, 1887, that is held by the Kansas State Historical Society.

66. As had been the case in 1859, money raised in Boston was not directly given to Mary. Instead, the committee appointed trustees to manage the money, to "hold the funds collected and dispose of the income for the benefit of Mrs. Brown and other members of the family as they should judge best, the purchase of an annuity for Mrs. Brown being recommended." If Mary thought back to the struggles she had had to exert control over money in the past she appears to have held her tongue. "John Brown's Widow," *Boston Journal*, October 26, 1882.

67. See "'Zekle's Wife'; the Entertainment in Aid of the John Brown Fund—Mrs. Amy Talbot Dunn's Character Sketch," *Boston Daily Advertiser*, November 9, 1882, p. 2; *Boston Journal*, November 8, 1882. A few months after this Boston event, the *Washington Post* reported that the sketch had been performed at a recent suffrage convention and compared its effect on the "present movement" to *Uncle Tom's Cabin*'s effect on the antislavery movement. "Woman's Suffragists Close Their Convention," *Washington Post*, January 26, 1883, http://www.iath.virginia.edu/utc/articles/n2ar19bat.html. For a description of the sketch see Elizabeth Cady Stanton, Susan B. Anthony, and Matilda Gage, *History of Woman Suffrage*, vol. 3, *1876–1885* (Rochester, NY: Charles Mann, 1887), 254–55.

68. Thomas K. Beecher, "Brother Anderson's Sermon," in *Shoemaker's Best Selections for Readings and Recitations*, no. 6 (1880) (Granger Index Reprint Series, Books for Libraries Press, 1970), 48–51, esp. 49.

69. "At the Hawthorne Rooms; Entertainment for the Benefit of the Mrs. John Brown Fund—Readings by Dr. Holmes and Others, and Music," *Boston Daily Advertiser*, November 23, 1882.

70. F. G. Adams to Mary Brown, October [31], 1882, Personal Papers, folder 26, box 2, John Brown Papers, KSHS. Franklin Sanborn may have had a hand in setting up this invitation. He had written to Adams, "Mrs John Brown here but will go westward next week. She thinks of spending a few days in Kansas. Can the friends there see that she sees the places and persons she [wants]?" Franklin Sanborn to F. G. Adams, October 23, 1882, "Manuscripts, Vol. 10 Letters (correspondence received), Jan. 1882–Aug. 1883," Records of the Kansas State Historical Society, KSHS.

71. F. G. Adams to John Brown Jr., January 2, 1882, MIC 50, JBJR.

72. Sarah Brown to Franklin Adams, as quoted in "John Brown: Interesting and Valuable Papers. A Description of the Relics, and Manuscripts Presented by Mrs. Mary A. Brown to the Kansas Historical Society," *Topeka Daily Capital*, December 20, 1881, STUTDB, http://www.wvculture.org/history/wvmemory/jbdetail. aspx?Type=Text&Id=5039.

73. For a full list of Mary's donated items, see *Transactions of the Kansas State Historical Society, 1883–1885*, 3rd and 4th Biennial Reports, vol. 3 (Topeka: George W. Martin, Kansas Publishing House, 1886), 38–42, 53, and 59. John Brown Jr. also made a few donations. See ibid., 53.

74. F. G. Adams to Mary Stearns, May 21, 1879, Stearns Papers, KSHS. Adams wrote her about a "cheap little picture of Capt. John Brown to present to persons calling in our room who express a special interest in his memory,—and these are of course many such."

75. By the 1890s, Adams would defend Pottawatomie as "a terrible blow struck against assassins who had, unchecked for months, carried on the work of butchery of defenceless settlers." Franklin Adams to Richard Hinton, ca. 1894, box 1, ELDR. Reproduced by permission of the Huntington Library.

76. G. W. Brown, *Reminiscences of Old Brown: Thrilling Incidents of Border Life in Kansas* (Rockford, IL: Abraham E. Smith, 1880), 12, 55–56.

77. In contrast to Mary Brown's quiet presence on the Topeka stage, Sara Robinson took an active role in the attempt to replace Brown with Robinson as Kansas's true hero. After Charles Robinson's death in 1894, Sara Robinson continued her advocacy, writing a biography of her husband and financing a second book by G. W. Brown called *False Claims of Kansas History Truthfully Corrected*. See Courtright, "'A Goblin That Drives Her Insane.'"

78. After its official start in 1875, Adams had become very important to the society's aim of preserving and collecting materials on Kansas history. Larry O. Jochims and Virgil W. Dean, "Pillars of Society: A Brief History of the Kansas State Historical Society," *Kansas History* 18 (Autumn 1995): 142–63. See also Edgar Langsdorf, "The First Hundred Years of the Kansas State Historical Society," *Kansas Historical Quarterly* 41 (Autumn 1975): 265–309.

79. He had accepted their donation and written to John Brown Jr. for help in "connect[ing] all the links" about Brown's life. F. G. Adams to John Brown Jr., January 2, 1882, MIC 50, JBJR. While Mary Brown was in Topeka, Adams enlisted her aid to weigh in on a debate about a portrait of John Brown done by Selden

Woodman. From Topeka, Mary Brown wrote to the *Century* to affirm her sense that the portrait was "a very good likeness of him, and the more I see it, the more I like it." A letter by Adams, written two weeks before Mary's visit, also appeared. Mary Brown, November 15, 1882, "Open Letters," *Century*, July 1883, 477.

80. F. G. Adams had already been working with Mary Stearns on their mutual desire to place a statue of Brown in Washington, DC. He assured Mary Stearns that the KSHS was "doing what it can to cultivate such sentiment," that Brown above all others deserved commemoration for his role in Kansas history. Franklin G. Adams to Mary Stearns, January 12, 1878, Stearns Papers, KSHS. They corresponded throughout the 1880s.

81. "Mrs. John Brown," *Daily Kansas State Journal*, November 14, 1882; "Mrs. John Brown: Her Arrival in This City—Arrangements for a Reception in Her Honor," *Topeka Daily Capital*, November 12, 1882.

82. *Daily Kansas State Journal*, November 13, 1882.

83. For the details of the planning, see "Mrs. John Brown," *Topeka Daily Capital*, November 14, 1882; "The Reception," ibid.; "Mrs. John Brown," *Daily Kansas State Journal*, November 14, 1882; ibid., November 15, 1882.

84. "Mrs. John Brown," *Daily Kansas State Journal*, November 15, 1882.

85. "The Reception," unidentified newspaper clipping, November 16, 1882, Franklin Sanborn scrapbooks, STUTDB, http://www.wvculture.org/history/wvmemory/jbdetail.aspx?Type=Text&Id=5015.

86. Details on decorations and general events of the night taken from "A Warm Welcome," *Topeka Daily Capital*, November 16, 1882; "Mrs. Brown's Reception," *Daily Kansas State Journal*, November 16, 1882; and "The Reception," unidentified newspaper clipping, November 16, 1882.

87. "Mrs. Brown's Reception," *Daily Kansas State Journal*, November 16, 1882.

88. "A Warm Welcome," *Topeka Daily Capital*, November 16, 1882.

89. F. G. Adams to Mary Stearns, November 18, 1882, Stearns Papers, KSHS.

90. "A Warm Welcome," *Topeka Daily Capital*, November 16, 1882.

91. "Mrs. Brown's Reception," *Daily Kansas State Journal*, November 16, 1882.

92. "A Warm Welcome," *Topeka Daily Capital*, November 16, 1882.

93. "The Reception," unidentified newspaper clipping, November 16, 1882.

94. "A Warm Welcome," *Topeka Daily Capital*, November 16, 1882.

95. "Mrs. Brown's Reception," *Daily Kansas State Journal*, November 16, 1882.

96. Roger D. Cunningham, *The Black Citizen-Soldiers of Kansas, 1864–1901* (Columbia: University of Missouri Press, 2008), 54.

97. Etcheson, *Bleeding Kansas*.

98. Robert G. Athearn, *In Search of Canaan: Black Migration to Kansas, 1879–80* (Lawrence: Regents Press of Kansas, 1978), 67, 199–202, 160. On this conflict, see also Scott McNall, *The Road to Rebellion: Class Formation and Kansas Populism, 1865–1900* (Chicago: University of Chicago Press, 1988), esp. 84.

99. Don W. Wilson, *Governor Charles Robinson of Kansas* (Lawrence: University Press of Kansas, 1975), esp. 121.

100. For a discussion of the 1879 letter, see Athearn, *In Search of Canaan*, 65–66. In the years prior to her trip, John Jr. had frequently commented on the situation of African Americans in the South and had even addressed a few groups in Ohio about

the matter. See, for example, John Brown Jr. to Horatio N. Rust, April 30, 1879, RU 303, box 1, RUST. Of all the Brown siblings, John Jr. seems to have kept the most abreast of issues of African American concern, and to have continued to think of himself as an activist on their behalf.

101. "The Reception," unidentified newspaper clipping, November 16, 1882. I have not found any indication that African Americans in Topeka tried to use Mary's visit to claim any rights or to combat prejudice either (unlike Rev. Podd in Chicago). The primary African American newspaper in Topeka, the *Colored American*, had ceased publication by the time of Mary's visit, and no other African American papers survive from 1882.

102. "The Reception," unidentified newspaper clipping, November 16, 1882. A second reception was held at the Congregational church the following evening, where again all Topekans were invited to meet and "to look upon one who was the companion and counselor of the grand old hero of Osawatomie." *Lawrence Daily Journal*, November 16, 1882. For outside reports on the Topeka reception, see *New York Times*, November 18, 1882; *Los Angeles Times*, November 17, 1882.

103. F. G. Adams to Mary Stearns, November 18, 1882, Stearns Papers, KSHS.

104. Ibid. Mary Brown's departure in no way ended the Kansas—or national—debate on John Brown. In fact, work on both sides only increased. In late October a group known as the John Brown Associates formed and met, vowing to "spare no pains in their efforts to hand down to future history such facts and experiences as we had with our worthy leader." Franklin Adams was corresponding secretary. See *Topeka Daily Capital*, November 22, 1882; and "John Brown Resolutions of the Meeting of the John Brown Associates in the Historical Society Room," published October 26, 1882, Personal Papers, folder 26, box 2, John Brown Papers, KSHS. Detractors also remained hard at work. David Utter as well as Amos Lawrence worked to track down Mahala Doyle. In Boston, Frank Stearns (son of George and Mary Stearns) took on Amos Lawrence, and the Massachusetts Historical Society, like KSHS, wound up in the middle of a debate on Brown's character. Jason Brown as well as John Jr. ultimately made visits to Topeka, and they worked to combat attacks on their father. Jason Brown to F. G. Adams, 1884, Personal Papers, folder 28, ibid.

105. Dwight Thatcher to Franklin Sanborn, March 30, 1885, in Sanborn, *Life and Letters*, 499.

106. Mary Brown to F. G. Adams, November 21, 1882, Personal Papers, folder 26, box 2, John Brown Papers, KSHS.

107. Likely owing to the patronage of government worker and abolitionist Horatio Rust, Sarah had obtained a position at the U.S. Mint in San Francisco—another effort by a Brown sympathizer to help lift the Browns out of poverty. Her job did not last long, though Franklin Sanborn and others advocated for her to keep the civil service post after the election of 1884 swept Republicans out of power. Carl Schurz to Franklin Sanborn, May 9, 1885, MS09–0111, STUTDB, http://www.wvculture.org/history/wvmemory/jbdetail.aspx?Type=Text&Id=1120.

108. Mary Brown to F. G. Adams, December 11, 1882, Personal Papers, folder 26, box 2, John Brown Papers, KSHS.

109. Mary Brown to Lucy Brown Clark, March 13, 1883, copy, folder 13, box 1, series 1, BGC.

110. Mary Brown to Franklin Sanborn, December 11, 1882, STUT, reel 2. John Jr. also assured Sanborn that she had spoken in "glowing terms" about her trip. John Brown Jr. to Franklin Sanborn, November 4, 1883, ibid.

111. Elizabeth T. Spring, "A Worthy Woman," *Topeka Daily Capital*, November 19, 1882. The second piece was Elizabeth T. Spring, "After Many Days: The Return of John Brown's Widow to Kansas," *Topeka Daily Capital*, November 19, 1882.

112. Spring, "Worthy Woman."

113. Nalty, *Browns of Madronia*, 26. Today the Saratoga Civic Center sits on the site of what had been their land. My thanks to Jean Libby for this information.

114. Ruth Brown Thompson to Thomas Featherstonhaugh, postscript of October 7, 1896, to letter of October 6, 1896, folder 18, box 6, OGL. Local Saratoga historian Damon Nalty declared the cause of Mary's death as likely liver cancer; great-granddaughter Elizabeth Huxtable said it was a kidney ailment. Nalty, *Browns of Madronia*, 26–27; Elizabeth Huxtable to Velma West Sykes, April 6, 1964, folder 3, box 1, Sykes Papers, LoC. For more details see Clarence Gee, notes from Stutler John Brown scrapbook, from *Portland (ME) Republican*, December 1884, folder 5, box 8, series 2, BGC.

115. Sarah's letter quoted in John Brown Jr. to Franklin Sanborn, March 4, 1884, MS04–0046, STUTDB, http://www.wvculture.org/history/wvmemory/jbdetail. aspx?Type=Text&Id=649.

116. Ellen's daughter Mary Fablinger remembered Mary's body being returned from San Francisco to Saratoga and laid out in the parlor of Ellen's home. Elizabeth Huxtable to Velma West Sykes, April 6, 1964, folder 3, box 1, Sykes Papers, LoC. Mary was buried in Saratoga in a small hilltop cemetery. It is unclear if the elder Brown siblings were consulted about this. About six weeks after her death, John Jr. wrote to Sanborn, "Ruth says that in a conversation she had with mother respecting her wish as to having her own grave at North Elba when she too should leave us, she then expressed the idea that the expense must be considered, and she prefered [*sic*] to leave the question to be determined at the time by the wishes and circumstances of her children. This talk I believe was had at North Elba when we were all there last. It would be a satisfaction to me to know that her remains are to rest, also, near that Rock in N. E., and yet her children in California should I think have their feeling determined in the matter, upon the supposition that the expense and difficulty of the undertaking at this time of the year did not have to be considered. Of course, these *must* be regarded, and may of themselves alone decide the question there. I shall send you the first word I receive further." John Brown Jr. to Franklin Sanborn, March 4, 1884, MS04–0046, STUTDB, http://www.wvculture.org/history/wvmemory/jbdetail.aspx?Type=Text&Id=649.

117. "Burial of Widow Described: Spectator at Funeral Tells of Services Held for Wife of Abolitionist," *National Tribune*, January 1, 1942, John Brown Scrapbooks, STUT, reel 7. The "spectator" was Stella Follett Hesse, who was seventeen at the time of Mary's death.

118. W. H. Cross, "John Brown's Wife: A Sketch of Her Life and Character," California news clipping, folder 10, box 2, series 3, BGC.

119. "Marching On: Death of the Widow of Old John Brown of Harper's Ferry Fame," *San Francisco Call*, March 1, 1884, news clipping, folder 12, box 2, series 3, BGC. Other obituaries included *Boston Journal*, March 1, 1884; *Sacramento Union*,

March 3, 1884; *San Jose Mercury*, March 1, 1884; *Chicago Tribune*, March 1, 1884; *San Francisco Bulletin*, February 29, 1884; *Owyhee Avalanche*, March 8, 1884; *Cincinnati Commercial Tribune*, March 1, 1884; *Las Vegas Daily Gazette*, March 1, 1884; *New Haven Register*, March 1, 1884; *Springfield (MA) Republican*, March 1, 1884; *Trenton Evening Times*, March 1, 1884. Some papers also printed an interview with William Still, an African American abolitionist who had been active in the Underground Railroad and published a memoir in the 1870s. Mary had stayed with Still around the time of Brown's execution, and the *Philadelphia Times* sought out Still to ask questions about Mary's behavior the day of Brown's execution. See "Mrs. Mary Brown," *Atchison Globe*, March 8, 1884; and *Chicago Tribune*, March 15, 1884.

120. Shirley A. Leckie, *Elizabeth Bacon Custer and the Making of a Myth* (Norman: University of Oklahoma Press, 1993), xiii. Leckie astutely notes how Custer was able to use her gender to make sure that her version of who Custer had been would go unchallenged, but she notes that her public widowhood came with "a very high price: her ability to live a fully autonomous life." Shirley A. Leckie, "Biography Matters: Why Historians Need Well-Crafted Biographies More Than Ever," in *Writing Biography: Historians and Their Craft*, ed. Lloyd E. Ambrosius (Lincoln: University of Nebraska Press, 2004), 8.

121. Varina Davis, *Jefferson Davis: Ex-President of the Confederate States of America, a Memoir by His Wife*, 2 vols. (New York: Belford Co., 1890), 2. For an assessment of the book, see Cashin, *First Lady of the Confederacy*, 266–69, esp. 266.

122. It is unclear how hard Spring worked to find a publisher. Both Stanford and the Huntington Library have (slightly different) typescript copies of her memoir.

123. Mary Brown to Salmon Brown, September 7, 1882, box 7, ELDR. Reproduced by permission of the Huntington Library.

7. Annie Brown Adams, the Last Survivor

1. Annie Brown Adams to editor of the *Transcript*, November 11, 1892, STUT, reel 2.

2. Annie Brown Adams to A. M. Ross, February 19, 1892, 3007 #30, GLC.

3. Paul A. Shackel, "John Brown's Fort: A Contested National Symbol," in Finkelman and Russo, *Terrible Swift Sword*, 179.

4. American Anti-Slavery Society, *Commemoration of the Fiftieth Anniversary of the Organization of the American Anti-Slavery Society, in Philadelphia* (Philadelphia: Thomas. S. Dando & Co., 1884), 47–48.

5. David Blight, "A Quarrel Forgotten or a Revolution Remembered? Reunion and Race in the Memory of the Civil War, 1875–1913," in Blight, *Beyond the Battlefield: Race, Memory, and the American Civil War* (Amherst: University of Massachusetts, 2002), 127.

6. Blight, *Race and Reunion*, 381. It is unclear where John Brown fits into Blight's argument, as he mentions Brown or the raid only four times in *Race and Reunion* and never discusses him in any depth.

7. On public memory of John Brown, see Peterson, *John Brown: The Legend Revisited*, and Gilpin, *John Brown Still Lives!* Julie Roy Jeffrey challenges us to remember that other abolitionists continued to insist on what Blight would call an "emancipationist" narrative of the war. Jeffrey, *Abolitionists Remember*.

8. Joseph Edgar Chamberlin, *John Brown* (Boston: Small, Maynard & Co., 1899), ix.

9. For an assessment of this de-radicalization of Brown among white Americans, see Gilpin, *John Brown Lives!*

10. For a representative piece about the Brown sons, see M. A. Batchelder, "John Brown's Brothers," *Christian Union*, March 21, 1889.

11. Eleanor Atkinson, "The Soul of John Brown: Recollections of the Great Abolitionist by His Son," *American Magazine*, October 1909, pp. 633–43.

12. *Salt Lake Semi-Weekly Tribune*, January 22, 1897, p. 4.

13. Thanks to Wendy Gamber, who used this term "submerged memory" in feedback on an early draft of this chapter.

14. "I like the work very well, though I never was strong enough to endure close confinement," she wrote to her eldest brother. Sarah Brown to John Brown Jr., 1882, STUT, reel 2.

15. While in later years she worked privately to solicit aid for her sister Annie, Sarah also denied to the world at large any need for such efforts, uncomfortable with any story that, as she stated, "puts me before thousands of people as a subject for pity and ridicule." Letter to editor of the *Springfield (MA) Republican*, May 22, 1905, news clipping, in folder "Brown, Miss Sarah," box 6, OGV; Sarah Brown to Franklin Sanborn, March 5, 1885, folder 2, box 2, series 2, BGC.

16. In 1890, Ruth wrote to Horatio Rust about the disposal of Brown's field glass. Asking him not to "mention this to any of the younger members of our family," she confided that she, John Jr., and Jason thought Rust should get the glass, adding that they felt that the majority should rule. This was an especially interesting rendering of what constituted a "majority," since there were three of them and four other Browns: Salmon, Annie, Ellen, and Sarah. Ruth Brown Thompson to Horatio Rust, June 26, 1890, RU 350, box 2, RUST. Reproduced by permission of the Huntington Library. See also Ruth Brown Thompson to Horatio Rust, November 25, 1892, RU 359, ibid.

17. McGlone, "Rescripting a Troubled Past."

18. Both Annie and Ruth in their letters refer to nervous states that seem to point to trauma about the family's antislavery violence. Ruth had spells throughout the 1880s; this was part of what led abolitionist Horatio Rust to fund a trip for her to Redondo Beach in 1891. For a description of the trip and her gratitude to Rust, see Ruth Brown Thompson to Horatio Rust, September 12, 1891, RU 356, RUST. Both Annie and Ruth relayed how difficult it was for them to write about the family past, that sometimes they were just not up to the task. Cathy Caruth's description of trauma as "an overwhelming experience of sudden, or catastrophic events, in which the response to the event occurs in the often delayed, and uncontrolled repetitive occurrence of hallucinations and other intrusive phenomena" is useful here. Caruth as quoted in Jenny Edkins, *Trauma and the Politics of Memory* (Cambridge: Cambridge University Press, 2003), 38. On trauma, history, and memory, see also Caruth, *Unclaimed Experience*; Nigel Hunt, *Memory, War, and Trauma* (Cambridge: Cambridge University Press, 2010); Mark Klempner, "Navigating Life Review Interviews with Survivors of Trauma," *Oral History Review* 27, no. 2 (Fall 2000): 67–83; and Daniel L. Schacter, *Searching for Memory: The Brain, the Mind, and the Past* (Basic Books, 1996).

19. Sarah consistently reminded the curious that she had "no desire to be put into the papers just because I am his daughter," while Ellen seems to have worked to disappear into private life and obscure herself from the public record. Her brother Salmon's daughter Agnes would eventually tell Brown researcher Clarence Gee that Ellen's daughter Mary also "shrank from public contacts." When Gee wrote to Ellen's daughter Mary (born in 1879), she claimed little knowledge of her aunt Annie and seemed to not know about the Kennedy farm. Sarah Brown, letter to editor (of *Springfield Republican*), May 15, 1905, in folder "Brown, Miss Sarah," box 6, OGV. Mary Fablinger to Clarence Gee, November 1, 1926, folder 6, Annie Brown Adams, box 2, series 2, BGC. Agnes Brown Evans to Clarence Gee, October 23, 1961, folder 5, Salmon Brown, ibid.

20. In an oral history interview from 1976, Beatrice Keesey, Annie's granddaughter, recalled her mother Bertha burning all kinds of papers after Annie's death. Oral history conducted by Donna Oden with Beatrice Keesey, April 29, 1976, folder 84, box 2, CC-SUNY. Another descendant of Annie, Alice Keesey Mecoy, only became aware of the connection at the age of sixteen when a researcher appeared on the family doorstep. She has been actively researching Annie Brown and her family ever since. Alice Keesey Mecoy, "John Brown Kin," blog, http://johnbrownkin.blogspot.com/.

21. For evidence of Annie's trip, see Annie Brown Adams to Horatio Rust, May 19, 1895, RU 263, box 3, RUST. Sarah had also visited, and Rust appears to have funded both trips. See Ruth Thompson Brown to Horatio Rust, May 14, 1890, RU 349, box 2, ibid.

22. Sarah would acknowledge as much to Katherine Mayo, who would write in her notes: "She has always been consumed with jealousy when any notice has been paid to any of the others, even to Mrs J B, as to the people of J. B. She feels that, by virtue of Kennedy Farm, she is the only one left entitled to recognition." Other siblings agreed. It may have been this that led Annie to scrawl "don't show Mrs Thompson" across the top of a letter in which she wrote of having "*always known more*" than most others about John Brown. Katherine Mayo, "Sarah Brown—Notes, Saratoga, CA, between Sept 16 and 20, 1908," folder "Brown, Miss Sarah," box 6, OGV; Salmon Brown to Franklin Sanborn, August 8, 1909, STUT, reel 2; Annie Brown Adams to Horatio Rust, ca. 1895, RU 268, box 3, RUST (reproduced by permission of the Huntington Library).

23. Petrolia had two general stores, two blacksmith shops, a butcher, cooper, and carpenter. It also had a church, post office, and schoolhouse. Owen C. Coy, *The Humboldt Bay Region, 1850–1875: A Study in the American Colonization of California* (Los Angeles: California State Historical Association, 1929), 247, 248.

24. In between were sixteen-year-old Bertha, eleven-year-old Samuel, eight-year-old Sarah, six-year-old Edith, and four-year-old Gus.

25. Annie Brown Adams to A. M. Ross, December 2, 1888, 3007.22, GLC.

26. For this information I am grateful to the innkeeper at Petrolia's Lost Inn. See http://redwoods.info/showrecord.asp?id=4254.

27. Annie Brown Adams to A. M. Ross, March 6, 1890, 3007.25, GLC.

28. For information on the Mattole Road, I thank Linda DeLong, archivist and reference librarian at the Humboldt County Historical Society. For additional in-

formation, see Mildred Hoover et al., *Historic Spots in California* (Palo Alto: Stanford University Press, 2002), 101–7.

29. Katherine Mayo, "Sturdy Children of John Brown," news clipping, *Saturday Evening Post*, 1909, S/AC.

30. Annie Brown Adams to A. M. Ross, October 19, 1887, 3007.16, GLC.

31. Annie Brown Adams to Franklin Sanborn, December 23, 1894, copy, folder [6?], box 2, series 2, BGC.

32. Annie Brown Adams to A. M. Ross, August 3, 1885, 3007.12, GLC.

33. She also noted that she had received $100 of the John Brown fund—perhaps requested to assist with the move. Annie Brown Adams to William Lloyd Garrison [Jr.], August 28, 1888, S/AC.

34. Annie Brown Adams to Horatio Rust, May 21, 1897, RU 274, box 4, RUST. Reproduced by permission of the Huntington Library. Annie had kept some property in her own name; she possibly used her portion from the sale of the "John Brown Cottage" in Red Bluff to purchase their home in Rohnerville. She purchased the home in Petrolia using funds from the sale of their home in Rohnerville and donations from "friends in Boston."

35. Annie Brown Adams to A. M. Ross, July 1, 1888, 3007.20, GLC.

36. It does not appear that any of her sisters ever suggested that Annie leave Samuel or come to live with them. From the beginning, historian Robert Griswold notes, California offered "wide-ranging grounds for divorce" that included, importantly for Annie, habitual intemperance, as well as cruelty. Though Griswold chronicles the (economic and other) obstacles to women in seeking a divorce, he also argues that many, on all ends of the economic spectrum—and particularly the lower end—did initiate divorce proceedings. Robert Griswold, *Family and Divorce in California, 1850–1890: Victorian Illusions and Everyday Realities* (Albany, NY: SUNY Press, 1982), 1, 79–80.

37. Ruth Brown Thompson to Franklin Sanborn, January 24, 1895, 8262, GLC.

38. Sarah Brown to Franklin Sanborn, March 5, 1885, folder 2, box 2, series 2, BGC.

39. Annie Brown Adams to Franklin Sanborn, December 23, 1894, STUT, reel 2. Embarrassed, she added, "Pardon me for airing my skeleton. I would not have mentioned him only that I could not make you comprehend how I was situated without lifting the curtain and giving you a glimpse."

40. Annie Brown Adams to Horatio Rust, April 29, 1897, RU 273, box 3, RUST. Reproduced by permission of the Huntington Library. On how the extreme situation had led her to have him arrested, see Annie Brown Adams to Horatio Rust, May 21, 1897, RU 274, box 4, ibid. Emphasis in the original.

41. Another Brown family rumor was that she became attracted to another of Brown's raiders there, possibly Aaron Stevens or Jeremiah Anderson, though nothing in Annie's later letters confirms any of these attachments. Horwitz, *Midnight Rising*, 120; Chapin, "Last Days of Old John Brown," 326. She did once express dislike for Aaron Stevens's friend (or fiancée, perhaps) Jennie Dunbar, describing her as "heartless." Annie Brown Adams to Alexander Ross, April 2, 1889, 3007.23, GLC.

42. For discussion of the 1906 earthquake, see Franklin Sanborn to G. H. D. Johnson, December 10, 1909, folder 21, box 47, CHS; Franklin Sanborn to Oswald Garrison Villard, February 3, 1910, folder 10, box 1A, OGV.

43. Annie Brown Adams to A. M. Ross, September 13, 1892, 3007.32, GLC.

44. In 1895, she wrote to Alexander Ross, "I was once threatened, seriously, with a suit for slander by a negro, of white descent because I objected to some of his lawbreaking and sins, large and small. Just think of the disgrace of John Brown's daughter, being sued for slander by a 'nigger.' That is the only reward I ever received from that race, for my labors in their behalf. I have told you this for consolation in your troubles, so you may see that you are not the only one who sows that others may reap." Annie Brown Adams to A. M. Ross, May 12, 1895, 3007.41, GLC. Annie may not have intended to slur African Americans with her use of a racial pejorative (John Brown had once used the term in a letter to his family as a way to highlight the prejudice against slaves), but her hardened attitude comes through nonetheless. For John Brown's use of the term, see John Brown to wife and children, November 8, 1859, in Sanborn, *Life and Letters*, 586.

45. Ida B. Wells-Barnett to Annie Brown Adams, January 4, 1896, folder 82, box 7, CC-SUNY.

46. A host of such letters sending money and others asking for confirmation of receipt are contained in both the Cotter Collection at SUNY–Plattsburgh and the Rust Papers at the Huntington. It is clear that Annie received a number of donations. A Mrs. T. H. Lyles wrote, "I have had your letter published in allmost every colored paper in the East, and it is awakening my people to a sence of gratitude that they have long owed to your father and his family, a week or so ago the colored people of Chicago Illinois sent to you Eleven Dollars and sixty cents ($11.60) which I hope came safely to hand, and I now send you Ten Dollars ($10.00) sent to me by the Womans Era Club of Boston I wish you would acknowledge the receipt of it direct to Mrs Ellen N. Taylor No. 19 Brewery St. Cambridgeport Mass. the colored people of Washington are asking all the churches to raise a colection for you we are making an effort to save your home and to help you in this hour of need I will send you some Papers containing the Notice." Mrs. T. H. Lyles to Annie Brown Adams, January 22, 1897, folder 82, box 7, CC-SUNY. More donations came in, but Annie's abolitionist patrons soon expressed frustration that she was not acknowledging them. Thomas Featherstonhaugh wrote to Horatio Rust, "There is one thing that Annie must attend to if she wants this thing to go on, and that is to promptly acknowledge the receipt of money. I sent her $56 some six weeks ago, and in this I acted simply as the agent of some friendly colored people. I have not yet got word to show that the money was received. You can see what a position this places me in. . . . and I have written her scolding letters to the effect that some form of receipt must be sent at once when money is sent. . . . If you are writing to Mrs. Adams, will you speak to her on this point. She may be sick or it may be thoughtlessness." Thomas Featherstonhaugh to Horatio Rust, March 6, 1897, RU 63, Box 3, RUST. Reproduced by permission of the Huntington Library.

47. Annie Brown Adams to Ida B. Wells-Barnett, June 7, 1897, the *Conservator*, in p. 98, Rust scrapbook, RU 371, RUST. Reproduced by permission of the Huntington Library.

48. An especially embarrassing reference comes in a 1908 letter that she wrote to Brown biographer Oswald Garrison Villard in which she confided, "The full blooded black is usually a docile and amiable creature." Annie Brown Adams to Oswald Garrison Villard, March 23 [25?], 1908, folder "Adams, Annie Brown," box 1A, OGV.

49. Both son Salmon and Ruth's daughter Mary Thompson made statements to interviewers that cast them as even more regressive than Annie. Each denied that Brown believed in interracial marriage, though there is evidence to the contrary. Mary Thompson asserted that her family all opposed interracial marriage, noting their shock at Frederick Douglass's late-in-life marriage to a white woman. She told interviewer Katherine Mayo "that it was a part of the family creed, inherited from J.B., that one of the ugliest features of slavery was the mingling of the races; but J.B. had regarded it as a monstrosity based on the coercion of slavery. He did not contemplate the possibility in a state of liberty." Salmon was quoted in a 1905 newspaper as stating, "It was a great mistake, a politician's mistake, to make an American citizen of the freed colored man. The American negro slave has and always had a God-given right to freedom, but few of his race are fit for citizenship." The *Humboldt Times* closed, "Salmon Brown justifies his father in all the acts of his life, but he believes there is no excuse for the politicians who took up the cause of the negro after his freedom was practically assured and put the ballot and citizenship in his hands." Katherine Mayo, notes from interview with Henry Thompson, 1908, folder "Brown Papers—Early Days—Vows against Slavery—Views on Race Amalgamation," box 3, OGV. As quoted in "John Brown's Life Recalled: His Son, Formerly a Citizen of Humboldt, Tells of Exciting Times—His Love of Negro Never Advocated Political Rights," *Humboldt Times*, August 9, 1905, p. 4, folder 74, box 6, CC-SUNY. On Mary Thompson's views, see also Mayo to Villard, August 25, 1908, and September 14, 1908, folder "Mayo, Katherine I," box 12, OGV. The closest actual evidence of Brown's viewpoint comes from a published account in the *New York Herald* when, interviewed in the Charles Town jail, he confided "that although he was opposed to it, yet he would much prefer a son or a daughter of his to marry an industrious and honest negro than an indolent and dishonest white man." "Interview with the Prisoners," *New York Herald*, November 24, 1859. Thanks to Tony Horwitz for this citation.

50. Only John Jr. and Sarah, oddly enough, seemed immune. John Jr. sent letters on behalf of the Kansas Exodusters. Sarah was accredited by the American Missionary Society in San Francisco, and she learned a "sufficient smattering" of Japanese to work with local immigrants. In 1911, she reflected that, upon beginning it, "I had really no purpose in life and something said to me here was my opportunity to accomplish good." But if Sarah, just thirteen when her father died in Virginia, saw connections to her father's equally unpopular antiracist stance or to childhood lessons in self-sacrifice and equity, she kept them to herself and even vehemently denied the connection when pressed by a reporter. "What [John Brown] did for slaves, she seeks to do for aspiring Japanese," one writer noted in 1909. Another writer pushed Sarah to link herself to her father, leading her to snap, "Yes, I'm John Brown's daughter. . . . But I've lived in California for twenty-seven years. That's really all there is to say, and you can't make a story out of that, can you?"

Mary Miller Chiao, "Sarah Brown" (working paper, 2007), 28; Gerald Beaumont, "Daughter of John Brown," news clipping, pp. 550–51, E. A. Housman Scrapbook, STUT, reel 5; Edward Sidney Williams, "John Brown's Spirit in the Santa Clara Foothills," *Overland Monthly and Out West Magazine* 54 (September 1909), 321; "Last in Family of Hero of Harper's Ferry Woman: John Brown's Aged Daughter Recluse: Lives Near San Jose and Occupies Time Teaching Class of Japanese," *San Francisco Examiner*, June 30, [19?], news clipping, in folder "Adams, Annie Brown," box 1A, OGV. Many thanks to Mary Chiao for providing a copy of her work on Sarah Brown.

51. Annie Brown Adams to Horatio Rust, December 2, 1894, RU 262, Box 3, RUST. Reproduced by permission of the Huntington Library.

52. Annie Brown Adams to Katherine Mayo, March 13, 1909, folder "Adams, Annie Brown," box 1A, OGV. This was not a new feeling for Annie. She had referred to Sanborn's book as publishing "an amount of family rubbish." Annie Brown Adams to A. M. Ross, July 31, 1887, 3007.15, GLC.

53. Annie Brown Adams to Thomas Featherstonhaugh, September 29, 1896, folder 18, box 6, OGL.

54. Annie Brown Adams to A. M. Ross, January 10, 1894, 3007.38, GLC.

55. Hunt, *Memory, War, and Trauma*, 7, 3.

56. Her eldest sister Ruth also looked to preserve favorable accounts and memorabilia for her children. Ruth Brown Thompson to Mary Stearns, May 23, 1888, Stearns Papers, KSHS; Ruth Brown Thompson to F. G. Logan, November 30, 1892, folder 17, box 47, CHS.

57. Quoted in Franklin Sanborn to William Elsey Connelly, August 6, 1900, copy, folder 5, box 1A, OGV.

58. Woodrow Wilson, *A History of the American People*, vol. 4 (New York: Harper & Row, 1902), 185, 160. A milder 1888 text referred to Brown as bearing "a conspicuous part as a free-state man in the murderous feuds of the Kansas struggle." Edward Eggleston, *A History of the United States and Its People for the Use of Schools* (New York: American Book Co., 1888). For a summary of textbook coverage of John Brown, see James W. Loewen, *Lies My Teacher Told Me: Everything Your American History Teacher Got Wrong* (New York: W. W. Norton, 1995), 165–72.

59. Libby, "John Brown's Family and Their California Refuge."

60. Annie Brown Adams to A. M. Ross, July 31, 1887, 3007.15, GLC.

61. Annie Brown Adams to A. M. Ross, February 25, 1882, 3007.11, GLC.

62. Annie Brown Adams to Horatio Rust, December 2, 1894, RU 262, box 3, RUST. Reproduced by permission of the Huntington Library.

63. Annie Brown Adams to A. M. Ross, July 31, 1887, 3007.15, GLC. Annie had long criticized Douglass, who she felt had betrayed her father and then mocked her family with accounts of their poverty. For her criticism of Douglass as "devoured by conceit & self-importance" as well as her assertion that he had betrayed his promise to "go with him & share his lot," see Annie Brown statement about Frederick Douglass, folder "Frederick Douglass," box 7, OGV.

64. Katherine Mayo, "The Trip to Annie Brown Adams," folder "Adams, Annie Brown," box 1A, OGV. Over time, many members of the Brown family banned unfavorable works from their homes. Like Annie, Salmon apparently banned negative

books. Even in the 1970s, one of Salmon's daughters informed Velma Sykes that if Stephen Oates's new Brown biography had a southern slant, "please do not send it to me, as we do not keep such books in our home library." Nell Brown Groves to Velma West Sykes, February 15, 1973, folder 6, box 1, Sykes Papers, LoC.

65. Included in a whole spate of biographies on Brown between 1885 and 1915 are Sanborn, *Life and Letters*; Hermann von Holst, *John Brown*, ed. Frank Preston Stearns (Boston: Cupples and Hurd, 1888); Eli Thayer, *The Kansas Crusade* (New York: Harpers Brothers, 1889); Hinton, *John Brown and His Men*; Featherstonhaugh, *John Brown's Men*; Chamberlin, *John Brown*; William E. Connelly, *John Brown* (1900; Freeport, NY, Books for Libraries Press, 1971); W. E. B. Du Bois, *John Brown* (Philadelphia: George W. Jacobs and Co., 1909); Villard, *John Brown: A Biography Fifty Years After*. Other works quite critical of John Brown also came out in this time, and these scholars rarely if ever consulted the Browns. See, for example, Charles Robinson, *The Kansas Conflict* (New York: Harper & Row, 1892); and Hill Peebles Wilson, *John Brown: Soldier of Fortune; a Critique* (Lawrence, KS: H. P. Wilson, 1913). Wilson even accused the Brown family of misrepresenting him. Wilson, *John Brown*, 15, 134, 395.

66. Annie Brown Adams to Ross, January 2, 1887, 3007.14, GLC.

67. Sanborn, *Life and Letters*, vii.

68. Merrill Peterson also points to a group of "self-promoting advocates." Peterson, *John Brown: The Legend Revisited*, 129. Brown biographer Louis DeCaro Jr. is convinced that Alexander Ross fabricated his closeness to John Brown to promote his own interests. Louis DeCaro Jr., "'Cheating at Solitaire': The Self-Made Myth of Alexander Ross, the Canadian Friend of John Brown," John Brown the Abolitionist: A Biographer's Blog, December 31, 2005, http://abolitionist-john-brown.blogspot.com/2005_12_01_archive.html.

69. Franklin Sanborn to R. J. Hinton, August 13, 1892, folder 4, box 1A, OGV. Villard and Sanborn would ultimately feud to the degree that one contemplated legal action against the other. Oswald Garrison Villard to Chauncey Ford, February 21, 1911, box 1, ibid.; Franklin Sanborn to Oswald Garrison Villard, September 11, 1909, folder 10, box 1A, ibid.

70. Annie Brown Adams to Richard Hinton, August 22, 1892, folder "Adams, Annie Brown," box 1A, OGV.

71. Richard Hinton to William Connelly, undated, ca. 1900–1901, STUT, reel 2.

72. Biographers from Sanborn to Villard also wrote to the Brown children to verify facts. See, for example, Sarah Brown to F. B. Sanborn, March 5, 1885, folder 23, series 3, Sanborn Papers, CFPL. Other times, Brown daughters Ruth, Annie, and Sarah, along with their brothers, were asked to provide statements about specific events or broad memories. Annie Brown Adams, statement written for Franklin Sanborn, November 1886, typescript copy, folder 8, box 46, CHS; Annie Brown Adams, Memories of KF, etc., 3007.49, GLC. Annie and the Brown sons were also frequently called upon to proof biographical pieces. Annie Brown Adams to Richard Hinton, May 23, 1893, folder 59, series A, group 1, box 3, Richard J. Hinton Papers, KSHS; Annie Brown Adams to "dear friend," September 24, 1893, STUT, reel 2; John Brown Jr. to Sanborn, March 24, 1885, March 27, 1885, April 8, 1885, April 10, 1885, ibid.

73. Annie Brown Adams to Garibaldi Ross, December 15, 1887, 3007.17, GLC.

74. Featherstonhaugh, *John Brown's Men*, 7.

75. Others who assisted Featherstonhaugh were Captain E. P. Hall of Washington and Professor O. G. Libby of the University of Wisconsin. Thomas Featherstonhaugh, "The Final Burial of the Followers of John Brown," *New England Magazine* 24 (April 1901): 128–34. Jeremiah Anderson's body had been taken along with Watson's to the medical school; it was never recovered.

76. Annie added that she had always hoped to use her expertise to secure the bodies herself—in fact, she claimed, that was part of the reason she had gone south during the war. Annie Brown Adams to Thomas Featherstonhaugh, September 29, 1896, folder 18, box 6, OGL.

77. Quoted in Featherstonhaugh, *John Brown's Men*, 22–23.

78. The nephew of Aaron Stevens also arranged to have the bodies of Stevens and Hazlett disinterred from Eagleswood and sent there. Featherstonhaugh, "Final Burial of the Followers of John Brown." For another account of the funeral, see "Honoring John Brown's Followers," *Mail and Express Illustrated Saturday Magazine*, September 9, 1899, box 3, OGV.

79. Featherstonhaugh, "Final Burial of the Followers of John Brown." Featherstonhaugh seems to have originally included text about Annie as well as the image, but it must have been taken out by the magazine editors. Thomas Featherstonhaugh to Horatio Rust, April 30, 1901, RU 68, box 4, RUST. Reproduced by permission of the Huntington Library.

80. Annie Brown Adams, statement written for Franklin Sanborn, November 1886, CHS.

81. Annie Brown Adams to Richard J. Hinton, June 7, 1894, folder 64, series A, group 1, box 3, Hinton Papers, KSHS.

82. Annie Brown Adams to A. M. Ross, April 13, 1879, 3007.08, GLC.

83. Ibid.

84. Annie Brown Adams to A. M. Ross, July 31, 1887, 3007.15, GLC.

85. Horatio Nelson Rust to Richard Hinton, January 19, 1893, folder 55, series A, group 1, box 2, Hinton Papers, KSHS. For a report on the exhibit, see "Relics That Thrill: They Center around John Brown and Abraham Lincoln," *Chicago Daily*, October 23, 1892, p. 33.

86. Paul Shackel, "The John Brown Fort: Unwanted Symbol, Coveted Icon," in *Memory in Black and White: Race, Commemoration, and the Post-Bellum Landscape* (Walnut Creek, CA: AltaMira, 2003), 51.

87. For skepticism, see Horatio Nelson Rust to Richard Hinton, January 19, 1893, Hinton MC 384, folder 55, series A, group 1, box 2, Hinton Papers, KSHS; and Mary Stearns to Franklin Sanborn, March 4, 1892, STUT, reel 3. For excitement, see "John Brown's Fort: Removal of the Historical Building to Chicago," *Chicago Daily*, August 4, 1892.

88. See Gail Bederman, *Manliness and Civilization: A Cultural History of Gender and Race in the United States, 1880–1917* (Chicago: University of Chicago Press, 1995); Neil Harris, *Grand Illusions: Chicago's World Fair of 1893* (Chicago: Chicago Historical Society, 1994); and Robert Muccigrosso, *Celebrating the New World: Chicago's Columbian Exposition of 1893* (Chicago: Ivan R. Dee, 1993).

89. Annie Brown Adams to A. M. Ross, September 13, 1892, 3007.32, GLC.

90. So did her sister. To Logan, Ruth wrote, "We all thought [her daughter Mary] had better not accept his offer," adding that "somehow we do not feel the confidence in that scheme that perhaps we ought to." Ruth Brown Thompson to Mr. [F. G.] Logan, November 6, 1892, folder 17, box 47, CHS.

91. The fort display was an unmitigated failure, costing the John Brown Fort Company $60,000. In 1909, Storer College purchased the fort and placed it on their grounds, and it remained there until 1968, when the National Park Service moved it to its present location. Shackel, "John Brown's Fort," esp. 61–72.

92. Annie Brown Adams to [Franklin Sanborn], 1892, STUT, reel 2. Two Brown sons, John Jr. and Jason, attended the fair. Ruth Brown Thompson to Mr. Frank Logan, November 6, 1892, folder 17, box 47, CHS; Mrs. A. M. Clark to [C. S. Cler?], August 31, 1893, MIC 50, JBJR.

93. Annie Brown Adams to Sanborn, February 28, 1894, STUT, reel 2.

94. She, like her siblings, was probably aware that other abolitionist children had capitalized on their relationships and published memoirs of their famous parents. But Annie was unable to get the Brown siblings together on this: some papers had been misplaced, the Brown siblings were somewhat disconnected, and Annie's proposed "the story of John Brown as seen by his children" never materialized. Ruth also worked on a manuscript that failed to materialize, in part because Brown biographers had mixed reactions to this project or, at least, to the idea of the Browns bearing the byline and having editorial control. For early correspondence about Ruth's manuscript and others' plans for a memorial volume, see Franklin Sanborn to R. J. Hinton, August 13, 1892, folder 4, box 1A, OGV; Ruth Brown Thompson to Horatio Rust, November 1, 1886, RU 353, box 1, RUST; Franklin Sanborn to Horatio Rust, March 15, 1892, RU 220, box 2, ibid.; Franklin Sanborn to Horatio Rust, July 17, 1892, RU 221, box 2, ibid.; Alexander Ross to Horatio Rust, December 26, 1892, RU 187, box 2, ibid.; Richard Hinton to Horatio Rust, January 25, 1893, RU 96, box 2, ibid.; Ruth Brown Thompson to Horatio Rust, January 26, 1893, RU 360, box 2, ibid. Ruth's manuscript also is referred to in Charles Wingate, "Boston Letter [from August 1, 1893]," *The Critic: A Weekly Review of Literature and the Arts* 20 (August 5, 1893): 90.

95. Annie Brown Adams to A. M. Ross, June 24, 1894, 3007.39, GLC.

96. Ibid.

97. Annie Brown Adams to Richard Hinton, May 11, 1895, folder "Adams, Annie Brown," box 1A, OGV.

98. Annie Brown Adams to "dear friend," September 24, 1893, STUT, reel 2.

99. Oswald Garrison Villard to Thomas Wentworth Higginson, November 18, 1907, no. 950, Higginson Correspondence, BMS Am 1162, Houghton.

100. Annie Brown Adams to Oswald Garrison to Villard, March 23 [25?], 1908, folder "Adams, Annie Brown," box 1A, OGV.

101. Mayo spent part of her adult life living abroad as well, and she had an avid interest in India in particular. From this interest came her most famous work, *Mother India* (1927). See Manoranjan Jha, *Katherine Mayo and India* (New Delhi: People's Publishing House, 1971).

102. Mayo, "Sturdy Children of John Brown."

103. Ellen defended herself, explaining that she had refused Mayo because she did not have any kind of credential and that "confidences concerning family matter have been abused on similar occasions." Mayo to Villard, June 22, 1908, folder "Mayo, Katherine I," box 12, OGV; Ellen Brown Fablinger to Villard, September 15, 1908, folder "Fablinger, Ellen Brown," box 8, ibid. For more information on Mayo's interviews with Brown's daughters and the Thompsons, see Bonnie Laughlin-Schultz, "'Could I Not Do Something for the Cause?' The Brown Women, Antislavery Reform, and Memory of Militant Abolitionism" (PhD diss., Indiana University, 2009); and Bonnie Laughlin-Schultz, "John Brown's Children in Southern California," unpublished manuscript.

104. Mayo to Villard, August 25, 1908, folder "Mayo, Katherine I," box 12, OGV.

105. Mayo to Villard, September 14, 1908, folder "Mayo, Katherine I," box 12, OGV.

106. Mayo, "Trip to Annie Brown Adams."

107. Ibid.

108. Her older children had long moved out, her two oldest daughters Vivian and Bertha having worked as housekeepers and nannies since the mid-1880s. It is possible that her life with Samuel—who was by then close to eighty years old—had calmed somewhat. "We two old birds," she wrote of herself and Samuel in 1909, "have lived here all alone this winter, in the old nest, from which the young ones have all flown." Annie Brown Adams to Katherine Mayo, March 13, 1909, folder "Adams, Annie Brown," box 1A, OGV.

109. Mayo to Villard, August 20, 1908, folder "Mayo, Katherine I," box 12, OGV.

110. Mayo, "Trip to Annie Brown Adams."

111. Annie Brown Adams to Oswald Garrison Villard, October 26, 1908, folder "Adams, Annie Brown," box 1A, OGV.

112. Oswald Garrison Villard, *Fighting Years: Memoirs of a Liberal Editor* (New York: Harcourt Brace, 1939), 99.

113. Villard, *John Brown*, 170.

114. Salmon also seems to have been angry with Annie, feeling that she had misconstrued facts in her eagerness to claim the role of eyewitness. Salmon Brown to Franklin Sanborn, June 8, 1911, STUT, reel 2.

115. Franklin Sanborn, letter to the *Transcript*, February 11, 1911, as quoted in Oswald Garrison Villard to Chauncey Ford, February 21, 1911, box 1, OGV.

116. Wilson's object was "to correct a perversion of truth, whereby John Brown has acquired fame, as an altruist and a martyr, which should not be attributed to him." Wilson, *John Brown, Soldier of Fortune*, 15. For Sanborn and others' outrage, see Franklin Sanborn to W. E. Connelly, February 18, 1913, STUT, reel 3.

117. The suit was by Nell Brown Groves, one of Salmon's daughters. See Janet Horne, untitled article, *Seattle Times*, July 25, 1972, news clipping, folder 5: Salmon Brown, box 2, series 2, BGC.

118. Owen died in 1889, John Jr. in 1895, and Ruth in 1904. After Owen's death, Jason Brown had moved back to Ohio to live with his son, and he died in Akron in 1912. After struggling with poverty and being bedridden for a number of years, Salmon Brown committed suicide in 1919. *Akron Beacon Journal*, December 25, 1912, p. 1; Abbie Brown to Emma Adair Remington, June 11, 1919, typescript copy, folder 5, Salmon Brown, box 2, series 2, BGC.

119. Clarence Gee, notes on Ellen Brown Fablinger genealogy, folder 7, box 2, series 2, BGC. Her children were Bessie, Sadie, Mary, Margaret, Frances, Vera, Winifred, and James Jr., her last child, who was born in 1896. Gee identifies another son, John, who died at the age of four months. Sarah lived off and on with the Fablingers while the children were young, and she later housed Ellen's three eldest daughters in San Jose while they attended normal school. In addition to working as teachers, Ellen's daughters—as well as Annie's two oldest daughters—held positions in San Francisco, likely in mills and factories, perhaps at the Levi Strauss and Co. that opened there in 1853. See William Issel and Robert W. Cherny, *San Francisco, 1865–1932: Politics, Power, and Urban Development* (Berkeley: University of California Press, 1986), esp. 53–79.

120. "Daughter of John Brown Dies Here: Death of Mrs. Ellen Fablinger Occurs Less Than Month after Sister's Passing," *San Jose Mercury*, July 25, 1916, p. 1; "Sarah Brown of Saratoga Dies: Was Daughter of Famous Abolitionist, John Brown of Harper's Ferry," *San Jose Mercury*, July 1, 1916, p. 1.

121. Samuel died October 27, 1914, according to W. E. Roscoe, *A History of the Mattole Valley*, typewritten MSS, 1940, in folder 84, box 2, CC-SUNY.

122. Alice Cook Hunt, handwritten reminiscence, written at the request of Bonnie Laughlin-Schultz, August 2008, in the possession of Bonnie Laughlin-Schultz.

123. Ibid.

124. The official cause of death was a fall and broken bones, though Annie had also been diagnosed with terminal cancer and had, according to granddaughter Alice Cook Hunt, lived her last months in tremendous pain. A broken neck also appears on the coroner's report. In his *Midnight Rising*, Tony Horwitz notes the irony of Brown's daughter dying in such a similar manner to her father's hanging. Horwitz, *Midnight Rising*, 284.

125. I originally had difficulty locating her grave—indicative of her forgotten place in Brown's story. My thanks to Ron Kuhnel, who has an ongoing project of photographing old graves in Humboldt County, for identifying and sending photos of it.

126. Notices of Annie's death included "John Brown's Daughter Dies," *Washington Post*, October 6, 1926, p. 8; "John Brown's Daughter Dead," *New York Times*, October 6, 1926, p. 25; untitled obituary, *Chicago Daily Tribune*, October 6, 1926, p. 1; "John Brown's Daughter Dies in California," *New York Amsterdam News*, October 13, 1926, p. 5; and "John Brown's Daughter Dies: Mrs. A. B. Adams Lived Fifty Years in California," *Los Angeles Times*, October 9, 1926, p. 3. The *Washington Post, New York Times, Los Angeles Times,* and *New York Amsterdam News* all erroneously reported that Annie saw her father hanged, and that she was the only representative of the family there.

127. "John Brown's Daughter Dies: Mrs. A. B. Adams Lived Fifty Years in California," *Los Angeles Times*, October 9, 1926, p. 3.

Epilogue

1. "Last Echo from John Brown's Grave," *Hartford Courant*, October 24, 1926, p. D6.

2. A notable exception is Tony Horwitz's new work on Brown's raid, which pays particular attention to Annie. In his biography of Brown, Evan Carton is also interested in the dynamics of his family. Horwitz, *Midnight Rising*; Carton, *Patriotic Treason*.

3. The Madronia Cemetery does list Mary Brown as one of its "notable gravesites." See http://www.madroniacemetery.com/about/notable/. More information on Jean Libby's pathbreaking work to recover the history of the Brown women can be found at http://www.alliesforfreedom.org/index.html.

4. Alice Keesey Mecoy, "John Brown Kin," http://johnbrownkin.blogspot.com/.

5. See http://www.sandraweber.com/author/trouble.htm for information on the performance. Weber is the author (with Peggy Lynn) of *Breaking Trail: Remarkable Women of the Adirondacks* (Purple Mountain Press, 2004). Peggy Eyres's song appears on the CD *Cloudsplitter* (Sleeping Giant / Rough House Records, 1997).

6. In addition to songs that highlight Brown, Magpie sings about raiders such as Jeremiah Anderson, John Henry Kagi, John Copeland, and Dangerfield Newby, as well as Frederick Douglass and Harriet Tubman. The duo also performs two songs about the Brown women. "Mary Brown, Abolitionist" is a cover of the Peggy Eyres song that tells Mary's story through a letter she wrote to Brown in prison. "Pretty Little Bird" recounts Annie's time at the Kennedy farm through the story of the birds that Brown saved. (This episode, used in Sanborn's *Life and Letters*, opens chapter 3 of this work.) For more information on Magpie's music, see http://www.magpiemusic.com/brown_cd.htm.

7. Greg Artzner, Terry Leonino, and Richard Henzel, *Sword of the Spirit: A One-Act Play Based on the Life and Letters of John and Mary Brown*. This well-researched play features Brown in jail giving one final interview in which he recounts his life and his transformation into a violent abolitionist, while Mary (from Lucretia Mott's house prior to seeing Brown) is on the other side of the stage telling her story. Their version of Mary Brown has an upper-middle-class sensibility that I believe she lacked, but I admire their commitment to bring both John and Mary's stories before the American public. See http://www.magpiemusic.com/spiritsword.html.

8. His father was a playwright in his own right. Kirke Mechem, *John Brown: A Play in Three Acts* (Manhattan, KS: Kansas Magazine, 1939).

9. Kirke Mechem Jr., *John Brown: Opera in Three Acts* (New York: Schirmer, 2006). The opera premiered May 3, 2008, at the Lyric Opera of Kansas City. Mechem consulted with Stephen Oates in the writing of his opera, and notes that he tried to be objective and historically accurate. See http://kirkemechem.com/johnbrown.html.

10. Statement of Annie Brown written for Franklin Sanborn, November 1886, typescript copy, folder 8, box 46, CHS.

11. The Garrison family poses a useful contrast here, as various generations of Garrisons since William Lloyd Garrison have worked on behalf of social justice issues and seemed to draw some of this from their heritage. Lloyd McKim Garrison, "Garrison at Two Hundred: The Family, the Legacy, and the Question of Garrison's Relevance in Contemporary America," in *William Lloyd Garrison at Two Hundred*, ed. James Brewer Stewart (New Haven, CT: Yale University Press, 2008), 119–28.

12. In an exchange in 1970–71 in the *New York Review of Books*, Willie Lee Rose was criticized for her hesitance about Brown's means despite his noble ideals, but I share her hesitation about Brown's use of violence—particularly that which he commanded from his sons and son-in-law in Kansas. Willie Lee Rose, "Killing for Freedom," *New York Review of Books*, December 3, 1970, http://www.nybooks.com/articles/10740.

✹ Bibliography

Manuscript Collections

Bancroft Library, University of California, Berkeley
Lucy Higgins and Sarah Brown Papers

Boston Public Library, Rare Books and Manuscripts Department
Anti-Slavery Manuscripts

Chicago Historical Society
John Brown Collection
Zebina Eastman Papers, 1841–85

Columbia University, Rare Book and Manuscripts Library, New York
John Brown (Oswald Garrison Villard) Manuscripts

Division of Rare and Manuscript Collections, Cornell University Library, Ithaca, NY
Samuel J. May Anti-Slavery Manuscript Collection

Elwyn B. Robinson Department of Special Collections, Chester Fritz Library, University of North Dakota, Grand Forks
Orin G. Libby Papers

Historical Society of Pennsylvania, Philadelphia
Ferdinand Julius Dreer Papers

Houghton Library, Harvard College, Cambridge, MA
Alcott Family Papers
Amos Bronson Alcott Papers
Garrison Family Papers
Thomas Wentworth Higginson Correspondence
Thomas Wentworth Higginson, Letters and Journals
Thomas Wentworth Higginson, Additional Papers
Wendell Phillips Papers, Series 2: Letters to Wendell Phillips
Letters Received by Franklin Benjamin Sanborn
Franklin Benjamin Sanborn and William Ellery Channing Papers

Hudson Library and Historical Society, Hudson, OH

Brown-Gee Collection
Brown-Clark Collection
Brown Family Reunion Papers

Humboldt County Historical Society, Eureka, CA

John Brown Family Folder

Huntington Library, San Marino, CA

(John) Brown Family Collection, 1838–1943
John Brown Jr. Letters
James William Eldridge Papers
Horatio Nelson Rust Papers, 1799–1906
Benjamin H. Smith Papers, 1859–65
Rebecca Spring, "Auld Acquaintances," typescript manuscript, HM 46944
Rebecca Spring Letters

Kansas State Historical Society, Topeka

Samuel Lyle and Florella Brown Adair Family Collection, 1831–1921
Zu Adams Papers, 1873–1911
Franklin George Adams Papers, 1872–1903
John Brown Papers, microfilm
Thomas Wentworth Higginson Collection, microfilm
Richard J. Hinton Papers, 1850–1905
Records of the Kansas State Historical Society, Correspondence Received
James Malin Papers
George L. and Mary E. Stearns Papers, 1856–1901, microfilm
Velma West Sykes Collection of John Brown Papers, 1832–1964, microfilm

Library of Congress, Washington, DC

Papers of Velma West Sykes, 1820–1975

Massachusetts Historical Society, Boston

John A. Andrew Papers, 1772–1895
John Brown Collection, 1861–1918
Dana Family Papers, 1654–1950
Thomas Bradford Drew Diaries, 1849–98
William Lloyd Garrison Papers, 1833–82
Jacob M. Manning Papers, 1853–1905
New England Emigrant Aid Co. Records, 1855–62
Theodore Parker Papers, 1826–65
Stevens Family Papers, 1770–1911

Mattole Valley Historical Society, Petrolia, CA

Annie Brown Adams Binder

New-York Historical Society, New York
Gilder Lehrman Collection

Ohio Historical Society, Columbus
John Brown Jr. Papers, 1830–1932, microfilm

Pasadena History Museum, Pasadena, CA
John Brown Family History, scrapbook, box 22, vol. 87

Rauner Special Collections Library, Dartmouth College, Hanover, NH
John Brown Correspondence

Saratoga Historical Museum, Saratoga, CA
Sarah Brown and Fablinger Family File, box 23B

Smith College Archives, Northampton, MA
Slavery/Antislavery Collection

Special Collections and University Archives, Stanford University Libraries, Palo Alto, CA
Rebecca Spring Papers, ca. 1830–1900

Special Collections, Feinberg Library, SUNY–Plattsburgh, Plattsburgh, NY
Edwin N. Cotter Jr. Collection on John Brown

St. Lawrence County Historical Association, Canton, NY
Miscellaneous Correspondence, 1818–1952

West Virginia State Archives, Charleston
Boyd Blynn Stutler collection of John Brown papers, 1821–1961, microfilm
John Brown / Boyd B. Stutler Collection Database, West Virginia Memory Project, http://www.wvculture.org/history/wvmemory/imlsintro.html

William Monroe Special Collections, Concord Free Public Library, Concord, MA
Collection of materials issued by or relating to the Concord School, Concord (1855–1862)
Franklin Benjamin Sanborn Papers, 1845–1936

Newspapers and Magazines

Atlantic Monthly
Banner of Light
Boston Commonwealth
Boston Daily Advertiser
Boston Evening Courier
Boston Journal

Boston Morning Journal
Boston Transcript
Chicago Daily Inter Ocean
Chicago Daily News
Chicago Tribune
Daily Kansas State Journal
Indianapolis Journal
Lawrence (KS) Daily Journal
Liberator
Los Angeles Times
The Nation
National Anti-Slavery Standard
New England Magazine
New York Times
New York Tribune
The Outlook
Overland Monthly
Red Bluff (CA) Independent
Red Bluff Semi-Weekly Independent
Red Bluff Sentinel
San Francisco Chronicle
Storer Record (Storer College, Harpers Ferry)
Topeka Daily Capital
Water-Cure Journal

Selected Published Primary Sources

Adams, Anne B. "Some Pleasant Recollections of Concord People." In "Three Contemporary Accounts of Louisa May Alcott, with Glimpses of Other Concord Notables," edited by Joel Myerson and Daniel Shealy. *New England Quarterly* 59 (March 1986): 109–22.

American Anti-Slavery Society. *Commemoration of the Fiftieth Anniversary of the Organization of the American Anti-Slavery Society, in Philadelphia.* Philadelphia: Thomas S. Dando & Co., 1884.

Anderson, Osborne. "A Voice from Harper's Ferry: A Narrative of Events at Harper's Ferry; with Incidents Prior and Subsequent to Its Capture by Captain Brown and His Men" (Boston, 1861). In *Black Voices from Harpers Ferry.* Edited by Jean Libby. Palo Alto, CA: by the editor, 1979.

The Anti-Slavery History of the John-Brown Year. New York: American Anti-Slavery Society, 1861.

Bowles, Samuel. *Our New West—Records of Travel between the Mississippi River and the Pacific Ocean.* Hartford, CT: Hartford Publishing Co., 1869.

Brown, G. W. *Reminiscences of Old Brown: Thrilling Incidents of Border Life in Kansas.* Rockford, IL: Abraham E. Smith, 1880.

Brown, Sarah. "A Reminiscence: School Days at Concord, Mass." In *After Harper's Ferry: John Brown's Widow—Her Family and the Saratoga Years.* Saratoga, CA: Saratoga Historical Foundation, 1964.

Carr, John. *Pioneer Days in California: Historical and Personal Sketches*. Eureka, CA: Times Publishing Co., 1891.

Chamberlin, Joseph Edgar. *John Brown*. Boston: Small, Maynard, and Co., 1899.

Chapin, Lou V. "The Last Days of Old John Brown." *Overland Monthly*, April 1899, 322–32.

Clarke, James Freeman. *Anti-Slavery Days: A Sketch of the Struggle Which Ended in the Abolition of Slavery in the United States*. New York: R. Worthington, 1884.

Constitution and By-laws of the Grand Lodge: Also of Subordinate Lodges of the Independent Order of Good Templars of the State of California. San Francisco: Francis, Valentine & Co., Printers, 1866.

———. San Francisco: Francis, Valentine & Co., Printers, 1867.

Correspondence between Lydia Maria Child, and Gov. Wise and Mrs. Mason, of Virginia. New York: American Anti-Slavery Society, 1860.

Dana, Richard Henry. "How We Met John Brown." *Atlantic Monthly*, July 1871, 1–9.

Danvers Historical Society. *Old Anti-Slavery Days: Proceedings of the Commemorative Meeting, Held by the Danvers Historical Society, at the Town Hall, Danvers, April 26, 1893*. Edited by A. P. Putnam. Danvers, MA: Danvers Mirror Printing, 1893.

DeCaro, Louis, Jr. *John Brown: The Cost of Freedom—Selections from His Life and Letters*. New York: International Publishers, 2007.

Douglass, Frederick. *Life and Times of Frederick Douglass*. Hartford, CT: Park Publishing Co., 1882. http://books.google.com/books?id=EQmknGd90hUC.

Du Bois, W. E. B. *John Brown*. Philadelphia: George W. Jacobs and Co., 1909.

Earle, Jonathan. *John Brown's Raid on Harpers Ferry: A Brief History with Documents*. Boston: Bedford / St. Martin's, 2008.

Featherstonhaugh, Thomas. *John Brown's Men; the Lives of Those killed at Harpers Ferry, with a Supplementary Bibliography of John Brown*. Southern History Association, October 1899, 281–306.

Garrison, Wendell Phillips, and Francis Jackson Garrison. *William Lloyd Garrison: The Story of His Life, Told by His Children*. New York: Century Co., 1889.

Gregg, Edith E. W., ed. *The Letters of Ellen Tucker Emerson*. Vol. 1. Kent, OH: Kent State University Press, 1982.

Hale, Nancy, and Ellen Wright Garrison. *Daughter of Abolitionists*. Northampton, MA: Smith College, 1964.

Hastings, Lansford W. *The Emigrants' Guide to Oregon and California* (1845). Princeton, NJ: Princeton University Press, 1932.

Hawley, A. T. *The Climate, Resources and Advantages of Humboldt County, Cal., Described in a Series of Letters to the* San Francisco Daily Evening Bulletin. Eureka, CA: *Daily and Weekly Humboldt Times*, J. E. Wyman & Son Publishers, 1879.

Higginson, Thomas Wentworth. *Cheerful Yesterdays*. Boston: Houghton Mifflin, 1898.

———. "A Visit to John Brown's Household in 1859." In Higginson, *Contemporaries*, 219–43. Boston: Houghton Mifflin, 1899.

Hinton, Richard. *John Brown and His Men, with Some Account of the Roads They Travelled to Reach Harper's Ferry*. New York: Funk & Wagnalls, 1894.

History of Santa Clara County, California, Including Its Geography, Geology, Topography, Climatography and Description . . .Also Incidents of Public life . . .and Biographical

Sketches of Early and Prominent Settlers and Representative Men. San Francisco: Alley, Bowen & Co., 1881.

Hume, John F. *The Abolitionists: Together with Personal Memories of the Struggle for Human Rights, 1830–1864.* New York: G. P. Putnam's Sons, 1905.

Illustrated Fraternal Directory Including Educational Institutions of the Pacific Coast, Giving a Succinct Description of the Aims and Objects of Beneficiary and Fraternal Societies. . . . San Francisco: Bancroft Co., 1889.

Invasion at Harper's Ferry. Washington, DC: Government Printing Office, 1860.

Irvine, Leigh H. *History of Humboldt County, California, with Biographical Sketches of the Leading Men and Women of the County Who Have Been Identified with Its Growth and Development from the Early Days to the Present.* Los Angeles: Historic Record Co., 1915.

Letters of Lydia Maria Child, with a Biographical Introduction by John G. Whittier and an Appendix by Wendell Phillips. Boston: Houghton Mifflin, 1883.

Lewis, E. J. *Tehama County, California, Illustrations Descriptive of Its Scenery, Fine Residences, Public Buildings, Manufactories, Hotels, Farm Scenes, Business Houses, Schools, Churches, Mines, Mills, Etc., . . .with Historical Sketch of the County.* San Francisco: Elliot and Moore, 1880.

Loughary, Harriet A. "Travels and Incidents" (1864). In *Covered Wagon Women: Diaries and Letters from the Western Trails, 1840–1890,* vol. 8, *1862–1865,* edited/compiled by Kenneth L. Holmes, 115–62. Spokane, WA: Arthur H. Clark, 1989.

May, Samuel J. *Some Recollections of Our Antislavery Conflict.* Boston: Fields, Osgood, and Co., 1869.

Memorial and Biographical History of Northern California: Illustrated, Containing a History of This Important Section of the Pacific Coast from the Earliest Period of Its Occupancy to the Present Time. . . . Chicago: Lewis Publishing Co., 1891.

Muir, John. *Picturesque California: The Rocky Mountains and the Pacific Slope.* New York: J. Dewing Co., 1888.

Myerson, Joel, and Daniel Shealy, eds. *The Journals of Louisa May Alcott.* Boston: Little, Brown, 1989.

Myerson, Joel, Daniel Shealy, and Madeleine B. Stern, eds. *The Selected Letters of Louisa May Alcott.* Boston: Little, Brown, 1987.

Pillsbury, Parker. *Acts of the Anti-Slavery Apostles.* Concord, MA: Clague, Wegman, Schlict, and Co., 1883.

Powell, Aaron M. *Personal Reminiscences of the Anti-Slavery and Other Reforms and Reformers.* New York: Caulon Press, 1899.

Proceedings of the Sixth Annual Session of the Grand Lodge of the Independent Order of Good Templars Held at Sacramento, September 1865. Sacramento: James Anthony & Co. Printers, 1865.

Proceedings of the Seventh Annual Session of the Grand Lodge of the Independent Order of Good Templars, Held at Sacramento, September 1866. Sacramento: Russell & Winterburn, Printers, Union Book and Job Office, 1866.

Proceedings of the Eighth Annual Session of the Grand Lodge of the Independent Order of Good Templars, Held at Sacramento, September 1867. Sacramento: Russell & Winterburn, Printers, Union Book and Job Office, 1867.

Redpath, James, ed. *Echoes of Harper's Ferry.* Boston: Thayer and Eldridge, 1860.

——. *The Public Life of Capt. John Brown, with an Auto-Biography of His Childhood and Youth.* Boston: Thayer and Eldridge, 1860.

Reid, Hiram A. *History of Pasadena . . .Being a Complete and Comprehensive Histo-cyclopedia of All Matters Pertaining to This Region.* Pasadena, CA: Pasadena History Co., 1895.

Ruchames, Louis, ed. *John Brown: The Making of a Revolutionary; the Story of John Brown in His Own Words and in the Words of Those Who Knew Him.* New York: Grosset & Dunlap, 1969.

——, ed. *A John Brown Reader: The Story of John Brown in His Own Words, in the Words of Those Who Knew Him, and in the Poetry and Prose of the Literary Heritage.* New York: Abelard-Schuman, 1959.

Sanborn, Franklin. *The Life and Letters of John Brown, Liberator of Kansas, and Martyr of Virginia.* Boston: Roberts Brothers, 1885.

——. *Memoirs of John Brown.* Concord, MA, 1878.

——. *Recollections of Seventy Years.* 2 vols. Boston: Gorham Press, 1909.

Sawyer, Eugene T. *History of Santa Clara County, California.* Los Angeles: Historic Record Co., 1922.

Southwick, Sarah H. *Reminiscences of Early Anti-Slavery Days.* Cambridge, MA: Riverside Press, 1893.

Spring, Rebecca Buffum. "A Visit to John Brown in 1859." In *Virtuous Lives: Four Quaker Sisters Remember Family Life, Abolitionism, and Women's Suffrage*, edited by Lucille Salitant and Eve Lewis Perera, 117–24. New York: Continuum, 1994.

Stauffer, John, and Zoe Trodd, eds. *Meteor of War: The John Brown Story.* New York: Brandywine Press, 2004.

Stearns, Frank Preston. *The Life and Public Services of George Luther Stearns.* Philadelphia: J. B. Lippincott, 1907.

Still, William. *The Underground Railroad, a Record of Facts, Authentic Narratives, Letters, & c., Narrating the Hardships Hair-breadth Escapes and Death Struggles of the Slaves in Their Efforts for Freedom, as Related by Themselves and Others, or Witnessed by the Author.* Philadelphia: Porter and Coates, 1872.

Tilton, Theodore. "A Personal Interview with Captain Brown's Wife." *Independent*, November 17, 1859.

Villard, Oswald Garrison. *John Brown: A Biography Fifty Years After.* Boston: Houghton Mifflin, 1910.

von Holst, Hermann. *John Brown.* Edited by Frank Preston Stearns. Boston: Cupples and Hurd, 1888.

Webb, Richard D. *The Life and Letters of Captain John Brown, Who Was Executed at Charlestown, Va., December 2, 1859, for an Armed Attack upon American Slavery; with Notices of Some of His Confederates, 1861.* London: Smith Elder and Co., 1861.

Wilson, Hill Peebles. *John Brown, Soldier of Fortune: A Critique.* Lawrence, KS: H. P. Wilson, 1913.

Woman's Christian Temperance Union. *Prohibition in California: Pasadena's Prohibitory Ordinance Sustained by the Supreme Court; History of the Case,—Difficulties Overcome,—the Ordinance Passed,—Contested in Court,—Sustained Four Times,—Text of the Ordinance, Decisions of the Courts.* Pasadena: H. N. Farey & Co., 1887.

Oral Histories

Alice Cook Hunt, handwritten reminiscence, written at the request of Bonnie Laughlin-Schultz, August 2008, in the possession of Bonnie Laughlin-Schultz.
Alice Cook Hunt to Bonnie Laughlin-Schultz, July 20, 2008, handwritten letter in the possession of Bonnie Laughlin-Schultz.

Secondary Sources

Aaron, Daniel, ed. *Studies in Biography*. Cambridge, MA: Harvard University Press, 1978.
Abzug, Robert H. *Cosmos Crumbling: American Reform and the Religious Imagination*. New York: Oxford University Press, 1994.
Adams, Rachel. "Caught Looking." *Common-Place* 4 (January 2004), http://www.common-place.org/vol-04/no-02/adams/.
——. *Sideshow U.S.A.: Freaks and the American Cultural Imagination*. Chicago: University of Chicago Press, 2001.
Alonso, Harriet. *Growing Up Abolitionist: The Story of the Garrison Children*. Amherst: University of Massachusetts Press, 2002.
Anderson, Mary Siler. *Backwoods Chronicle: A History of Southern Humboldt, 1849–1920*. Redway, CA: Southern Humboldt County Press, 1985.
Andrews, Stephen. "'Which Threatens to Tear Our Fabric Asunder': The Opposition to Modern American Spiritualism, 1848–60." PhD diss., Stanford University, 2005.
Apostol, Jane. "Horatio Nelson Rust: Abolitionist, Archaeologist, Indian Agent." *California History* (Winter 1979–1980): 304–15.
Applegate, Debby. *The Most Famous Man in America: The Biography of Henry Ward Beecher*. New York: Doubleday, 2006.
Athearn, Robert G. *In Search of Canaan: Black Migration to Kansas, 1879–80*. Lawrence: Regents Press of Kansas, 1978.
Atkin, Andrea M. "'When Pincushions Are Periodicals': Women's Work, Race, and Material Objects in Female Abolitionism." *ATQ* 11, no. 2 (1997): 93–113.
Bach, Jennifer L. "Acts of Remembrance: Mary Todd Lincoln and Her Husband's Memory." *Journal of the Abraham Lincoln Association* 25, no. 2 (2004): 25–49.
Bailey, Fred Arthur. "The Textbooks of the 'Lost Cause': Censorship and the Creation of Southern State History." *Georgia Historical Quarterly* 75 (Fall 1991): 507–35.
Baker, Jean H. *Mary Todd Lincoln: A Biography*. New York: W. W. Norton, 1987.
Baker, Thomas N. *Sentiment and Celebrity: Nathaniel Parker Willis and the Trials of Literary Fame*. New York: Oxford University Press, 1999.
Banner, Lois. "Biography as History." *American Historical Review* 114 (June 2009): 579–86.
Bederman, Gail. *Manliness and Civilization: A Cultural History of Gender and Race in the United States, 1880–1917*. Chicago: University of Chicago Press, 1995.
Blackwell, Alice Stone. *Lucy Stone Blackwell: Pioneer of Woman's Rights*. Charlottesville: University Press of Virginia, 2000. First published in 1930.
Blair, William A. *Cities of the Dead: Contesting the Memory of the Civil War in the South, 1865–1914*. Chapel Hill: University of North Carolina Press, 2004.

Blake, David Haven. *Walt Whitman and the Culture of American Celebrity*. New Haven, CT: Yale University Press, 2006.

Blight, David. *Beyond the Battlefield: Race, Memory, and the American Civil War*. Amherst: University of Massachusetts Press, 2002.

———. *Race and Reunion: The Civil War in American Memory*. Cambridge, MA: Harvard University Press, 2001.

Blue, Frederick J. *No Taint of Compromise: Crusaders in Antislavery Politics*. Baton Rouge: LSU Press, 2005.

Bourdieu, Pierre. "Structures, Habitus, Power: Basis for a Theory of Symbolic Power." In *Culture/Power/History: A Reader in Contemporary Social Theory*, edited by Nicholas B. Dirks, Geoff Eley, and Sherry B. Ortner, 155–99. Princeton, NJ: Princeton University Press, 1994.

Bowman, Shearer Davis. *At the Precipice: Americans North and South during the Secession Crisis*. Chapel Hill: University of North Carolina Press, 2010.

Boyer, Richard O. *The Legend of John Brown: A Biography and a History*. New York: Alfred A. Knopf, 1973.

Brakebill, Tina Stewart. *"Circumstances Are Destiny": An Antebellum Woman's Struggle to Define Sphere*. Kent, OH: Kent State University Press, 2006.

Braudy, Leo. *The Frenzy of Renown: Fame and Its History*. New York: Oxford University Press, 1986.

Browning, Judkin. "'Bringing Light to Our Land . . .When She Was Dark as Night': Northerners, Freedpeople, and Education during Military Occupation in North Carolina, 1862–1865." *American Nineteenth-Century History* 9 (March 2008): 1–17.

Butchart, Ronald E. *Northern Schools, Southern Blacks, and Reconstruction: Freedmen's Education, 1862–1875*. Westport, CT: Greenwood Press, 1980.

———. *Schooling the Freed People: Teaching, Learning, and the Struggle for Black Freedom, 1861–1876*. Chapel Hill: University of North Carolina Press, 2010.

Butler, Jon. *Awash in a Sea of Faith: Christianizing the American People*. Cambridge, MA: Harvard University Press, 1990.

Bynum, Caroline Walker. "Introduction: The Complexity of Symbols." In *Gender and Religion: On the Complexity of Symbols*, edited by Caroline Walker Bynum et al., 1–20. Boston: Beacon Press, 1986.

Cameron, Kenneth Walter. "Sanborn's Preparatory School in Concord (1855–1863)." *American Renaissance Literary Report* 3 (1989): 34–84.

Carton, Evan. *Patriotic Treason: John Brown and the Soul of America*. New York: Simon & Schuster, 2006.

Caruth, Cathy. *Unclaimed Experience: Trauma, Narrative, and History*. Baltimore: Johns Hopkins University Press, 1996.

Cashin, Joan. *First Lady of the Confederacy: Varina Davis's Civil War*. Cambridge, MA: Belknap Press of Harvard University Press, 2006.

Casper, Scott E. *Constructing American Lives: Biography and Culture in Nineteenth-Century America*. Chapel Hill: University of North Carolina Press, 1999.

Cayleff, Susan. *Wash and Be Healed: The Water-Cure Movement and Women's Health*. Philadelphia: Temple University Press, 1987.

Chiao, Mary Miller. "Sarah Brown." Working paper, 2007.

Cherches, Peter. "Star Course: Popular Lectures and the Marketing of Celebrity in Nineteenth-Century America." PhD diss., New York University, 1997.

Clark, Elizabeth. "'The Sacred Rights of the Weak': Pain, Sympathy, and the Culture of Individual Rights in Antebellum America." *Journal of American History* 82 (September 1995): 463–93.

Clavin, Matthew. "A Second Haitian Revolution: John Brown, Toussaint Louverture, and the Making of the American Civil War." *Civil War History* 54 (June 2008): 117–45.

Clinton, Catherine. *Harriet Tubman: The Road to Freedom.* New York: Little, Brown, 2004.

——. *Mrs. Lincoln: A Life.* New York: HarperCollins, 2009.

Coontz, Stephanie. *The Way We Never Were: American Families and the Nostalgia Press.* New York: Basic Books, 2000.

Courtwright, Julie. "'A Goblin That Drives Her Insane': Sara Robinson and the History Wars of Kansas, 1894–1911." *Kansas History* (Summer 2002): 102–23.

Cox, Robert. *Body and Soul: A Sympathetic History of American Spiritualism.* Charlottesville: University of Virginia Press, 2003.

Coy, Owen C. *The Humboldt Bay Region, 1850–1875: A Study in the American Colonization of California.* Los Angeles: California State Historical Association, 1929.

Creighton, Margaret. *The Color of Courage: Gettysburg's Forgotten History.* Basic Books, 2004.

Cunningham, Florence. *Saratoga's First Hundred Years.* Edited by Frances L. Fox. Fresno, CA: Valley Publishers, 1967.

Cunningham, Roger D. *The Black Citizen-Soldiers of Kansas, 1864–1901.* Columbia: University of Missouri Press, 2008.

Curry, Richard O. "The Abolitionists and Reconstruction: A Critical Appraisal." *Journal of Southern History* 34 (November 1968): 527–45.

Donald, David Herbert. *Lincoln.* New York: Simon & Schuster, 1995.

DeCaro, Louis, Jr. *"Fire from the Midst of You": A Religious Life of John Brown.* New York: NYU Press, 2002.

——. *John Brown: The Man Who Lived—Essays in Honor of the Harper's Ferry Raid Sesquicentennial, 1859–2009.* Morrisville, NC: Lulu, 2009.

Demos, John. "The Antislavery Movement and the Problem of Violent 'Means.'" *New England Quarterly* 37 (December 1964): 501–26.

Dilworth, Leah, ed. *Acts of Possession: Collecting in America.* New Brunswick, NJ: Rutgers University Press, 2003.

Dixon, Chris. *Perfecting the Family: Antislavery Marriages in Nineteenth-Century America.* Amherst: University of Massachusetts Press, 1998.

Donegan, Jane B. *"Hydropathic Highway to Health": Women and Water-Cure in Antebellum America.* New York: Greenwood Press, 1986.

Duberman, Martin, ed. *The Antislavery Vanguard: New Essays on the Abolitionists.* Princeton, NJ: Princeton University Press, 1965.

Edelstein, Tilden G. *Strange Enthusiasm: A Life of Thomas Wentworth Higginson.* New Haven, CT: Yale University Press, 1968.

Edkins, Jenny. *Trauma and the Politics of Memory.* Cambridge: Cambridge University Press, 2003.

Emerson, Jason. "In His Father's Shadow: Searching for the Real Robert Todd Lincoln." *Civil War Times* 47, no. 5 (2008): 54–57.

———. *The Madness of Mary Lincoln.* Carbondale: Southern Illinois University Press, 2007.

Emilio, John D., and Estelle Friedman. *Intimate Matters: A History of Sexuality in America.* New York: Harper & Row, 1988.

Endres, Kathleen L. *Akron's "Better Half": Women's Clubs and the Humanization of the City, 1825–1925.* Akron, OH: University of Akron Press, 2006.

Enstad, Nan. *Ladies of Labor, Girls of Adventure: Working Women, Popular Culture, and Labor Politics at the Turn of the Century.* New York: Columbia University Press, 1999.

Etcheson, Nicole. *Bleeding Kansas: Contested Liberty in the Civil War Era.* Topeka: University Press of Kansas, 2004.

———. "John Brown, Terrorist?" *American Nineteenth Century History* 10 (March 2009): 29–48.

———. "'Labouring for the Freedom of the Territory': Free-State Kansas Women in the 1850s." *Kansas History* 21 (Spring 1998): 68–87.

Fahey, David M. *Temperance and Racism: John Bull, Johnny Reb, and the Good Templars.* Lexington: University Press of Kentucky, 1996.

Fairbain, Charlotte J. *John Brown's Fort: Armory Engine and Guard House.* Harpers Ferry, WV: Harpers Ferry National Historical Park, 1961.

Faragher, John Mack. *Women and Children on the Overland Trail.* New Haven, CT: Yale University Press, 1979.

Farrell, James. *Inventing the American Way of Death, 1830–1920.* Philadelphia: Temple University Press, 1980.

Faulkner, Carol. *Lucretia Mott's Heresy: Abolition and Women's Rights in Nineteenth-Century America.* Philadelphia: University of Pennsylvania Press, 2011.

———. "The Root of the Evil: Free Produce and Radical Antislavery, 1820–1860." *Journal of the Early Republic* 27, no. 3 (2007): 277–405.

Faust, Drew Gilpin. *This Republic of Suffering: Death and the American Civil War.* New York: Random House, 2008.

Finkelman, Paul. "Manufacturing Martyrdom: The Anti-Slavery Response to John Brown's Raid." In *His Soul Goes Marching On: Responses to John Brown and the Harpers Ferry Raid,* edited by Paul Finkelman, 98–116. Charlottesville: University of Virginia Press, 1995.

Finkelman, Paul, and Peggy Russo, eds. *Terrible Swift Sword: The Legacy of John Brown.* Athens: Ohio University Press, 2005.

Fletcher, Holly Berkley. *Gender and the American Temperance Movement of the Nineteenth Century.* New York: Routledge, 2008.

Flood, Charles Bracelen. *Lee: The Last Years.* Boston: Houghton Mifflin, 1981.

Foster, Gaines. *Ghosts of the Confederacy: Defeat, the Lost Cause, and the Emergence of the New South.* New York: Oxford University Press, 1987.

Frank, Stephen M. *Life with Father: Parenthood and Masculinity in the Nineteenth-Century American North.* Baltimore: Johns Hopkins University Press, 1998.

Friedman, Lawrence J. "Antebellum American Abolitionism and the Problem of Violent Means." *Psychohistory Review* 9, no. 1 (1980): 23–58.

——. *Gregarious Saints: Self and Community in American Abolitionism, 1830–1870.* Cambridge: Cambridge University Press, 1982.

Frohman, Charles. *Put-in-Bay: Its History.* Columbus: Ohio Historical Society, 1971.

Gabrial, Brian. "A Woman's Place: Defiance and Obedience; Newspaper Stories about Women during the Trial of John Brown." *American Journalism* 25 (Winter 2008): 7–29.

Gac, Scott. *Singing for Freedom: The Hutchinson Family Singers and the Nineteenth-Century Culture of Antebellum Reform.* New Haven, CT: Yale University Press, 2007.

Gallagher, Gary W. *Causes Won, Lost, and Forgotten: How Hollywood and Popular Art Shape What We Know about the Civil War.* Chapel Hill: University of North Carolina Press, 2008.

Gallagher, Gary, and Alan Nolan, eds. *The Myth of the Lost Cause and Civil War History.* Bloomington: Indiana University Press, 2000.

Gallagher, Gary, and Joan Waugh, eds. *Wars within a War: Controversy and Conflict over the American Civil War.* Chapel Hill: University of North Carolina Press, 2009.

Gamber, Wendy. *The Boardinghouse in Nineteenth-Century America.* Baltimore: Johns Hopkins University Press, 2007.

Gannon, Barbara A. *The Won Cause: Black and White Comradeship in the Grand Army of the Republic.* Chapel Hill: University of North Carolina Press, 2011.

Garrod, R. V. *Saratoga Story.* Saratoga, CA: Saratoga Historical Foundation, 1961.

Geffert, Hannah N. "John Brown and His Black Allies: An Ignored Alliance." *Pennsylvania Magazine of History and Biography* 126 (October 2002): 591–610.

Geffert, Hannah, and Jean Libby. "Regional Black Involvement in John Brown's Raid on Harpers Ferry." In *Prophets of Protest: Reconsidering the History of American Abolitionism*, edited by Timothy Patrick McCarthy and John Stauffer, 165–82. New York: New Press, 2006.

Getz, Lynne. "Partners in Motion: Gender, Migration, and Reform in Antebellum Ohio and Kansas." *Frontiers* 27, no. 2 (2006): 102–35.

Gilbert, Benjamin Franklin. "The Confederate Minority in California." *California Historical Society Quarterly* 20 (June 1941): 154–70.

Gilpin, R. Blakeslee. *John Brown Lives! America's Long Reckoning with Violence, Equality, and Change.* Chapel Hill: University of North Carolina Press, 2011.

Ginzberg, Lori. "The Pleasures (and Dangers) of Biography." *Journal of Women's History* 19, no. 3 (2007): 205–12.

——. *Untidy Origins: A Story of Women's Rights in Antebellum New York.* Chapel Hill: University of North Carolina Press, 2005.

——. *Women and the Work of Benevolence: Morality, Politics, and Class in the 19th-Century United States.* New Haven, CT: Yale University Press, 1990.

Godine, Amy. "Home Truth: The Saga of African-Americans in the Adirondack Past." *Adirondack Life* (January/February 1994): 46–64.

Gold, Susanna W. "'Fighting It Over Again': The Battle of Gettysburg at the 1876 Centennial Exhibition." *Civil War History* 54 (September 2008): 277–310.

Goodman, Paul. *Of One Blood: Abolitionism and the Origins of Racial Equality.* Berkeley: University of California Press, 1998.

Gopnik, Adam. "John Brown's Body: A New Biography Restores Brown's Central-
ity to the Civil War." *New Yorker*, April 25, 2005, http://www.newyorker.com/
archive/2005/04/25/050425crbo_books.

Griswold, Robert. *Family and Divorce in California, 1850–1890: Victorian Illusions and
Everyday Realities*. Albany, NY: SUNY Press, 1982.

Halberstadt, April Hope. "Sarah Brown, Artist and Abolitionist." July 2006, http://
www.saratogahistory.com/History/sarah_brown.htm.

Halttunen, Karen. *Confidence Men and Painted Women*. New Haven, CT: Yale University Press, 1982.

Hansen, Debra Gold. *Strained Sisterhood: Gender and Class in the Boston Female Anti-
Slavery Society*. Amherst: University of Massachusetts Press, 1993.

Hardin, David. *After the War: The Lives and Images of Major Civil War Figures after the
Shooting Stopped*. Chicago: Ivan R. Dee, 2010.

Harris, M. Keith. "Slavery, Emancipation, and Veterans of the Union Cause: Commemorating Freedom in the Era of Reconciliation, 1885–1915." *Civil War
History* 53 (September 2007): 264–90.

Harrold, Stanley. *Border War: Fighting over Slavery before the Civil War*. Chapel Hill:
University of North Carolina Press, 2010.

——. "John Brown's Forerunners: Slave Rescue Attempts and the Abolitionists,
1841–1851." *Radical History Review* 55 (1993): 88–110.

——. *The Rise of Aggressive Abolitionism: Addresses to the Slaves*. Lexington: University
Press of Kentucky, 2004.

Harrold, Stanley, and John McKivigan, eds. *Antislavery Violence: Sectional, Racial, and
Cultural Conflict in Antebellum America*. Knoxville: University of Tennessee
Press, 1999.

Heller, Charles. *Portrait of an Abolitionist: A Biography of George Luther Stearns*. Westport, CT: Greenwood Press, 1996.

Hewitt, Nancy. *Women's Activism and Social Change: Rochester, New York, 1822–1872*.
Ithaca, NY: Cornell University Press, 1984.

Hickey, James T. "Robert Todd Lincoln and the 'Purely Private' Letters of the Lincoln Family." *Journal of the Illinois State Historical Society* 74, no. 1 (1981): 59–79.

Hirrel, Leo P. *Children of Wrath: New School Calvinism and Antebellum Reform*. Lexington: University Press of Kentucky, 1998.

Hirsh, Seymour. "Servile Insurrection and John Brown's Body in Europe." *Journal of
American History* 80 (September 1993): 499–524.

Hodes, Martha. *The Sea Captain's Wife: A True Story of Love, Race, and War in the Nineteenth Century*. New York: W. W. Norton, 2006.

Hodges, Graham Russell Gao. *David Ruggles: A Radical Black Abolitionist and the Underground Railroad in New York City*. Chapel Hill: University of North Carolina
Press, 2010.

Hoffert, Sylvia. *Jane Grey Swisshelm: An Unconventional Life, 1815–1884*. Chapel Hill:
University of North Carolina Press, 2004.

Hoganson, Kristin. "Garrisonian Abolitionists and the Rhetoric of Gender, 1850–
1860." *American Quarterly* 45, no. 4 (1993): 558–95.

Holt, Michael. *The Fate of Their Country: Politicians, Slavery Extension, and the Coming
of the Civil War*. New York: Hill & Wang, 2004.

Horwitz, Tony. *Midnight Rising: John Brown and the Raid That Sparked the Civil War.* New York: Henry Holt, 2011.

Hunt, Nigel. *Memory, War, and Trauma.* Cambridge: Cambridge University Press, 2010.

Izant, Grace Goulder. *Hudson's Heritage: A Chronology of the Founding and Flowering of the Village of Hudson, Ohio.* Kent, OH: Kent State University Press, 1985.

James, Michael E. "The City on the Hill: Temperance, Race, and Class in Turn-of-the-Century Pasadena." *California History* 80, no. 4 (2001–2): 186–203.

Jeffrey, Julie Roy. *Abolitionists Remember: Antislavery Autobiographies and the Unfinished Work of Emancipation.* Chapel Hill: University of North Carolina Press, 2008.

——. *Frontier Women: "Civilizing" the West? 1840–1880.* Rev. ed. New York: Hill & Wang, 1998.

——. *The Great Silent Army: Ordinary Women in the Antislavery Movement.* Chapel Hill: University of North Carolina Press, 1998.

——. "The Liberty Women of Boston: Evangelicalism and Antislavery Politics." *New England Quarterly* 85 (March 2012): 38–77.

——. "'Stranger, Buy . . . Lest Our Mission Fail': The Complex Culture of Women's Abolitionist Fairs." *American Nineteenth Century History* 4, no. 1 (2003): 1–24.

Jensen, Joan. *Loosening the Bond: Mid-Atlantic Farm Women, 1750–1850.* New Haven, CT: Yale University Press, 1988.

Jensen, Joan, and Darlis Miller. "The Gentle Tamers Revisited: New Approaches to the History of Women in the American West." In *Women and Gender in the American West*, edited by Mary Ann Irwin and James F. Brooks, 9–36. Albuquerque: University of New Mexico Press, 2004.

Jochims, Larry O., and Virgil W. Dean. "Pillars of Society: A Brief History of the Kansas State Historical Society." *Kansas History* 18 (Autumn 1995): 142–63.

Jordan, Brian. "Living Monuments: Union Veteran Amputees and the Embodied Memory of the Civil War." *Civil War History* 57 (June 2011): 121–52.

Karcher, Carolyn. *The First Woman in the Republic: A Cultural Biography of Lydia Maria Child.* Durham, NC: Duke University Press, 1994.

Kasson, Joy. *Buffalo Bill's Wild West: Celebrity, Memory, and Popular History.* New York: Hill & Wang, 2000.

Kelly, Catherine. *In the New England Fashion: Reshaping Women's Lives in the Nineteenth Century.* Ithaca, NY: Cornell University Press, 1999.

Kerber, Linda. "Separate Spheres, Female Worlds, Woman's Place." *Journal of American History* 75 (June 1988): 9–39.

Kerr, Andrea Moore. *Lucy Stone: Speaking Out for Equality.* New Brunswick, NJ: Rutgers University Press, 1992.

Kessler-Harris, Alice. "Why Biography?" *American Historical Review* 114 (June 2009): 625–30.

Lachman, Charles. *The Last Lincolns: The Rise and Fall of a Great American Family.* New York: Sterling Publishing Co., 2008.

Laderman, Gary. *The Sacred Remains: American Attitudes toward Death, 1799–1883.* New Haven, CT: Yale University Press, 1996.

Lang, Amy Schrager. *The Syntax of Class: Writing Inequality in Nineteenth-Century America.* Princeton, NJ: Princeton University Press, 2003.

Langsdorf, Edgar. "The First Hundred Years of the Kansas State Historical Society." *Kansas Historical Quarterly* 41 (Autumn 1975): 265–309.

Larson, Kate Clifford. *Bound for the Promised Land: Harriet Tubman, Portrait of an American Hero.* New York: Ballantine, 2004.

Lasser, Carol. "Beyond Separate Spheres: The Power of Public Opinion." *Journal of the Early Republic* 21 (Spring 2001): 115–23.

Laurie, Bruce. *Beyond Garrison: Antislavery and Social Reform.* Cambridge: Cambridge University Press, 2005.

Leavitt, Judith Walzer. *Brought to Bed: Childbearing in America, 1750 to 1950.* New York: Oxford University Press, 1986.

Leckie, Shirley A. "Biography Matters: Why Historians Need Well-Crafted Biographies More Than Ever." In *Writing Biography: Historians and Their Craft,* edited by Lloyd E. Ambrosius, 1–26. Lincoln: University of Nebraska Press, 2004.

———. *Elizabeth Bacon Custer and the Making of a Myth.* Norman: University of Oklahoma Press, 1993.

Lepore, Jill. "Historians Who Love Too Much: Reflections on Microhistory and Biography." *Journal of American History* 88 (June 2001): 129–44.

Lerner, Gerda. *The Grimké Sisters from South Carolina: Rebels against Slavery.* Boston: Houghton Mifflin, 1967.

Levine, Bruce. *Half Slave and Half Free: The Roots of Civil War.* New York: Hill & Wang, 1992.

Libby, Jean. "John Brown's Family and Their California Refuge." *Californians* 7, no. 1 (1989): 14–23.

Loewen, James W. *Lies My Teacher Told Me: Everything Your American History Teacher Got Wrong.* New York: W. W. Norton, 1995.

Lowenthal, David. *The Past Is a Foreign Country.* Cambridge: Cambridge University Press, 1985.

Lubet, Steven. "John Brown's Trial." *Alabama Law Review* 52 (Winter 2001): 425–66.

MacKenzie, Mary. *The Plains of Abraham: A History of North Elba and Lake Placid.* Edited by Lee Manchester. Utica, NY: Nicholas Burns Publishing, 2007.

Madison, James H. "Taking the Country Barefooted: The Indiana Colony in Southern California." *California History* 69, no. 3 (1990): 236–49.

Malin, James Claude. *John Brown and the Legend of Fifty-Six.* Philadelphia: American Philosophical Society, 1942.

Marshall, Nicholas. "'In the Midst of Life We Are in Death': Affliction and Religion in Antebellum New York." In *Mortal Remains: Death in Early America,* edited by Nancy Isenberg and Andrew Burstein, 176–86. Philadelphia: University of Pennsylvania Press, 2002.

Masur, Louis. *1831: Year of Eclipse.* New York: Hill & Wang, 2001.

———. *Rites of Execution: Capital Punishment and the Transformation of American Culture.* New York: Oxford University Press, 1989.

Matzke, Jason P. "The John Brown Way: Frederick Douglass and Henry David Thoreau on the Use of Violence." *Massachusetts Review* 46 (Spring 2005): 62–75.

Mayer, Henry. *All on Fire: William Lloyd Garrison and the Abolition of Slavery.* New York: St. Martin's Press, 1998.

McGinty, Brian. *John Brown's Trial.* Cambridge, MA: Harvard University Press, 2009.

McGlone, Robert E. *John Brown's War against Slavery*. Cambridge: Cambridge University Press, 2009.

———. "Rescripting a Troubled Past: John Brown's Family and the Harpers Ferry Conspiracy." *Journal of American History* 75, no. 4 (1989): 1179–1200.

McKivigan, John. *Forgotten Firebrand: James Redpath and the Making of Nineteenth-Century America*. Ithaca, NY: Cornell University Press, 2008.

McPherson, James. *The Abolitionist Legacy: From Reconstruction to the NAACP*. Princeton, NJ: Princeton University Press, 1975.

———. *The Struggle for Equality: Abolitionists and the Negro in the Civil War and Reconstruction*. Princeton, NJ: Princeton University Press, 1964.

Merish, Laurie. *Sentimental Materialism: Gender, Commodity Culture, and Nineteenth-Century American Literature*. Durham, NC: Duke University Press, 2000.

Million, Joelle. *Woman's Voice, Woman's Place: Lucy Stone and the Birth of the Woman's Rights Movement*. Westport, CT: Praeger, 2003.

Mintz, Steven. *Huck's Raft: A History of American Childhood*. Cambridge, MA: Belknap Press of Harvard University Press, 2004.

Mintz, Steven, and Susan Kellogg. *Domestic Revolutions: A Social History of American Family Life*. New York: Free Press, 1989.

Mitchell, Laura L. "More Meteor Than Martyr: The Legacy of John Brown." In *The Problem of Evil: Slavery, Freedom, and the Ambiguities of American Reform*, edited by Steven Mintz and John Stauffer, 287–97. Amherst: University of Massachusetts Press, 2007.

Morrison, Michael. *Slavery and the American West: The Eclipse of Manifest Destiny and the Coming of the Civil War*. Chapel Hill: University of North Carolina Press, 1997.

Mullaney, Marie Marino. "Feminism, Utopianism, and Domesticity: The Case of Rebecca Buffum Spring, 1811–1911." In *A New Jersey Anthology*, edited by Maxine N. Lurie, 161–86. New Brunswick, NJ: Rutgers University Press, 2002.

Nalty, Damon. *The Browns of Madronia*. Saratoga, CA: Saratoga Historical Foundation, 1995.

Neff, John. *Honoring the Civil War Dead: Commemoration and the Problem of Reconciliation*. Lawrence: University Press of Kansas, 2005.

Newbury, Michael. "Eaten Alive: Slavery and Celebrity in Antebellum America." *English Literary History* 61, no. 1 (1994): 159–87.

Newman, Richard S. *The Transformation of American Abolitionism: Fighting Slavery in the Early Republic*. Chapel Hill: University of North Carolina Press, 2002.

Noll, Mark. *America's God: From Jonathan Edwards to Abraham Lincoln*. New York: Oxford University Press, 2002.

Nudelman, Franny. *John Brown's Body: Slavery, Violence, and the Culture of War*. Chapel Hill: University of North Carolina Press, 2004.

Oates, Stephen. "John Brown and His Judges: A Critique of the Historical Literature." In *Beyond the Civil War Synthesis: Political Essays on the Civil War Era*, edited by Robert P. Swierenga, 57–72. Westport, CT: Greenwood Press, 1975.

———. *To Purge This Land with Blood: A Biography of John Brown*. New York: Harper & Row, 1971.

Oertel, Kristin Tegtmeier. *Bleeding Borders: Race, Gender, and Violence in Pre–Civil War Kansas*. Baton Rouge: LSU Press, 2009.

Ousley, Laurie. "The Business of Housekeeping: The Mistress, the Domestic Worker, and the Construction of Class." *Legacy: A Journal of American Women Writers* 23, no. 2 (2006): 132–47.

Painter, Nell Irvin. *Exodusters: Black Migration to Kansas after Reconstruction.* New York: Alfred A. Knopf, 1977.

Parker, Alison M. *Purifying America: Women, Cultural Reform, and Pro-Censorship Activism, 1873–1933.* Urbana: University of Illinois Press, 1997.

Parramore, Thomas C., with Peter C. Stewart and Tommy L. Bogger. *Norfolk: The First Four Centuries.* Charlottesville: University Press of Virginia, 1994.

Pease, Jane H., and William H. Pease. "Confrontation and Abolition in the 1850s." *Journal of American History* 58 (March 1972): 923–72.

Perry, Lewis, and Michael Fellman, eds. *Antislavery Reconsidered: New Perspectives on the Abolitionists.* Baton Rouge: LSU Press, 1979.

Perry, Mark. *Lift Up Thy Voice: The Grimké Family's Journey from Slaveholders to Civil Rights Leaders.* New York: Viking, 2003.

Peterson, Merrill. *John Brown: The Legend Revisited.* Charlottesville: University of Virginia Press, 2002.

Peterson, Robert H. *Altadena's Golden Years: More Than 250 Photographs of the Community's Early Landmarks, Events, and People.* Alhambra: Sinclair Printing & Lithograph, 1976.

Petrulionis, Sandra Harbert. *To Set This World Right: The Antislavery Movement in Thoreau's Concord.* Ithaca, NY: Cornell University Press, 2006.

Pfaelzer, Jean. *Driven Out: The Forgotten War against Chinese Americans.* New York: Random House, 2007.

Phay, Wilbert. "John Brown's Family in Red Bluff, 1864–1870." MA thesis, Chico State College, 1986.

Poole, Scott. "Memory and the Abolitionist Heritage: Thomas Wentworth Higginson and the Uncertain Meaning of the Civil War." *Civil War History* 51, no. 2 (2005): 202–17.

Portnoy, Alison. *Their Right to Speak: Women's Activism in the Indian and Slave Debates.* Cambridge, MA: Harvard University Press, 2005.

Quarles, Benjamin. *Allies for Freedom: Blacks and John Brown.* New York: Oxford University Press, 1974.

Renehan, Edward. *The Secret Six: The True Tale of the Men Who Conspired with John Brown.* New York: Crown, 1995.

Reynolds, David. *John Brown, Abolitionist: The Man Who Killed Slavery, Sparked the Civil War, and Seeded Civil Rights.* New York: Alfred A. Knopf, 2005.

Rice, Stephen P. *Minding the Machine: Languages of Class in Early Industrial America.* Berkeley: University of California Press, 2004.

Richards, Leonard L. *The California Gold Rush and the Coming of the Civil War.* New York: Alfred A. Knopf, 2007.

Richardson, Joe M. *Christian Reconstruction: The American Missionary Association and Southern Blacks, 1861–1890.* Athens: University of Georgia Press, 1986.

Robertson, Stacey. *Hearts Beating for Liberty: Women Abolitionists in the Old Northwest.* Chapel Hill: University of North Carolina Press, 2010.

——. *Parker Pillsbury: Radical Abolitionist, Male Feminist.* Ithaca, NY: Cornell University Press, 2000.

Romero, Lora. *Home Fronts: Domesticity and Its Critics in the Antebellum United States.* Durham, NC: Duke University Press, 1997.

Ronda, Bruce A. *Reading the Old Man: John Brown in American Culture.* Knoxville: University of Tennessee Press, 2008.

Rose, Willie Lee. "Killing for Freedom." *New York Review of Books*, December 3, 1970, http://www.nybooks.com/articles/10740.

Rosenberg, Daniel. *Mary Brown: From Harpers Ferry to California.* Occasional Paper no. 17, American Institute for Marxist Studies, 1975.

Rossbach, Jeffery S. *Ambivalent Conspirators: John Brown, the Secret Six, and a Theory of Slave Violence.* Philadelphia: University of Pennsylvania Press, 1982.

Roth, Michael S. *The Ironist's Cage: Memory, Trauma, and the Construction of History.* New York: Columbia University Press, 1995.

Rotundo, E. Anthony. *American Manhood: Transformations in Masculinity from the Revolution to the Modern Era.* New York: Basic Books, 1993.

——. "Learning about Manhood: Gender Ideals and the Middle-Class Family in Nineteenth-Century America." In *Manliness and Morality: Middle-Class Masculinity in Britain and America, 1800–1940*, edited by J. A. Morgan and James Walvin, 35–51. Manchester: Manchester University Press, 1987.

Ryan, Mary. *The Empire of the Mother: American Writing about Domesticity, 1830–1860.* New York: Haworth Press, 1982.

Salerno, Beth. *Sister Societies: Women's Antislavery Organizations in Antebellum America.* DeKalb: Northern Illinois University Press, 2005.

Salomon, Ronald. "Being Good: An Abolitionist Family Attempts to Live Up to Its Own Standards." *Vermont History* 69 (2001): 32–47.

Sappol, Michael. *A Traffic of Dead Bodies: Anatomy and Embodied Social Identity in Nineteenth-Century America.* Princeton, NJ: Princeton University Press, 2002.

Schacter, Daniel L. *Searching for Memory: The Brain, the Mind, and the Past.* Basic Books, 1996.

Schlissel, Lillian. *Women's Diaries of the Westward Journey.* 3rd rev. ed. New York: Schocken Books, 2004.

Shackel, Paul. *Memory in Black and White: Race, Commemoration, and the Post-Bellum Landscape.* Walnut Creek, CA: AltaMira, 2003.

Silber, Nina. "A Compound of Wonderful Potency: Women Teachers of the North in the Civil War South." In *The War Was You and Me: Civilians in the American Civil War*, edited by Joan E. Cashin, 35–59. Princeton, NJ: Princeton University Press, 2002.

——. *The Romance of Reunion: Northerners and the South, 1865–1900.* Chapel Hill: University of North Carolina Press, 1995.

Sklar, Kathryn Kish. *Catharine Beecher: A Study in American Domesticity.* New York: W. W. Norton, 1976.

Smith-Rosenberg, Carroll. "The Female World of Love and Ritual." *Signs* 1, no. 1 (1975): 1–29.

Sprague, Julia A., compiler. *History of the New England Women's Club, from 1868 to 1893.* Boston: Lee and Shepard, 1894.

Stauffer, John. *The Black Hearts of Men: Radical Abolitionists and the Transformation of Race.* Cambridge, MA: Harvard University Press, 2002.

——. *Giants: The Parallel Lives of Frederick Douglass and Abraham Lincoln*. New York: Twelve, 2008.

Stauffer, John, and Timothy McCarthy, eds. *Prophets of Protest: Reconsiderations of American Abolitionism*. New York: Free Press, 2006.

Stewart, James B. *Holy Warriors: The Abolitionists and American Slavery*. New York: Hill & Wang, 1976.

——. *Wendell Phillips, Liberty's Hero*. Baton Rouge: LSU Press, 1986.

Strasser, Susan. *Never Done: A History of American Housework*. New York: Pantheon, 1982.

Strouse, Jean. "Semiprivate Lives." In *Studies in Biography*, edited by Daniel Aaron, 113–31. Cambridge, MA: Harvard University Press, 1978.

Taylor, Barbara. "Separation of Soul: Solitude, Biography, History." *American Historical Review* 114 (June 2009): 640–51.

Taylor, Harriet, and Eldrid Herrington, eds. *The Afterlife of John Brown*. New York: Palgrave Macmillan, 2005.

Thelen, David, ed. *Memory and American History*. Bloomington: Indiana University Press, 1990.

Thornton, Tamara Plakins. "Sacred Relics in the Cause of Liberty: A Civil War Memorial Cabinet and the Victorian Logic of Collecting." *Dublin Seminar for New England Folklife Annual Proceedings* 29 (2004): 188–98.

Trodd, Zoe. "Writ in Blood: John Brown's Charter of Humanity, the Tribunal of History, and the Thick Link of American Political Protest." *Journal for the Study of Radicalism* 1, no. 1 (2006): 1–29.

Tuchman, Barbara. "Biography as a Prism in History." In *Telling Lives: The Biographer's Art*, edited by Marc Pachter, 132–47. Philadelphia: University of Pennsylvania Press, 1981.

Turner, Victor. *The Forest of Symbols: Aspects of Ndembu Ritual*. Ithaca, NY: Cornell University Press, 1970.

Tyrell, Ian. *Woman's World, Woman's Empire: The Woman's Christian Temperance Union in International Perspective*. Chapel Hill: University of North Carolina Press, 1991.

Varon, Elizabeth. *Disunion! The Coming of the American Civil War, 1789–1859*. Chapel Hill: University of North Carolina Press, 2008.

Venet, Wendy Hamand. "'Cry Aloud and Spare Not': Northern Anti-Slavery Women and John Brown's Raid." In *His Soul Goes Marching On: Responses to John Brown and the Harpers Ferry Raid*, edited by Paul Finkelman, 41–66. Charlottesville: University of Virginia Press, 1995.

——. *Neither Ballots nor Bullets: Women Abolitionists and the Civil War*. Charlottesville: University Press of Virginia, 1991.

von Frank, Albert J. "John Brown, James Redpath, and the Idea of Revolution." *Civil War History* 52, no. 2 (2006): 142–60.

Walters, Ronald. *American Reformers, 1815–1860*. Rev. ed. New York: Hill & Wang, 1997.

——. *The Antislavery Appeal: American Abolitionism after 1830*. Baltimore: Johns Hopkins University Press, 1978.

Warren, Robert Penn. *John Brown: The Making of a Martyr*. Nashville, TN: Payson and Clark, 1929.

Waugh, Joan. *U.S. Grant: American Hero, American Myth.* Chapel Hill: University of North Carolina Press, 2009.

Wellman, Judith. "Women and Radical Reform in Antebellum Upstate New York: A Profile of Grassroots Female Abolitionists." In *Clio Was a Woman: Studies in the History of American Women*, edited by Mabel E. Deutrich and Virginia C. Purdy, 113–27. Washington, DC: Howard University Press, 1980.

White, Elizabeth Alice. "Charitable Calculations: Fancywork, Charity, and the Culture of the Sentimental Market, 1830–1880." In *The Middling Sorts: Explorations in the History of the American Middle Class*, edited by Burton J. Bledstein and Robert D. Johnston, 73–85. New York: Routledge, 2001.

White, Richard. *"It's Your Misfortune and None of My Own": A History of the American West.* Norman: University of Oklahoma Press, 1991.

White, Ronald. *A. Lincoln.* New York: Random House, 2009.

Whites, LeeAnn. "Forty Shirts and a Wagonload of Wheat: Women, the Domestic Supply Line, and the Civil War on the Western Border." *Journal of the Civil War Era* 1 (March 2011): 56–78.

——, ed. *Occupied Women: Gender, Military Occupation, and the American Civil War.* Baton Rouge: LSU Press, 2009.

Wilentz, Sean. "Homegrown Terrorist." *New Republic*, October 24, 2005, http://www.tnr.com/doc.mhtml?i=20051024&s=wilentz102405.

Wills, Brian Steel. *The War Hits Home: The Civil War in Southeastern Virginia.* Charlottesville: University Press of Virginia, 2001.

Wineapple, Brenda. *White Heat: The Friendship of Emily Dickinson and Thomas Wentworth Higginson.* New York: Alfred A. Knopf, 2008.

Winter, Jay. *Remembering War: The Great War between Memory and History in the Twentieth Century.* New Haven, CT: Yale University Press, 2006.

Wood, Ann Douglas. "'The Fashionable Diseases': Women's Complaints and Their Treatment in Nineteenth-Century America." *Journal of Interdisciplinary History* 4 (Summer 1973): 25–52.

Woodworth, Steven E. *Manifest Destinies: America's Westward Expansion and the Road to Civil War.* New York: Alfred A. Knopf, 2010.

Wyatt-Brown, Bertram. "Abolition and Antislavery in Hudson and Cleveland: Contrasts in Reform Styles." In *Cleveland: A Tradition of Reform*, edited by David D. Van Tassel and John J. Grabowski, 92–112. Kent, OH: Kent State University Press, 1986.

Yellin, Jean Fagan, and John C. Van Horne, eds. *The Abolitionist Sisterhood: Women's Political Culture in Antebellum America.* Ithaca, NY: Cornell University Press, 1994.

INDEX

Italics indicate that the page contains an image of the person.